TOPIC	MENU PATH AND/OR COM1	
Indexed Fields		
Inserting a Line	F8	၁
Mailing Labels		14
Modifying a Form	Form Definition/View or Modify Form	6
Moving Text or Fields	F3/F6	6
Multi-Form	Alt-F10	7
Multi-Form Reports		7
Multi-View	F10	7
Page Numbering		5
Placing or Modifying a Field	F10	2
Printing a Record	Shift-F9	6
Printing a Report		5
Printer Configuration	System Administration/Define Printers	1
Recalculation	Ctrl-F9	9
Record Searches		4
Reorganizing a Form	Form Definition/Reorganize Form	17
Report Formats		5
Required Fields		2
Restoring a Database	Database Maintenance/Restore Database	17
Saving a Field Definition	F2	2
Saving a Form Definition	F2	2
Saving a Record	F2	3
Screen Styles	System Administration/Define Screen Styles	18
Selecting Fields for Reports		5
Selecting Records for Reports		5
Signing On to DataEase		1
Soundex Searches	~	4
Starting DataEase		1
Subforms		9
Table View	Shift-F1	4
Unique Fields		2
Updating a Record	F8	4
User Passwords		1
Wild Card Searches		4

Mastering DataEase

Mastering DataEase®

Susan Harmon

SAN FRANCISCO   PARIS   DÜSSELDORF   SOEST

Acquisitions Editor: Dianne King
Developmental Editor: Eric Stone
Editor: Savitha Pichai
Technical Editor: Linwood P. Beacom
Word Processors: Scott Campbell, Winnie Kelly, Deborah Maizels, Lisa Mitchell
Chapter Art and Layout: Charlotte Carter
Screen Graphics: Cuong Le
Typesetter: Len Gilbert
Proofreader: R.M. Holmes
Indexer: Ted Laux
Cover Designer: Thomas Ingalls + Associates
Cover Photographer: Michael Lamotte
Screen reproductions produced by XenoFont.

XenoFont is a trademark of XenoSoft.

SYBEX is a registered trademark of SYBEX, Inc.

TRADEMARKS: SYBEX has attempted throughout this book to distinguish proprietary trademarks from descriptive terms by following the capitalization style used by the manufacturer.

SYBEX is not affiliated with any manufacturer.

Every effort has been made to supply complete and accurate information. However, SYBEX assumes no responsibility for its use, nor for any infringement of the intellectual property rights of third parties which would result from such use.

The text of this book is printed on recycled paper.

Copyright ©1990 SYBEX Inc., 2021 Challenger Drive, Alameda, CA 94501. World rights reserved. No part of this publication may be stored in a retrieval system, transmitted, or reproduced in any way, including but not limited to photocopy, photograph, magnetic or other record, without the prior agreement and written permission of the publisher.

Library of Congress Card Number: 90-70874
ISBN: 0-89588-689-8

Manufactured in the United States of America
10 9 8 7 6 5 4 3

ACKNOWLEDGMENTS

Many thanks to the staff at SYBEX who contributed to the inception, development, and production of this book. In particular, thanks to Dianne King for guiding me through the initial stages; Eric Stone for his clear thoughts; and Savitha Pichai for her keen eyes, patience, and courtesy.

Many thanks also to Lin Beacom for his precise and careful technical edits.

And finally, thanks to the technical and marketing staff at DataEase, in particular Randy Newell and Jeff Roberts, for patiently answering my questions and attending to my requests.

CONTENTS AT A GLANCE

INTRODUCTION   xix

CHAPTER   ONE   A First Look at Databases and DataEase   1

TWO   Creating Your First Form   19

THREE   Entering Records   47

FOUR   Working with Your Records   65

FIVE   Creating Queries and Quick Reports   95

SIX   Modifying Your Form   141

SEVEN   Working with Multiple Forms   169

EIGHT   Advanced Form Design   207

NINE   Keeping Track of Sales   245

TEN   Keeping Track of Payments   277

ELEVEN   Creating Reports with the Data Query Language   301

TWELVE   Creating High Level Queries   337

THIRTEEN   Modifying Your Database with High Level Queries   355

FOURTEEN   Creating Customer Statements and Form Letters   379

FIFTEEN   Automating Sales and Order Entry   401

SIXTEEN   Creating Your Own Menus   425

SEVENTEEN   Maintaining Your Database   447

EIGHTEEN   System Configuration and Administration   471

NINETEEN   Tips and Shortcuts   491

APPENDIX   A   Installing DataEase   495

B   Converting Files from Other Programs   503

C   Exporting to GrafTalk   509

INDEX   517

TABLE OF CONTENTS

INTRODUCTION — **xix**

CHAPTER ONE	**A First Look at Databases and DataEase**	**1**

Fast Track	2
What Is a Database?	3
Database Terminology	4
So What Is Database Management?	5
What You Should Know about DataEase on a Network	7
Sharing Data	7
Database Security	7
Building a Simple Database	8
Starting DataEase	9
Signing On	10
The DataEase Opening Screen	10
Creating and Naming a New Database	11
The DataEase Main Menu	14
Making Menu Selections	15
Selecting Your Printer	16

CHAPTER TWO	**Creating Your First Form**	**19**

Fast Track	20
The Form Definition Screen	22
Using the Command Help Menus—F4	23
Getting More Help—Alt-F1	25
Designing Your Form	26
Field Definition	28
Placing Text and Fields	29
Entering the Text into Your Form	30
Correcting Errors	31
Defining the Fields—F10	33
Special Attributes: Required, Indexed, Unique	36
Creating Ranges	39
Creating a Calculated Field	40
Creating Field Help	42
Displaying Field Attributes	43
Printing Your Form Definition—Shift-F9	44

x

Saving Your Form—F2	45
Security Notes	46
LAN Notes	46

CHAPTER THREE — Entering Records · 47

Fast Track	48
The Records Menu	49
The Record Entry Screen	50
Entering Records	51
Entering Your First Record	51
Correcting Errors	54
Testing Field Attributes	57
Data Entry Shortcuts	59
Using Information from the Previous Record—Shift-F5 and Shift-F6	59
Creating and Using a Default Record—Shift-F2 and Shift-F5	60
Printing a Record—Shift-F9	63
Leaving Record Entry	63
Security Notes	64
LAN Notes	64

CHAPTER FOUR — Working with Your Records · 65

Fast Track	66
Viewing Records in Form View	68
Viewing Records in Entry Order—F3	69
Viewing Records in Reverse Order—Shift-F3	70
Viewing Records in Index Order	71
Searching for Particular Records	75
Searching for a Record Number—Ctrl-F3	75
Searching for Exact Matches	76
Searching for Partial Matches	80
Using Wild Cards to Match Values	80
"Sounds Like" Searches	81
Notes about Searches	83
Making Changes to Your Records	84
Modifying Records—F8	84
Deleting Records—F7	85

Working with Records in Table View—Shift-F1	87
Entering and Saving Records in Table View	89
Displaying Table View Records in Index Order	90
Displaying Selected Records in Table View	91
Modifying Records in Table View	92
Security Notes	93
LAN Notes	94

CHAPTER FIVE   Creating Queries and Quick Reports   95

Fast Track	96
DataEase Query by Example	98
Report Formats	99
The Quick Reports Menu	100
Creating a Quick Report of Inventory Items	101
Selecting the Fields for Your Report	101
Defining the Format	105
Running Your Report	107
Modifying the Format	109
Changing the Report Width	110
Adding a Header and Footer	112
Adding a Date to the Report Header	113
Adding a Page Number to Your Report Footer	114
Saving the Report	117
Printing the Report	117
Printing to a File	118
Selecting Records for Your Report	119
Entering Text Criteria	119
Selecting Numeric Ranges	123
Printing the Report Definition	124
Creating a Report Grouped by Manufacturer	127
Including Group Headers and Trailers in Your Report	127
Copying Information—F5 and F6	132
Creating a Calculated Field	134
Quick Reports from Record Entry	136
Loading an Existing Report	137
A Finishing Touch	138
Returning to the Main Menu	139
Security Notes	139
LAN Notes	139

CHAPTER SIX	**Modifying Your Form**	**141**
	Fast Track	142
	Changing a Field Length	146
	Adding a Comments Field	147
	Moving Fields	150
	Creating a Default Entry	153
	Inserting and Deleting Lines in Your Form	154
	Recovering from Mistakes	156
	Saving Your Changes	156
	Enhancing Your Form	157
	Changing Field Highlights	157
	Adding Borders to Your Form—Alt-F10	159
	Highlighting Your Text	161
	Adding Special Print Attributes	163
	Adding Field Values in Record Entry	164
	Printing a Record	167
	Notes about Modification	167

CHAPTER SEVEN	**Working with Multiple Forms**	**169**
	Fast Track	170
	Creating a Vendors Form	172
	Creating an Orders Form	174
	Including Two Unique Fields	174
	Form Relationships	178
	Creating Relationships	180
	Relating ITEMS to ORDERS	180
	Relating ORDERS to VENDORS	182
	Relating ITEMS to VENDORS	183
	Displaying Relationship Records	184
	Using Multi-View to Display Multiple Forms	186
	Matching Multiple Records in the Related Form	188
	Adding Records to the Related Form	189
	Displaying a Table of Related Records	190
	Searching for Records in a Subform	191
	Adding and Modifying Records in Multi-Form	193
	Displaying Multiple Subforms	195
	Using Dynamic Lookup to Copy Field Values	196
	Creating a Second Relationship between Two Forms	198
	Creating Reports from Related Forms	203
	Security Notes	206

xiii

CHAPTER EIGHT	**Advanced Form Design**	**207**
	Fast Track	208
	Entering Dates	210
	Looking Up Field Values in Another Form	212
	Using the IF Function to Make Decisions	213
	Using the IF Function to Determine the Amount Back-Ordered	214
	Combining IF and LOOKUP in a Derivation Formula	215
	Entering Records with the Help of Formulas and Functions	216
	Creating a Salesperson Form	218
	Using Functions to Control Case and Order	219
	Using the PROPER Function	219
	Using the UPPER Function	220
	Using SEQUENCE to Increment Field Values	220
	Data Entry with Text Conversion and Sequencing	223
	Using the LASTFIRST Function	223
	Combining Text Conversion Functions	225
	Testing the FIRSTLAST Function	227
	Creating Choice Fields	228
	Using Choice Fields in Data Entry	230
	Modifying a Choice Field	231
	Choice Fields and Reports	234
	The DataEase DICTIONARY Form	235
	Copying Fields from the DICTIONARY Form	236
	Changing the Pitch for a Report	240
CHAPTER NINE	**Keeping Track of Sales**	**245**
	Fast Track	246
	Designing the Invoice Form	247
	Defining the Subform	249
	Defining the Main Form	250
	Hiding Fields from Table View	252
	Using SUM OF to Total Records in a Related Form	252
	Creating the Relationships	256
	Adding the Subform to Complete the Invoice—F9	259
	Entering Records into the Subform	263
	Printing Your Invoice	267
	Using SUM OF to Keep Track of Sales	271
	Using Ctrl-F9 to Recalculate Formulas	274

CHAPTER TEN	**Keeping Track of Payments**	**277**
	Fast Track	278
	Creating the PAYMENTS Form with Multiple Subforms	279
	Creating the PAYLIST Form	280
	Creating the PAYMENTS Form	281
	Calculating BALANCE DUE for Each Invoice	282
	Creating the Relationships	283
	Including the Subforms with the PAYMENTS Form	284
	Entering Payment Records	288
	Creating a Report with Multiple Groups	290
	Suppressing Field Spaces	293
	Changing the Report Layout	297
	Selecting Records with a Referential Formula	298
	Adding Fields to the Field Selection List	298

CHAPTER ELEVEN	**Creating Reports with the Data Query Language**	**301**
	Fast Track	302
	The DQL Menu	305
	Converting a Quick Report to DQL	305
	Creating a Single Form Report	307
	Defining Queries	308
	Using Interactive Menus	308
	Creating a DQL Report Using Two Related Forms	314
	Modifying a Procedure	319
	Using Other Relational Operators in Reports	322
	Creating a DQL Report Using Three Related Forms	326
	Using the Data Entry Form to Select Records	330
	Modifying a Data Entry Form	333
	Security Notes	335

CHAPTER TWELVE	**Creating High Level Queries**	**337**
	Fast Track	338
	The High Level Query Menu	339
	Including Calculated Fields in a Report Query	340
	Comparing Field Values	342
	Adding an Ad Hoc Relationship to a Procedure	346
	Modifying the Print Style Before Running the Procedure	351
	Printing Your Procedures	353

xv

CHAPTER THIRTEEN	**Modifying** **Your Database with High Level Queries**	*355*
	Fast Track	356
	Using a High Level Query to Make Global Changes	357
	Typing Query Statements with the Menus Active	359
	Using a High Level Query to Record Shipments	362
	Creating a Relationship Based on Two Fields	363
	Switching to Quick Reports	365
	Using a DQL Procedure to Place Orders	368
	Using an **if** Statement in Your Query	369
	Using **input** to Select Records for a Report	375
	Security Notes	378

CHAPTER FOURTEEN	**Creating Customer Statements and Form Letters**	*379*
	Fast Track	380
	Creating the Query	382
	Naming Ad Hoc Relationships	383
	Designing a Custom Format	386
	Creating a Form Letter	390
	Printing to a Disk File	395
	Creating Mailing Labels	396

CHAPTER FIFTEEN	**Automating Sales and Order Entry**	**401**
	Fast Track	402
	Using the Case Command for Multiple Conditions	405
	Using Current Status	406
	Copying Data from Another Form	408
	Displaying Messages	409
	Adding a New Customer	410
	Using Variables to Enter Data	412
	Using **while** to Repeat Query Statements	414
	Preparing and Running a Converted Procedure	417
	Using Control Procedures to Run Multiple Procedures	419
	Running a Control Procedure	420
	Consolidating the Orders	422
	An Optional Method for Entering Orders	423
	Security Notes	424

xvi

CHAPTER SIXTEEN	**Creating Your Own Menus**	**425**
	Fast Track	426
	Creating a Menu for Invoice Entry	429
	Loading the Menus	433
	Calling a Menu	433
	Calling One Menu from Another	436
	Creating Chain Menus	438
	Changing the Start-up Menu	441
	Printing Your Custom Menus	443
	Optional Menu Configurations	445
	Security Notes	446
CHAPTER SEVENTEEN	**Maintaining Your Database**	**447**
	Fast Track	448
	Copying Forms and Records	450
	Deleting Groups of Records with DQL	452
	Copying Fields from Another Form	453
	Form Reorganization	454
	Deleting and Resequencing	456
	Copying Records between Forms	456
	Copying DataEase Files between Databases	457
	Determining DataEase DOS File Names	458
	Installing a Single Form or Procedure	460
	Installing Applications	462
	Backing Up Your Database	465
	Restoring Your Database	467
	Performing DOS Functions from DataEase	468
	Security Notes	469
	LAN Notes	469
CHAPTER EIGHTEEN	**System Configuration and Administration**	**471**
	Fast Track	472
	The System Administration Menu	474
	Defining Your System Configuration	475
	Creating a Custom Printer Definition	479
	Defining a Custom Screen Style	480

	Assigning User Security Levels	484
	Modifying Record Entry Security Requirements	485
	Establishing Field Security Levels	487
	User Passwords	489

CHAPTER NINETEEN — Tips and Shortcuts — 491

Signing On from DOS	492
Copying Queries	492
Sorting Your Database	493
Multiple Headers and Footers in Reports	494

APPENDIX A — Installing DataEase — 495

Hardware and Software Requirements	496
General Installation Guidelines	497
Installing DataEase on a Single Computer	498
Upgrading from Version 4.1 or 4.0	500
Upgrading from Version 2.5 or Lower	501

APPENDIX B — Converting Files from Other Programs — 503

Transferring from Lotus or Symphony	504
Converting dBASE Files	505
Converting Paradox Files	506

APPENDIX C — Exporting to GrafTalk — 509

The GrafTalk Export Format	510
Creating a Graph from DataEase Data	511
The GrafTalk Chart Format	513

INDEX — 517

INTRODUCTION

DataEase is a powerful database management and application development system written for the DOS single user or multiuser environment. Its use of simple fill-in forms combines user-friendliness and power in such a way that anyone from a novice to a sophisticated user can develop complex applications without prior programming knowledge. You can also step into the world of programming with the elegantly simple yet powerful Data Query Language, which is enhanced by an optional menu system that takes you step by step through the programming commands.

WHO THIS BOOK IS FOR

This book is written for those of you who are new to database management or new to computers. However, if you are familiar with databases in general or with DataEase in particular, especially an earlier version, you can use this book to sprint across the basics and into the more advanced features.

The exercises in this book start you off at the very beginning, with creating the first database form. As you learn more about DataEase, you will create a working application that will grow into a powerful information management tool. The concepts you'll learn here can be applied to your own work environment.

Although this book is based on DataEase version 4.2, you can also use it to learn DataEase version 4.0 or 4.01. The new features of version 4.2 are discussed later in this introduction. And throughout the book, any commands, concepts, or screen images that are exclusive to version 4.2 will be clearly noted.

THE NEW DATAEASE

In July of 1989, DataEase introduced version 4.0, which enhanced version 2.53 by introducing more than 70 new features, including:

- Multi-Form viewing and editing.
- Multi-Form quick reports.
- Formulas and group totals in quick reports.
- Eighteen new Data Query Language commands.
- Increased processing speed.
- Improved LAN performance and better memory management.
- Improved file conversion features, including direct exporting to MultiMate and WordPerfect.
- Support for expanded memory.
- More reports and forms per database and more records per form.
- Up to 13 languages from which to select at sign-on time.

In the spring of 1990, DataEase version 4.2 was introduced; it contains an expanded addressable memory of 16Mb of RAM on 80286- and 80386-based computers. In addition, referential integrity was introduced, improving links between multiple forms. Now key field values changed in one form can automatically be changed in a related form.

All of these features, both new and old, combine to make Data-Ease one of the most powerful and flexible database management programs on the market today.

HOW THIS BOOK IS ORGANIZED

Chapter 1 introduces you to database management and DataEase. Chapters 2–6 concentrate on creating and modifying forms; entering, editing, and displaying records; and creating reports from your records. Chapters 7 and 8 show you the basics of working with multiple forms. In Chapters 9 and 10, you'll begin to create Multi-Form applications. Chapters 11–15 start by showing you how to use Data Query

Language to build a simple report and end with an automated invoice/order entry/accounts receivable system. Chapter 16 shows you how to build your own menu system that allows users to interface with your application. Chapter 17 shows you how to manage your files and Chapter 18 is dedicated to configuring DataEase for use in a single user or multiuser environment. Finally, Chapter 19 includes hints and shortcuts that can assist you in your work and save you time.

If you haven't installed DataEase on your computer yet, you can refer to Appendix A for instructions. In Appendix B, you will find instructions for converting your Lotus 1-2-3, Symphony, dBASE, or Paradox files into DataEase. Appendix C covers exporting DataEase data into the GrafTalk export format so that you can create graphs from your numeric data.

HOW TO USE THIS BOOK

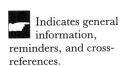
Indicates general information, reminders, and cross-references.

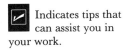
Indicates tips that can assist you in your work.

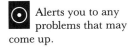
Alerts you to any problems that may come up.

The purpose of this book is to provide you with helpful reference information and to assist you in learning DataEase. Most of the chapters begin with "Fast Track" sections that provide a quick reference to the major features of DataEase. Throughout the text, you will find margin notes, indicated by the icons shown to the left, that point out general information, tips, and warnings. Most sections include tutorial exercises consisting of bulleted lists that provide general steps for performing DataEase tasks; and numbered lists to guide you through the exercise and help you understand what is happening on the screen. The chapters will end, when appropriate, with sections called "LAN Notes" and "Security Notes." These sections will discuss the ways in which topics covered in the chapter may be affected in a local area network or by security issues.

It will help you to become familiar with some of the words, phrases, and keys that are used consistently throughout the book:

- *Type* is generally followed by keyboard characters in boldface, indicating that you should type these characters. For example, Type **San Francisco** means you should type the words **San Francisco**. If the characters are surrounded by < > (brackets), you should type the informtion requested *xxii*

within the brackets. For example, Type **<your name>** means you should type your name (without the brackets).

- *Press* is always followed by a special keyboard function key and indicates that you should press that key. For example, Press **F6** means you should press the function key labeled **F6**. Press **Shift-F6** means that you should press the **Shift** key first and hold it down as you press **F6**. **Ctrl**, **Shift**, and **Alt** are "silent" function keys that are often used with other function keys to access special commands.

- ◄─┘ often follows a Type instruction and indicates that you should press **Enter** to complete the command or phrase. For example, Type **San Francisco**◄─┘ means you should type the words **San Francisco** and press **Enter**.

CHAPTER ONE

A First Look at Databases and DataEase

Fast Track

To start DataEase,   9

type **dease** at the DOS prompt, followed by the directory path that contains your database files, if different from the DataEase directory.

To create a new database,   11

select NONE from the Sign On box in the Opening Screen, and enter the name of your new database. If you want to protect the database from other users, enter your user name and an optional password.

To select an existing database,   11

select the database you want to work with from the Sign On box in the Opening Screen. If any user records have been created for this database, you must also enter a valid user name; if that user name has been assigned a password, you must also enter the correct password.

To change the default printer,   16

select System Administration from the Main Menu, then select Define Configuration from the Administration menu. Fill in the fields requesting your PORT TYPE and PORT NUMBER, and select your PRINTER DEFINITION from the list of printers. Seek technical assistance if you are unsure of how to answer the prompts.

CHAPTER 1

IF THIS IS YOUR FIRST EXPERIENCE WORKING WITH databases, you no doubt have many questions, beginning perhaps with, "What is a database, anyway?" If you have any previous experience with databases, you may still have questions about DataEase's approach to database management. The first part of this chapter addresses these and other special considerations, such as data security and using DataEase on a network.

Once you have a basic understanding of the concepts, you'll be ready to start using DataEase. In the remaining sections of this chapter, you'll learn how to start the program and create your first database. Let's begin with some basic definitions.

WHAT IS A DATABASE?

Quite simply, a database is an organized list of information that is important to you. It could be your address book, or the telephone book. On a grander scale, if you are a United States taxpayer, you are part of a large database kept by the Internal Revenue Service. Have you ever gone into an auto parts store and watched the clerk look up the serial number of the thingamabob you held in your hand to check for a price? That clerk is using another kind of database—an unwieldy paper database, but nonetheless a database.

DataEase allows you to maintain *electronic* databases. If you keep birthdays in your address book, wouldn't it be nice if you could somehow glean from all those pages a list of everyone whose birthdays fall in the current month? Or, if you are planning a trip to Dallas, can your address book come up with a list of all your friends and acquaintances who live there? An electronic database can give you that information in seconds.

Is your address book designed in a way that is easy to read, with enough room for those long names and addresses? Does it have space for *all* the information you like to keep (like those birthdays)? If you could design your own, would it be different? You *can* design your own entry form with an electronic database.

At your office, a database can be used to keep lists of customers, employees, inventory items, books and literature, etc. At your home a database could organize not only your addresses, but your checkbook, or your insured belongings.

DATABASE TERMINOLOGY

The very word *terminology* scares away many potential computer users. However, many database terms are found in everyday English. Whether a database is paper or electronic, it has a definitive structure. If you have experience with other database products, you will find that DataEase organizes its database structure somewhat differently from many of the products on the market and makes use of some different terms. However, DataEase conforms to the true meaning of the term *database*.

A database is composed of a number of related lists. Each one of these lists is referred to by its data entry *form*, much like the form you use to enter someone's name in your address book:

FIRST NAME: _____ LAST NAME: _____
ADDRESS: _____
CITY: _____ STATE: _____ ZIP CODE: _____
BIRTHDAY: _____

A DataEase form is composed of *fields*, and can contain at least one and as many as 255 fields. For example, the city and the state are each fields in your name and address database. The example above has seven fields. The text that precedes each field is called the field prompt, and describes the information that must be entered. These prompts may also enhance the cosmetic appearance of the form.

You must also assign a *name* to each field, which DataEase uses to identify the field. The field prompt can be used as the name, but it can be more convenient to have a shorter name. For example:

FNAME, LNAME, ADD, CITY, STATE, ZIP, BDAY

might be used as field names in the address database.

Each time you fill in a form, you create a record. For example, you have a record for each person in your address book.

FIRST NAME: Edward   LAST NAME: Jones
ADDRESS: 23 Elm Street
CITY: Cleveland   STATE: OH   ZIP CODE: 44303
BIRTHDAY: 01/12/60

A DataEase form can have at least one and as many as 16 million records.

A sales database may contain several data entry forms, one each for customers, salespeople, invoices, and products. And although these forms are maintained separately, you can establish *relationships* between one or more of them so that if, for example, you are working with a customer's record, you can easily get information about his or her latest invoice. Similarly, if you are working with an invoice record, you can quickly access information about the availability of a product.

SO WHAT IS DATABASE MANAGEMENT?

Database management involves the daily activities of maintaining and accessing the information stored in your forms and records. These can be divided into five types of tasks:

Entering records   This involves adding new information. When you first create your forms, this is the primary task that will keep you busy for a while.

Editing records   You will need to update your records as information changes; people move, salaries increase, positions change. Records are also removed as employees leave or products are discontinued.

6 MASTERING DATAEASE

CH. 1

Sorting your database	You might organize your records alphabetically by state, city, or last name, or numerically from highest to lowest sale.
Querying the database	You will do this in order to retrieve information about your records, such as which customers live in New York; who has purchased the most of Product A this month; which employees are due for a review or promotion.
Printing reports	The information you gather can be printed in a variety of formats. In addition, you can use sort and Query to alphabetize and select your records for each report.

In some way or another, you already perform most of these tasks on your address book as you add names alphabetically, cross out old ones, change addresses and phone numbers, and look up information. And eventually, when it starts looking messy or you run out of room, you must start over with a new address book and add the information all over again. As you'll learn in the following chapters, you can avoid this inconvenience with an electronic database.

In addition to the data entry forms that *you* create, DataEase comes with many of its own forms. Instead of learning a complicated command structure to tell DataEase what to do, you simply fill out a special form that DataEase displays. Because of this, you can use DataEase for your simplest database requirements with very little effort. You can also create specialized applications with the DataEase Data Query Language (DQL) for a variety of purposes, from inventory control to sophisticated accounting transactions such as posting to multiple forms. This book will take you gradually from the basics to the complex.

Later in the chapter you will learn how to create your database, and you will design your first form in Chapter 2. First, if you are operating DataEase on a local area network or are sharing your computer with several DataEase users, you should read over the following sections.

WHAT YOU SHOULD KNOW ABOUT DATAEASE ON A NETWORK

Although DataEase is used by many on a single computer, Data-Ease also operates on a local area network (LAN) where the software can be accessed from a single disk (the file server) by multiple users. If you operate DataEase on a LAN, there are a few DataEase features you should understand as you learn how to use the product.

SHARING DATA

If you are using DataEase on a LAN, you may be sharing your database with a number of other users. To maintain the integrity of the data stored in each form, DataEase allows you to create your own *locking rules*. For example, if someone else is making a change to the record you may look at the record; however DataEase will prevent you from storing any changes until the other person finishes. This is called *record locking*, and is one locking restriction DataEase imposes. However, your systems administrator may impose even tighter restrictions, and not allow you even to look at a record that another person is using. If someone is modifying a form or running a report, you may be restricted from accessing that form. This is called *file locking*.

The point is, if you attempt to gain access to a record or form that is locked for some reason, DataEase will display a *resource conflict message* and will continue to attempt to access the form or record until it becomes available.

DATABASE SECURITY

When more than one person shares the same database, either on a LAN or simply on the same computer, you can establish a *user information record* for each user. A user information record includes the name, an optional password used to gain access to the database, and a security level. You will learn more about names and passwords in the next chapter. Your security level determines what tasks you may perform or what records or forms you can access. For example, you must have a high security level to create a form. A systems administrator may require a high security level even to view or print certain

CH. 1

fields in a form. A person with a high security level can perform any task, while a person with a low 3 security level can usually only view or print information. For detailed information about security levels and their limitations, refer to Chapter 3, Volume 2 of your DataEase documentation.

These user information records are strictly optional, but are useful when protecting sensitive data or sophisticated applications from users who are unfamiliar with them. If your security level is not high enough to perform a particular task or access a record, an appropriate message will be displayed. There are seven security levels available, listed below in order of precedence:

- High
- Medium 1
- Medium 2
- Medium 3
- Low 1
- Low 2
- Low 3

If you are a systems administrator, you can refer to volume 2 of your DataEase documentation as well as Chapter 18 of this book for more information about establishing security levels.

BUILDING A SIMPLE DATABASE

The best way to learn a program is to create a practical application for yourself or someone else. Furniture Palace, a fictional chain of furniture stores serving the Great Lakes region of the Midwest, could use your help. Lately, Furniture Palace has had problems that many growing businesses face. Prices change, but salespeople are often unaware of them; sales are high, but inventory is always low; in addition, accounting is falling behind in its paperwork. Your mission is to create for Furniture Palace a better way to maintain current sales and pricing, to make sure that the inventory level is high enough to support the orders, and to help keep track of customer payments and sales commissions.

In the course of this book, you'll learn how to solve Furniture Palace's problems using DataEase. The exercises in each chapter will show you how to:

- Create a database called INVENTORY that contains a number of forms for storing information about the furniture inventory, customers, payments, and furniture sales.

- Link all these forms so that information about inventory items, customers, and accounts receivable is current and available to Furniture Palace employees.

- Generate reports that track sales, invoice payments, and inventory levels.

- Design a more efficient sales order system that checks the inventory supply and automatically reorders when inventory is low.

This chapter will start you off with the basics and you'll learn how to start the DataEase program, create your first database, and define your first form. Before you begin, you should have completed the following tasks:

- Install DataEase.
- Create a subdirectory called DEASE\SYBEX.

If you have not done so, please turn to Appendix A for instructions.

STARTING DATAEASE

Once you have completed the installation procedure and created your working directory, you are ready to begin the DataEase program. If the DEASE subdirectory is not current:

1. Type **cd\dease**
2. Press **Enter**

10 MASTERING DATAEASE

CH. 1

To start DataEase:

1. Type **dease sybex**
2. Press **Enter**

Dease instructs the computer to load the DataEase program. **Sybex** tells DataEase which subdirectory you will use to store your database forms and records. If you omit the subdirectory from the command, DataEase will store your files in the Dease directory.

From now on, if a numbered instruction requires you to press the Enter key after typing characters, the symbol ← will follow the text to indicate that you complete the command by pressing Enter. For example, the instruction *Type your name* ← means you should type your name and press Enter.

SIGNING ON

Each time you start the program, DataEase waits for you either to select an existing database to work with or create a new one. This process is called *signing on*.

THE DATAEASE OPENING SCREEN

The Opening Screen, pictured in Figure 1.1, includes some important information you should note. At the top right of the screen is the serial number of your program. You will be asked for this number if you call DataEase for technical assistance. The telephone number for DataEase is displayed on the left.

> If you press Esc from the Opening Screen you will return to DOS.

The available function key commands are listed across the bottom of the screen. Later on in this chapter, you will learn about these and other commands. At the very bottom of this and every other DataEase menu screen is the current time and date. Of course, the date and time on your screen will always be different from those in the screens depicted in this book.

A FIRST LOOK AT DATABASES AND DATAEASE   11

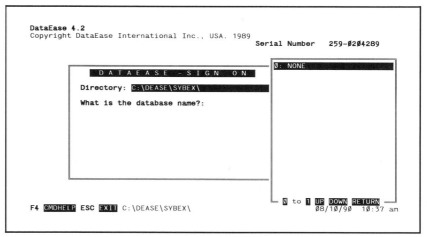

Figure 1.1: The DataEase Opening Screen

CREATING AND NAMING A NEW DATABASE

The most significant areas of the Opening Screen are the Sign On box and, immediately to the right, the list of database names. The Sign On box displays the current directory, *C:\dease\sybex*, and asks:

What is the database name?:

DataEase waits for you to select the name of the database from the list on the right. Since this directory does not contain any databases, NONE is the only option listed.

Before you can design your forms, you'll need to create the database and give it a name. Before you can name your new database, you need to tell DataEase you don't want a database from the existing list by selecting NONE:

1. Press **Enter** to select NONE. Now you can type the name of your new database:
2. Type **INVENTORY** ⏎

When you name your new database, you can enter any name containing 2–19 characters.

> To change your directory select NONE, press ↑ to move to the Directory prompt, and enter the directory name.

CH. 1

Since this is a new database, DataEase responds with:

**Database does not exist in specified directory
Create a new database (y/n)?**

3. Type **y** ⬅ to create a new database.

Next, DataEase displays the following message:

New database will use the filename letter I

What does this mean? Well, each time you create a form for this database and enter records, DataEase creates a number of different DOS files to hold the information. This letter will be included in all DOS file names associated with this database. For more information on DataEase forms and their DOS file names, see the section on Database Status in Chapter 17.

Entering Your Name

After you select or create your database, DataEase asks:

What is your name :_

A user name can be entered in either uppercase or lowercase.

Before you answer this question, you should understand its significance. When you first create a database, you are asked for a user name. You may enter any name up to 15 characters. This is strictly optional and you can skip it by simply pressing Enter. If you do enter a name, DataEase automatically creates a user information record under your name with a *high* security rating. From that point on anyone who wants to use this database must enter your user name. After the database has been created, other user information records may be created with access to this database. User information records are covered in Chapters 16 and 18, and may be of interest to you only if you work on a multiuser system, are a systems administrator, or share your computer with other users.

For this exercise, go ahead and create a user information record for yourself.

1. Type **<your name>** ⬅

Entering Your Password

After you enter your name, DataEase asks for your password:

What is your security password   :_

You can enter any password up to eight characters. Again, this is strictly optional. If you *do* enter a password, it will be assigned to your user information record, and anyone signing in under your user name must enter your password. Whenever you type a password, the letters never display, so when entering it the first time, be sure you type the correct characters.

If you type the incorrect name or password when trying to reenter the database, DataEase will return you to the name prompt and you must enter them both again. If you enter either of them incorrectly on the second attempt, DataEase exits the program and returns you to DOS.

Some good advice: if you are the only user and security is not an issue, the best idea is just to omit the name and password. Each time you create or select your database, you will be asked for your name and password. If you assigned no name or password, simply press Enter to skip these prompts.

1. Press **Enter** to bypass the password.

At this point, DataEase takes a few seconds to create your new database. Following that, the Main Menu is displayed.

Notes to Administrators

If you assign no user name to a database, a user information record is created without a name and with a *high* security rating.

When you initially create a database and assign a user name, this is the *only* name that can be used to open the database. However, once you open the database, you can add, delete, and change user names or passwords. For more information, as well as helpful hints about how to protect yourself against password peril, see the section on user information records in Chapter 18.

You can enter your password in either uppercase or lowercase.

Passwords can be added to user information records after the database is created.

THE DATAEASE MAIN MENU

After you sign on, DataEase displays the Main Menu, pictured in Figure 1.2. All of the DataEase functions are available from one of these numbered selections described briefly below:

1. Form Definition and Relationships. Define, revise, delete forms; establish relationships between forms.

2. Record Entry. Enter, edit, view, and delete records.

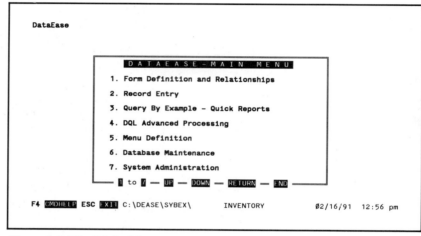

Figure 1.2: The Main Menu

3. Query By Example–Quick Reports. Design custom reports for viewing or printing. (In version 4.0, the selection simply reads Quick Reports.)

4. DQL Advanced Processing. More sophisticated report processing; allows access to DataEase's procedural language, which you can use to design custom applications.

5. Menu Definition. Create custom menus for users and special applications.

6. Database Maintenance. Back up your database; perform DOS functions.

7. System Administration. Define users, screen styles, printers, and hardware configurations.

MAKING MENU SELECTIONS

The Main Menu is an example of a *task* menu. Task menus always contain numbered selections. You can select an item from the menu using one of two methods:

- Press the ↑ or ↓ key to highlight the desired selection and press **Enter**.

- Type the number next to the selection. This is the faster way, since you do not need to press **Enter**.

Although typing the number may be faster, when you are first getting comfortable with a program it is wiser to be cautious than quick. If you prefer to type the selection number, you certainly may. If you accidentally type the wrong number and encounter an unfamiliar screen, simply press Esc to return to the previous menu.

When an exercise step requires that you make a menu selection, this book will use the term *Select* in the instructions. For example, if the instruction says *Select Record Entry*, you can either highlight Record Entry and press Enter or type the number next to Record Entry.

At the bottom of the menu is a list of keys that you can press at this point. See Table 1.1 for a complete list of keys you can use when making a menu selection. Please note that if you press Esc from the Main Menu you will exit the program.

Table 1.1: Keys for Menu Selection

PRESS:	TO:
↓	Highlight next item.
↑	Highlight previous item.
Home	Highlight first item.
End	Highlight last item.
Enter	Select highlighted item.
Any number in list	Select item.
Esc	Leave menu.

SELECTING YOUR PRINTER

When you first install the program, DataEase selects the Epson MX-80 as the default printer. If this is compatible with your printer, or if your printer has already been configured, you can skip this next section. To change the printer selection, follow the steps below. If you are a new computer user, or are unfamiliar with your hardware, enlist the aid of someone who understands hardware and can help you complete the form before proceeding.

1. Select **System Administration**; DataEase displays the System Administration menu.

2. Select **Define Configuration**; DataEase displays the Configuration form pictured in Figure 1.3.

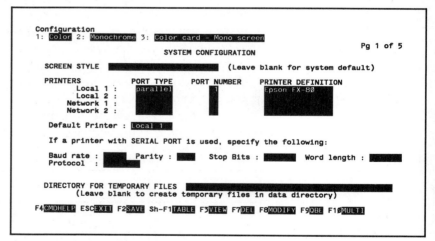

Figure 1.3: Printer Definition form

3. Press **Tab** to skip to the next field, under PRINTERS, which asks you for your PORT TYPE.

4. Type one of the following:

    - **1** if your printer is parallel.
    - **2** if your printer is serial.

Your printer is cabled to one of the numbered ports in the back of your computer. The next field asks you for the PORT NUMBER:

5. Type the number of the port your printer is cabled to and press **Enter**

The next field asks you for your PRINTER DEFINITION, which is the name of your printer. You can select your printer from the alphabetical list of printers:

6. Press **F1** to display the list of printers.

7. Press ↓ until the name of your printer is highlighted.

8. Press **Enter**

The last step is to save this information:

9. Press the **F2** function key. DataEase returns you to the System Configuration menu.

10. Press **Esc** twice to return to the Main Menu.

You have accomplished three tasks in this first chapter:

- You have started and signed on to DataEase.
- You have created and named your first database.
- You have, if necessary, changed the selected printer.

In the next chapter, you'll create your first form.

CHAPTER TWO

Creating
Your First Form

Fast Track

To define a new form,   21

select Form Definition and Relationships from the Main Menu. Then select Define a Form from the Form Definition menu, and enter the name of your new form. You can place explanatory text and field prompts anywhere on the screen. Place your fields next to your field prompts. When the form is complete, press **F2** to save it.

To define a field,   28

position the cursor, and press **F10**. You can either accept the field prompt as the field name, or enter a particular field name. Select the field type, and follow the prompts to complete any other information about the type and length of the field. The remaining fields are optional. When the field is complete, press **F2** to save the definition.

To print your form definition,   44

press **Shift-F9**.

CHAPTER 2

THE NEXT STEP TOWARD BUILDING YOUR DATABASE
is to design the forms you use to enter the data. You can create up to
2000 forms per database. There are five basic steps to create any
new form:

- Design the layout of the form.
- Name your form.
- Enter your form text.
- Place and define your fields.
- Save your definition.

In addition, you can add cosmetic enhancements such as borders and
special screen highlights. In this section, you will learn the basic steps
to design a simple form: entering text and defining fields.

The first form you will create in your INVENTORY database will
be called ITEMS and will contain the different items sold by Furniture Palace, the amount they cost, the amount they sell for, and the
number of pieces currently in stock.

Begin from the Main Menu:

1. Select **Form Definition and Relationships**

The Form Definition menu, pictured in Figure 2.1 contains a list of
form definition tasks. The next step is to:

2. Select **Define a Form**; DataEase asks you to:

   Please enter the Form name to be defined:

You can enter any name up to 20 characters, beginning with a letter.
All text characters, numbers, or spaces are allowed in form names,
except [,],{, or }. In addition, the first eight characters should be a

CH. 2

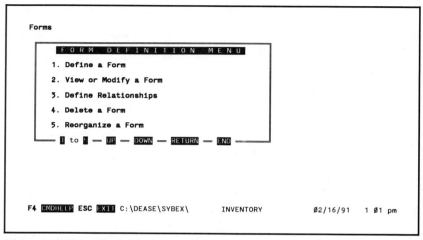

Figure 2.1: Form Definition menu

unique combination, in order to conform to DOS file naming conventions. Names can be entered in uppercase or lowercase.

3. Type **ITEMS** ←

THE FORM DEFINITION SCREEN

After you enter the name of your form, DataEase displays the Form Definition screen, as shown in Figure 2.2. The first thing you'll see is the name of your form in the top left corner of the screen:

Form: ITEMS

DataEase uses the first two lines of the screen to display information. The top line is divided into three sections:

- The *title area* on the left where DataEase displays the current task or form name.

- The *mode/cursor position* in the middle where DataEase displays the position of the cursor in terms of Row (R) and Column (C).

- The *message area* on the right where DataEase displays special messages, including error messages.

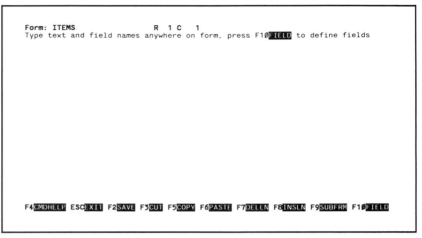

Figure 2.2: Form Definition screen

The second line is the *prompt line*, where DataEase displays special menus or choices.

The blank area of the Form Definition screen is where you design the layout of your form. Right now, the only thing you see in this area is the blinking cursor, which, as indicated by the cursor position area, is shown to be in R 1 C 1, or Row 1, Column 1. As you move around the screen, this indicator will change to reflect your current position. An exercise in this book may contain an instruction that tells you to move your cursor to a specific position, as in the following example:

1. Move the cursor to Row 2, Column 5.

Finally, at the bottom of the screen, DataEase lists the function keys.

USING THE COMMAND HELP MENUS—F4

Most of the commands available to you are assigned to the function keys. For your convenience, the most commonly used function key commands for the current screen are always listed across the bottom of the screen. You will eventually become familiar with most of them.

However, if you ever need assistance remembering a command, you can use the Command Help menus to select your command. No matter where you are in DataEase, the F4 function key will display the Command Help menu for the current screen.

Take a look:

1. Press **F4**

DataEase displays the list of menu names across the top of the screen, as shown in Figure 2.3. Each name represents a pull-down menu of related commands. The first of these pull-down menus, Exit, is displayed. One at a time, display the other menus:

2. Press → three times.

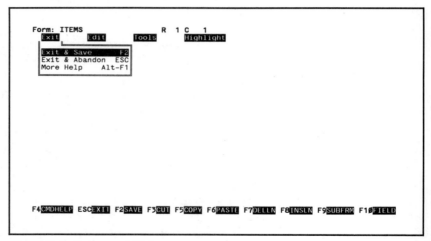

Figure 2.3: Command Help menu

Each time you press →, a different menu is displayed. To the right of each command is the function key shortcut to the command. You can use either the command menus or the function keys to execute a command. To use the Command Help menu:

- Press → or ← to select a menu.
- Press ↑ or ↓ followed by **Enter** to select a command listed in the menu.
- Press **Esc** to clear the menus.

CREATING YOUR FIRST FORM   25

Let's exit Command Help and return to the Form Definition screen and take a look at another form of help.

3. Press **Esc** to clear the screen.

GETTING MORE HELP—ALT-F1

> You clear any help screen by pressing any key other than F1.

DataEase offers additional assistance in the form of Help screens, which display information about cursor movement, editing, saving your work, and other commands that relate to the current screen. You can display help screens by pressing Alt-F1 or by using Command Help. Let's use Command Help to display additional help screens:

1. Press **F4** to display the menus.
2. Select **More Help**

The first help screen, which lists available commands, is pictured in Figure 2.4. The numbers displayed in the message area refer to pages in the DataEase Reference Manual related to this topic. If more help screens are available you can ask to see them by pressing F1. Try it:

3. Press **F1**

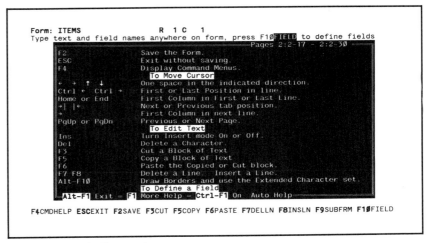

Figure 2.4: Help Screen 1

DataEase displays another help screen with more commands. Let's see if there is another help screen.

    4. Press **F1** again.

The Form Definition screen returns, indicating that no more help is available.

One last item about available help: You can also press Alt-F1 from the Command Help menu to display help on the currently highlighted menu command. Let's look for help with an Edit command:

1. Press **F4**
2. Select the **Edit** menu.
3. Highlight (do *not* select) the **Copy** command.
4. Press **Alt-F1** for help. (Remember to hold down the **Alt** key before pressing **F1**.)

DataEase displays a help box, pictured in Figure 2.5, which contains information about the command. Now you can clear the menus:

    5. Press **Esc**

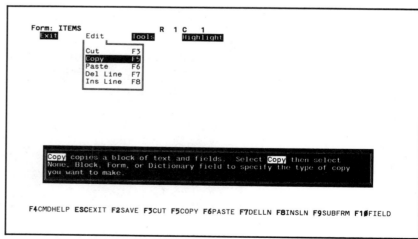

Figure 2.5: Help box for Copy command

Later in this chapter, you will learn how to create your own help screens to assist the operator in entering the records.

DESIGNING YOUR FORM

Before creating your form on the screen, imagine what the form might look like on a piece of paper. In fact, it is an excellent idea to design your form on paper before creating it on the screen. You'll save time later if you can decide exactly what information you want to keep and in what order. The form you define will be used to enter the data and therefore should be clear and easy to follow. In addition, as you will see in the next chapter, this form provides the format when later viewing individual records. So you may want to give some thought as to how you want the information to appear on the screen.

A form is composed of two types of entries: form text and record entry fields. You can see an example of this in Figure 2.6.

Record entry fields are the areas where you enter data. Fields are usually represented on your paper forms by blank lines; on the screen they are shown in highlight, generally light brown on a blue background for color monitors and grey or white on a black background

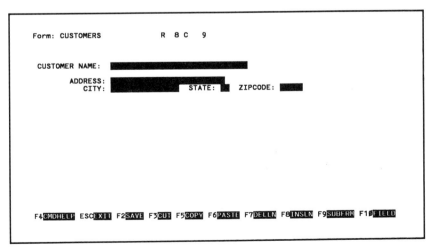

Figure 2.6: A sample form

28 MASTERING DATAEASE

CH. 2

for non-color monitors. Form text is anything you want to type on the form, including field prompts, explanatory text, titles, or any other text you want to add. In addition, if you have a color monitor, you can design your form to display fields and text in a variety of colors.

The screen has 22 lines available. Each form can be up to 16 screens, or pages, in length and can contain up to 255 fields.

FIELD DEFINITION

Record entry fields must not only be placed on the screen, they must also be defined. Fields are assigned characteristics, or attributes, that help DataEase determine what kind of data you want entered and how you want it to look. Although you will be learning about many field characteristics, there are three things you must tell DataEase about each field:

The field name	Each field is assigned a name that DataEase will use when referencing that field. You can use the text you entered as the field prompt, or any name you choose up to 20 characters.
Data type	This determines the type of information that is accepted. For example, if a field is defined as number, no letters can be entered. See Table 2.1 for examples of each data type.
Field length	DataEase needs to know the maximum number of characters for text, number, or numeric string fields. Lengths of the other field types are automatically calculated by DataEase. When defining field lengths, remember that DataEase limits each record to 4000 characters. Table 2.1 also includes information about maximum field lengths.

CREATING YOUR FIRST FORM 29

Table 2.1: Samples of Field Types

TYPE	CONTENTS	DESCRIPTION	MAXIMUM LENGTH
Text	Any character	Names; Addresses; Titles.	255
Number	0–9; – ; .	Entries with true numeric values.	
Integers		Whole numbers.	14
Fixed Point		Decimal position is fixed.	39, ?
Floating Point		Decimal position varies; decimal entered by user	14
Numeric String	0–9	Numbers with no numeric value: Zip Codes, Social Security Numbers, Phone Numbers.	255
Date	0–9/	Valid dates only.	8
Time	0–9:	Valid times only.	8
Yes/No	yes or no		3
Choice	255	List of choices determined by user.	255

Note: All numbers are stored to a precision of 14 characters. For Integers, DataEase inserts commas in numbers that contain 4 digits or more and adds characters to the length for each comma; for Fixed Point, DataEase adds characters to the length for both commas and the decimal place; for Floating Point, you must account for the decimal point in the field length.

PLACING TEXT AND FIELDS

DataEase displays the following message in the prompt area of the screen:

Type text and field names anywhere on form

30 MASTERING DATAEASE

CH. 2

As you can see, DataEase gives you the freedom to place your text and fields anywhere on the screen that you like. At the top of the Form Definition area you can see the *cursor*, currently in Row 1, Column 1. You tell DataEase where you want to place a field or text by moving the cursor there.

Before you begin creating your form, take a look at Table 2.2 for a list of keys you can use in the Form Definition screen.

Table 2.2: Keys for Form Definition

CURSOR MOVEMENT KEYS	
PRESS:	**TO MOVE TO:**
←	Left one character.
→	Right one character.
↑	Up one line.
↓	Down one line.
Home	First column in first line.
End	Last column in last line.
Tab	Right one tab stop (6 spaces).
Shift-Tab	Left one tab stop.
PgDn	Next page (screen).
PgUp	Previous page (screen).
EDITING KEYS	
PRESS:	**TO:**
Ins	Add characters.
Del	Remove character.

ENTERING THE TEXT INTO YOUR FORM

When you type form text, remember it will appear later exactly as you type it, upper or lowercase. In your first form, you'll be typing your text in uppercase to make the field prompts stand out. When you create your own, you can type them any way you like. In

CREATING YOUR FIRST FORM **31**

addition, it makes no difference whether you place your text first, then your fields, or your text and fields at the same time. However, for this exercise you will enter the form text first, then place the fields.

Using the cursor position indicator in the status line as a guide, follow the steps below to place the form text. Let's start with the form title:

1. Move the cursor to Row 2, Column 31.
2. Type **MASTER INVENTORY LIST**

Next, enter your field prompts:

3. Move the cursor to Row 5, Column 7.
4. Type **ENTRY DATE:**

CORRECTING ERRORS

If you make a mistake while entering text, it is easy to correct. If you have experience with word processing, you will find the concepts familiar. Just in case you make an error, let's practice correcting text by typing the next prompt incorrectly:

1. Move the cursor to Row 7, Column 7.
2. Type **STROCK NMBER:**

Obviously, the prompt should be STOCK NUMBER. Table 2.2 listed the two important editing keys for form definition: Del and Ins. In this case, you can use the Del key to remove the R, and the Ins key to add the U:

3. Move the cursor to the first **R**, as shown below:

   ST<u>R</u>OCK NMBER:
4. Press **Del**. Notice that the **R** disappears and the following characters shift to the left to fill in its place.
5. Move the cursor to the **M** (where the **U** should be):

   N<u>M</u>BER:
6. Press **Ins**. When Insert mode is active, Ins appears in the mode area, temporarily replacing the Row and Column indicators.

7. Type **U**. The **U** is inserted and the other characters shift to the right.

8. Press **Ins** again to cancel Insert mode.

Insert mode is now cancelled and the Row and Column indicators reappear. Your screen should look like the one in Figure 2.7.

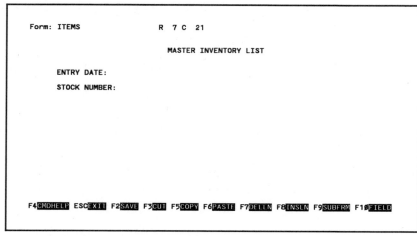

Figure 2.7: Screen after two field prompts

Now you can continue entering the remaining field prompts:

1. Move the cursor to Row 7, Column 31.
2. Type **ITEM:**
3. Move the cursor to Row 9, Column 7.
4. **MANUFACTURER:**
5. Move the cursor to Row 9, Column 45.
6. Type **OUR COST:**
7. Move the cursor to Row 11, Column 7.
8. Type **MARKUP%:**
9. Move the cursor to Row 11, Column 24.
10. Type **SELLING PRICE:**

11. Move the cursor to Row 11, Column 51.
12. Type **QUANTITY ON HAND:**

When you finish entering text, your form should look like Figure 2.8.

DEFINING THE FIELDS—F10

The next step is to place and define your fields. Let's begin with the first field, ENTRY DATE, which is the date the item was first entered into inventory:

1. Move the cursor to Row 5, Column 19.
2. Press **F10**

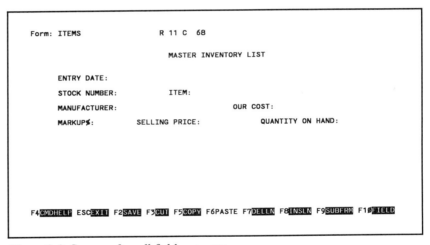

Figure 2.8: Screen after all field prompts

Your form disappears and DataEase displays the Field Definition form pictured in Figure 2.9. This screen is basically another form with field prompts and entry fields. Notice that ENTRY DATE is entered as the field name and that the next prompt is for the field type. Table 2.3 lists the function keys you can use in the Field Definition screen.

34 MASTERING DATAEASE

CH. 2

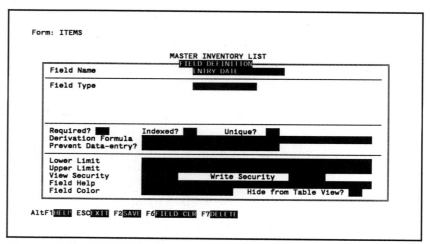

Figure 2.9: Field Definition form for ENTRY DATE

Table 2.3: Keys for Field Definition

CURSOR MOVEMENT KEYS	
PRESS:	**TO MOVE TO:**
Tab or Enter	Next field.
Shift-Tab	Previous field.
Home	First field.
End	Last field.
EDITING KEYS	
PRESS:	**TO:**
F6	Erase the current field.
F2	Clear the screen and save the definition.
Esc	Clear the screen without saving the definition.
F7	Delete the current field definition.
F1	Display more information.

Although you can change the field name, here we will accept it and move to the next field:

3. Press **Tab** to move to Field Type.

You are prompted to enter a field type. A partial list of numbered field types is displayed on the prompt line, as shown in Figure 2.10. Let's stop a moment and discuss this type of menu. F1 (More) at the far right of the prompt line tells you that there are more selections, but the one we want, Date, is visible. To make a selection from a menu that appears across the top of your screen, you must type the number next to your choice.

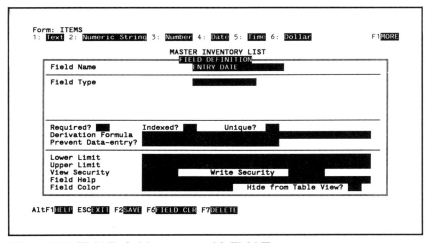

Figure 2.10: Field Definition screen with Field Type menu

4. Type **4** to select **Date**

Date is entered as the field type. DataEase accepts only valid date entries in date fields. Field lengths for date fields are automatically eight characters, to accommodate a format of mm-dd-yy, e.g., 07-12-91.

5. Press **F2** to save the definition.

CH. 2

Once again, the form is displayed and the ENTRY DATE field appears as a highlighted box. The color or shading of your field will depend on the type of monitor you have.

SPECIAL ATTRIBUTES: REQUIRED, INDEXED, UNIQUE

The next field, STOCK NUMBER, has a few more characteristics:

1. Move the cursor to Row 7, Column 21.

2. Press **F10**

From now on, after we abbreviate a field name, we will refer to that field by its shorter name. In this case, we'll refer to this field as STOCK#, since that is the name DataEase will use.

As you know, DataEase automatically enters the field prompt as the field name. However, the field prompt is a description or an operator prompt and is not always an appropriate field name. You can save space in the database if you select shorter names for your fields. Later, when you learn how to use DataEase's Data Query Language, you will be grateful for shorter field names. In this case, let's change the field name to STOCK#.

3. Press → to move the cursor to the space after the **K**:

   STOCK_NUMBER

4. Type #

   STOCK_#NUMBER

5. Press **Del** six times to delete NUMBER.

6. Press **Tab** to move to Field Type.

STOCK# is an example of a numeric string field. Only numbers are accepted into this type of field, although they are treated as characters with no numeric value. A zip code would be another example of a numeric string field. A telephone or Social Security number would be an example of a specially formatted numeric string.

7. Select **Numeric String**

8. Select **No** (for no special format).

CREATING YOUR FIRST FORM 37

9. Type **5** for the length.

10. Press **Tab** to move to the Required? field.

Required Fields

Some fields provide essential information about a record. For example, your Social Security number is vital to the IRS. Such fields should require operator entry. Since each item must be assigned a STOCK# before it can be a part of the inventory, this is required information in your ITEMS form. DataEase will not save a record until all required fields are filled.

The Required? field displays a Yes/No menu in the prompt line:

1: No 2: Yes

To make a selection from the Yes/No menu, you can type 1 or N; 2 or Y.

1. Select **Yes** for the Required? field.

Indexed Fields

Some fields are used to organize records. For example, you may want to alphabetize by MANUFACTURER but probably not by MARKUP%. You may want to organize your records by ITEM, but probably not by ENTRY DATE. Indexing a field allows you to alphabetize your records by a text or character string and also assists DataEase in finding information quickly. You can create up to 254 field indexes per form. Since STOCK# is an important field, you'll want to create an index for it.

1. Select **Yes** for the Indexed? field.

Unique Fields

Each record should have at least one field that is used to distinguish it from other records. For example, your Social Security number identifies you and only you. Accordingly, when you create a form, you should include at least one unique field. These unique fields are

38 MASTERING DATAEASE

CH. 2

usually required as well as indexed. In ITEMS, you'll use the STOCK# field to identify each item.

1. Select **Yes** for the Unique? field.

Your completed definition should look like the one pictured in Figure 2.11.

2. Press **F2** to save the definition.

The Form Definition screen returns and the new field is added.

The next two fields you'll define, ITEM and MANUFACTURER, are examples of text fields, in which any character is allowed. These fields will also be indexed. Use the information below to define these two fields:

> The **R, C** column contains the row and column positions at which you should place the fields.

FIELD	R, C	TYPE	LENGTH	IND?
ITEM	7,37	Text	25	yes
MANUFACTURER	9,21	Text	20	yes

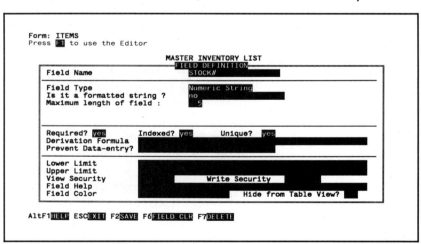

Figure 2.11: Completed definition for STOCK#

> DataEase will increase the size of number fields if it adds dollar signs and commas. Make sure you have enough room in your form for the extra characters.

The next field, COST, is a dollar field. DataEase automatically assigns two decimal places to dollar fields; you need only enter the number of characters to the left of the decimal. DataEase adds commas where necessary and dollar signs. Following COST is

MARKUP%, a number field. DataEase recognizes three types of number fields:

Integer   Whole numbers without decimal places.

Fixed Point   Where you define the number of places to the left *and* right of the decimal point.

Floating Point   Where decimal point is not defined; you enter the number of digits including the decimal point, but you must enter the decimal point.

MARKUP% is a fixed point number field.

Use the information below as a guide to define these fields. (Notice that you will change the name of the OUR COST field.)

FIELD	*R, C*	*NAME*	*TYPE*	*DECIMAL PLACES*
OUR COST	9,55	COST	Dollar	4 (to the left)
MARKUP%	11,16	MARKUP%	Number, Fixed Point	1 (to the left) ;1 (to the right)

Now your form should look like the one pictured in Figure 2.12.

CREATING RANGES

If you want a numeric entry to fall within a certain range, you must set upper and lower limits. For example, if salaries are never below $15,000 or above $75,000, you would set a lower limit of 15,000 and an upper limit of 75,000. DataEase would then prevent the operator from entering a number outside of this range.

In the case of your ITEMS form, markups are never less than 1.3% or higher than 2.5%. Let's return to the MARKUP% field and set the limit:

1. If necessary, move the cursor to the MARKUP% field.

2. Press **F10**

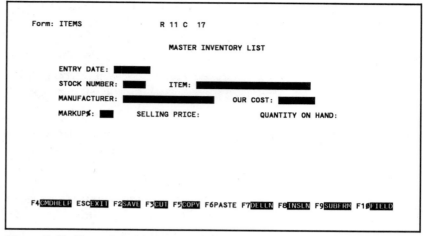

Figure 2.12: Form definition after MARKUP%

3. Move the cursor to the Lower Limit field.
4. Type **1.3**
5. Move to the Upper Limit field.
6. Type **2.5**
7. Press **F2** to save the changes.

CREATING A CALCULATED FIELD

Calculated fields are derived from a derivation formula entered in the Field Definition screen. There are four different types of derivations, (the last three of which will be discussed in Chapter 8):

Calculation

Lookup

Sequence

Default

A calculation formula may consist of field names in the current form or numeric constants. PRICE, for example, is derived from multiplying the MARKUP% field by the COST field. Table 2.4 lists the arithmetic operators used in formulas.

Table 2.4: Arithmetic Operators

OPERATOR	TYPE	EXAMPLES
+	Addition	Subtotal + Tax
–	Subtraction	Subtotal – Discount
*	Multiplication	Subtotal * .06
/	Division	Salary / 12

1. Move the cursor to Row 11, Column 39 and press **F10**
2. Using Figure 2.13 as a guide, define the field name, type, and length, and enter the formula for PRICE.
3. **Tab** to the Prevent Data-entry? field.

DataEase displays the following menu choices in the prompt line:

1:No 2:Yes 3:Yes and do not save (virtual)

As a general rule, you should select Y to prevent operator entry in a calculated field. However, there are exceptions. For example, the

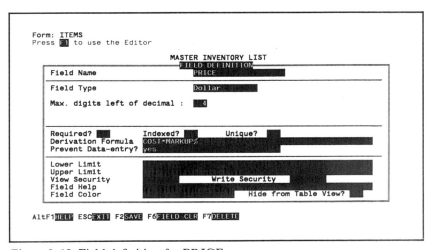

Figure 2.13: Field definition for PRICE

42 MASTERING DATAEASE

CH. 2

operator should be able to override the formula in a tax field for non-taxable items. You would select the third option, Yes and do not save (virtual), if you wanted only to display the results of the formula and *not* save the information with the record. In this case operator entry is not allowed, but the data will be stored with the record:

4. Select **Yes** to prevent data entry and save the results.

5. Press **F2** to save the definition.

The last field is QUANTITY ON HAND:

1. Use the information below to enter the field definition (and notice that you will change the name of the field):

R, C	NAME	TYPE	LENGTH
11,69	QTY ONHAND	Number, Integer	3

2. Save the definition.

CREATING FIELD HELP

Sometimes field prompts do not provide enough information about what to enter in a field. In that case, you can create your own help screen that the operator can display when entering records. For example, in order to sort the ITEM field properly the item description should follow the name, e.g., *Bed, Water* instead of *Water Bed*. Otherwise, the record would be sorted under W for water, instead of B for bed. Follow the steps below to create a help screen for the ITEM field:

1. Move the cursor to the ITEM field.

2. Press **F10**

3. Press **Tab** to move the cursor to the Field Help field.

> You are limited to 1330 characters per Field Help field.

You will need additional space to enter the field help message. Pressing F1 displays a full-page editing screen:

4. Press **F1**

CREATING YOUR FIRST FORM 43

5. Type

    ENTER THE ITEM NAME FIRST, FOLLOWED BY THE DESCRIPTION;
    i.e. Table, Kitchen or Bed, King

Your help screen should look like the one in Figure 2.14.

6. Press **F2** to save the help message.

7. Press **F2** to save the definition.

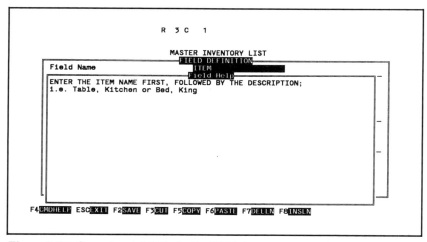

Figure 2.14: Completed field help for ITEM

DISPLAYING FIELD ATTRIBUTES

You've seen how easy it is to delete and type over form text. But what if you accidentally press Del or type over a field? Fortunately, DataEase won't let you. When you press any key other than F10 or Ins while your cursor is on a field, DataEase lets you know you have run into a field by displaying the field name and characteristics in the prompt line.

Try it and see:

1. Move the cursor to the STOCK# field.

2. Press **Spacebar**

44 MASTERING DATAEASE

CH. 2

DataEase displays field information in the prompt line:

FIELD: STOCK#,Num.String,5,Required,Indexed,Unique

Congratulations! You have completed your first form definition. It should look like the one pictured in Figure 2.15.

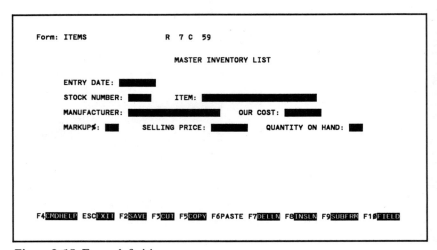

Figure 2.15: Form definition

PRINTING YOUR FORM DEFINITION—SHIFT-F9

> It is also a good idea to save a paper copy of your work just in case all your electronic copies disappear.

Any experienced computer user will tell you to save a copy of your work on another disk. Printing a copy of your form definition is the best way to guarantee accuracy in case you need to recreate this form some day. Pressing Shift-F9 will print the definition for your form. If you have a printer, make sure it is on *and* on line. Then go ahead and print your form definition. (Remember to hold down the Shift key before pressing F9.)

1. Press **Shift-F9**

If you don't have a printer, you can refer to Figure 2.16 to see what your form definition looks like.

CREATING YOUR FIRST FORM   45

```
┌─────────────────────────────────────────────────────────────────────────┐
│                                                                           │
│        FORM    ITEMS                              07/30/90  10:43          │
│        ---------------------------                -----------------        │
│                                                                           │
│   1       10      20      30      40      50      60      70      80       │
│   ----+----+----+----+----+----+----+----+----+----+----+----+----+----+  │
│                           MASTER INVENTORY LIST                           │
│                                                                           │
│        ENTRY DATE: _____                                               │
│                                                                           │
│        STOCK NUMBER: _____    ITEM: _____                   │
│                                                                           │
│        MANUFACTURER: _____    OUR COST: _____                │
│                                                                           │
│        MARKUP%: ___   SELLING PRICE: _____    QUANTITY ON HAND: ___     │
│   ----+----+----+----+----+----+----+----+----+----+----+----+----+----+  │
│   1       10      20      30      40      50      60      70      80       │
│                                                                           │
│        FIELD DESCRIPTIONS                                                 │
│        ------------------                                                 │
│                                                                           │
│   No. Name                 Type      Len Req In- Uni Der Rng Pre- Hide Record │
│                                      gth uir dex que ive Chk vent Tbl size offset │
│   ─────────────────────────────────────────────────────────────────────────── │
│     1 ENTRY DATE           Date       8  no  no  no  no  no  no   no    6     3 │
│     2 STOCK#               Num.String 5  yes yes yes no  no  no   no    5     9 │
│     3 ITEM                 Text      25  no  yes no  no  no  no   no   25    14 │
│         Field Help:                                                       │
│   ENTER ITEM FIRST FOLLOWED BY THE DESCRIPTION;                           │
│   i.e. Table, Kitchen or Bed, King                                        │
│     4 MANUFACTURER         Text      20  no  yes no  no  no  no   no   20    39 │
│     5 COST                 Number     8  no  no  no  no  no  no   no    8    59 │
│         Number Type : Fixed point                                         │
│         Digits to left of decimal = 5                                     │
│     6 MARKUP%              Number     3  no  no  no  yes no  no   no    4    67 │
│         Number Type : Fixed point                                         │
│         Digits to left of decimal = 1                                     │
│         Lower Range : 1.3                                                 │
│         Upper Range : 2.5                                                 │
│     7 PRICE                Number     8  no  no  no  yes no  yes  no    8    71 │
│         Number Type : Fixed point                                         │
│         Digits to left of decimal = 5                                     │
│         Field calculation formula : COST*MARKUP%                          │
│     8 QTY ONHAND           Number     3  no  no  no  no  no  no   no    2    79 │
│         Number Type : Integer                                             │
│   ─────────────────────────────────────────────────────────────────────────── │
│   Record size 81                                                          │
│                                                                           │
│   Memory required for form: Text  426, Fields 373, Total 799 bytes.       │
│                                                                           │
└─────────────────────────────────────────────────────────────────────────┘
```

Figure 2.16: Form definition printout

SAVING YOUR FORM—F2

Perhaps the most crucial step in form definition is saving your form. If you miss that step, you'll lose everything—not a pleasant thought. Right now, your form resides in the computer's memory; saving the form puts it permanently on your disk.

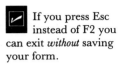

If you press Esc instead of F2 you can exit *without* saving your form.

1. Press **F2** to save your form. DataEase returns you to the Form Definition menu and displays in the message area:

   Form Definition Saved

   From here you can return to the Main Menu:

2. Press **Esc**

Now that you have completed your first form, you are ready to enter information into your database. In the next chapter, you will see how your field attributes help you enter records.

SECURITY NOTES

You must have a *high* security level to create a form. If your security level is not high enough for the task you want to perform, the message area will display:

Security access denied

LAN NOTES

No forms in the same database may share the same name. If you attempt to use a name already used by yourself or another user, the message area displays:

Form <formname> already exists

You must enter another name or press **Esc** to cancel the command.

CHAPTER THREE

Entering Records

Fast Track

To enter a record,   49

select Record Entry from the Main Menu; select the form name from the Records menu. Enter data in the first field, and press **Tab** to move to the next field. Press **Alt-F1** to see any available help screens for the current field.

To save the record and enter another,   53

press **F2** (to save your current record), then press **F5** (to clear the form for the next record). Press **Esc** when you are done to return to the Records menu.

To print your record,   63

press **Shift-F9**.

CHAPTER *3*

AFTER YOU HAVE DEFINED YOUR FORM, THE NEXT STEP is to enter some records. Each form you create can contain up to 16 million records. (We hope you'll never need to enter that many.) Your records are the heart of your database. They are the source of all the information generated from your database. Therefore, entering records accurately and efficiently is a top priority.

In this chapter, you'll get enough practice to be comfortable with this most important task. And of course you'll learn how to save your records, and along the way learn some shortcuts that will eliminate unnecessary typing. From the Main Menu:

    1. Select **Record Entry** ⏎

THE RECORDS MENU

DataEase displays the Records menu pictured in Figure 3.1. On the right is the list of available forms. DataEase asks you to:

> Please select a Form.
> Enter a number from 0 to 2:

A list is a vertical menu of items or item names. To make selections from a list, you can either use the directional arrow keys to highlight your selection or type the number preceding the selection. However, whether you highlight the item or type the number, you must always confirm by pressing Enter.

    1. Select **ITEMS**

50 MASTERING DATAEASE

CH. 3

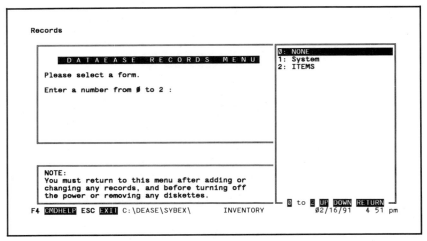

Figure 3.1: The Records menu

THE RECORD ENTRY SCREEN

Your ITEMS form, pictured in Figure 3.2, appears as you originally created it. However, there are some differences. Did you notice them?

- The date field contains the date separators (/).
- The decimal points are showing for three of your number fields.

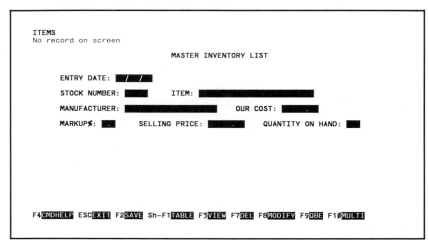

Figure 3.2: The blank ITEMS form

ENTERING RECORDS **51**

ENTERING RECORDS

There are three basic steps to entering records:

- Enter the information into each field.
- Press **F2** to save the record.
- Press **F5** to clear the form for another record.

While entering your records, keep in mind the following guidelines:

- When you have completed a field entry, press **Tab** or **Enter** to move to the next field.
- If you fill a field completely, the cursor automatically moves to the next field.
- If you make a mistake in a field, you can press the **Backspace** key to erase the previous character(s).
- If you press **Esc** while entering a record, DataEase will ask you if you want to abandon (lose) this entry. Just answer **N** to return to your record.

Although DataEase does not distinguish between UPPERCASE and lowercase, your reports will look unprofessional if your data is entered in mixed cases.

One of the most important things to remember when entering records is to be consistent, particularly in text fields. The way you enter data is the way it will appear in printed reports. Instructions on how you want your data entered can be included in the entry form. In Chapter 9, you will learn about some ways you can control the way text is entered.

ENTERING YOUR FIRST RECORD

Let's continue to build your database by entering your first record. Follow the steps below, starting with the ENTRY DATE field:

1. Type **011588**

DataEase displays the message:

New Record on Screen

and the cursor automatically moves to STOCK NUMBER when you fill the date field:

2. Type **98765** for STOCK#.

Your cursor now moves to the ITEM field.

Displaying Field Help—ALT-F1

Normally, when you press Alt-F1 DataEase displays help for the current screen. However, if a help screen was created for the current field, pressing Alt-F1 displays that instead. Let's display the help screen you created for ITEM in the last chapter:

1. Press **Alt-F1**

DataEase displays your help screen, as pictured in Figure 3.3. More Data Ease help screens can be displayed by pressing F1.

2. Press **Esc** to clear the help screen.

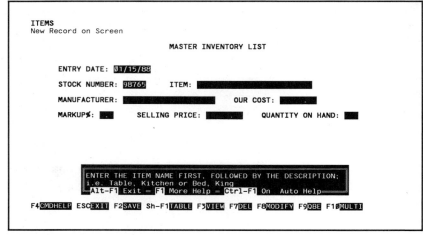

Figure 3.3: Field help for ITEM

3. Starting with the ITEM field, fill in the next four fields using the information below:

ITEM:	Table, Kitchen ⏎
MANUFACTURER:	Realco ⏎
OUR COST:	350 ⏎
MARKUP%:	1.5

As soon as you type the MARKUP% value, DataEase calculates PRICE and the cursor moves to QUANTITY ON HAND.

4. Type *3* ⏎

Now your screen should appear as in Figure 3.4.

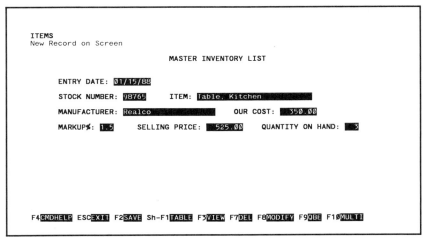

Figure 3.4: Completed first record

Saving Your Record and Clearing the Screen—F2 and F5

Records are saved one at a time after entry. After you fill in all the fields for one record, you must save it on the disk with the F2 key and clear the screen by pressing F5 before entering the next record. First

54 MASTERING DATAEASE

CH. 3

save the current record:

1. Press **F2**; DataEase displays this information in the message area:

New Record Written

Record 1 on screen

and the record remains on the screen.

2. Press **F5** to clear the screen. The screen clears and the cursor returns to the first field, ENTRY DATE.

CORRECTING ERRORS

You can always stop and correct any mistakes during record entry. Table 3.1 provides a list of cursor movement and editing keys you can use in record entry. Just for practice, let's make some mistakes:

1. Use the following information to enter your next record:

ENTRY DATE:	052587
STOCK NUMBER:	12335
ITEM:	Bed, King
MANUFACTURER:	Regal Furniture ←
OUR COST:	800 ←
MARKUP%:	2 ←
QUANTITY ON HAND:	2 ←

Before you save your record, let's correct the errors. First, the STOCK# is incorrect: it should be 12345. You need to replace the 3 with 4. To replace a character, simply type over it:

1. Press **Home** to move to the first field.

2. Press **Tab** to move to STOCK#.

3. Press the → key to move the cursor under the second 3:

STOCK NUMBER: 123_35

4. Type **4**

Table 3.1: Keys for Record Entry

CURSOR MOVEMENT KEYS	
PRESS:	**TO MOVE TO:**
→	Next character in field.
←	Previous character in field.
↓	Down one field to right.
↑	Up one field to left.
Tab	Next field.
Shift-Tab	Previous field.
Home	First field.
End	Last field.
PgDn	Next screen (page).
PgUp	Previous screen (page).
EDITING KEYS	
PRESS:	**TO:**
Del	Delete current character.
Backspace	Delete previous character.
Ins	Turn on/off insert mode (on—add characters to field; off—replace characters).

The Ins key is used when you want to add one or more characters to a field. It works just as it does when you are editing a form. The ITEM should be: Bed, Water, King:

1. Move to the ITEM field and place the cursor under the K:

   ITEM: Bed, <u>K</u>ing

2. Press **Ins**

3. Type **Water,**

56 MASTERING DATAEASE

CH. 3

The field should now display:

ITEM: Bed, Water, King

4. Press **Ins** to cancel Insert mode.

And finally, the MANUFACTURER should be Real, not Regal Furniture. Let's use Del to fix it:

1. Press **Tab** to move to the MANUFACTURER field.
2. Move the cursor to the **g**
3. Press **Del**

The field should now display:

MANUFACTURER: Real Furniture

Your corrected record should look like the one pictured in Figure 3.5. Now you can save the record and clear the screen for the next record:

1. Press **F2** to save the record.
2. Press **F5** to clear the form.

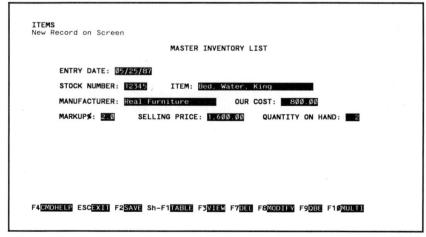

Figure 3.5: Corrected second record

Add the remaining records to your database as shown in Table 3.2. If you notice any mistakes in the list, just leave them in for now. When you complete the last record, save it and clear the screen.

Table 3.2: Records to Be Entered

ENTRY DATE	STOCK#	ITEM	COST	MARKUP%	QTY ON HAND	MANUFACTURER
04/15/86	87654	Bed, Queen	550.00	2.0	3	Picklepot Furniture
12/01/85	23456	Table, Bedside	300.00	1.5	1	ABC Company
02/25/89	65432	Table, Coffee	300.00	1.7	2	Picklepot Furn
07/24/88	45678	Chair, Lounge	300.00	1.8	4	Real Furniture
12/13/86	56789	Table, Side	250.00	1.5	5	ABC Company
11/19/89	78920	Armoire, Teak	700.00	1.5	2	Realico
09/18/89	78921	Table, Kitchen	450.00	1.5	3	Picklepot Furniture

TESTING FIELD ATTRIBUTES

You assigned two special attributes to STOCK#: unique and required. Let's test them to make sure they work. First, you'll leave out STOCK#, then you will enter a number already used:

1. Enter the following information into a new record:

ENTRY DATE:	090988
ITEM:	Bed, Twin
MANUFACTURER:	Terrahaute Furniture
OUR COST:	600 ↵
MARKUP%:	2 ↵
QUANTITY ON HAND:	4 ↵

2. Press **F2** to save the record.

58 MASTERING DATAEASE

CH. 3

DataEase catches the oversight and beeps at you and displays in the message area:

FIELD 'STOCK NUMBER' Must be Filled

3. Type **12345** as the STOCK#.

4. Press **F2** to save the record.

DataEase once again catches the mistake and displays the message:

Record already exists as 2
Do you want to modify that record? (Y/N)

If you say Y, DataEase will change Record 2 with the information you just typed on the screen. And you don't want that, so:

5. Type **N**

6. Move back to STOCK# and type **78923**

7. Save the record and clear the screen.

You now have ten records in your database.

You also assigned a special attribute to MARKUP%—you set a lower limit of 1.3, and an upper limit of 2.5. Let's test this by adding another record:

1. Enter the following information for your next record:

ENTRY DATE:	040588
STOCK NUMBER:	73456
ITEM:	Sofa, Modern ⏎
MANUFACTURER:	Terrahaute Furniture
OUR COST:	500 ⏎
MARKUP%:	3 ⏎

DataEase warns you:

MARKUP% FIELD value is too high
Highest value allowed 2.5

ENTERING RECORDS 59

2. Type **1.2**; as soon as you fill up the field, DataEase warns you again:

> MARKUP% FIELD value is too low
> Lowest value allowed 1.3

3. Type **1.8** ⏎

4. Type **2** in the QTY ONHAND field.

5. Save the record and clear the screen.

DATA ENTRY SHORTCUTS

In any database the same information is often repeated in multiple records. For example, city and state may be the same for many records in a personnel or customer database. DataEase offers several time-saving features which allow you to copy information from another record.

USING INFORMATION FROM THE PREVIOUS RECORD—SHIFT-F5 AND SHIFT-F6

If you find that certain information is repeated in several consecutive records, you can copy information from the previous record:

- Shift-F5 copies the information from the previous record.

- Shift-F6 copies the information from the previous field.

> Another way to use information from the previous record is *not* to clear the screen with F5.

Then you can simply change the fields that are different. For example, in the next record, the ENTRY DATE, MANUFACTURER, QTY ONHAND and MARKUP% are the same.

1. Press **Shift-F5** to copy the previous record.

2. Enter the following changes:

STOCK NUMBER:	78928
ITEM:	Table, Coffee ⏎
OUR COST:	300 ⏎

DataEase recalculates the PRICE.

60 *MASTERING DATAEASE*

CH. 3

3. Use **F2** and **F5** respectively to save the record and clear the screen.

In the next record, only the ITEM is the same:

1. Enter the first two fields:

   ENTRY DATE: 082388
   STOCK NUMBER: 65789

2. Press **Shift-F6** to copy the item from the previous record.

DataEase copies the previous item, Table, Coffee, into the current record.

3. Enter the remaining fields:

   MANUFACTURER: ABC Company ↵
   COST: 250 ↵
   MARKUP%:   1.5
   QUANTITY ON HAND: 3 ↵

4. Save the record and clear the screen.

CREATING AND USING
A DEFAULT RECORD—SHIFT-F2 AND SHIFT-F5

A default record may be the most commonly entered record, or a collection of the most commonly entered fields.

If you find that many of your records contain identical field values, you can store these field values in a special record, called a *default* record. If you create a default record, Shift-F5 copies the default record information and Shift-F6 copies the current field from the default record. You can create one default record per form. If you create another one, it replaces the previous default record.

To create and save a default record:

- Press **Alt-F5** to clear the form.

- Enter the record (you needn't fill in each field).

- Save the record with **Shift-F2**.

Alt-F5, referred to as *unchecked mode*, clears the form of all data, like F5; however, Alt-F5 also prevents DataEase from checking for and performing any automatic calculations, like PRICE, as you move around your form.

After you create the default record, you can:

If no default exists, Shift-F5 copies the previous record and Shift-F6 copies the previous field.

- Press **Shift-F5** to copy the default record into the current form.

- Press **Shift-F6** to copy the current field from the default record.

- Press **Shift-F7** to delete the default record.

Let's create a default record that consists of the most commonly entered field values. First,

1. Press **Alt-F5** to clear the screen unchecked. DataEase displays **Unchecked** in the mode area.

2. Enter the following field values:

ITEM:	Table, Side
MANUFACTURER:	ABC Company
MARKUP%:	1.5
QUANTITY ON HAND:	2

3. Press **Shift-F2** to save the record. DataEase displays the message:

   Default Record Written

4. Press F5 to clear the screen.

Now you can save some typing time by copying these default values. The next record contains all of the default record values, so you can copy the entire record:

1. Press **Shift-F5**

All of the field values from the default record are copied, as pictured in Figure 3.6.

62 MASTERING DATAEASE

CH. 3

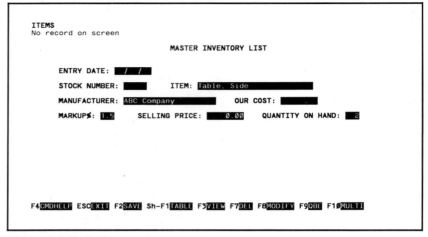

Figure 3.6: Default record copy

2. Complete the record by entering the following values:

   ENTRY DATE: 070686
   STOCK NUMBER: 13456
   OUR COST: 375 ⏎

3. Save the record and clear the screen.

In the next record, only the MANUFACTURER field is the same as the default.

1. Type in the values for the first fields:

   ENTRY DATE: 030487
   STOCK NUMBER: 79876
   ITEM: Bed, Water, Queen ⏎

Your cursor should now be on the MANUFACTURER field. Copy the default value for that field:

2. Press **Shift-F6**. Your field should display:

   MANUFACTURER: ABC Company

3. Move to OUR COST and enter the remaining fields:

   OUR COST: 500 ⏎
   MARKUP%:   2.5
   QUANTITY ON HAND: 3 ⏎

4. Save the record and clear the screen.

DataEase stores the default record only for the duration of the current record entry. Each time you leave record entry, the default is cleared.

You should now have 15 records in your database. (You can press Shift-F3 to check the number of the last record.)

PRINTING A RECORD—SHIFT-F9

You can print an individual record with Shift-F9. DataEase will print the record exactly as you see it on the screen, with underlines representing the field spaces. (Make sure your printer is on and on line.)

1. Press **Ctrl-F3** and type **1** to display the first record.
2. Press **Shift-F9**

Your form is printed and includes the record number in the top left corner.

LEAVING RECORD ENTRY

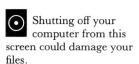

Shutting off your computer from this screen could damage your files.

After you complete your record entry for each work session, you should always return at least to the Record Entry menu before shutting off your computer. Leave Record Entry and return to the Main Menu:

1. Press **Esc** to leave the Record Entry screen.
2. Press **Esc** to return to the Main Menu.

Your Inventory database now contains a form called ITEMS with 15 records. In the next chapter, you will learn how to display these records in a variety of ways: alphabetically, individually or in groups, and selectively.

SECURITY NOTES

The default minimum security level is medium 3, which means that if you are assigned any lower level you cannot enter records. However, this can be changed by the systems administrator. If your security level is not high enough for the task you want to perform, this message will be displayed:

Security access denied

LAN NOTES

There are no locking restrictions for entering records. However, the systems administrator has the option of locking files while they are being used for a report. If that is the case, you will not be allowed access to a form whose records are being processed in a report. In addition, there may be restrictions for viewing or changing records. That is covered in the next chapter.

CHAPTER FOUR

Working with Your Records

Fast Track

To view records in entry order,   69

select the form from the Records menu. When the blank screen is displayed, press **F3** to display Record 1. Continue to press **F3** to display each record until the message **No more records** is displayed. You can press **F3** to return to Record 1.

To view records in reverse order,   70

press **Shift-F3** from Record Entry to display the previous record. Continue to press **Shift-F3** until the message **No more records** is displayed. Then press **Shift-F3** if you want to view the last record.

To view records in index order,   71

press **Alt-F5** to clear the screen. Move the cursor to the indexed field and type * (asterisk). (This field must be created as an indexed field in Form Definition. Only text or numeric string fields can be displayed in their indexed order.) Press **F3** to view the first record. Press **Alt-F3** to view each remaining record in index order.

To search for a particular record by record number,   75

press **Ctrl-F3**. Type the record number and press **Enter**.

To search for a particular record using search criteria,   76

clear the form with **Alt-F5**. Move to the field on which the search is based. Enter the exact characters or numbers to match (the case is not significant). Press **F3** to display the first record match. Press **Alt-F3** to display other matching records. You can use * (asterisk) to represent multiple unknown characters and ? (question mark) to represent a single unknown character.

To modify a record,   84

display the record you want to change and make the modifications. Press **F8** to update the database.

To display records in Table View,   87

press **Shift-F1** to switch from Form to Table View.

To add a record in Table View,   89

press **Shift-F1** to switch to Table View, and press **End** to move to the next blank record. Enter the record(s); to save them, press **F2**.

To modify records in Table View,   92

press **Shift-F1** to switch to Table View, and make your modifications. To save your changes, press **F2**, **F8**, or **Shift-F1** to switch back to Form View.

68

CHAPTER 4

ONCE YOU HAVE BUILT YOUR DATABASE BY CREATING your forms and entering records, most of your tasks will involve maintaining your database: accessing information, editing records, and printing reports. In this chapter, you will learn how to view your records, search for specific records, and make changes to your database.

DataEase simplifies working with your records by using the Record Entry screen for multiple tasks. In addition to entering records, you can:

- View your records in entry or index order.
- Search for specific records.
- Make changes to records.
- Remove records from your database.
- Display records individually or in a table.

VIEWING RECORDS IN FORM VIEW

Databases are dynamic entities, so you may spend much of your time changing records and adding new ones. However, sometimes you will want to look at your records to verify information, such as a customer balance or the status of an inventory item. So it is important to understand how to retrieve information from your database quickly and efficiently.

Records can be viewed individually from the Record Entry screen. This is called Form View and each record appears exactly as you entered it. DataEase offers a variety of methods for displaying your records in Form View.

VIEWING RECORDS IN ENTRY ORDER—F3

After you enter a batch of records you may want to review them and check for errors. You can display your records from Form View in the order you entered them. This is sometimes referred to as entry order or record number order, since numbers are assigned sequentially as you enter them.

So to start with, let's take a look at all those records you added to your database. Since you exited to the Main Menu at the end of the last chapter, begin from the Main Menu. (If you have exited the program, please load DataEase again and sign on. If you need assistance, refer to Chapter 1.)

1. Select **Record Entry**

2. Select **ITEMS** from the Records Menu Form List.

Notice that no record is currently displayed, indicating that you are at the end of the database. At this point you can either enter a new record or display a previously entered record.

Display the records you have entered, one at a time, beginning with Record 1:

1. Press **F3**

DataEase displays Record 1, as pictured in Figure 4.1, and displays in the message area at the top of the screen:

Record found

Record 1 on screen

2. Continue to press **F3** and each record will appear in consecutive order. After you reach the last record, DataEase sounds a beep and tells you:

No More Records

3. Press **F3** again to return to Record 1.

CH. 4

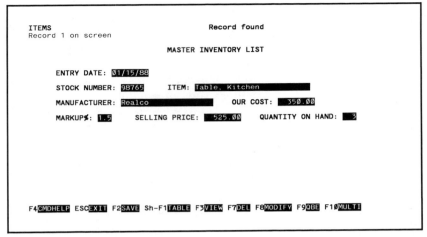

Figure 4.1: Display of Record 1

VIEWING RECORDS IN REVERSE ORDER—SHIFT-F3

You can reverse the display order at any time by pressing Shift-F3. If you are displaying the first record, press Shift-F3 twice; otherwise, press Shift-F3 once to display the previous record. Beginning with the first record, display your records in reverse order:

1. Press **Shift-F3**. Since you are at the beginning of your records, DataEase tells you:

   No More Records

2. Press **Shift-F3** again. The last record, Record 15, is displayed.

3. Press **Shift-F3** four more times, and notice that the record numbers display in reverse order.

4. Press **F3** a few times to display them again in entry order.

5. Press **Shift-F3** to reverse the view order until Record 1 is displayed again.

▶ New records are always added to the end of your database.

Any time you are entering records, you can stop and display your previously entered records with F3 or Shift-F3. And whenever you are displaying records you can clear the screen and enter a new record. So let's add another record:

1. Clear the screen with **F5**, and add the following record:

ENTRY DATE:	090387
STOCK NUMBER:	45234
ITEM:	Chair, Rocker
MANUFACTURER:	Real Furniture
OUR COST:	200
MARKUP%:	2
QUANTITY ON HAND:	2

2. Save the record, using the **F2** key.

3. Press **F3**; DataEase sounds a beep and displays:

   No More Records

   telling you that you are now at the end of the database.

4. Press **F3** again to display Record 1.

5. Continue to press **F3** and see that the newest record, Record 16, has been added at the end.

VIEWING RECORDS IN INDEX ORDER

Records are often entered in random order. However, when you are displaying records, you may prefer to view them in some type of alphabetical or numerical sequence. This is often referred to as *sorting* and is one reason why you create indexed fields.

DataEase can display records in the Record Entry screen sorted by any text or numeric string field which has been indexed. It does not physically reorder your database, but only changes the order temporarily for viewing purposes. But remember, DataEase can do this only if you index the field in Form Definition.

When you defined your ITEMS form, you established several index, or key, fields: STOCK#, ITEM, and MANUFACTURER.

72 MASTERING DATAEASE

CH. 4

When you did this, DataEase created a special index file for each of these fields, like an index file in a library. This allows you to sort by ITEM, STOCK#, or MANUFACTURER, and to display them in groups if there are duplicate entries. For example, because you indexed the MANUFACTURER field, you can display all of the items from the same company grouped together.

Text fields are displayed from A to Z with no distinction between uppercase and lowercase; numeric string fields are displayed from the lowest to the highest number. Text is sorted in the following order of precedence:

Ascending   spaces, special characters, numbers, letters

Descending   letters, numbers, special characters, spaces

To display records in index order:

Remember, always use Alt-F5 (unchecked mode) instead of F5 to clear any derived or calculated fields. Use Alt-F3 after F3 to display remaining indexed or selected records.

- Press **Alt-F5** to clear the form.
- Move the cursor to the indexed field.
- Type the * character in the field.
- Press **F3** to display the first record in alphabetical or numeric order.
- Press **Alt-F3** to continue displaying the records in index order.

Follow the steps below to display your item records in STOCK# order:

1. Press **Alt-F5** to clear the form.
2. Press **Tab** once to move the cursor to the STOCK# field.
3. Type the * character. Your screen should now look like Figure 4.2.
4. Press **F3** to display the first record.

DataEase displays Record 2, with STOCK# 12345, as the first record in the STOCK# index.

WORKING WITH YOUR RECORDS 73

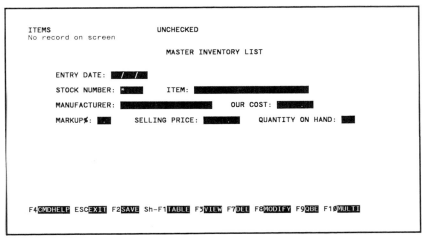

Figure 4.2: Form sorted by STOCK#

▰ Since you are viewing in index order, *not* entry order, the record numbers are no longer displayed sequentially.

5. Press **Alt-F3** to display the next record in sequence—STOCK# 13546.

6. Continue pressing **Alt-F3** to display the remaining records until the message **No More Records** appears.

7. Press **F3** to return to Record #1.

Since each STOCK# must be unique, you'll notice that there are no duplicates. However, there are several duplicate furniture listings in the ITEM index, such as Beds, Tables, etc. And since the name is the first word in the ITEM field, it's easy to reorganize the records into groups.

1. Clear the form again with **Alt-F5**
2. Place the * in the ITEM field.
3. Press **F3** to display the first record (Armoire).
4. Press **Alt-F3** to display the remaining records.

When you display your records in ITEM order, notice two things:

- The records are grouped together by type: Beds, Chairs, Tables, etc.

74 *MASTERING DATAEASE*

CH. 4

- If there are duplicate items, such as water beds or coffee tables, the records within each group are displayed in Record Number order.

Adding Another Record to the Index

So now what happens when you enter another record? DataEase assigns it the next number in sequence and adds the record to each index so that the record is positioned correctly when you view your database in index order. Let's see how quickly that happens.

1. Clear the form with **F5** and enter the following record:

ENTRY DATE:	082589
STOCK NUMBER:	56123
ITEM:	Sofa, Modern
MANUFACTURER:	Realco
OUR COST:	600
MARKUP%:	2
QUANTITY ON HAND:	1

2. Save the record by pressing **F2**
3. Press **F3** to redisplay each of your records.

The new record is assigned the number 17 and displayed at the end of the database. Now sort the records by MANUFACTURER:

1. Clear the form with **Alt-F5**
2. Place the * in the MANUFACTURER field.
3. Press **F3** to display the first record.
4. Press **Alt-F3** to display remaining records.

Your new record is displayed with the other items purchased from Realco.

Even more powerful sorting techniques are available to you in DataEase Quick Reports. You will learn more about that in Chapter 5.

WORKING WITH YOUR RECORDS **75**

Notes on Indexing

- You cannot display sorted records in reverse order.

- Although you can create an index for any field, you can sort from Record Entry only on text or numeric string fields.

- Once all records have been displayed in index order, Data-Ease returns to displaying records in entry order. To redisplay in index order, you must repeat the previous steps.

SEARCHING FOR PARTICULAR RECORDS

If the number of records you maintain should grow into the hundreds, it would no longer be efficient to search for records by displaying them one at a time in entry order, or even in index order. For example, what if you needed to see a specific bed that you purchased from Real Furniture? Or what if you wanted to see all the tables that you have in stock? Wouldn't you want to go directly to these records without having to view all those that precede them? The DataEase Search commands allow you to find a record by its record number or by a value contained in one or more fields.

SEARCHING FOR A RECORD NUMBER—CTRL-F3

In the section on entering records, you learned that each record is saved with a unique record number. If you know the number of the record you want to view, you can use Ctrl-F3 (View Record Number) to search for a record by its number. As an example, let's view Record 4:

> You do not have to clear the screen first when searching for a record by number.

1. Press **Ctrl-F3**

DataEase asks you to:

> Enter the Record number to view ?

2. Type **4**

3. Press **ENTER**; DataEase tells you:

   Record found

   and Record 4 is displayed.

   You may be thinking that it is unlikely you will know all your record numbers; however, Ctrl-F3 is a good way to get quickly to the beginning, middle, or end of your database. The use of record numbers will become more relevant when you learn about deleting records later in this chapter.

SEARCHING FOR EXACT MATCHES

DataEase will find only records whose field values match the search criteria *exactly*.

DataEase can also find records that match a certain value in one or more fields. The value that you enter is referred to as the *search criteria*. For example, if you type Realco in the MANUFACTURER field, as indicated in Figure 4.3, DataEase will search for and display the first record that contains Realco in that field, as shown in Figure 4.4. DataEase will not, however, find Realco, Inc. or Realco Furniture Company.

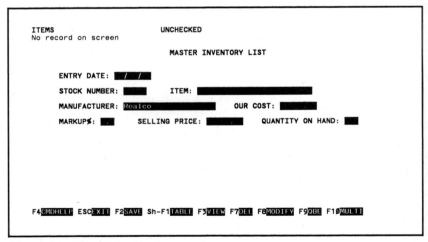

Figure 4.3: Criteria for Realco search

WORKING WITH YOUR RECORDS 77

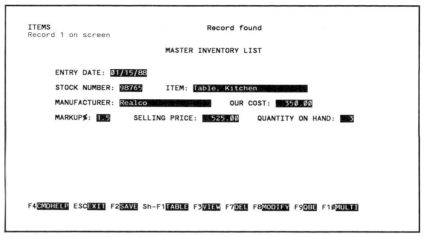

Figure 4.4: Realco record found

After the first matching record is displayed, you can continue displaying other records that contain a matching value in the selected field. The procedure for finding exact matches is outlined below:

- Press **Alt-F5** to clear all fields unchecked.
- Move to the appropriate field and enter the search criteria.
- Press **F3** to view the first record that matches.
- Press **Alt-F3** to display the next record that matches.
- Continue to press **Alt-F3** until the message area displays **No More Records**.
- To return to viewing all records, press **F3**.

For your first search, follow the steps below to find the record for STOCK# 23456:

1. Press **Alt-F5**
2. Move the cursor to the STOCK# field.
3. Type **23456**
4. Press **F3**; the record for STOCK# 23456 will be found and displayed.

5. Press **Alt-F3** and you'll see that there is only one record with that STOCK#.

Next, display the items purchased from Picklepot:

1. Clear the record with **Alt-F5**
2. Using Figure 4.5 as a guide, enter the search criteria.
3. Press **F3**

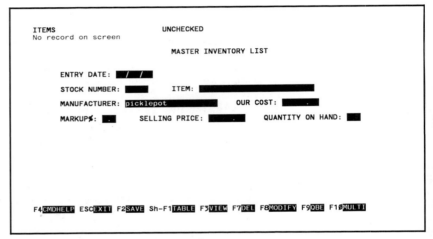

Figure 4.5: Picklepot criteria record

When you pressed F3, did the screen respond with **No More Records**? Or did you catch the mistake in Figure 4.5? The *exact* name of the company is Picklepot Furniture. Follow the previous steps to try the search again, this time using the corrected criteria shown in Figure 4.6.

If you continue to press Alt-F3, you will find two records for Picklepot Furniture. And notice that although you entered the criteria all in lowercase, you still find the records which have been entered with initial capital letters. As you can see, DataEase ignores any case distinction when searching for values. If you enter the search criteria in uppercase, it will find both uppercase and lowercase occurrences.

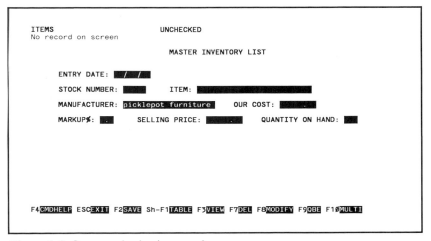

Figure 4.6: Corrected criteria record

SEARCHING FOR MULTIPLE CRITERIA

You can include as many fields in your search criteria as you want. For example, you may want to display all side tables purchased from ABC Company. In that case, you need to enter the search criteria in both the ITEM *and* the MANUFACTURER field.

Try it! Display all records for side tables purchased from ABC Company. Enter the criteria as shown in Figure 4.7. You should find two records for ABC's side tables.

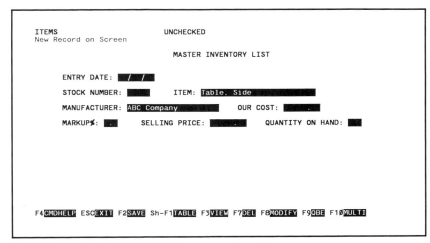

Figure 4.7: Criteria for ABC Company side tables

80 MASTERING DATAEASE

CH. 4

——— SEARCHING FOR PARTIAL MATCHES ——

What if you wanted to view all of your tables, whether kitchen or dining room or whatever? In that case you would need to search for a partial match: all records that begin with Table in the ITEM field. Or what if you weren't quite sure how to spell the search criteria? In that case, DataEase will search for a match based on your best guess.

USING WILD CARDS TO MATCH VALUES

The wild card can be used when you don't remember part of a field value or when an abbreviated form of the field value will do just as well.

Two characters, * and ?, are referred to as *wild card* characters. They can be included in the search criteria to substitute for any unknown character or group of characters. The * can represent one or more characters, while the ? stands for only a single character. Table 4.1 lists examples of wild cards in search criteria.

Table 4.1: Wild Cards in Search Criteria

SEARCH CRITERIA:	WOULD FIND:	WOULD NOT FIND:
Bed*	Bed, Water	Water Bed
	Bed, Queen	Queen Bed
	Bed, King	King Bed
*Dining room	Table, Dining Room	Dining room Table
	Chair, Dining Room	Dining Room Chair
North??st	NorthWest	North West
	NorthEast	North Eastern
*North??st	EastNorthEast	East North East
	WestNorthWest	WestNorth West
Sm?th	Smith	Smythe
	Smyth	Smyrnth
Sm?th*	Smithers	McSmith
	Smythe	Smaithers

Remember the problem you had earlier, when you did not enter Picklepot Furniture *exactly* and found no records? This could have been prevented by using a wild card character:

1. Search for Picklepot items again, this time using the wild card in the criteria, as shown in Figure 4.8.

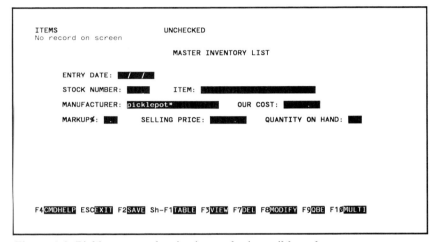

Figure 4.8: Picklepot search criteria employing wild card

This time you should have found three records for Picklepot. Why? Because one of your records was entered as Picklepot Furn, and therefore *not* found when you searched for Picklepot Furniture. This is obviously an error, but leave it for now and we'll fix it later.

2. Enter **Real*** in the MANUFACTURER field and find all records for Real Furniture.

This time, because the characters **Real** were unique to more than one company, you should find records for *three* different companies: Real Furniture, Realco, and Realico.

"SOUNDS LIKE" SEARCHES

"Well, I'm not sure how to spell it but it sounds like...." How many times have you said that when you had to look up someone's

CH. 4

name or a word in the dictionary? The DataEase Soundex search allows you enter the search value as it *sounds*, using as many characters as you like. Values entered for a Soundex search are preceded by the ~ (tilde) character.

For example, you are searching for a customer by the name of Dobiesky. You can't quite remember how to spell it, although you know that it begins with a D and has b,s,k sounds. If you entered ~ **dbsk** in the name field, you might find:

Dobieski

Dobrowsky

Dubrisky

Dabrinski

If the last name is preceded by a first name, you can precede the entry with the * character. For example, entering * ~ dbsk would find:

Tom Dobiesky or

John Dobrowsky

You can also use the ? character. However the * or ? must be entered *before* the Soundex search values, not in the middle or at the end of the entry.

Try this out on your inventory records. One of the manufacturers is named after a city in Indiana, something like Torahote or Tarahat.

1. Clear the form with **Alt-F5**

2. Enter the Soundex search value in the MANUFACTURER field, as shown in Figure 4.9.

3. Display each record.

Did you find all three records for Terrahaute Furniture?

And how does one spell armoire? Well, that is how it's spelled, but what if you weren't sure, but you knew you bought them from Pickle something? On your own, try filling out the form for a Soundex search on armoires from Real something. Did it work? If not, refer to Figure 4.10.

WORKING WITH YOUR RECORDS 83

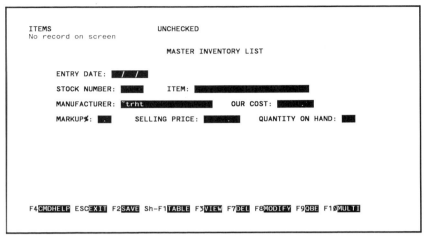

Figure 4.9: ~trht search criteria

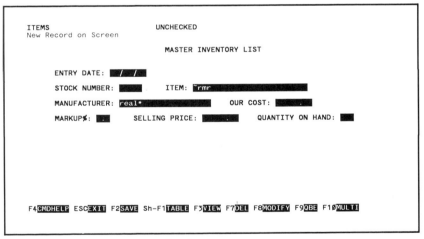

Figure 4.10: ~rmr real* search criteria

NOTES ABOUT SEARCHES

- It takes less time for DataEase to find records when searching for values in an indexed field. Therefore, when you create a form, it is a good idea to index those fields you plan to use often in search criteria.

84 MASTERING DATAEASE

CH. 4

- You cannot display selected records in reverse order.

- Once you have displayed all the selected records, the search is cancelled and all records are returned to entry order. To redisplay the selected records, you must repeat the steps.

MAKING CHANGES TO YOUR RECORDS

One of the most common database tasks involves editing or modifying your records. For example, if the cost of an item increases, you need to modify that record and update your database. If you discontinue an item, you will want to delete that record. And, of course, typos must be hunted down and eliminated.

In the previous exercises you learned all the various ways to retrieve records. In this section you will learn how to make changes to your records.

MODIFYING RECORDS—F8

Earlier, you used Ins and Del to make changes as you enter data. The following are additional editing commands used in record entry:

PRESS:	TO:
F6	Clear an entire field.
F8	Update the modified record.
Ctrl-F5	Undo the changes to the current record before updating with **F8**.

In one of the records, the MANUFACTURER was entered as Realico instead of Realco, and the COST should have been entered as 350. Follow the steps below to change the record (or try it on your own without looking!).

1. Clear the form unchecked.

2. Enter **Realico** in the MANUFACTURER field and press **F3**

3. Use **Del** to delete the **i**

4. **Tab** to the COST field.

5. Press **F6** to clear the field.

6. Type **350**

7. Press **Enter** to automatically recalculate PRICE. DataEase displays the message:

   Record 8 revised on screen

8. Press **F8** to update the record. DataEase tells you:

   Record 8 Updated

CANCELING CHANGES—CTRL-F5

You can always cancel your changes before you update the record. To see how easy this is:

1. Use **Ctrl-F3** to display Record 11 and make the following changes:

   OUR COST: 400

   QUANTITY ON HAND: 3

2. Press **Ctrl-F5**

> You must press Ctrl-F5 *before* pressing F8 and updating records.

DataEase restores all the fields to their previous values and displays the message:

   Disregard record changes

DELETING RECORDS—F7

From time to time, you need to remove records from your database as employees leave the company, or inventory items are discontinued. To delete a record from your database:

> You should never delete a record without first making sure you have a copy of that record in a backup database. For more information, see Chapter 17.

- Use **F3** (entry order Form View) or **Ctrl-F3** (Search) to display the record you want to delete.

- Press **F7**

- Select **2** to confirm the deletion.

86 *MASTERING DATAEASE*

CH. 4

STOCK# 45678 has been dropped from inventory, so you should delete that record:

1. Press Alt-F5 to clear the form.
2. Enter **45678** in the STOCK# field and press **F3**; DataEase will display Record 6 for STOCK# 45678.
3. Press **F7**
4. Select **2** to confirm the deletion. The message area will display:

Record Deleted

When you delete a record from the Record Entry screen, you can no longer display it by searching or pressing F3. Follow the steps below and you will see that there is no Record 6:

1. Use **Ctrl-F3** to display Record 1.
2. Press **F3** to display all the records in sequence, and notice that DataEase skips from Record 5 to Record 7.

RESTORING DELETED RECORDS

It would appear that Record 6 is gone forever. However, all is not lost. Deleted records remain in your database until you reorganize your form. You'll learn how to reorganize your forms in Chapter 17. Until then, you can restore a deleted record to your database, *but only if you know the number of the record.* To restore a deleted record, there are two steps you must follow:

- Use **Ctrl-F3** (View Record Number) to display the deleted record.
- Press **F8** (Update Record).

Follow the steps below to restore Record 6 to your database:

1. Use **Ctrl-F3** to redisplay Record 6. A beep sounds and the message area displays:

This is a Deleted Record

WORKING WITH YOUR RECORDS **87**

2. Press **F8**; DataEase tells you:

Record 6 Updated

3. Use **F3** to display your records in sequence again and see that Record 6 has been returned to your database.

In the previous exercise you learned that when you delete a record, the record number is not reassigned. In other words, the remaining records are not renumbered to adjust to the missing record. To permanently remove deleted records from your database and renumber your records you must *reorganize* your database form. For more information on form reorganization, see Chapter 17.

WORKING WITH RECORDS IN TABLE VIEW—SHIFT-F1

The first time you display Table View in a work session, Record 1 is current, regardless of your current record in Form View. After that, whenever you switch to Table View, the current record will match that in Form View.

Up to this point you have been displaying records in Form View, one at a time. This can be an efficient method of working with individual records. However, there may be times when you prefer to view multiple records. For example, you may want to see an instant list of all the items you buy from Real Furniture, especially if they raised all their prices! DataEase's Table View displays up to 15 records at a time in a columnar format.

To move from Form View to Table View and back again, press Shift-F1. Table View, pictured in Figure 4.11, displays your records starting with the first record from Form View. The cursor is at the beginning of Record 1. Depending on the number and size of your fields, you may be able to see only a few fields. However, you can use Tab or Enter to scroll to the remaining fields. For a list of all the keys you can use in Table View, refer to Table 4.2. Take a few minutes to become familiar with using these keys. Note that when you press ↓, the current record number is always displayed in the status line.

When you return to Form View, the current record from Table View is always displayed, as the following procedure demonstrates:

1. Move to Record 8.

2. Press **Shift-F1** to display Record 8 in Form View.

88 MASTERING DATAEASE

CH. 4

```
ITEMS
Record 1 on Line 1 of 17

ENTRY DA STOCK ITEM                 MANUFACTURER        COST   MAR PRIC
01/15/88 98765 Table, Kitchen       Realco              350.00 1.5   52
05/25/87 12345 Bed, Water, King      Real Furniture     800.00 2.0 1,60
04/15/86 87654 Bed, Queen            Picklepot Furniture 550.00 2.0 1,10
12/01/85 23456 Table, Bedside        ABC Company         300.00 1.5   45
02/25/89 65432 Table, Coffee         Picklepot Furniture 300.00 1.7   51
07/24/88 45678 Chair, Lounge         Real Furniture      300.00 1.8   54
12/13/86 56789 Table, Side           ABC Company         250.00 1.5   37
11/19/89 78920 Armoire, Teak         Realco              350.00 1.5   52
09/18/89 78921 Table, Kitchen        Picklepot Furniture 450.00 1.5   67
09/09/88 78923 Bed, Twin             Terrahaute Furniture 600.00 2.0 1,20
04/05/88 73456 Sofa, Modern          Terrahaute Furniture 500.00 1.8   90
04/05/88 78928 Table, Coffee         Terrahaute Furniture 300.00 1.8   54
08/23/88 65789 Table, Coffee         ABC Company         250.00 1.5   37
07/06/86 13456 Table, Side           ABC Company         375.00 1.5   56
03/04/87 79876 Bed, Water, Queen     ABC Company         500.00 2.5 1,25
09/03/87 45234 Chair, Rocker         Real Furniture      200.00 2.0   40
08/25/89 56123 Sofa, Modern          Realco              600.00 2.0 1,20

F4 CMDHELP  ESC EXIT  F2 SAVE  Sh-F1 FORM  Ctrl-F5 UNDO  F7 DELETE  F10 MULTI
```

Figure 4.11: Table View

Table 4.2: Keys in Table View

PRESS:	TO MOVE TO:
→	Character on right in current field.
←	Character on left in current field.
Tab or Enter	Next field.
Shift-Tab	Previous field.
↓	Next record.
↑	Previous record.
Ctrl-→	Last field in current record.
Ctrl-←	First field in current record.
Home	First field of first record.
End	Next blank record.

PRESS:	TO:
PgDn	Scroll forward (if more than 15 records).
PgUp	Scroll backward.

WORKING WITH YOUR RECORDS 89

3. Press **F3** twice to move to Record 10.

4. Press **Shift-F1** to return to Table View. Now Record 10 will also be current in Form View.

ENTERING AND SAVING RECORDS IN TABLE VIEW

You can enter records from Table View as well as from Form View. Follow the steps below to add another record in Table View:

1. Press **End** to move to the first blank row after the last record.

2. Type the following record as you would in Form View:

ENTRY DATE: 101289

STOCK NUMBER: 67891

ITEM: Bed, Queen ⬅

MANUFACTURER: Real Furniture ⬅

OUR COST: 350 ⬅

MARKUP%:   2.5

QUANTITY ON HAND: 1 ⬅

Notice that when you press Tab or Enter after the last field, the cursor automatically returns to the first field of the next blank record.

Notice that the MANUFAC-TURER is the same as in the previous record; use Shift-F6 to enter it for you.

3. Enter this last record.

ENTRY DATE: 121590

STOCK NUMBER: 93845

ITEM: Table, Dining Room ⬅

MANUFACTURER: Real Furniture ⬅

OUR COST: 500 ⬅

MARKUP%:   2 ⬅

QUANTITY ON HAND: 2 ⬅

New records are saved only when you press F2, or when you return to Form View by pressing Shift-F1. If you are entering many records in Table View, it is a good idea to use F2 to save frequently in case of an interruption of power. Save your new records and return to Form View:

4. Press **Shift-F1**

When DataEase returns you to Form View, the message area displays:

Saved all changes

If you enter a new record in Form View, and switch to Table View *without* saving it first, you will *lose* the record. Pressing Esc in Table View will return you to the Record Entry menu if you have saved all your changes. If not, this message will appear:

Do you want to abandon changes on the screen? (Y/N)

If you answer **Y**, you will return to the Record Entry menu and lose the changes made since the last save.

DISPLAYING TABLE VIEW RECORDS IN INDEX ORDER

To display a Table View of your records in index order:

- In Form View, place the * in the indexed field.
- Press **Shift-F1** immediately.

For example, you can display a Table View of your records in ITEM order:

1. Place the * in the ITEM field.
2. Press **Shift-F1** to return to Table View.

Your records are displayed in ITEM order, as pictured in Figure 4.12.

```
ITEMS
Record 8 on line 1 of 19
ENTRY DA STOCK ITEM                    MANUFACTURER         COST     MAR PRIC
11/19/89 78920 Armoire, Teak          Realco               350.00   1.5    52
04/15/86 87654 Bed, Queen             Picklepot Furniture  550.00   2.0  1,10
05/18/90 67891 Bed, Queen             Real Furniture       350.00   2.5    87
09/09/88 78923 Bed, Twin              Terrahaute Furniture 600.00   2.0  1,20
05/25/87 12345 Bed, Water, King       Real Furniture       800.00   2.0  1,60
03/04/87 79876 Bed, Water, Queen      ABC Company          500.00   2.5  1,25
07/24/88 45678 Chair, Lounge          Real Furniture       300.00   1.8    54
09/03/87 45234 Chair, Rocker          Real Furniture       200.00   2.0    40
04/05/88 73456 Sofa, Modern           Terrahaute Furniture 500.00   1.8    90
08/25/89 56123 Sofa, Modern           Realco               600.00   2.0  1,20
12/01/85 23456 Table, Bedside         ABC Company          300.00   1.5    45
02/25/89 65432 Table, Coffee          Picklepot Furniture  300.00   1.7    51
04/05/88 78928 Table, Coffee          Terrahaute Furniture 300.00   1.8    54
08/23/88 65789 Table, Coffee          ABC Company          250.00   1.5    37
05/18/90 93845 Table, Dining Room     Real Furniture       500.00   2.0  1,00
01/15/88 98765 Table, Kitchen         Realco               350.00   1.5    52
09/18/89 78921 Table, Kitchen         Picklepot Furniture  450.00   1.5    67
12/13/86 56789 Table, Side            ABC Company          250.00   1.5    37
07/06/86 13456 Table, Side            ABC Company          375.00   1.5    56

F4 CMDHELP  ESC EXIT  F2 SAVE  Sh-F1 FORM  Ctrl-F5 UNDO  F7 DELETE  F10 MULTI
```

Figure 4.12: Table View indexed by ITEM

DISPLAYING SELECTED RECORDS IN TABLE VIEW

To display the selected records in Table View:

- Enter the criteria in Form View.

- Press **Shift-F1** immediately to switch to Table View.

Let's display all items from ABC Company in Table View:

1. Return to Form View using Shift-F1.

2. Clear the form with **Alt-F5**

3. Enter **ABC*** in the MANUFACTURER field.

4. Press **Shift-F1**

All ABC Company items are now displayed in Table View, as pictured in Figure 4.13.

Return now to the Main Menu:

1. Press **Esc**; DataEase will return you to the Records menu.

2. Press **Esc** once more to return to the Main Menu.

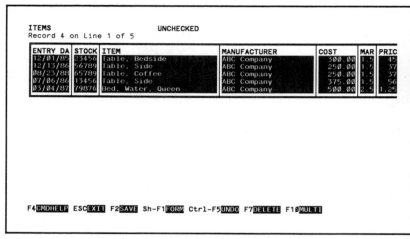

Figure 4.13: ABC Company items in Table View

When you return to Form View after displaying selected or sorted records in Table View, the current record from Table View is displayed, as always; however, the search or index order is cancelled and all records are once again selected.

MODIFYING RECORDS IN TABLE VIEW

If you are modifying multiple records, using Table View can be more efficient than Form View, since you can see up to a full screen of records. Each time you modify a record, the entire record is highlighted as soon as you move to another record. This allows you to keep track of the records you have changed.

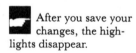 After you save your changes, the highlights disappear.

You can save your modifications by pressing Shift-F1 (return to Form View), F2 (save), or F8 (modify). Your changes are also automatically saved if you scroll to another screen. If you save your changes or new records by scrolling to another screen, and then press Esc to leave Record Entry, DataEase will ask you if you want to abandon your changes, implying that they are *not* saved. However, this message is misleading: all your changes and new records will be saved.

Unlike Form View, Table View allows you to undo your modifications to all or selected records *before* you save your changes.

To undo changes to the current record:

1. Press **Alt-F5**

To undo all modifications made before the last save:

1. Press **F5**; in this case, DataEase will ask:

Do you want to discard the entered data?

and you must confirm by pressing either y or n. You can also use F5 or Ctrl-F5 to remove new records before you save them. However, once you have saved your changes, you cannot undo them.

In the next chapter, you will learn how to create quick reports from the records you have entered.

SECURITY NOTES

- You can view records regardless of your security level. To enter, modify, or delete records, the default security level must be at least a medium. However, the systems administrator can override these by assigning a higher level to any of these tasks. If you attempt to perform a task above your security level, a warning message will appear indicating that you are not authorized for that task.

- When a form is designed, a field may be assigned a View or Write security level. If the View security required for a field is higher than your level, the information in that field will not be displayed. If the Write security for a field is higher than your level, you will be able to view the value but the cursor will not move to that field and you cannot enter information or modify it.

- When your systems administrator is performing maintenance functions on the database, he or she will usually lock the database, denying access to all users. If you attempt to access a locked database, this message is displayed:

Access not allowed - Database locked

94 *MASTERING DATAEASE*

CH. 4

and you must wait until the systems administrator has unlocked the database before you can use it. For more information, see Chapter 17.

LAN NOTES

If you are operating DataEase on a network and are sharing files, you should be aware of certain restrictions on accessing records. These restrictions are based upon the Record Selection locking rule in effect for that database.

RULE:	*RECORD AVAILABILITY:*
None	All records in the current form are available.
Shared	All users can access the same record; however, only the *first* user to access the record can modify or delete the record. If you attempt to modify or delete a record which was first accessed by another user, the following error message is displayed: **Record in use by Another User**
Exclusive	Only one user at a time can view a record. If you attempt to access a record currently in use, this error message is displayed: **Record in use by Another User**

Even if no locking rule is in effect, if you attempt to modify a record that has been modified by another user while you are viewing the record, the message area reads

Record Modified Since it was Read

and the revised record will appear on your screen. You will have to reenter any changes you made.

These and other locking rules are established in the System Configuration menu. If you have a systems administrator, please contact him or her for more information.

CHAPTER FIVE

Creating Queries and Quick Reports

Fast Track

To create a quick report, 101

select Query by Example–Quick Reports from the Main Menu. If you want to include all records and all fields, then just select Define Format to select the form the report is based on. Select the report format, or press **Enter** to accept the default columnar report. Make modifications to the report format if necessary. Press **F2** to save the format. Select Run Report to display the report on the screen.

To select fields for the report, 101

select Define List Fields. Move to the first field for the report and press **Spacebar**, or type **1** to select the field. Type **Order** to sort in ascending order, or **Reverse** to sort in descending order. Type **Group** to organize records with duplicate field values together. If the field is numeric, you can also include one or more statistics from the list. Move to the next field and press **Spacebar** or type **2**; enter any sort, group, or statistics commands. Repeat this for each field, and press **F2** to save the field selection.

To include special formatting commands in your report format, 112

select Modify or Define Format from the Quick Reports menu. Press . (period) and select the formatting command from the menu.

To print the report, 117

select Define Print Style, then select Printer. Select **y** to display the style screen each time you run the report. Enter the definition or press **F3** to display the default printer. Press **F2** to save.

To save the report, 117

select Save Report and enter a report name.

To select records for the report,   119

  select Define Record Selection. Enter the selection criteria in the appropriate
  field. Press **F2** to save the selection.

To move or copy text or fields in the report format,   132

  move to the beginning of the text you want to move or copy. Press **F3** to begin
  the cut or **F5** to begin the copy. Move the cursor to the end of the text you want
  to move or copy. Press **F3** to define the end of the cut area or **F5** to define the
  end of the copy area. Move the cursor to the new location for the text and press
  F6 to paste.

To create a quick report for the current form from Record Entry,   136

  press **F9** from the Record Entry screen to display the Quick Reports menu.
  Define the report. When you are finished, press **Esc** to return to the Record
  Entry screen.

To load an existing report,   137

  select Load Report and select the name of the report from the list.

CHAPTER 5

ONE OF THE PRIMARY REASONS PEOPLE IN BUSINESS maintain electronic databases is that databases provide quick access to information about their companies. This information is usually produced in the form of printed reports. For example, in the case of Furniture Palace:

- The Vice President of Sales wants monthly lists of sales for each salesperson along with monthly totals to generate commission reports and determine which salespeople are producing the most revenue.

- The Operations Manager needs a weekly report on inventory levels and projected orders. She needs to keep track of how much they buy from each vendor, how their prices vary, and how quickly they respond to orders.

- The Vice President of Marketing wants a quarterly report of total sales for each item to determine which products are selling the most and which should be discontinued. He also requests customer sales reports by city and state, which will indicate the weaker marketing areas.

- The Controller wants a monthly list of overdue accounts to make sure that receivables and collections are handled properly.

DATAEASE QUERY BY EXAMPLE

Retrieving selected information from a database, as in the above examples, is often referred to as "querying" the database and sometimes requires programming knowledge. However, DataEase's technique of Query by Example allows you to use forms, such as your ITEMS form, to select records, fields, and calculations for your reports. These query results may be displayed on the screen for you or printed in a report.

REPORT FORMATS

Report formats determine the layout of records and fields on the printed page. You can select from one of seven different predesigned report formats or you can create your own custom report. The default report format is columnar, as in the example shown in Figure 5.1.

```
==================================================================
  STOCK#    MANUFACTURER           ITEM             COST   PRICE
------------------------------------------------------------------
  79876  ABC Company          Bed, Water, Queen   550.00 1,375.00
  23456  ABC Company          Table, Bedside      330.00   495.00
  65789  ABC Company          Table, Coffee       275.00   412.50
  13456  ABC Company          Table, Side         412.50   618.75
  56789  ABC Company          Table, Side         275.00   412.50
  87654  Picklepot Furniture  Bed, Queen          550.00 1,100.00
  93847  Picklepot Furniture  Loveseat, Modern    300.00   600.00
  65432  Picklepot Furniture  Table, Coffee       300.00   510.00
  78921  Picklepot Furniture  Table, Kitchen      450.00   675.00
  67891  Real Furniture       Bed, Queen          350.00   875.00
  12345  Real Furniture       Bed, Water, King    800.00 1,600.00
  45678  Real Furniture       Chair, Lounge       300.00   540.00
  45234  Real Furniture       Chair, Rocker       200.00   400.00
  93845  Real Furniture       Table, Dining Room  500.00 1,000.00
  78920  Realcc               Armoire, Teak       350.00   525.00
  56123  Realcc               Sofa, Modern        600.00 1,200.00
  98765  Realcc               Table, Kitchen      350.00   525.00
  78923  Terrahaute Furniture Bed, Twin           600.00 1,200.00
  73456  Terrahaute Furniture Sofa, Modern        500.00   900.00
  78928  Terrahaute Furniture Table, Coffee       500.00   900.00
------------------------------------------------------------------
  sum
  mean                                            424.62   793.19
  count
==================================================================
```

Figure 5.1: Example of columnar report

You can generate mailing labels from your name and address lists using the mailing label format or use your Record Entry form as a report format. In addition, you can easily modify any DataEase predesigned format to accommodate your report requirements. Or you can select the custom report format to design special applications such as form letters.

In this chapter, you will create a variety of quick reports using the columnar format. In Chapter 8, you will learn how to print mailing labels and work with other special formats.

If you have exited the program, please load DataEase again and sign on. If you need assistance, refer to Chapter 1. Otherwise, the Main Menu should be displayed.

1. Select **Query by Example–Quick Reports** from the Main Menu.

THE QUICK REPORTS MENU

The Quick Reports menu, pictured in Figure 5.2, contains all the selections you need to create, print, and save a report. The report can include records from one or more forms in your database. Later on you will learn how to create a report from multiple forms. For now you'll concentrate on a single form, ITEMS. To begin with, let's summarize the steps for creating a report:

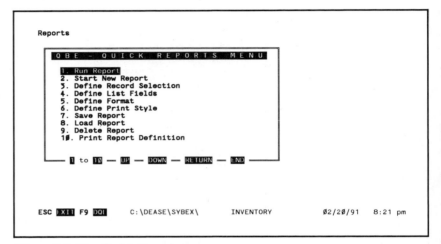

Figure 5.2: The Quick Reports menu

Define record selection	Enter selection criteria to select records, such as all items purchased from ABC Company. If you define no selection, all records in the form will be included.
Define list fields	Select the fields you want included in the report and their order. If you skip this step, all fields are included in the order they appear in your form.
Define format	Select one of the predefined or custom formats. If you do not select a format, the report will appear in columnar format.
Define print style	Select the destination of the report: either screen, printer, or disk file. If you make

	no selection, the report will be displayed on the screen.
Run report	After you have defined at least one of the above, you are ready to produce the report. If you defined no print style, the report will be displayed on the screen.
Save report	If you intend to produce this report again, you must save these specifications under a report name.

DataEase asks you for the name of the form when you select your first definition. So you must define at least one of the first four selections in order to choose the form.

CREATING A QUICK REPORT OF INVENTORY ITEMS

Let's begin with a simple report listing all the items in our inventory, which includes a total for QTY ONHAND at the end of the report. You'll select a field list, preview the format, and then run the report.

Since the report will include all your items, you won't need to define record selection.

SELECTING THE FIELDS FOR YOUR REPORT

Your first report will list your inventory items, sorted by ITEM. Duplicate items will sorted by MANUFACTURER, like the sample report pictured in Figure 5.3. Your report will also include the QTY ONHAND field. Since you don't need to include all your fields, you'll begin by selecting your field list:

1. Select **Define List Fields** from the Quick Reports menu.

2. Select **ITEMS** from the list of form names.

```
                                                              02/20/91
    ===================================================================
    STOCK#       ITEM              MANUFACTURER        COST    PRICE   QUANTITY
    -------------------------------------------------------------------
    78920   Armoire, Teak         Realco              350.00   525.00       2
    87654   Bed, Queen            Picklepot Furniture 550.00 1,100.00       3
    67891   Bed, Queen            Real Furniture      350.00   875.00       1
    78923   Bed, Twin             Terrahaute Furniture 600.00 1,200.00      4
    12345   Bed, Water, King      Real Furniture      800.00 1,600.00       2
    79876   Bed, Water, Queen     ABC Company         550.00 1,375.00       3
    45678   Chair, Lounge         Real Furniture      300.00   540.00       4
    45234   Chair, Rocker         Real Furniture      200.00   400.00       2
    56123   Sofa, Modern          Realco              600.00 1,200.00       1
    73456   Sofa, Modern          Terrahaute Furniture 500.00  900.00       2
    23456   Table, Bedside        ABC Company         330.00   495.00       1
    65789   Table, Coffee         ABC Company         275.00   412.50       3
    65432   Table, Coffee         Picklepot Furniture 300.00   510.00       2
    78928   Table, Coffee         Terrahaute Furniture 500.00  900.00       2
    93845   Table, Dining Room    Real Furniture      500.00 1,000.00       2
    78921   Table, Kitchen        Picklepot Furniture 450.00   675.00       3
    98765   Table, Kitchen        Realco              350.00   525.00       3
    56789   Table, Side           ABC Company         275.00   412.50       2
    13456   Table, Side           ABC Company         412.50   618.75       2
    -------------------------------------------------------------------
                                                                         44
                                                      431.18   803.36   2.32
                                                                         19
    ===================================================================
```

Figure 5.3: ITEM report

The Define List Fields form, pictured in Figure 5.4, is exactly like the one you created. The cursor is in the ENTRY DATE field and a menu of choices is displayed across the top.

For each selected field, you can specify one or more of the following statistics:

Order	Sort records by selected field in ascending alphabetical or numeric order: A–Z; 0–9.
Reverse	Sort records by selected field in descending alphabetical or numeric order: Z–A; 9–0.
Group	Group together records with duplicate field values.

For numeric fields only, you can specify one or more of the following:

Count	Count total number of records for each report and each group.
Sum	Group and report totals.
Mean	Group and report averages.

CREATING QUERIES AND QUICK REPORTS 103

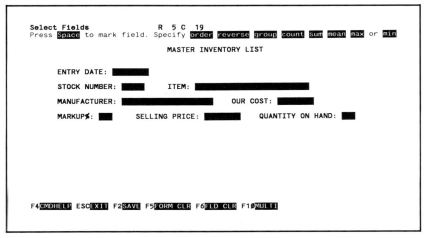

Figure 5.4: The Define List Fields screen

    Max   Largest number for each group and for report.

    Min   Smallest number for each group and for report.

These are the steps for selecting fields:

- **Tab** to the field you want displayed in the first column.
- Press **Spacebar** (the number 1 will appear).
- If you want records alphabetized by this field, type **Order** or **Reverse.**
- If there are duplicate field values and you want them grouped together, type **Group.**
- If you are selecting a numeric field, you can type any or all of the calculation options listed.
- **Tab** to the next field and repeat the above steps.

For this report, you will include STOCK#, ITEM in order, MANUFACTURER in order, an average for COST and PRICE, and the count, average, and sum for QTY ONHAND. Keep in

104 MASTERING DATAEASE

CH. 5

mind that the first field you select to be ordered or reversed is the primary sort field. For example, if you want to sort by zip code within each city, and by city within each state, select state first, then city, then zip code.

The cursor movement keys are the same as those used in Record Entry. Follow the steps below to select your fields, beginning with STOCK#:

1. Press **Tab** to move to STOCK NUMBER.
2. Press **Spacebar** to select the field.

Next, select ITEM as field 2, the primary sort field:

1. Press **Tab** to move to ITEM.
2. Press **Spacebar** to select the field.
3. Type **Order**

Select MANUFACTURER as the secondary sort field:

1. Press **Tab** to move to MANUFACTURER.
2. Press **Spacebar** to select the field.
3. Type **Order**

Next, select COST and SELLING PRICE:

1. Press **Tab** to move to OUR COST.
2. Press **Spacebar** to select the field and type **Mean**
3. Press **Tab** to move to SELLING PRICE.
4. Press **Spacebar** and type **Mean**

Finally, select QTY ONHAND and include sum and average statistics:

1. Press **Tab** to move to QUANTITY ON HAND.
2. Press **Spacebar**
3. Type **Sum Mean Count**

CREATING QUERIES AND QUICK REPORTS   *105*

> From any screen in Report Definition, pressing Esc will also save your changes, not cancel them. To start a new Field Selection, press F5 to clear the form.

Notice that the field size for QTY ONHAND temporarily expanded to accommodate the statistical information. Now your form should look like the one pictured in Figure 5.5, and you are ready to save the Field Selection form:

1. Press **F2**

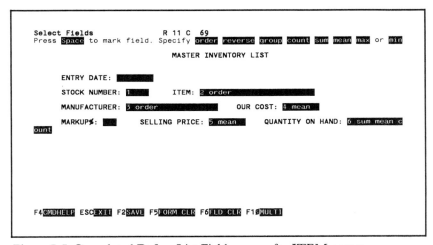

Figure 5.5: Completed Define List Fields screen for ITEM report

DataEase returns you to the Quick Reports Menu; notice that Selection 4 now reads Modify List Fields, instead of Define List Fields.

DEFINING THE FORMAT

After you select your fields or records, DataEase creates a default columnar format for displaying your report. Let's take a look at the layout:

1. Press **Enter** to select Define Format.

DataEase asks you for the report format:

    Minimum line length for a columnar report is 81
    What type of report format do you want: Columnar

106 MASTERING DATAEASE

CH. 5

This tells you that the report you created has a line length of 81 characters. The columnar format is entered as the default and a partial list of formats is displayed across the top of the screen.

2. Press **Enter** to accept the columnar format.

Next, you are asked for the report width:

What line length do you desire for the report?: 80

A report width of 80 is displayed as the default. 80 characters is the width of the screen, approximately the same width as 8½'' wide paper, (an estimated 10 characters to the inch). Most reports are wider than that, but require a wide-track printer and wide paper. You can change the line length to match the width of your paper. And since DataEase told us our report is 81 characters, let's change the default width:

3. Type **81** ⏎

Later, you will learn how to change the character *size* so that you can fit more characters on a line when printing.

DataEase will display your report format in columns, as shown in Figure 5.6. Your report is divided into several areas on the screen. At the top of the report, your field names are displayed as column headings. Below the column headings is the .items area, preceded by:

.items

The .items area, not to be confused with your form name, is defined by DataEase to contain the fields you selected for your report. Each field is a separate column. You can check the contents of the current field by pressing any key, just as you did in Form Definition. Try it:

1. Move the cursor to the ITEMS field.

2. Press **Spacebar** to display field characteristics.

CREATING QUERIES AND QUICK REPORTS   107

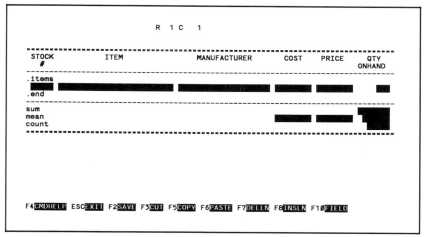

Figure 5.6: Report format

DataEase displays the field contents in the prompt line:

FIELD ITEM, Type Text

The end of the .items area is marked by:

.end

The last area includes the statistics you requested and will appear at the end of the report.

In the next section, you will learn how to make changes to the format. For now, let's save this by pressing F2 and see how it looks.

RUNNING YOUR REPORT

Since you'll display this report on the screen, you can skip Define Print Style and go right to Run Report:

1. Select **Run Report**

108 MASTERING DATAEASE

CH. 5

DataEase takes a few seconds to process the information, and voila! your report appears with all your records on the screen, as it is pictured in Figure 5.7.

Notice that the items appear in alphabetical order and the manufacturers are sorted alphabetically within each set of duplicate items. The first column in the report is the first field you selected, STOCK#. The next field you selected, ITEM, appears in the second column and the items are alphabetized because you included Order in the field selection. Since you also included Order for MANUFACTURER, the third field you selected, duplicate items are sorted by manufacturer in the third column. So, as you can see, your columns are displayed in the order in which you selected them, and the records are displayed alphabetically according to the Order you included in your field selection. If your report is longer than 22 lines, only a partial listing is displayed. To scroll back and forth through your report:

2. Press **PgDn** to see more of the report.

3. Press **PgUp** to see the previous sections.

If you compare this report to the one back in Figure 5.3, you can see that this report is not yet ready to print. We need to go back and change some things.

> If you had included no Order in your field selection, your records would have been displayed in record number, or entry, order.

Figure 5.7: First ITEM report

CREATING QUERIES AND QUICK REPORTS   *109*

4. Press **Esc** to clear the report and return to the Quick Reports menu.

MODIFYING THE FORMAT

If you have experience using a word processing program, you are familiar with the concepts of text editing and formatting. When modifying a report format you can insert and delete text, type over text, move and copy text, add and delete lines, and even include headers, footers, and page numbering. Whether you have experience or not, you will find that modifying a report format is easy.

1. Select **Modify Format** from the Report menu.

If we had changed the Define List Fields selection, we would answer N, so that DataEase could redesign the format with the new information.

This time DataEase asks you:

> **Do you want to keep existing report format ?: (Y/N)**

2. Select **Y** (Since no changes were made) to accept the old format.

In this section you will attend to the following problems:

- The report needs a heading.

- The report is a little too wide for printing.

- The row headings for the statistics at the end of the report should be more meaningful.

First, let's take a look at the width of the report. Remember, what appears on the screen will fit on 8½" wide paper when it prints. What you can't see on the screen will wrap around when it prints. Our report is 81 characters. Since you can see all your fields, the extra character is probably at the end of the dashed lines that separate your report areas. Let's just delete that extra dash in each line:

The cursor movement and basic editing keys are the same ones you used in Form Definition.

1. Move your cursor to Row 2.

2. Press **Ctrl-→** to move to the end of the line.

3. Move the cursor to Column 80 and observe that the dashed line extends to Column 81.

4. Press **Del** to delete the extra dash.
5. Repeat step 4 for Rows 5, 9, and 13.
6. Press **Home** to return to the top of the report.

CHANGING THE REPORT WIDTH

Since standard 8½" wide paper has a line length of only 85 characters, you have only 2.5 characters or a .25" margin on each side. One way to alter the width of a report is to change the width of one or more fields, just for the report. You may have noticed that the ITEM column is more than wide enough to fit the longest item. So let's modify the width of the ITEM field. You can modify a field the same way you do in a form—with the F10 key:

1. Move the cursor to the ITEM field.
2. Press **F10** to display Report Field Definition.

> Changes to the report width will not affect the field width in your form; that must be changed separately, as you'll see in Chapter 6.

The Report Field Definition box, as pictured in Figure 5.8, has only four characteristics displayed. You can change only the field name, width, and space suppression. You'll learn the purpose of suppressing spaces in Chapter 8.

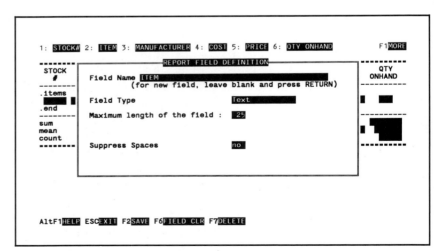

Figure 5.8: Report Field Definition for ITEM

CREATING QUERIES AND QUICK REPORTS 111

3. Press **Tab** to move to Maximum length of the field.

4. Type **20** as the new field length.

5. Press **F2** to save changes.

Now the field is shorter and you can use the Del key to close the gap between ITEM and the other fields:

1. Move the cursor to Row 7, Column 28.

2. Press **Del** five times.

However, the report column headings and calculated fields in the QTY ONHAND column are not lined up. Let's fix that, starting with the column headings:

3. Move the cursor to Row 3, Column 28.

4. Press **Del** five times.

5. Repeat step 4 at Column 28 for Rows 10, 11, and 12 to line up the sum, mean, and count fields.

The right edges of the numeric fields in the QTY ONHAND column should be lined up. (You'll fix Row 4 a little later.)

Next, while you're in the neighborhood, change the row headings for your statistical fields so they are more meaningful. Using Figure 5.9 as a guide:

6. Change the heading STOCK to STOCK#.

7. Change the heading QTY ONHAND to QUANTITY.

8. Move to Row 4 and press **F7** twice to delete two rows.

9. Change the row headings in Rows 10, 11, and 12 respectively, to TOTAL QUANTITY, AVERAGE, and NUMBER OF ITEMS.

Now let's see what your new report looks like:

10. Press **F2** to save the format.

11. Select **Run Report** to display the new report.

112 MASTERING DATAEASE

CH. 5

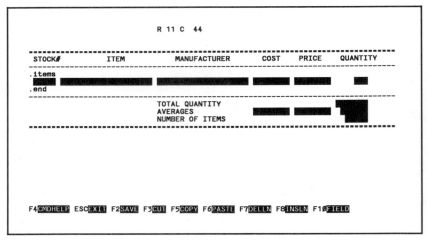

Figure 5.9: Format edit of column and row headings

The report looks good. However, some informational lines at the top and bottom of the report would improve it.

ADDING A HEADER AND FOOTER

Headers and footers are features often used in word processing. A header is one or more lines of text printed at the top of each page. A footer is text printed at the bottom of each page. Headers and footers typically contain the date, document title, and a page number. For this report, you will create a header with the report title and date, and a footer with the page number.

.items and .end are just two of several formatting commands that mark the different areas of the report. Two more, .header and .footer, begin the header and footer areas, and like all formatting commands must appear on a separate line by themselves. The text for the header and footer are entered on the line(s) below the command. The end of the header is marked by the .items formatting command. The .footer command is usually placed at the very end of the document.

1. Press **Esc** to clear the report.
2. Select **Modify Format** and type **Y** to keep the existing format.

CREATING QUERIES AND QUICK REPORTS   113

First, let's place the header:

1. Move the cursor to Row 1, Column 1.
2. Type . (period).

Whenever you type a period at the beginning of a line, DataEase displays the menu of formatting commands pictured in Figure 5.10.

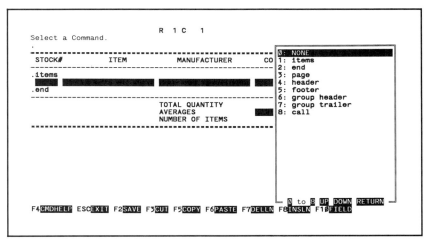

Figure 5.10: Format menu

3. Select **header**

The .header formatting command appears on your screen. Now, you need to insert a line for the header text.

4. Press **Enter** to move the cursor to Row 2.
5. Press **F8** to insert a line.
6. Move to Column 22.
7. Type **INVENTORY REPORT FOR FURNITURE PALACE**

ADDING A DATE TO THE REPORT HEADER

DataEase will print the current date on your report when you include a special field for it in your report format. You can place the

CH. 5

CURRENT DATE field in your report format using the F10 key:

1. Move the cursor to Row 2, Column 61.
2. Type **DATE:**
3. At Column 67, press **F10** to define the field.

DataEase displays the Report Field Definition box. The list of fields you selected for the report is displayed across the top in the prompt line. The message under the NAME field tells you:

For New Field, Leave Blank and Press RETURN

> You can also enter the name of a field that you did not originally select in Define List Fields.

This allows you to select an additional field from your form or create a derived field. In this case you are going to create a system-derived field called CURRENT DATE. System fields are derived from information kept current by DataEase, and include date, page, time, user, and item number.

1. Press **Enter** to enter the new field.
2. Type **CURRENT DATE**
3. Press **F2** to confirm.

As indicated on your screen, and also in Figure 5.11, DataEase recognizes this field and fills in the type for you.

4. Press **F2** to save the field definition.

The new field appears in the header area where you placed it.

ADDING A PAGE NUMBER
TO YOUR REPORT FOOTER

Next, you will create a footer area and include the current page number field:

1. Press **End** to move to the end of the report.
2. Press ↓ to move down one row.

CREATING QUERIES AND QUICK REPORTS **115**

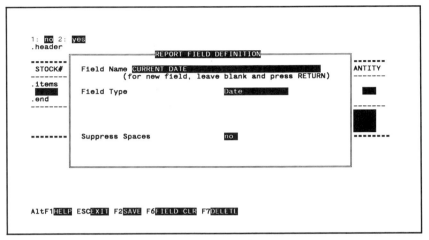

Figure 5.11: CURRENT DATE Definition form

3. Type **.** to begin the formatting command.

4. Select **footer** from the list. The .footer formatting command appears on your screen.

5. Move the cursor to Row 15, Column 29.

6. Type **PAGE:**

7. At Column 35, press **F10** to begin definition.

8. Press **Enter** to enter the new field.

9. Type **CURRENT PAGE NUMBER**

DataEase recognizes your entry and fills in the remaining fields, as shown in Figure 5.12.

10. Press **F2** twice.

Your completed format should look like the one in Figure 5.13.

Now you are ready to save your format and display your report again:

1. Press **F2** to save the format.

2. Select **Run Report**

116 MASTERING DATAEASE

CH. 5

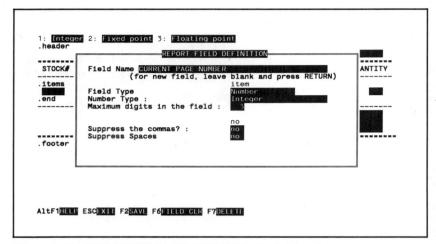

Figure 5.12: CURRENT PAGE NUMBER Definition form

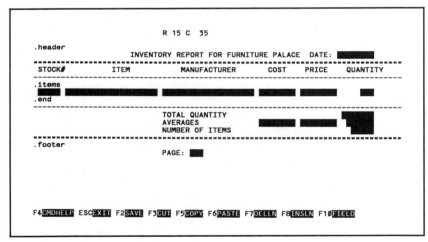

Figure 5.13: Format with date and page

Your report should look like the one in Figure 5.14, except that your date should be current.

3. Press **PgDn** and see that the page number falls at the bottom of the page.

```
 SPACE or PgDn: Continue report  EXIT : Abort report  PgUp : Scroll
                                                                  02/18/91
 ===========================================================================
  STOCK#     ITEM            MANUFACTURER         COST     PRICE    QUANTITY
 ---------------------------------------------------------------------------
  78920   Armoire, Teak       Realco             350.00    525.00      2
  87654   Bed, Queen          Picklepot Furniture 550.00 1,100.00      3
  67891   Bed, Queen          Real Furniture     350.00    875.00      1
  78923   Bed, Twin           Terrahaute Furniture 600.00 1,200.00     4
  12345   Bed, Water, King    Real Furniture     800.00 1,600.00      2
  79876   Bed, Water, Queen   ABC Company        550.00 1,375.00      3
  45678   Chair, Lounge       Real Furniture     300.00    540.00      4
  45234   Chair, Rocker       Real Furniture     200.00    400.00      2
  56123   Sofa, Modern        Realco             600.00 1,200.00      1
  73456   Sofa, Modern        Terrahaute Furniture 500.00   900.00     2
  23456   Table, Bedside      ABC Company        330.00    495.00      1
  65789   Table, Coffee       ABC Company        275.00    412.50      3
  65432   Table, Coffee       Picklepot Furniture 300.00    510.00     2
  78928   Table, Coffee       Terrahaute Furniture 500.00   900.00     2
  93845   Table, Dining Room  Real Furniture     500.00 1,000.00      2
  78921   Table, Kitchen      Picklepot Furniture 450.00    675.00     3
  98765   Table, Kitchen      Realco             350.00    525.00      3

 F4  CMDHELP  ESC  EXIT  C:\DEASE\SYBEX\        INVENTORY       05/18/91   8 04 am
```

Figure 5.14: Modified ITEM report

SAVING THE REPORT

As you can see, this report is much improved and certainly ready for printing. However, your report currently resides only in the computer's memory. If you should lose power you would also lose the report. So to be on the safe side, let's save this report specification on disk. That way you can retrieve it later and print or modify it:

1. Press **Esc** to clear the report.

2. Select **Save Report** from the Quick Reports menu. DataEase requests that you:

   Please enter the report procedure name

3. Type **INVLIST** ←.

PRINTING THE REPORT

Even if you don't have a printer available, read over this section for some important information that it contains.

Before you start, make sure your printer is on and on line:

1. Select **Define Print Style**

The Print Style Specification screen, pictured in Figure 5.15, is displayed. The menu across the top of the screen asks you to select the destination of the report:

1. Select **Printer**
2. Tab twice to the Printer Name field.

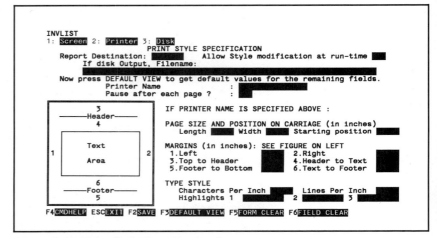

Figure 5.15: Print Style Specification form

3. Press **F3** to select your default printer.
4. Press **F2** to save the specifications.
5. Run the report.

PRINTING TO A FILE

One of the options in the Report Destination of the Print Style Specification screen is File. You can create a file on the disk that contains the report exactly as you see it printed or displayed on the screen. It is stored in ASCII format, which can be read by almost every word processing program on the market. Then you can include it with another document or just print it by itself, using some of the more sophisticated features offered by word processing software. Check the documentation that comes with your word processor for instructions on reading ASCII files.

SELECTING RECORDS FOR YOUR REPORT

You learned how to select records in Record Entry by searching for exact matches. You can use the same procedure for selecting records in Report Definition. However, you can also search for records that fall within numeric ranges. For example, you can search for items that cost greater than $500, or between $500 and $1000. You can also use selection operators in text fields to list, for example, records that include either tables or beds; or records that include everything but desks.

Refer to Table 5.1 for a list of selection operators and to Table 5.2 for examples of how they can be used.

For the sake of clarity in these tables, spaces are included between operators. However, they are not required.

Table 5.1: Selection Operators

=	Equal to.
>	Greater than.
<	Less than.
> =	Greater than or equal to.
< =	Less than or equal to.
Between .. to	Between and including.
And	Both conditions must be true.
Or	Either condition can be true.
Not	Not the condition.

ENTERING TEXT CRITERIA

Let's begin with a simple request by reporting only on items purchased from ABC Company:

1. Select **Modify Record Selection**

DataEase displays a form just like the one you used in Define List Fields.

CH. 5

120 MASTERING DATAEASE

Table 5.2: Example Usages

NUMERIC SELECTIONS	
CONDITION:	**SELECTED RECORDS:**
> 500	Numbers larger than 500 in search field.
> = 500	Numbers equal to or greater than 500 in search field.
< 500	Numbers less than 500 in search field.
< = 500	Numbers less than or equal to 500 in search field.
Between 100 to 500	Numbers between (and *including*) 100 and 500.
> = 100 and < = 500	Same as above.
> 100 and < 500	Numbers between (but *not including*) 100 and 500.
Not between 100 to 500	Numbers less than 100 and greater than 500; numbers that do *not* fall within that range.
< 100 or > 500	Same as above.
TEXT SELECTIONS	
CONDITION:	**SELECTED RECORDS:**
= "abc" or "xyz"	Records with either abc or xyz in search field.
Not = "abc"	Records *without* abc in search field.
= "TABLE*" or "BED*"	Records that begin with either table or bed in the search field.

CREATING QUERIES AND QUICK REPORTS   *121*

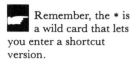
Remember, the * is a wild card that lets you enter a shortcut version.

2. Move the cursor to the MANUFACTURER field.
3. Type **ABC***
4. Press **F2** to save the selection.

If you printed the last report and prefer to display this one on the screen:

1. Select **Modify Print Style**
2. Type **1** to select the screen.
3. Press **F2**. Now you are ready to run the report.
4. Select **Run Report**

Your report lists only the records from ABC Company, as shown in Figure 5.16.

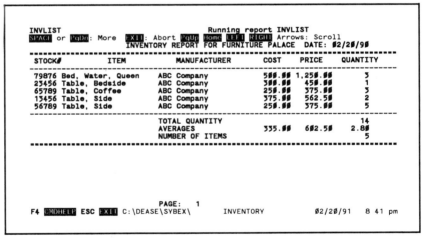

Figure 5.16: ABC Company report

Let's add another manufacturer to our list:

1. Press **Esc** to clear the screen.
2. Select **Modify Record Selection**
3. Move the cursor to the MANUFACTURER field.

4. Press **F6** to clear the field.
5. Type = "**ABC***" OR = "**REALCO**"

If you refer back to the examples in Table 5.2, you will notice that when you use an operator in your search criteria, you must enclose text values in quotes. But why not enter Real* as a shortcut for Realco? Because you also have a company called Real Furniture. Now you can save your changes and run the report again:

1. Press **F2**
2. Select **Run Report**

Now your records include items from both ABC Company and Realco, as shown in Figure 5.17. However, the companies are not listed in order. Remember, you selected ITEM as the primary field and MANUFACTURER as the secondary field in the sort order. Let's reverse that:

1. Clear the report.
2. Select **Modify List Fields**

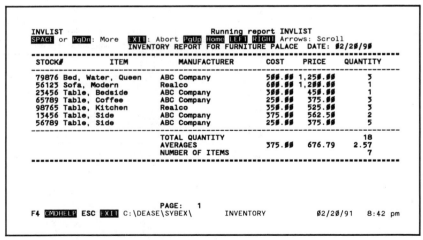

Figure 5.17: ABC Company and Realco report

CREATING QUERIES AND QUICK REPORTS   **123**

3. Edit the form so that 2 is the order of the MANUFAC-TURER field and 3 is the order of the ITEM field, as in the example below:

ITEM: 3 ORDER

MANUFACTURER: 2 ORDER

4. Save your changes and run the report again.

Now, your report is listed in order of MANUFACTURER, as shown in Figure 5.18.

```
INVLIST                                    Running report INVLIST
SPACE or PgDn: Continue report  EXIT: Abort report  PgUp: Scroll
                                                                     05/18/91
========================================================================
   STOCK#      ITEM            MANUFACTURER      COST    PRICE    QUANTITY
------------------------------------------------------------------------
   79876   Bed, Water, Queen   ABC Company     500.00 1,250.00        3
   23456   Table, Bedside      ABC Company     500.00   450.00        1
   65789   Table, Coffee       ABC Company     250.00   375.00        3
   13456   Table, Side         ABC Company     375.00   562.50        2
   56789   Table, Side         ABC Company     250.00   375.00        2
   78920   Armoire, Teak       Realco          350.00   525.00        2
   56123   Sofa, Modern        Realco          600.00 1,200.00        1
   98765   Table, Kitchen      Realco          350.00   525.00        3
------------------------------------------------------------------------
                               TOTAL QUANTITY                        17
                               AVERAGES         371.87   657.81    2.12
                               NUMBER OF ITEMS                        8
========================================================================


                               PAGE:   1
  F4 CMDHELP  ESC EXIT  C:\DEASE\SYBEX\      INVENTORY      05/18/91   8 26 am
```

Figure 5.18: Reordered ABC Company and Realco report

SELECTING NUMERIC RANGES

Next, let's search for values that fall within a numeric range. List just the items that sell for between $400 and $800:

1. Press **Esc** to clear the report.

2. Select **Modify Record Selection**

3. Press **F5** to clear the form.

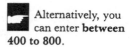
Alternatively, you can enter **between** 400 to 800.

4. Move the cursor to the SELLING PRICE field.
5. Type > = 400 and < = 800
6. Press **F2** to save the changes.
7. Run the report.

Please note that spaces are not necessary within the selection criteria; you could have entered > =400and< =800. Save your selection and run the report again to see that no SELLING PRICE is less than $400 or greater than $800.

Let's try one more. Display all tables that sell for less than $600. Try this one on your own. If you need assistance, refer to Figure 5.19 for the correct form entry. Your completed report should look like the one in Figure 5.20.

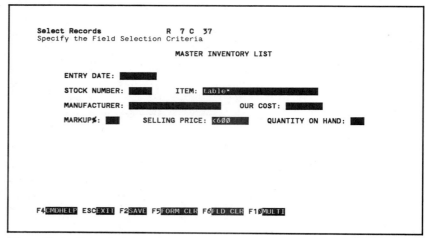

Figure 5.19: Selection for tables selling for less than $600

PRINTING THE REPORT DEFINITION

In the last chapter, you printed your report definition to maintain a detailed record of your report design and field characteristics. The sample report definition shown in Figure 5.21 includes record and

CREATING QUERIES AND QUICK REPORTS **125**

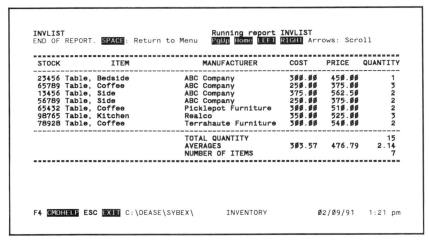

Figure 5.20: Report for tables selling for less than $600

field selections as well as a representation of the report format. If you should lose the report form file, you can easily redefine the report from this information.

So before you begin another report, print your report definition:

1. Select **Print Report Definition**

Notice that your report includes your last record selection. In the next section you will learn how to group your records for a report. Before you move on, save your report specification with the latest changes:

> If you don't want to save your record selection with the report, just select Modify Record Selection and press F5 to clear the form.

2. Select **Save Report**

DataEase asks you:

> Do you want to save modified report procedure under another name?(Y/N)

3. Type **N** to save it under the current name.

CH. 5

```
REPORT INVLIST
-----------------------------

RECORD SELECTION
----------------
  File ITEMS
  -------------------------
ITEM                    : TABLE*
PRICE                   : <600

FIELD SELECTION
---------------
STOCK#                  : 1
MANUFACTURER            : 2 order
ITEM                    : 3 order
COST                    : 4 mean
PRICE                   : 5 mean
QTY ONHAND              : 6 sum mean count

        REPORT FORMAT
        -------------

1       10      20      30      40      50      60      70      80
----+----+----+----+----+----+----+----+----+----+----+----+----+----+----+----+
.header
                    INVENTORY REPORT FOR FURNITURE PALACE   DATE: _____
========================================================================
  STOCK#        ITEM            MANUFACTURER       COST    PRICE   QUANTITY
------------------------------------------------------------------------
.items

.end    _____  _____  _____  _____      ____
------------------------------------------------------------------------
                    TOTAL QUANTITY                              _____
                    AVERAGES                    _____  _____  _____
                    NUMBER OF ITEMS                              _____
========================================================================
.footer
                    PAGE: ___
----+----+----+----+----+----+----+----+----+----+----+----+----+----+----+----+
1       10      20      30      40      50      60      70      80

        FIELD DESCRIPTIONS
        ------------------

                                                        Remove
No.  Name                   Type            Length  Spaces?
     _____ _____   _____  _____
  1  CURRENT DATE           Date               8    no
  2  STOCK#                 Numeric String     5    no
  3  ITEM                   Text              20    no
  4  MANUFACTURER           Text              20    no
  5  COST                   Number             8    no
       Number Type : Fixed point
       Digits to left of decimal = 5
  6  PRICE                  Number             8    no
       Number Type : Fixed point
       Digits to left of decimal = 5
  7  QTY ONHAND             Number             3    no
       Number Type : Integer
  8  QTY ONHAND             Number             7    no
       Number Type : Integer
  9  COST                   Number             8    no
       Number Type : Fixed point
       Digits to left of decimal = 5
 10  PRICE                  Number             8    no
       Number Type : Fixed point
       Digits to left of decimal = 5
```

Figure 5.21: Printed report definition

CREATING QUERIES AND QUICK REPORTS 127

```
    11  QTY ONHAND                Number            6      no
           Number Type : Fixed point
           Digits to left of decimal = 3
    12  QTY ONHAND                Number            5      no
           Number Type : Integer
    13  CURRENT PAGE NUMBER       Number            3      no
           Number Type : Integer

    Memory required:
       Report Definition:      1675
```

Figure 5.21: Printed report definition (continued)

CREATING A REPORT GROUPED BY MANUFACTURER

> Groups are not automatically alphabetized. If you want them sorted, you must select Order or Reverse.

You may recall that one of the options in the Select Fields menu is Group, which prints records together with duplicate field values. Order appears to do the same thing. However, grouped reports can also include separate statistics for each group. In your next report, you will group together items from the same manufacturer. Let's clear the current report and start over:

1. Select **Start New Report**

DataEase clears the current report, INVLIST, from memory and the menu selections change from Modify back to Define.

2. Select **Define List Fields**
3. Select **ITEMS**

Using Figure 5.22 as a guide, select the fields for your report. When you are finished, save your selections and return to the Quick Reports menu.

INCLUDING GROUP HEADERS AND TRAILERS IN YOUR REPORT

The next step is to define the format, which will be a bit different from the previous one. Refer to Figure 5.23 and notice that there are special text lines at the beginning of each manufacturer. These are called the group header and the group trailer. They are strictly

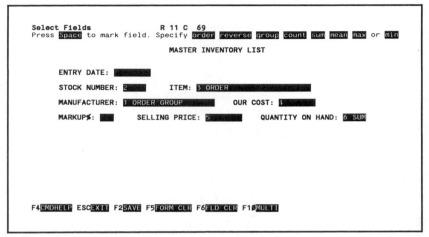

Figure 5.22: Selection field for MANUFACTURER report

optional; however, since the purpose of grouping is to provide statistical data for related records, the header and footer are important.

Let's begin:

1. Select **Define Format**
2. Press **Enter** to accept the columnar format. DataEase then asks:

   Do you want Group Headers and Group Trailers?

3. Type **Y** to accept the headers and trailers.

Your new report format, pictured in Figure 5.24, is displayed.

Notice that the group header also includes the field MANUFACTURER. And the group trailer includes the sum of QTY ONHAND for each group. However, as you can see, some editing is needed to make this report look like the one in Figure 5.23.

To start with, you'll change the heading for the statistics in Row 14 and you will add the manufacturer's name to the group trailer. This may seem repetitious, since you already have the MANUFACTURER name in the group header, but if you have a large inventory, the trailer may be separated from the header by several pages.

```
=================================================================
           STOCK#          ITEM              COST      PRICE     QTY
                                                                 ONHAND
-----------------------------------------------------------------
MANUFACTURER ABC Company
           79876     Bed, Water, Queen        500.00  1,250.00      3
           23456     Table, Bedside           300.00    450.00      1
           65789     Table, Coffee            250.00    375.00      3
           13456     Table, Side              375.00    562.50      2
           56789     Table, Side              250.00    375.00      5
                     TOTAL QUANTITY FOR ABC Company                14

-----------------------------------------------------------------
MANUFACTURER Picklepot Furn
           65432     Table, Coffee            300.00    510.00      2
                     TOTAL QUANTITY FOR Picklepot Furn             2

-----------------------------------------------------------------
MANUFACTURER Picklepot Furniture
           87654     Bed, Queen               550.00  1,100.00      3
           78921     Table, Kitchen           450.00    675.00      3
                     TOTAL QUANTITY FOR Picklepot Furniture        6

-----------------------------------------------------------------
MANUFACTURER Real Furniture
           12345     Bed, Water, King         800.00  1,600.00      2
           45678     Chair, Lounge            300.00    540.00      4
           45234     Chair, Rocker            200.00    400.00      2
                     TOTAL QUANTITY FOR Real Furniture             8

-----------------------------------------------------------------
MANUFACTURER Realco
           56123     Sofa, Modern             600.00  1,200.00      1
           98765     Table, Kitchen           350.00    525.00      3
                     TOTAL QUANTITY FOR Realco                     4

-----------------------------------------------------------------
MANUFACTURER Realico
           78920     Armoire, Teak            700.00  1,050.00      2
                     TOTAL QUANTITY FOR Realico                    2

-----------------------------------------------------------------
MANUFACTURER Terrahaute Furniture
           78923     Bed, Twin                600.00  1,200.00      4
           73456     Sofa, Modern             500.00    900.00      2
           78928     Table, Coffee            500.00    900.00      2
                     TOTAL QUANTITY FOR Terrahaute Furniture       8

-----------------------------------------------------------------
-----------------------------------------------------------------
           TOTAL QUANTITY IN INVENTORY:                           44
=================================================================
```

Figure 5.23: MANUFACTURER report with group headers and trailers

1. Move to Row 14 and use the **Spacebar** to move to Column 11.

2. Type **TOTAL QUANTITY IN INVENTORY:**

3. Move to Row 11, use the **Spacebar** to move to Column 11, and type **TOTAL QUANTITY FOR**

4. Move to Column 30 and press **F10**

5. Select **MANUFACTURER** from the menu.

6. Press **F2** to confirm and save.

130 MASTERING DATAEASE

CH. 5

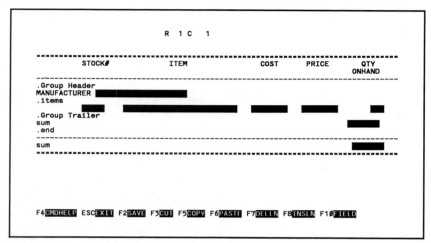

Figure 5.24: Format with group headers and trailers

There is one other minor change to make. Notice that your **TOTAL QUANTITY** field in the group trailer isn't quite lined up under QTY ONHAND. That's easy to fix:

1. Move the cursor to Row 11, Column 52.
2. Press **Ins** and press **Spacebar**
3. Press **Ins** again to cancel Insert mode.

After your modifications, your format should look like the one in Figure 5.25.

Let's look at the results of your work so far:

1. Press **F2** to save your changes and run the report.

Your report, pictured in Figure 5.26, looks good, but the groups are too close together, making the report difficult to read. That can be fixed by inserting some blank lines and separating the groups by adding dashed lines (which you will accomplish in the next section).

1. Clear the report.
2. Select **Modify Format** and keep the old format.

CREATING QUERIES AND QUICK REPORTS **131**

```
                        R 11 C  54

------------------------------------------------------------------
               STOCK#         ITEM            COST     PRICE    QTY
                                                              ONHAND
------------------------------------------------------------------
.Group Header
MANUFACTURER
.items

.Group Trailer
               TOTAL QUANTITY FOR
.end
------------------------------------------------------------------
               TOTAL QUANTITY IN INVENTORY:
==================================================================




    F4 CMDHELP  ESC EXIT  F2 SAVE  F3 CUT  F5 COPY  F6 PASTE  F7 DELLN  F8 INSLN  F10 FIELD
```

Figure 5.25: Format with group headers and trailers after edit

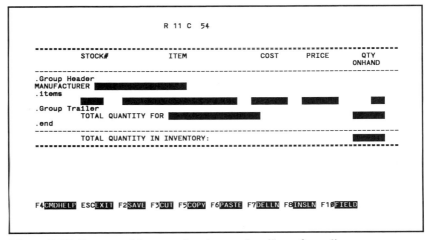

Figure 5.26: Completed report

Next, insert two blank lines after the group trailer to create a space between each group:

3. Move the cursor to Row 12.

4. Press **F8** twice to insert two blank lines.

132 MASTERING DATAEASE

CH. 5

COPYING INFORMATION—F5 AND F6

The Copy and Paste commands are used when you want to copy any text or fields within your report format. To use Copy and Paste:

- Move the cursor to the beginning of the text you want to copy.
- Press **F5** to enable the Copy command.
- Move the cursor one space past the last character you want to copy.
- Press **F5** to mark the end of the area being copied.
- Move the cursor to the location for the copy.
- Press **F6** to enable the Paste command.

To separate each group in the report, let's add a dashed line after each group to the end of the footer area. To save time, you can copy the dashed line from line 5 of the report:

1. Move the cursor to Row 5, Column 1.
2. Press **F5** to begin the copy. DataEase displays a message across the top of the screen instructing you to:

   Move cursor to the end of the block & press F5

3. Press **Ctrl-→** to move to the end of the line.
4. Press **F5** to mark the end of the copy area.
5. Move the cursor to Row 13, Column 1.
6. Press **F6** to paste the copy.

Your format should now look like the one in Figure 5.27.

1. Save the format.
2. Run the report.

Your new report should look like the one in Figure 5.28. However, you are not quite finished with this report. There is one more special

Figure 5.27: Format after Copy and Paste

addition: a field which calculates the dollar investment for each inventory item.

3. Clear the report.
4. Select **Modify Format** again and keep the old format.

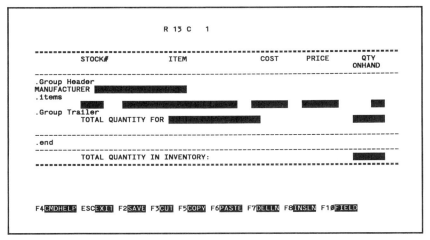

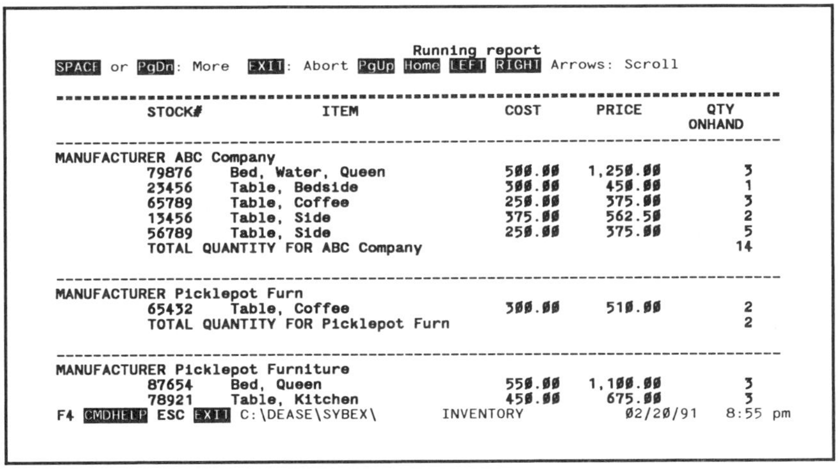

Figure 5.28: Completed report with separated groups

134 MASTERING DATAEASE

CH. 5

CREATING A CALCULATED FIELD

You can place three types of fields in your reports: form fields, system-derived fields, and calculated fields. You have already placed the first two. A calculated field in your report is just like a calculated field in your form: an expression or formula that is composed of values or numeric fields that exist in your form.

For this report, you will create a new column called INVEST-MENT and the field will be the product of COST * QTY ONHAND. But first, you have to make room for it and you can do that by moving the fields in the .items area to the left nine spaces:

1. Move the cursor to Row 9, Column 1.

2. Press **Del** nine times.

3. Repeat step 2 for Rows 3 and 4.

4. Repeat step 2 at Row 11, Column 51 and at Row 15, Column 51.

5. Move the cursor to Row 9, Column 70 and press **F10** to begin definition.

6. Press **Enter** to enter a new field.

7. Type **COST * QTY ONHAND**

8. Press **F2** two times.

The last step is to add a column heading for your calculated field. Then you can save your changes and print your new report:

1. Move the cursor to Row 3, Column 69.

2. Type **INVESTMENT**

Your format screen should now look like the one in Figure 5.29.

3. Press **F2** to save the format.

4. Save the report under the name **INVMFR**

5. Run the report.

Your completed report should look like the one in Figure 5.30.

CREATING QUERIES AND QUICK REPORTS   *135*

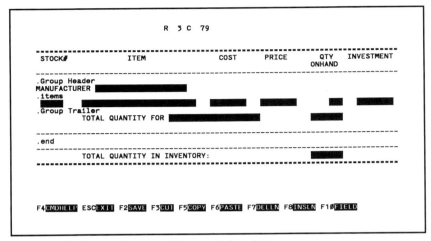

Figure 5.29: Report format with calculation field

Notice that INVESTMENT is not included in the statistics. Calculated fields can only be placed in the .items area of Quick Reports; you cannot include them in group statistical functions.

Figure 5.30: Completed report after adding INVESTMENT field

In the last chapter, an error was found in one of the records for Picklepot Furniture: Picklepot Furn was typed instead. As a result, it appeared in your report by itself when you grouped your records by MANUFACTURER.

136 MASTERING DATAEASE

CH. 5

In the next section, you will correct this and learn another access route to Quick Reports. Before continuing, return to the Main Menu:

1. Press **Esc** to clear the report.

2. Press **Esc** to exit Quick Reports.

If you have not saved your latest report definition, DataEase will ask

Are you sure?

just to remind you that you made changes you have not saved.

QUICK REPORTS FROM RECORD ENTRY

You can also access the Quick Reports directly from Record Entry and then return to Record Entry when you are finished by pressing Esc. This can be convenient when you want to create a report after entering your records. Or, if while running a report you find a mistake in one of your records, you can exit back to the Main Menu, get into Record Entry, fix your mistake, and with one keystroke return to Quick Reports. Let's try it:

1. Select **Record Entry**

2. Select ITEMS from the list of form names.

Now you can fix that Picklepot error and then quickly run the report again:

1. Type **Picklepot Furn** in the MANUFACTURER field and press **F3** to display the record for Picklepot Furn.

2. Change the MANUFACTURER to **Picklepot Furniture**

3. Update the record with **F8**

Look at the function key listing at the bottom of the screen and notice that F9 is QBE (Query by Example). Now let's go directly to

CREATING QUERIES AND QUICK REPORTS   **137**

Quick Reports and run the INVMFR report again:

4. Press **F9**

LOADING AN EXISTING REPORT

DataEase immediately displays the Quick Reports menu. However, the selections all say Define, waiting for you to create a new report. In order to run a previously created report, you must first load it:

1. Select **Load Report**

DataEase displays a list of the reports you have created so far and asks you to:

> Please select the report to load:
> Enter a number from 0 to 2

2. Select **INVMFR** from the list of report names.

3. Run the report.

Now Picklepot Furniture has three records, as pictured in Figure 5.31.

```
INVMFR                                  Running report INVMFR
SPACE or PgDn: More   EXIT: Abort  PgUp Home LEFT RIGHT Arrows: Scroll
================================================================================
    STOCK#           ITEM            COST      PRICE      QTY    INVESTMENT
                                                          ONHAND
--------------------------------------------------------------------------------
MANUFACTURER ABC Company
    79876       Bed, Water, Queen     500.00   1,250.00      3    1,500.00
    23456       Table, Bedside        300.00     450.00      1      300.00
    65789       Table, Coffee         250.00     375.00      3      750.00
    13456       Table, Side           375.00     562.50      2      750.00
    56789       Table, Side           250.00     375.00      5    1,250.00
                TOTAL QUANTITY FOR ABC Company                14

--------------------------------------------------------------------------------
MANUFACTURER Picklepot Furniture
    87654       Bed, Queen            550.00   1,100.00      3    1,650.00
    65432       Table, Coffee         300.00     510.00      2      600.00
    78921       Table, Kitchen        450.00     675.00      3    1,350.00
                TOTAL QUANTITY FOR Picklepot Furniture         8

--------------------------------------------------------------------------------
MANUFACTURER Real Furniture
F4 CMDHELP ESC EXIT C:\DEASE\SYBEX\       INVENTORY       02/20/91   9 01 pm
```

Figure 5.31: Report after Picklepot Furniture edit

138 MASTERING DATAEASE

CH. 5

A FINISHING TOUCH

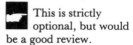 This is strictly optional, but would be a good review.

Now to make this report really shine, you should add a report header and footer, just as you did for the last one, with a title, current date, and page number. Figure 5.32 shows the finished format and Figure 5.33 shows the finished report. Remember to save your report again.

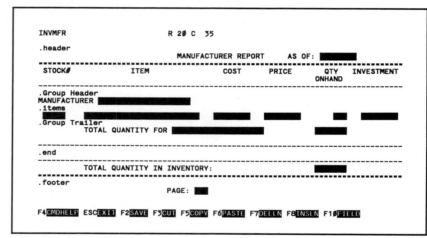

Figure 5.32: Format with headers and footers

Figure 5.33: Report with headers and footers

CREATING QUERIES AND QUICK REPORTS **139**

RETURNING TO THE MAIN MENU

When you are finished, you must exit through Record Entry to return to the Main Menu:

1. Press **Esc**

DataEase returns you to Record Entry and displays the last current record for Picklepot Furniture.

2. Press **Esc** to return to the Records menu.
3. Press **Esc** to return to the Main Menu.

> ⊙ If you have created or modified a report from Record Entry, remember to save the report before pressing Esc. DataEase will not remind you to save the report if you forget to do so.

Believe it or not, we have covered the most basic elements of DataEase. You now know how to create and modify a form; enter, view and modify records; and create and run a report. In the next chapter, you will learn how to make modifications to your form, including adding fields, moving text and fields, and adding special enhancements to your form.

SECURITY NOTES

You must have at least a high security level to run an existing report from the Quick Reports menu. If you have a medium or low level, you can create and run reports, but not save them.

LAN NOTES

If the Record Entry locking rule is exclusive:

- Your report is denied access to a record that another user is already viewing.

- Another user is denied access to a record being processed by your report.

While a report is being run, no form referenced by the report can be modified or deleted. If an attempt is made, DataEase will display

CH. 5

the following Resource Conflict message:

The resource you selected is currently in use:

By user: "Username"
Computer: "Computername"

Waiting for form "Formname"
n attempts to access resource, Press Esc to abort

If the administrator has assigned a Shared Report Definition locking rule, any number of users can load the same report. However, no one can save the modifications if more than one user has loaded a shared report. If an attempt is made to save the modifications, the Resource Conflict message is displayed.

If the locking rule is exclusive, only one user can load the report. If another user attempts to load the exclusive report, the Resource Conflict message is displayed.

CHAPTER SIX

Modifying
Your Form

Fast Track

To modify a form,   145
select Form Definition and Relationships from the Main Menu. Select View or Modify a Form and select the form from the list. Make any changes necessary. Press **F2** to save the form or press **Esc** to cancel all changes. If you save the form, you are asked if you want to save the form under a different name. If so, type **y** and enter a name not already used.

To change a field definition,   146
move the cursor to the field you want to change and press **F10**. Make any changes and press **F2** to save.

To create a comments, or multiline, field,   147
position the cursor and press **F10**. Enter a name beginning with **Long:** and followed by at least one alphabetic character. Define the type as text and for the length enter the number of characters you want for each line. Press **F2** to save the definition. Copy the field to the rows beneath the field as many times as necessary for the number of lines you specified.

To copy a field or text,   148
move the cursor to the beginning of the text or field you want to copy. Press **F5** to mark the beginning of the area to be copied. Move the cursor to the end of the area you want to move and press **F5** again. Move the cursor to the new location and press **F6**.

To move a field or text,   150
move the cursor to the beginning of the text or field you want to move. Press **F3** to mark the beginning of the area to be cut. Move the cursor to the end of the area you want to move and press **F3** again. Move the cursor to the new location and press **F6**.

To create a default entry, 153

move the cursor to the field which will display the default and press **F10**. Move to the Derivation Formula field, and enter the default. If the default is text, surround it with double quotes, e.g., "married". If the default is the value of another field, enter that field name, e.g., fname. If the default is a number, enter the number without quotes.

To create a special highlight for a field, 158

move the cursor to the field you want to highlight. Press **F10** and move the cursor to Field Color. Select the highlight from the Field Color menu. Press **F2** to save.

To add a border to your form, 159

move the cursor to the position for the top left corner of the border. Press **Alt-F10** and select Single or Double Border from the list. Move the cursor to the position for the bottom right corner of the border and press **Alt-F10**.

To erase a border, 161

move the cursor to the top left corner of the border. Press **Alt-F10** and select Erase Border. Move the cursor to the bottom right corner of the border and press **Alt-F10**.

To underline, boldface, or italicize text, 163

move the cursor to the beginning of the text. Press **Alt-B** to begin bold, **Alt-U** to begin underline, or **Alt-I** to begin italics. Move the cursor to the end of the text and press **Alt-E** to end the enhancement.

To print a record from Record Entry, 167

display the record you want to print and press **Shift-F9**.

CHAPTER 6

ONE OF THE ABSOLUTE TRUTHS ABOUT LIFE IS THAT *things change,* which is one of the reasons we use computers. For example, in Chapter 2 you learned how information stored in your database changes constantly and how easy it is to modify your records. You also may find that your form needs to undergo changes.

You can change any aspect of your form:

Add fields	You may find that you need to keep more information about an item, such as a vendor contact.
Delete fields	You may find that some information you have been keeping is never used, or is duplicated in another form. Be cautious; deleting the field also removes the data.
Move fields	You may want to change the order of fields for cosmetic reasons or to make field selections for reports easier; you may find you need to move fields around if you add or delete fields. Moving fields will have no ill affect on the data.
Add characteristic	You can at any time make a field unique, indexed, or required, or add any other attribute, without affecting the data.
Change field length	You can also change the maximum number of characters for any text or numeric field.

Change field type	If you change a field type, DataEase will make any necessary conversions within the limits of the data type allowed. This is covered more thoroughly in Chapter 8.
Field enhancements	And, of course, you can add any cosmetic enhancements, such as lines, boxes, highlights, and character enhancements such as boldface and italics.

In this chapter, you will make most of these changes to your ITEMS form. Let's begin from the Main Menu:

1. Select **Form Definition & Relationships**

2. Select **View or Modify a Form** from the Form Definition menu.

3. Select **ITEMS** from the list of form names.

Your original form, shown in Figure 6.1, appears on the screen displaying the rather cryptic message:

Form has 19 records, each 81 bytes, in file ITEMIAAA.DBM

This simply tells you that each of your 19 records is 81 bytes (computerese for characters) and your records are contained in a DOS file called ITEMIAAA.DBM. A message relaying this type of information displays each time you modify a form definition.

In this chapter, you will make the following changes to your form:

- Change the width of the ITEM field.

- Add a comments field.

- Add a field called SOURCE with a default entry.

- Rearrange the existing fields to make room for the SOURCE field.

CH. 6

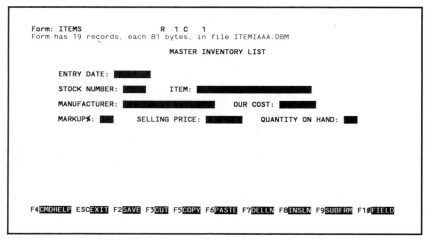

Figure 6.1: Form before edit

- Insert and delete lines.
- Add field and character enhancements.

CHANGING A FIELD LENGTH

You can increase the maximum length of any field to make room for more characters. You can also decrease the length if you find that it is longer than necessary.

The first change to your form is a simple one. You changed the length of the ITEM field for your report. Since it is longer than necessary, you can change it permanently in your form as well:

1. Move your cursor anywhere on the ITEM field.
2. Press **F10**
3. **Tab** to the Maximum Length field.
4. Type **20**

Your Field Definition box should look like the one in Figure 6.2.

⊙ If you decrease the length and some data is longer, it will be truncated, so be careful that you don't lose information.

MODIFYING YOUR FORM **147**

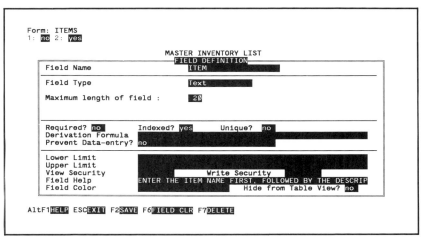

Figure 6.2: Field definition for ITEM

5. Save the definition.

Notice that the ITEM field is shorter by five characters.

ADDING A COMMENTS FIELD

A text field is a single line field with a maximum length of 255 characters, and usually contains information that is brief and descriptive. If you want to create a multiline field that holds more than 255 characters and allows you to enter text in a paragraph format, then you should create long:text fields. A long:text field

- Contains up to 4000 characters.
- Can consist of multiple lines in your form.
- Cannot be on the same line as any other field.
- Can be indexed and used in a search.
- Can be included in reports.

To create a long:text field:

- Begin on a line that contains no other fields.
- Place the field using **F10**, as you would any other field.

148 MASTERING DATAEASE

CH. 6

- Assign it a name beginning with **long:** followed by at least one alphabetic character.

- Assign a line length; this then becomes the line length for each line in the long:text field.

- Add any other characteristics you want to include.

- Save the definition.

- Use **F5** to copy the line, and **F6** to paste each additional line, starting directly below the first line.

You can enter the text as a paragraph, using word-wrap, if you like.

Each line in a long:text field is considered by DataEase to be a separate field, and each additional line is assigned the name of the long:text field with the line number added at the end of the name. For example, if you named your long:text field long:comments, the second line would be long:comments2, the third, long:comments3, etc. This allows you to sort and search separately on these lines. These fields can be used in reports, but each line would appear as a separate column.

Let's add a comments field that is four lines long to your form. It will contain ordering information about each item and will be called LONG:ORDER.

1. Move the cursor to Row 13, Column 7.

2. Type **ORDERING INFORMATION:** reduce for the field description.

3. At Column 29, press **F10** to begin definition.

4. Press **F6** to clear the field name.

5. Type **long:order** ⏎

6. Select **Text** as the type.

7. Type **35** for the width.

8. Press **F2** to save the definition.

Next, you'll use F5 (Copy) and F6 (Paste), to add the other three lines, just as you did when you copied the line in your report format.

MODIFYING YOUR FORM   **149**

1. Move to the beginning of the field (Column 29).

2. Press **F5** to begin the copy. DataEase asks:

   0:NONE 1:BLOCK 2:FORM 3:DICTIONARY FIELD
   Copy a Block, a Form or a Dictionary Field?

In form modification you can copy:

- Text or fields in the current form.

- Another form into the current form.

- A field from the Dictionary form, which will be discussed in Chapter 8.

In this case you want to copy a block:

3. Select **Block**

4. Move the cursor to Column 64, the last space *past* the end of the field.

5. Press **F5** to mark the end of the copy area.

6. Move the cursor directly below the field, Row 14, Column 29.

7. Press **F6** to paste the copy.

8. Move the cursor down to Row 15, Column 29.

9. Press **F6** to paste the copy.

10. Repeat steps 8 and 9 to copy the field one more time.

When you have finished, your screen should look like the one in Figure 6.3.

So that you can see that each field is named separately, display the field characteristics:

1. Move the cursor to the beginning of the second line of the ORDERING INFORMATION field.

2. Press **Spacebar**

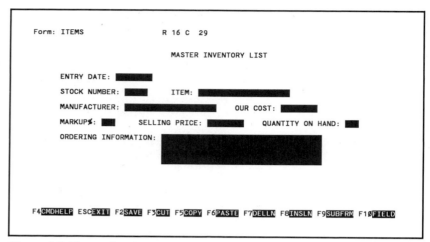

Figure 6.3: Form after long:order placed

DataEase displays the field characteristics in the top left corner of the screen:

FIELD:LONG:ORDER2,Text,35

3. Repeat steps 1 and 2 for the last two fields and notice that they are named *long:order3* and *long:order4*.

You can sort or search on any line in your long:text field. To delete a line in a long:text field, press Shift-F7. To insert a line in a long:text field, move the cursor to the row where you want the line, and press Shift-F8.

MOVING FIELDS

You can move text, fields or a combination of both. Moving is similar to copying, except that you use F3 (Cut) instead of F5 (Copy) before you paste. F3 deletes the designated text or field, and lets you insert it in a new location. The procedure for moving is outlined below:

- Move the cursor to the beginning of the text or field you want to move.
- Press **F3** to begin the cut.

MODIFYING YOUR FORM **151**

- Move the cursor to the first space past the end of the copy area.
- Press **F3** to cut.
- Move the cursor to the new location.
- Press **F6** to paste.

In the next section, you will add a field called SOURCE in front of OUR COST. This means that you'll need to move some fields out of the way. STOCK#, and then MANUFACTURER, can each be moved up a line. Let's start by moving STOCK# to the same line as ENTRY DATE:

1. Move the cursor to Row 7, Column 7, under the S in STOCK NUMBER.

2. Press **F3** to begin the cut. DataEase asks you to:

   Move cursor to the end of the block and press F3

3. Move to the space after the end of the STOCK# field.

4. Press **F3** to complete the cut.

5. Move the cursor to Row 5, Column 41.

6. Press **F6** to paste.

Now your form should look like the one in Figure 6.4: the STOCK NUMBER prompt has relocated and ITEM has moved over. Let's finish the job and move ITEM to the beginning of the line to make room for MANUFACTURER.

7. Move the cursor to Row 7, Column 7 and press **Del** five times to move ITEM over.

Next, move MANUFACTURER up to row 7:

1. Move the cursor to Row 9, Column 7, under the M in MANUFACTURER.

2. Press **F3** to begin cut.

3. Move to the space after the end of the MANUFACTURER field (Column 41).

152   MASTERING DATAEASE

CH. 6

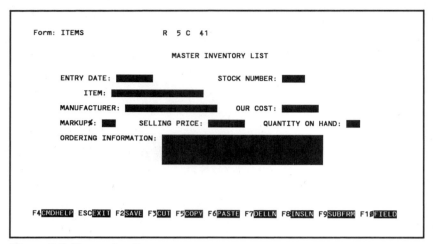

Figure 6.4: Form after first move

4. Press **F3** to complete the cut.
5. Move the cursor to Row 7, Column 41.
6. Press **F6** to paste.

Now your form should look like the one in Figure 6.5. You'll change the position of OUR COST after you add the new field.

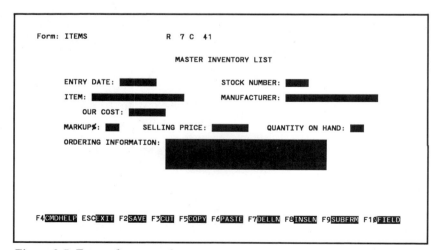

Figure 6.5: Form after second move

CREATING A DEFAULT ENTRY

In Chapter 2, you created a default record that contained commonly used field values. A default is also another type of derivation formula. The default entry automatically appears in the field during record entry. If the default entry is text, it must be enclosed in quotes: "". For example, in this case, you are going to add a new field called SOURCE, which will contain the vendor from whom the item is purchased. This is usually the manufacturer, but may be a third-party distributor. To save room in the database, the default entry will be "MFR" to indicate the manufacturer; and because the source may *not* be the manufacturer, you'll allow operator entry to override the default.

1. Move the cursor to Row 9, Column 7.

2. Press **Ins** and type **SOURCE:** and press **Spacebar**

3. Press **F10**

4. Using the information below as a guide, define the field:

				DERIV.
NAME	*TYPE*	*LENGTH*	*IND?*	*FORM.*
SOURCE	Text	15	yes	"MFR"

When completed, your definition screen should look like the one in Figure 6.6. (Did you remember to index the field?)

5. Save the definition.

6. Insert spaces in front of OUR COST to move it under MANUFACTURER.

7. Press **Ins** to cancel Insert mode.

The new field is placed, and your form should look like the one in Figure 6.7.

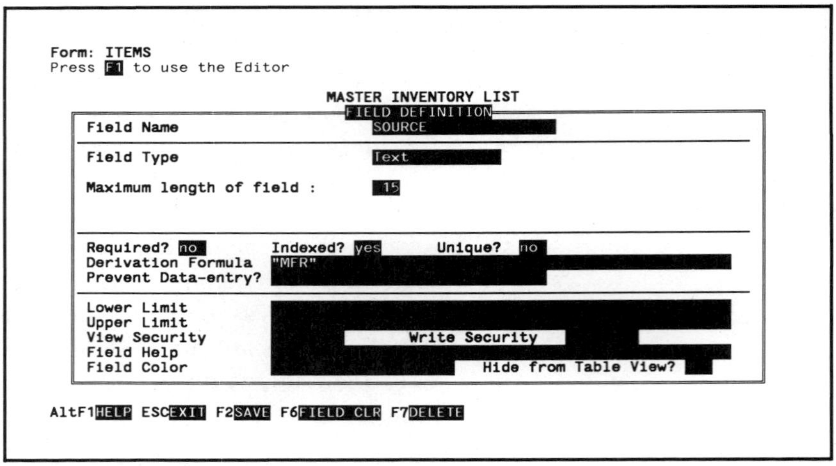

154 MASTERING DATAEASE

CH. 6

Figure 6.6: Completed definition of SOURCE

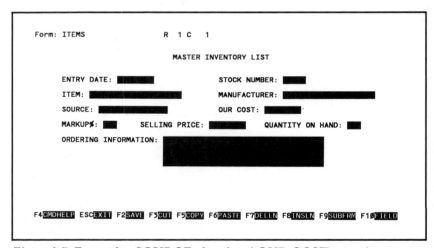

Figure 6.7: Form after SOURCE placed and OUR COST moved

INSERTING AND DELETING LINES IN YOUR FORM

When you modified your report format, you used F7 and F8 to delete and insert lines. You can do the same in form modification.

⊙ Remember when you delete a row, all information on that row goes with it. You will lose any fields or text on that row, with no opportunity to change your mind. So, be very careful.

Let's add one more field to your form called TOTSOLD. This will represent the total units sold to date. In Chapter 7 you will learn about a special formula that will give us that figure.

1. Move your cursor to Row 12, Column 1.
2. Press **F8** twice to insert two new rows.
3. Move the cursor to Row 13, Column 7.
4. Type **total sold to date:**
5. At Column 27, press **F10** and place the field with the following characteristics:

NAME	TYPE	LENGTH	PREVENT DATA-ENTRY?
TOTSOLD	Number, Integer	4	yes, and do not save (virtual)

Your definition should look like the one in Figure 6.8.

6. Save the definition.

Now that your new fields have been added and your other fields rearranged, your form should look like the one in Figure 6.9.

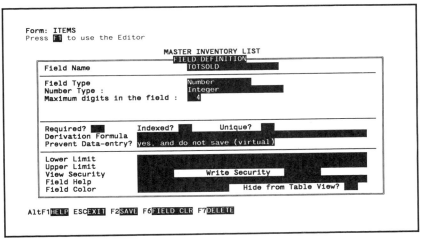

Figure 6.8: Definition of TOTSOLD

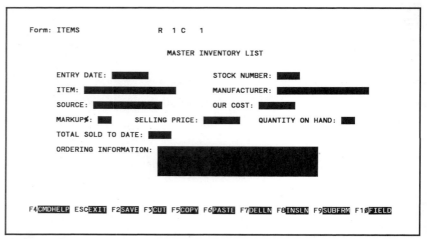

Figure 6.9: Form after definition saved

RECOVERING FROM MISTAKES

If you should accidentally delete a line of fields, or if some other mishap should occur, you can return the form to its original state. If you press Esc, DataEase will give you the opportunity to leave Form Definition without saving your form. If you have made any changes, DataEase will ask you:

Do you want to abandon modified form/data (Y or N):

If you answer Y, DataEase will return you to the Form Definition menu *without* saving any of your changes. If you answer N, you will remain in the Form Definition screen.

So, obviously, if you make a major mistake, you can recover by pressing Esc, but you will also lose any other changes you made. The moral is be careful, and look before you press.

SAVING YOUR CHANGES

Mistakes and power failures are a nuisance, but they can happen. One way to lose less information is to save as you go along. After you

MODIFYING YOUR FORM **157**

One good rule of thumb is: when you get to the point where you wouldn't want to repeat what you have just done, SAVE.

make a number of changes, press F2 to save and exit, then return to your form again by selecting Modify Form. It's an extra step, but could save you valuable time in the long run.

Since you have made quite a few changes *and* still have a few more to go, let's save the form, then return to editing it:

1. Press **F2** to save the form. DataEase asks:

    Do you want to save the form under another name (Y/N)?

This allows you to make a new form without changing anything in the current form. If you say Y, you can also choose whether or not to transfer the records over.

2. Type **N**
3. Select **View or Modify a Form**
4. Select **ITEMS** from the list.

Now your changes are safely stored on the disk and you can continue with the final modifications.

ENHANCING YOUR FORM

Colors, shadings, and print attributes can enhance the look of your form as well as draw attention to certain areas. If you have a color monitor, you can display your text areas and record entry fields in different colors. If you have a monochrome monitor, you can experiment with different shadings. Later in this section, you will learn about printing records from Form View; these printouts can be improved with the addition of text enhancements such as underscore and italic print.

CHANGING FIELD HIGHLIGHTS

On a color monitor, fields in Record Entry are normally displayed in light brown with a blue background. On a monochrome monitor, fields are displayed in white/grey on a black background.

However, you may want to draw attention to some fields by displaying them in a different background color or shading. For example, you might want the stock number to appear with a red background; and a dollar field to display in a green backgroud. In monochrome you can reverse the field display: black against a grey/white background.

If your monitor is color, you can change the background color of a field by selecting one of 11 different colors and highlights.

Let's display the STOCK# field in the same background color as the function keys (referred to in the menu as Key Names), which is red on a color monitor and light gray on a monochrome.

1. Move the cursor to the STOCK# field and press **F10**

2. Press the **End** key, then ← to move quickly to Field Color.

3. Press **F1** to display the entire menu. DataEase displays a menu of field highlights and colors, as shown in Figure 6.10.

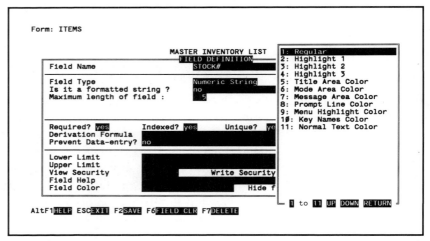

Figure 6.10: Color menu

4. Select **Key Names Color**

5. Save the definition.

The new color for STOCK# will be visible in Record Entry. In the meantime, you can ask DataEase to display temporarily the selected

MODIFYING YOUR FORM **159**

colors in Form Definition by pressing Alt-S (Show Colors). Try it:

1. Press **Alt-S**

The STOCK# field appears in red (or light grey) and DataEase displays the following message at the top of the screen:

> Press PgUp, PgDn, Home or End to scroll; Press any other key to continue

You can use these keys to scroll through a multipage form to see all the fields. You can then press any key to return to the normal display:

1. Press **Spacebar**

ADDING BORDERS TO YOUR FORM—ALT-F10

If you move fields after erasing borders, extra rows may be inserted that cannot be deleted without losing rows of text. The manufacturers of DataEase are aware of this problem.

A border is a single or double line drawn around your entire form or a portion of it. You should wait until *after* you have completed all your modifications to draw your border since moving, deleting, and adding fields, as well as text enhancements, will "rearrange" your border. However, you should always draw your border *before* adding any text enhancements and print attributes (covered next) to your form text that falls within the borders. This allows DataEase to compensate for the extra codes inserted before and after the text. If you wait until after you have added enhancements to draw your border, the border will not be aligned correctly in the Record Entry screen.

But for now, to draw a box around your form:

-   Move the cursor to the top left corner for the box.
-   Press **Alt-F10**.
-   Select Single or Double border.
-   Move the cursor to the bottom right corner for the box.
-   Press **Alt-F10**.

Let's complete your first form by creating a double border around the body of the form. This time, let's use Command Help to create our border. You'll begin the command through the Command Help menu:

1. Move the cursor to Row 3, Column 3 (top left corner of the box).
2. Press **F4** to display Command Help.
3. Select **Tools**
4. Select **Borders & Ext Char Set**
5. Select **Double Border**; DataEase asks you to:

   Move cursor to the opposite corner & press Alt-F10

Complete the border:

6. Move the cursor to Row 21, Column 78.
7. Press **Alt-F10**

Your form should now include a border, as depicted in Figure 6.11.

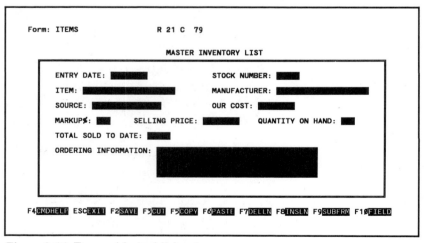

Figure 6.11: Form with double border

As mentioned previously, a border should be drawn *after* you have placed all your fields and text. If you need to add or delete a field, you should erase your border first. The procedure for erasing the border is similar to that of drawing it:

- Place the cursor at the top left corner of your border.
- Press **Alt-F10** and select **Erase border.**
- Move the cursor to the bottom right corner of the border and press **Alt-F10**.

HIGHLIGHTING YOUR TEXT

You can also highlight form text. The Highlight menu, shown in Figure 6.12, displays a list of colors to enhance the look of your text in Record Entry. Let's display the STOCK# field in the same color used for the prompt line: black on green for color, and grey on black for monochrome. There are no function keys to select text background color, so you must use the Command Help menu:

1. Move the cursor to the first character in the STOCK NUMBER prompt, under the S.

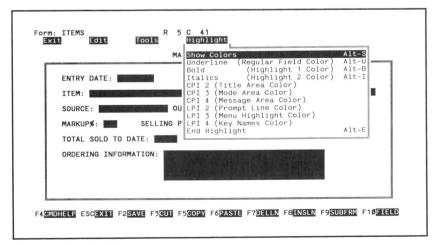

Figure 6.12: Highlight menu

2. Press **F4** and move the cursor to **Highlight**

3. Highlight **LPI 2 (Prompt Line Color)** and press **Enter**; DataEase prompts you for the next step:

   Move cursor to end of LPI2 area & press Alt-E

4. Move the cursor to the space after the last character in the prompt:

   STOCK NUMBER:_

5. Press **Alt-E** to end the selected area.

Whoops! DataEase adds some special coding to your title to indicate the special highlight, and appears to offset part of your border, as shown in Figure 6.13. However, these codes do not appear in Record Entry and your border will return to normal then. If you decide to delete any codes within the form, the border will automatically readjust any lines that appear offset now because of the codes.

Use Show Colors (Alt-S) to see how your form will display in Record Entry:

6. Press **Alt-S**

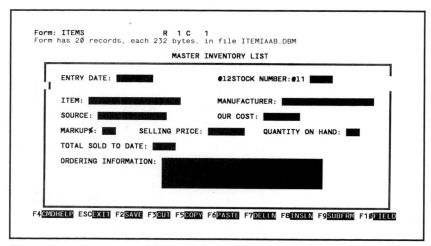

Figure 6.13: Form after STOCK# text highlight

MODIFYING YOUR FORM **163**

Both the STOCK# field and the form title display in the appropriate highlight color. And the borders are back in place.

7. Press **Spacebar** to return to the normal form display.

ADDING SPECIAL PRINT ATTRIBUTES

Special print attributes—such as boldface, underline, and italic print—will improve the look of your printed record. Text selected for bold will be printed twice so that it appears darker than the other text. Let's add the bold and underline attributes to your form title:

1. Move the cursor to the first character of the title, under the M in MASTER INVENTORY LIST.

2. Press **F4** and select **Highlight**

Notice that next to each attribute is the color used to represent that attribute in Record Entry. Notice also the function key shortcuts: Alt-U for underline; Alt-B for bold; Alt-I for italic.

3. Select **Underline**

4. Move the cursor to the space after the last character in the title.

5. Press **Alt-E** to end the selected area.

6. To select the bold attribute, place the cursor under the M in MASTER INVENTORY LIST and press **Alt-B**, then move the cursor to the first space to the right of the T in LIST and press Alt-E.

If you select a print attribute for text, the attribute color overrides any text highlight color you might have selected.

DataEase adds special coding to your title to indicate the special attribute, as shown in Figure 6.14. Use Show Colors to see how your form will display in Record Entry.

7. Press **Alt-S**

164 MASTERING DATAEASE

CH. 6

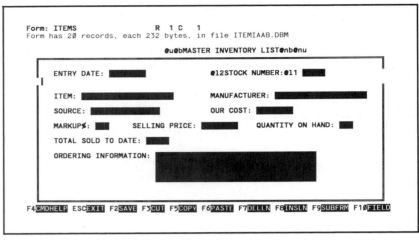

Figure 6.14: Form with print attributes

As you can see, text selected for special print attributes is displayed on the screen in special colors. This time the text is red, the color used to represent bold, the last attribute you selected.

8. Press **Spacebar** to return to the normal display.

Now that you have completed your modifications, it's time to go into Record Entry and see the results:

1. Press **F2** to save your form.
2. Type **N** to save it under the *same* name.
3. Press **Esc** to return to the Main Menu.

■ When you save your form, DataEase will display messages indicating that it is reorganizing fields and updating indexes with the changes you made. This process will only take a few seconds in this case since you only have a few records. However, as your database grows, this could take considerably longer.

ADDING FIELD VALUES IN RECORD ENTRY

The only drawback to adding a new field to your form is that someone has to add the data! Well, it's certainly no problem to add data to new fields in Record Entry. Just for practice, you'll add only a couple of comments. And while you're at it, you can change the SOURCE

MODIFYING YOUR FORM **165**

fields that do not use the default entry. Some tricks you learned earlier will make this easy. First:

1. Select **Record Entry** from the Main Menu.

2. Select **ITEMS** from the Record Entry screen. DataEase displays your newly modified form with the new fields and highlights.

3. Press **F3** to display the first record.

Notice that even though you added fields and moved them around, the data is displayed in the right place.

As you can see, MFR automatically appears as the default entry for the SOURCE field. However, a few of the items are purchased from a source other than the manufacturer. One way to make changes in the SOURCE field efficiently is to use Table View. However, if you have a very large database, it would be more practical to search for the STOCK# and follow these general steps to make the changes:

- Clear the screen with **Alt-F5**.

- Enter the STOCK# of the record that needs to be changed.

- Press **F3**.

- Enter the new SOURCE and press **F8** to modify the record.

- Repeat the above steps for each record.

In the next exercise, you'll do just the above, using the following steps:

1. Change the SOURCE fields for the following records:

STOCK#	*SOURCE*
12345	Country Cousins
23456	Beds 'n Things
45678	Carver's Chairs
78921	Table Tops
78923	Beds 'n Things
65789	Table Tops
45234	Country Cousins

Next, add a couple of comments in your LONG:ORDER field just to see how easy it is. When you type the information, you will not press Enter until you have finished the entire entry. A process called "word-wrap" will take care of formatting it into your four-line field as you type.

1. Display Record 1.
2. Move the cursor to LONG:ORDER and type the following:

   We are trying the MFR as new source. We will review shipments after 3 months (6/91)

Your form should look like the one in Figure 6.15. Notice that DataEase has added carriage return characters at the end of each field line.

Figure 6.15: Form after first comment entry

3. Press **F8** to update the record and **F5** to clear the screen.
4. Display Record 2 and type the following into the LONG:ORDER field:

   This product is a big seller but the source is slow so order way ahead of time.

5. Update the record but do not clear the screen.

Your screen should look like the one in Figure 6.16.

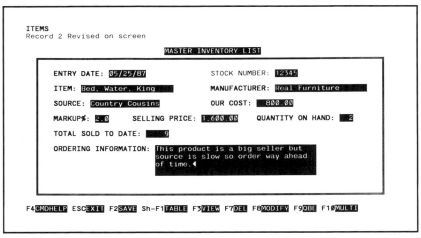

Figure 6.16: Form after second comment entry

PRINTING A RECORD

Printing from Record Entry is one way to print records containing long:text fields that do not easily fit into a columnar report format.

Now that you have included some text enhancements in your form, let's print it again and you'll see that the form title will appear boldfaced and underscored as you defined it when you modified your form.

Your printer may not print the border with straight lines, but may instead use some special characters. If so, you may not want to include a border in your Form Definition. Let's print the first record with the LONG:ORDER field information (make sure your printer is on and on line).

1. Use **Ctrl-F3** to display the first record.
2. Press **Shift-F9**

Your record is printed with the text enhancements.

NOTES ABOUT MODIFICATION

If you make a field unique after you have entered records and already have duplicate field entries, DataEase will not discover this until you make a modification to one of the duplicate records. If that happens, when you try to update, DataEase will not save it until the duplicate field value has been changed.

168 MASTERING DATAEASE

CH. 6

Before making any changes to your field characteristics, please refer to the section on "Modifying Field Definitions" in Chapter 2 of Volume 2 of your DataEase documentation for information on the effects of form modification on data already stored. Modifications made incorrectly can adversely affect your data; this section tells you how to avoid this. Errors caused by incorrect form modification are written to special DOS files called *exception files*, also discussed in this section. If DataEase has had to create an exception file because of an error, the message area of your screen will display the name of that file. You can see the contents of this file by using the *type* command from DOS.

As you can see, basic modifications to your form are easily made. In the next chapter, you will learn how to work with multiple forms. If you use DataEase on a LAN, be aware that the Security and LAN notes on form definition also apply to form modification. You can refer to Chapter 2 if you need to reread that material.

CHAPTER SEVEN

Working with Multiple Forms

Fast Track

To create a relationship between two forms,   180

select Form Definition and Relationships from the Main Menu. Select Define Relationships from the Form Definition menu. Fill in the relationship form, selecting Form 1, Form 2, and at least one set of fields from Forms 1 and 2 that contain common values that will be used to match records in both forms. Press **F2** to save the relationship record.

To display matching records from related forms in Form View,   186

use Record Entry to open the primary form. Press **F10** (Multi-View) and select the related form from the list. Press **F3** to continue displaying records in the related form. To return to the primary form, press **Esc**. The second time you use **F10**, if the cursor is on the linking field and no other forms are related by that field, DataEase will display the matching record immediately.

To display matching records from related forms in Table View,   190

use Record Entry to open the primary form. Press **Alt-F10** (Multi-Form) and select the related form from the list. Press **F3** to display the next record in the primary form and matching records in the subform. If you modify or add a record in the subform, press **F8** to update. Press **Esc** to clear the subform.

To use Dynamic Lookup   196

to copy values from a related field in a related form, use Record Entry to open the primary form. Move the cursor to the field you want to copy into. Press **Ctrl-F10** (Dynamic Lookup) and select the related form from the list. Move the cursor to the record that contains the value you want to copy, and press **Enter**. DataEase copies the value from the related field only.

To create a second relationship between two forms, 198

select Form Definition and Relationships from the Main Menu. Select Define Relationships from the Form Definitions menu. Fill in the relationship form, selecting Form 1, Form 2, and at least one set of fields from Forms 1 and 2 that contain common values that will be used to match records in both forms. In the last two fields of the relationship record, enter the optional name for Form 1 and the optional name for Form 2. These names will be used in place of the form names when DataEase displays a list of related forms.

To include fields from a related form in a report, 203

select Query By Example–Quick Reports from the Main Menu, and select the field list for the primary form. While still displaying the primary form, press **F10** and select the related form from the list; select the fields. Press **F2** to save the selection and return to the Quick Reports menu or press **Esc** to return to the primary form.

CHAPTER 7

SO FAR YOU HAVE CREATED A FORM THAT CONTAINS the current status of each inventory item. However, a database usually consists of many related forms. Furniture Palace could also use forms for customer sales, accounts receivable, product orders, and vendor and customer information.

Each of these forms would contain information related to another form. For example, a VENDORS form would contain name, address, and contact information for each manufacturer and source contained in the ITEMS form. An ORDERS form would contain information about orders placed for each inventory item. In this chapter, you will learn how to work with records from several related forms. But first, you'll need to create more forms.

CREATING A VENDORS FORM

The next form you'll create is VENDORS, which will keep information about each of Furniture Palace's suppliers. This is a simple form comprised primarily of field types you have used before. The NAME field will be used as the unique field, since no two vendors have the same name.

1. Use the example in Figure 7.1 to place field prompts and fields.

2. Then use the information below to place and define the first seven fields next to their prompts.

VENDORS FORM

FIELD NAME	TYPE	LENGTH	REQ?	IND?	UNI?
NAME	Text	25	Yes	Yes	Yes
DESCRIPTION	Text	4	No	No	No

WORKING WITH MULTIPLE FORMS   *173*

VENDORS FORM

FIELD NAME	*TYPE*	*LENGTH*	*REQ?*	*IND?*	*UNI?*
ADDRESS	Text	20	No	No	No
CITY	Text	15	No	No	No
STATE	Text	2	No	No	No
ZIP	Numeric String	5	No	No	No
CONTACT	Text	25			

```
Form: VENDORS                    R 12 C  17
Type text and field names anywhere on form, press F10 FIELD to define fields

                         CURRENT VENDORS

     NAME:                            DESCRIPTION:

     ADDRESS:

     CITY:              STATE:     ZIP:

     CONTACT:

     TELEPHONE:




  F4 CMDHELP  ESC EXIT  F2 SAVE  F3 CUT  F5 COPY  F6 PASTE  F7 DELLN  F8 INSLN  F9 SUBFRM  F10 FIELD
```

Figure 7.1: Text for VENDORS form

From now on, when you are asked to create a form, you won't be given the exact row and column coordinates for the prompts and fields. Instead, you will use the indicated figure as a guide to the approximate positions for the text. The fields will then follow the prompts, separated by a space.

The last field, TELEPHONE, is another numeric string field. However, this time you will select DataEase's predefined format for telephone numbers:

1. Use **F10** to place the field next to the TELEPHONE: prompt.

2. Press **F10** to begin the definition and press **Enter** to accept the name.

3. Select **Numeric String**
4. Select **phone no**
5. Press **F2** to save the definition.

The completed form is pictured in Figure 7.2.

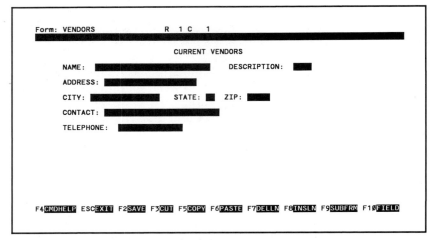

Figure 7.2: Completed VENDORS form

CREATING THE ORDERS FORM

Next, you'll create a form called ORDERS to keep records of product orders placed with vendors. This form will contain two unique fields.

INCLUDING TWO UNIQUE FIELDS

Each time you save a record, DataEase will check to see if another record contains both the same order number *and* the same stock number before the record is accepted.

In the ITEMS form, you defined only the STOCK# as unique, since no two products can have the same stock number. In the ORDERS form a combination of *two* fields will make each record unique: ORDER# and STOCK#. Each order placed with a vendor includes an order number. However, a single order might include several different products. Since each product will be entered as a separate record, an order number may be repeated in several records. So the combination of order number and stock number will make each record unique.

1. Use the form in Figure 7.3 as a guide to place the field prompts.
2. Use the information in Table 7.1 to place and define each field after its prompt.

The completed order form is pictured in Figure 7.4.

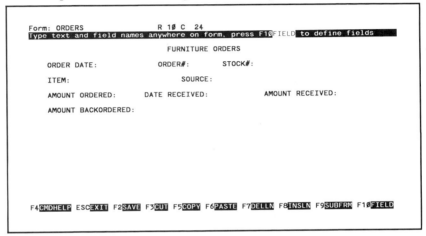

Figure 7.3: Field prompts for ORDERS

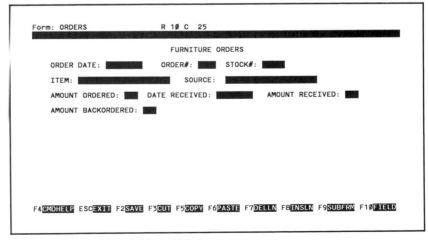

Figure 7.4: Completed ORDERS form

Table 7.1. Field Definition for ORDERS

FIELD NAME	TYPE	LENGTH	REQ?	IND?	UNI?	DERIV. FORM.	PREVENT DATA-ENTRY?
DATEORD	DATE		Yes	No	No		
ORDER#	Numeric String	4	Yes	Yes	Yes		
STOCK#	Numeric String	5	Yes	Yes	Yes		
ITEM	Text	20	No	No	No		
SOURCE	Text	20	No	No	No		
AMTORD	Number, Integer	3	No	No	No		
DATEREC	Date		No	No	No		
AMTREC	Number, Integer	3	No	No	No		
AMTBACK	Number, Integer	3	No	No	No	AMTORD-AMTREC	Yes, and do not save (virtual)

When you have completed the forms, add the following records in the VENDORS form. (You'll leave the DESCRIPTION field blank for now.)

DATE-ORD	ORDER#	STOCK#	ITEM	SOURCE	AMT-ORD
01/15/91	0001	23456	Table, Bedside	Beds 'n Things	3
01/17/91	0002	56123	Sofa, Modern	Realco	3
01/17/91	0002	78920	Armoire, Teak	Realco	1
01/01/91	0003	56123	Sofa, Modern	Realco	1
02/05/91	0004	23456	Table, Bedside	Beds 'n Things	1
02/22/91	0005	78920	Armoire, Teak	Realco	1
02/23/91	0006	45234	Chair, Rocker	Country Cousins	2
02/23/91	0006	12345	Bed, Water, King	Country Cousins	1
03/01/91	0007	65789	Table, Coffee	Table Tops	2
03/05/91	0008	45234	Chair, Rocker	Country Cousins	1
03/15/91	0009	79876	Bed, Water, Queen	ABC Company	1
03/17/91	0010	98765	Table, Kitchen	Realco	2

178 **MASTERING DATAEASE**

CH. 7

Remember, press F2 to save each record, F5 to clear the form, and Esc to exit Record Entry.

Next, you'll add records to the ORDERS form, using the information in Table 7.2; you'll have several opportunities to use Shift-F6 to copy the field from the previous record.

When you have completed entering records, return to the Main Menu.

FORM RELATIONSHIPS

A relationship is a link between two forms based on common field values. What field values do your ITEMS, ORDERS, and VENDORS forms have in common?

- Many of the same stock numbers are found in both ITEMS and ORDERS.

- Source names are found in both ORDERS and ITEMS.

- And the name of the manufacturer and/or source is in ITEMS, ORDERS, and VENDORS.

The field names might be different, but the values match.

These common fields can be used to *link* forms to one another so you can work simultaneously with records from more than one form. The link between two forms creates a relationship. DataEase has three commands that you can use when working with related forms:

Multi-View   To view individual records from related forms. For example, if you are viewing a record in ORDERS that shows a shipment is overdue, you can quickly view the source's record from the VENDORS form to look up the contact and phone number.

Multi-Form   To view a table of records from a related form. If you are viewing a product record in the ITEM form, you can at the same time view a table of orders placed for that product.

Table 7.2: Records to be Entered

NAME	DESCR	ADDRESS	CITY	STATE	ZIP	CONTACT	PHONE
ABC Company	MFR	120 W. Maple	Milwaukee	WI	34932	Elmer Johnston	(414) 342-3333
Carver's Chairs	DIST	4040 Parkway	Gary	IN	64529	Mary Dore	(216) 363-4092
Realco	MFR	606 E. 56th St.	Cleveland	OH	44323	Bill Topps	(216) 363-2131
Table Tops	DIST	509 S. Bush	Chicago	IL	60603	Tom Tripp	(312) 435-2342
Picklepot Furniture	MFR	100 Picklebarrel Way	Ames	IA	75354	Larry Jones	(515) 235-1111
Real Furniture	MFR	300 W. Madison	Chicago	IL	60543	Marcia Hunter	(312) 542-2222
Beds 'n Things	DIST	302 Wellen Way	Detroit	MI	54232	Sam Turner	(313) 266-3222
Terrahaute Furniture	MFR	405 Maple Way	Carmel	IN	55423	Clara Green	(317) 432-2255
Country Cousins	DIST	50 Mayfair	Louisville	KY	65223	Joe Jones	(502) 311-1333

180 MASTERING DATAEASE

CH. 7

Dynamic Lookup	To copy a field value from a record in a related form. If you are ordering an item and can't remember the stock number, you can display a table of records from ITEMS, then locate and copy the stock number of the item you want to order.

You can also create reports that contain fields from multiple related forms.

CREATING RELATIONSHIPS

Before you can work with two or more forms, you must establish at least one relationship.

> You can have up to 100 active form relationships in a database.

The procedure for establishing a relationship is quite simple:

- Select **Form Definitions and Relationships** from the Main Menu.

- Select **Define Relationships** from the Form Definition menu to display the Form Relationship screen.

- Select Form 1 from the menu.

- Select Form 2 from the menu.

- Select the field from Form 1 that contains the common field value.

- Select the field from Form 2 that contains the common field value.

- Press F2 to save the relationship.

RELATING ITEMS TO ORDERS

To work with both ITEMS and ORDERS records, you'll create a relationship between these two forms based on the STOCK# fields in both forms. Begin from the Main Menu:

1. Select **Form Definitions and Relationships**

2. Select **Define Relationships** from the Form Definition menu.

The Form Relationship form, pictured in Figure 7.5, is used to record the relationship between two forms (Form 1 and Form 2) based on at least one set of fields being equal, or containing the same values. Each form you select represents a different side of the relationship.

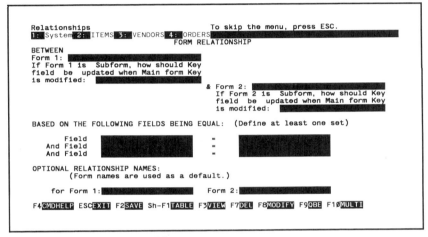

Figure 7.5: Form Relationship screen

Please note that DataEase version 4.2 includes additional fields after the Form 1: and Form 2: prompts in the relationship form. If you have an earlier version, these two additional fields are not included, and therefore your screen will be slightly different from the one shown in Figure 7.5.

The first field prompts you for the name of Form 1 and a numbered list of your current form names is displayed in the prompt line area of the screen.

Each side of the relationship must have a name. Normally the form names are used; however, as you will learn later, this is not always the case. Relationships work in both directions, so it does not matter which you select as Form 1 or Form 2.

3. Select **ITEMS**

4. Press **Tab** to move to the Form 2 field.

5. Select **ORDERS**

182 MASTERING DATAEASE

CH. 7

The cursor moves to the subform field. The topic of the subform field is covered in Chapter 9, so you'll skip this field.

6. Press **Tab** to skip this and move to the next field. The next two fields ask for the set of related fields:

   BASED ON THE FOLLOWING FIELDS BEING EQUAL:
   (Define at least one set)

The first field prompts you to select from a displayed list of fields from Form 1 (ITEMS).

7. Select **STOCK#**; the second field prompts you to select from the fields from Form 2 (ORDERS).

8. Select **STOCK#**

You have now established a relationship between ITEMS and ORDERS, linking records in which the stock numbers are the same. The completed record is pictured in Figure 7.6. The relationship between ITEMS and ORDERS is referred to as a one-to-many relationship, because each STOCK# has only one record in ITEMS, but may appear several times in ORDERS. The relationship between ORDERS and ITEMS is the reverse, an example of a many-to-one relationship.

9. Press F2 to save the record.

RELATING ORDERS TO VENDORS

Next, to work with records from ORDERS and VENDORS, you'll relate these forms based on the SOURCE field in ORDERS and the NAME field in VENDORS.

1. Press **F5** to clear the form.

2. For Form 1, select **ORDERS** from the menu of form names.

3. Press **Tab** to move to the Form 2 field.

4. Select **VENDORS**

5. Press **Tab** to skip the next field.

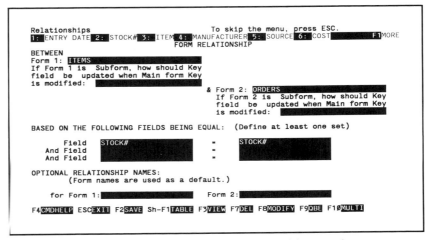

Figure 7.6: Completed ITEMS-ORDERS relationship record

6. Select **SOURCE** from the list of fields from VENDORS.

7. Select **NAME** from the list of fields from ORDERS.

The relationship between ORDERS and VENDORS links records where the value of the SOURCE field in ORDERS is equal to the value of the NAME field in VENDOR. The completed record is pictured in Figure 7.7. ORDERS to VENDORS is a many-to-one relationship; VENDORS to ORDERS is a one-to-many.

8. Press **F2** to save the record.

RELATING ITEMS TO VENDORS

Finally, to work with VENDORS and ITEMS records, you'll relate those forms based on the NAME field in the VENDORS form and MANUFACTURER field in the ITEMS form.

1. Press **F5** to clear the form.

2. For Form 1 select **VENDORS** from the menu of form names.

3. Press **Tab** to move to the Form 2 field.

4. Select **ITEMS**

184 MASTERING DATAEASE

CH. 7

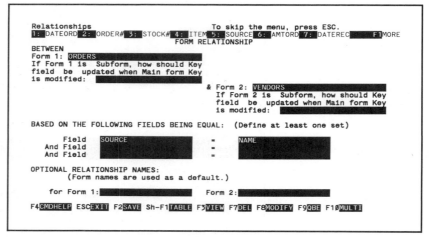

Figure 7.7: Completed VENDORS-ORDERS relationship record

5. Press **Tab** to skip the next field.
6. Select **NAME** from the menu of fields from VENDORS.
7. Select **MANUFACTURER** from the menu of fields from ORDERS.

You have now established your third relationship which links records where the value of the NAME in VENDORS is identical to the value of MANUFACTURER in ITEMS. The completed record is pictured in Figure 7.8.

DISPLAYING RELATIONSHIP RECORDS

The same commands for displaying records in Record Entry are available to you when working with Relationship records. You can display all or selected records in Form or Table View.

1. Press **F3** several times to display your records.
2. Press **Shift-F1** to display a Table View of your records. Then, press **Shift-F1** again to return to Form View.

> You can also press F9 and use Quick Reports to create a report of your relationship records. You can then sort your relationships by any field. (You cannot display the records in any sorted order in Record Entry.)

WORKING WITH MULTIPLE FORMS 185

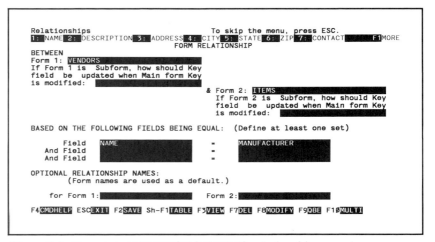

Figure 7.8: Completed VENDORS-ITEMS relationship record

Search for the record linked by STOCK#:

1. Press **Alt-F5** to clear the form.
2. Press Tab four times to move to the field selection for Form 1.
3. Type **STOCK#**
4. Press **Tab** and type **STOCK#** in the field selection for Form 2.
5. Press **F3** to display the relationship record linked by **STOCK#** at the top of the screen.

As you continue building your database, you will be creating more form relationships. However, for now leave Form Relationship and return to the Main Menu:

1. Press **Esc** to clear the menu.
2. Press **Esc** to return to the Form Definition menu.
3. Press **Esc** to return to the Main Menu.

186 **MASTERING DATAEASE**

CH. 7

USING MULTI-VIEW
TO DISPLAY MULTIPLE FORMS

Now that you have created your relationships, you can display records from related forms. To start, you'll work with ORDERS and display information from VENDORS. In this case, ORDERS is referred to as the primary form, and VENDORS, the related form.

1. Select **Record Entry**

2. Select **ORDERS**

3. Press **F3** to display Record 1.

Record 1 is displayed showing Beds 'n Things as the SOURCE. Since the SOURCE field links ORDERS and VENDORS, you can also display the VENDOR record for Beds 'n Things. When you are in Record Entry, use F10, the Multi-View key, to display records from a related form.

4. Press **F10**

A list of the relationships you created for ORDERS is displayed to the right of the screen, as shown in Figure 7.9. DataEase prompts you to:

Select the relationship to view

5. Select **VENDORS**

DataEase immediately displays the record for Beds 'n Things. Notice that VENDORS is displayed in the mode area.

When you press F10, the first record you see in the related form is *always* the record that contains the matching field value, in this case Beds 'n Things. However, once you display the matching record, you are completely free to display, modify, delete, or add *any* records in the related form, just as if it were the primary form. When you are ready to return to the primary form, simply press Esc. Notice that

WORKING WITH MULTIPLE FORMS   187

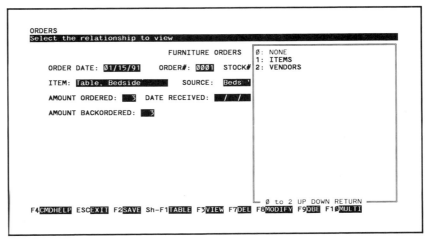

Figure 7.9: Relationship menu in Record Entry

Beds 'n Things is Record 7:

1. Press **F3** and notice that Record 8 displays next.

2. Press **F3** several more times to display the remaining records in record-number order.

3. Press **Esc** to return to the primary form.

When you return to ORDERS, this message appears in the message area:

Returned to ORDERS

and Record 1 is still displayed. DataEase does not lose your place in the primary form, no matter what record you last displayed in the related form.

The first time you press F10 in a work session, the list of relationships is displayed. After that, if the cursor is on the field which links the two forms, DataEase displays the matching record immediately. Try it:

1. Move the cursor to the SOURCE field and press **F3** to display the next record, which shows Realco in the SOURCE field.

2. Press **F10**; the record for Realco is displayed.

3. Press **Esc** to return to the primary form.

4. Press **Alt-F5** to clear the form, and enter **Pickle*** in the SOURCE field.

5. Press **F10**; the record for Picklepot Furniture is displayed.

6. Press **Esc** to return to the primary form.

As you can see, the related record is displayed immediately if the cursor is in the common field. There are two exceptions to this rule:

- If the current field is linked to more than one form, the menu will always display. We'll see an example of that later in this chapter.

- If you have prevented data entry in the linked field, your cursor will not move to that field.

Now you may be asking, does this work in reverse? Can I work with VENDORS as the primary form and ORDERS as the related form? Let's try it.

1. Press **Esc** to return to the Records menu.

Since you entered a value before exiting, without saving the record, DataEase asks if you want to abandon the record.

2. Type **Y**

3. Select **VENDORS** from the Records menu.

4. Press **F3** until the record for Beds 'n Things is displayed.

5. Press **F10** and select ORDERS.

The first order placed with Beds 'n Things is displayed.

MATCHING MULTIPLE RECORDS IN THE RELATED FORM

Each SOURCE in the ORDERS form has only one matching record in the VENDORS form. But what if there is more than one record that matches the field value in the primary form? Have more orders been placed with Beds 'n Things? Let's see:

1. Press **Alt-F3**

The next order placed with Beds 'n Things is displayed. When you press Alt-F3 instead of F3, the next *matching* record is displayed in the related form.

Let's see how many orders have been placed with Realco.

1. Press **Esc** to return to VENDORS.

2. Press **F3** until Realco's record is displayed.

3. Press **F10**

Even though your cursor is in the related field, the list is displayed again. Why? Because NAME is used to relate VENDORS to both ORDERS *and* ITEMS.

4. Select **ORDERS**

The first order for Realco is displayed.

5. Press **Alt-F3** until **No more records** is displayed.

Did you find a total of five records?

ADDING RECORDS TO THE RELATED FORM

Not only can you *display* records from a related form, you can also *add* records to the related form. While you have ORDERS on the screen, add another record:

1. If necessary, press **F5** to clear the form and add the following record:

DATEORD: 032091

ORDER#:   11

STOCK#:   45678

ITEM: Chair, Lounge

190 MASTERING DATAEASE

CH. 7

> SOURCE: Carver's Chairs
>
> AMTORD: 2

2. Save the record.

3. Press **F3** until all records are displayed, and see that your record has been added.

4. Press **Esc** to return to VENDORS.

DISPLAYING A TABLE OF RELATED RECORDS

DataEase displays up to three records for each subform in a Table View.

When several records in the related form contain matching field values, it may be more convenient to display multiple records in a Table View. Multi-Form displays multiple related forms on the screen together. The primary form acts as the main form; the related forms act as a subform. You can display a related form as a temporary subform by pressing Alt-F10. Later, in Chapter 9, you will learn how to create permanent subforms.

Some of the stock numbers appear several times in ORDERS, so let's work with ITEMS as the primary form and ORDERS as the related form.

1. Press **Esc** to return to the Records menu and select ITEMS from the relationship list.

2. Move to the STOCK# field and enter **23456**

3. Press **F3** to find the record.

The Multi-Form menu in Command Help includes all the commands for working with related forms. Let's use Command Help to display your multiform:

4. Press **F4** and select the **Multi-Form** menu.

5. Select **Multi-Form (Alt-F10)**

6. Select **ORDERS** from the list of forms.

A table appears in the middle of your form displaying two records from ORDERS that match STOCK# 23456, as displayed in Figure 7.10.

WORKING WITH MULTIPLE FORMS **191**

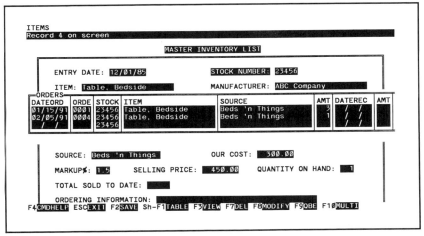

Figure 7.10: Using Multi-Form with ITEMS to show ORDERS

7. Continue to press **F3**

Notice that as the STOCK# changes in ITEMS, the records in the table also change. If no record in ORDERS matches the current STOCK#, the record appears blank except for the STOCK# field.

SEARCHING FOR RECORDS IN A SUBFORM

If you want to search for a record in the main form, you must first clear the subform:

1. Press **Esc** to clear the related form.

2. Press **Alt-F5** to clear the main form.

3. Move to the STOCK# field and type **45234**

4. Press **F3** to find the record.

5. Move the cursor back to the STOCK# field.

6. Press **Alt-F10** and select ORDERS; DataEase displays the matching records from ORDERS.

192 MASTERING DATAEASE

CH. 7

If you are using DataEase version 4.2, you can use the following keys to move back and forth between the subform and the main form:

- **Ctrl-PgDn** from a field in the main form that is *above* the subform, moves the cursor to the first field in the subform that allows data entry.

- **Ctrl-PgDn** from the subform moves the cursor to the next field in the main form that allows data entry.

- **Ctrl-PgUp** from a field in the main form that is *below* the subform, moves the cursor backwards to the nearest field in the subform that allows data entry.

- **Ctrl-PgUp** from a field in the subform moves the cursor backwards to the nearest field in the main form that allows data entry.

Regardless of the version you are using, you can always use the arrow keys or the Tab key to move between the subform and the main form. If you are using DataEase 4.2:

1. Press **Ctrl-PgDn** to move to the DATEORD field in the first record of the subform.

If you are using an earlier version:

1. Press ↓ until the cursor is on the DATEORD field in the first record of the subform.

Notice that this message displays in the prompt line:

SubRecord 7 on line 1 of 2

What does this mean? This tells you that the current subform record is number 7 in the ORDERS file and that it is one of two records in the subform.

2. Press ↓ and notice that the message changes:

SubRecord 10 on line 2 of 2

WORKING WITH MULTIPLE FORMS 193

3. Press **F3**; DataEase displays the next record in the *primary* form. Even though your cursor is in the subform table, F3 still moves you from record to record in the primary form.

If you are using DataEase version 4.2:

4. Press **Ctrl-PgUp** to move back to the main form.

If you are using an earlier version:

5. Press ↑ until the cursor has returned to the main form.

ADDING AND MODIFYING RECORDS IN MULTI-FORM

In Multi-View, you can move independently within the related form. In Multi-Form, however, the records displayed in the table are directly dependent upon the value of the matching field in the primary form.

Although you can add and modify records in Multi-Form also, the procedure is slightly different. Let's try it by correcting the current AMTORD for STOCK# 45678 and adding a new order:

1. Press **Esc** to clear the subform and display the record for STOCK# 45678.

2. Press **Alt-F10** and select **ORDERS**

3. When the subform is displayed, press ↓ and then Tab to move to the AMTORD field.

4. Type **1**

5. Press **F8**

This message displays:

Saved all changes

DataEase updates the record in the subform. Next, let's add another order for the lounge chair:

1. Move to the beginning of the blank row below the second record and enter the following field values:

   DATEORD: 033091

   ORDER#:   12

2. Press **Tab** to move to ITEM.
3. Press **Shift-F6** to copy the ITEM from the previous record.
4. Press **Shift-F6** to copy the SOURCE from the previous record.
5. Type **1** for AMTORD.
6. Press **F8** again.

The STOCK# is already displayed.

Although you have added a record in ORDERS, you must press F8. If you press F2, you will add another *primary* form record as well. The current primary form record would still exist with only two subform records; the new primary form record would contain *three* subform records. In addition, you would add three additional records to the ORDERS form.

Let's verify that the changes were made in the ORDERS form:

1. Press **Esc** to clear the subform.
2. Press **F10** and select **ORDERS**; the first subform record is displayed, showing the updated AMTORD.
3. Press **F3**; the new record entered in the subform with ORDER# 0012 is displayed.
4. Press **Esc** to return to the primary form.

As you can see, there are several differences between Multi-Form and Multi-View:

- In Multi-View, you can move independently through the records in the related form.

WORKING WITH MULTIPLE FORMS 195

- In Multi-Form, you can display and work with multiple records on the same screen as the primary form.

- The records in Multi-Form are temporarily part of the current record as a subform and you cannot move independently within the records, although you can add and modify records.

DISPLAYING MULTIPLE SUBFORMS

You can use Multi-Form to display more than one table of records related to the primary form. For example, ITEMS is also related to VENDORS by the MANUFACTURER field. Let's redisplay the ORDERS subform, then display the vendor record for Real Furniture.

1. Press **Alt-F5** to clear the form and search for the record with STOCK# 98765.

2. Press **Alt-F10** and select **ORDERS** from the list.

3. Move to the MANUFACTURER field.

4. Press **Alt-F10** and select **VENDORS** from the list. The record for Realco is displayed and the subform for ORDERS moves near the bottom of the screen, as shown in Figure 7.11.

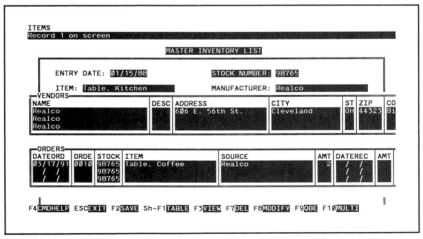

Figure 7.11: ITEMS with two multiforms: VENDORS and ORDERS

196 MASTERING DATAEASE

CH. 7

5. Press **Esc** to clear the VENDORS subform. The VENDORS subform clears and the ORDERS subform moves up.

6. Press **Esc** to clear the ORDERS subform.

USING DYNAMIC LOOKUP TO COPY FIELD VALUES

Another command from the Multi menu is Dynamic Lookup (Ctrl-F10). This command *copies* a value from the common field of any record in the related record. To use Dynamic Lookup:

- Press **Ctrl-F10** and select the relationship name.

- Move the cursor to the record that contains the value you want to copy.

- Press Enter.

DataEase will copy the value from the related field.

For example, what if you are placing an order for an item and you can't remember the STOCK#? In this case, someone wants you to place an order for the queen-sized bed purchased from Real Furniture. Since ORDERS and ITEMS are related by STOCK#, it's easy to look up the information.

1. Press **Esc** to exit ITEMS and select **ORDERS** from the list of forms.

2. Enter the first two fields:

   ORDER DATE: 040591

   ORDER#:   13

3. Press **Ctrl-F10** and select **ITEMS** from the list.

DataEase displays the first 18 records in the ITEMS form, shown in Figure 7.12. Although only the first three fields are displayed, you can press Tab to see the other fields.

WORKING WITH MULTIPLE FORMS   197

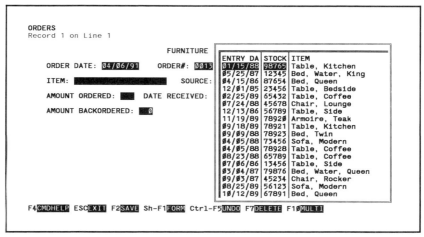

Figure 7.12: Dynamic Lookup menu

4. Press ↓ until the cursor is on the first record shown for Bed, Queen.

5. Press **Tab** three times to display the MANUFACTURER and see that it is **not** Real Furniture.

6. Press ← to return to the first field.

Another record for Bed, Queen is at the bottom of the list.

7. Press ↓ to move to the last record and **Tab** three times to see that the company *is* Real Furniture.

8. Press **Enter** to copy the STOCK#.

The STOCK# is copied and the list of records disappears.

DataEase copies only the value for the related field, no matter where the cursor is in the record.

9. Enter the remaining field values:

    ITEM: Bed, Queen
    SOURCE: Real Furniture
    AMOUNT ORDERED: 1

10. Save the record and clear the screen.

198 MASTERING DATAEASE

CH. 7

Let's use Dynamic Lookup to enter one more order, for a dining room table purchased from Real Furniture.

> Since the ORDER# and SOURCE are the same as in the previous record, you can use Shift-F6 to copy the previous field.

1. Press **Shift-F6** twice to copy the first two fields from the previous record.

2. Press **Ctrl-F10** and press **PgDn** to see the record for Dining Room Table.

3. Move the cursor to the record and press **Enter** to copy the STOCK# value.

4. Enter the remaining fields:

    ITEM: Table, Dining Room

    SOURCE: Real Furniture (or use Shift-F6)

    AMOUNT ORDERED: 1

5. Save the record and clear the screen.

CREATING A SECOND RELATIONSHIP BETWEEN TWO FORMS

From ITEMS, you have displayed records in VENDORS that match the manufacturer name. However, you could not display records in VENDORS that match the source name in ITEMS because there is no link to VENDORS based on the SOURCE field. If you want to relate ITEMS and VENDORS by SOURCE as well, you must create another relationship.

As you know, each side of a relationship is assigned a name, using the names you entered for Form 1 and Form 2. DataEase cannot use the same relationship names for two different sets of relationships. In other words, if you can create a relationship record using the form names VENDORS and ITEMS, DataEase cannot use these as names for another relationship.

If you want to create a second relationship, you must enter an optional form name that DataEase can use when listing the relationships. It is a good idea to use the name of the common field as the

WORKING WITH MULTIPLE FORMS   199

optional form name. When you display the list of relationships, you can tell by the name which one refers to the field you want to match. This may sound a little complicated, but hang in there. By the time you are finished with the exercise, it should be clear.

In the first part of the next exercise you will:

- Modify the existing relationship between ITEMS and VENDORS based on MANUFACTURER, giving ITEMS the optional form name of MFRI and VENDORS the optional form name of MFRV.

- Create a new relationship between ITEMS and VENDORS based on SOURCE, giving ITEMS the optional form name of SRCI and VENDORS the optional form name of SRCV.

From now on, DataEase will use these new optional names when displaying the relationship list.

The optional form names used here are an abbreviation of the field name, followed by the first character of the form name. You can use any name you wish, as long as it is *not* the same as a form name in the current database. Let's begin by modifying the existing relationship:

1. Press **Esc** twice to return to the Main Menu.

2. Select **Form Definition and Relationships**

3. Select **Define Relationships** from the Form Definition menu.

Remember, relationship records can be displayed and modified using the same commands you learned in Record Entry.

4. Press **F3** until the record for VENDORS and ITEMS is displayed.

5. Press **End**, then ← to move quickly to the OPTIONAL RELATIONSHIP NAMES field for Form 1 at the bottom of the screen:

    OPTIONAL RELATIONSHIP NAMES:
    (Form names are used as default)

    for Form 1 _____   Form 2 _____

6. Type **MFRV**

7. **Tab** to the next field and type **MFRI**

The optional names used in the record should help you remember that this relationship links NAME in VENDORS to

MANUFACTURER in ITEMS. MFRV is the VENDOR side and MFRI is the ITEMS side.

The completed record is pictured in Figure 7.13.

8. Press F8 to update the record.

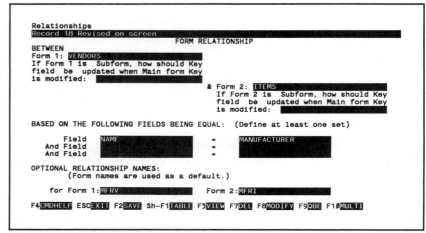

Figure 7.13: Relationship record with the optional form names MFRV and MFRI

Next, you'll create a new relationship and enter its optional names:

1. Press **F5** to clear the form.
2. Using Figure 7.14 as a guide, fill in the screen.
3. Press **F2** to save the record.

The optional names used in this record should help you remember that this relationship links NAME in VENDORS to SOURCE in ITEMS: SRCV is the VENDORS side and SRCI is the ITEMS side.

4. Press **Esc** twice to return to the Main Menu.

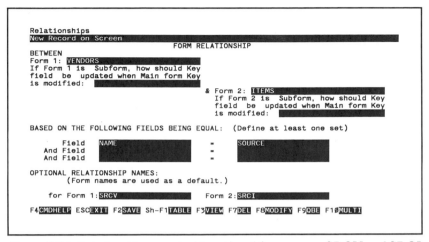

Figure 7.14: Relationship record with optional form names SRCV and SRCI

Now you are ready to test your new relationships in both ITEMS and VENDORS:

1. Select **Record Entry** and select **ITEMS** from the list.
2. Press **F3** until Record 2 is displayed with Country Cousins in the SOURCE field.
3. Press **F10**

The new list includes both SRCV and MFRV. Since you are looking for a NAME in ITEMS that matches the SOURCE in VENDORS:

4. Select **SRCV** to select the relationship linked by SOURCE.

The record for Country Cousins is displayed. Next, display a record in VENDORS that matches the current manufacturer:

1. Press **Esc** to return to the primary form.
2. Press **F10** and this time select **MFRV** to select the relationship linked by MANUFACTURER.

CH. 7

The record for the manufacturer, Real Furniture, is displayed.

Next, let's display a Table View of items manufactured by Picklepot Furniture:

1. Press **Esc** twice to return to the Records menu.
2. Select **VENDORS** from the list.
3. Press **F3** until the record for Picklepot Furniture is displayed.
4. Press **Alt-F10**

Now the list includes SRCI and MFRI, both of which connect to the ITEMS form.

1. Since Picklepot Furniture is a manufacturer, select **MFRI** from the list.

The table of records, pictured in Figure 7.15, contains Picklepot Furniture in the MANUFACTURER field.

Now, how do you think you would display a list of records in ITEMS that show the manufacturer as the source? Think about it. You can follow the steps below, but try it on your own first.

1. Press **Esc** to clear the subform.
2. Press **Alt-F5** to clear the form unchecked.

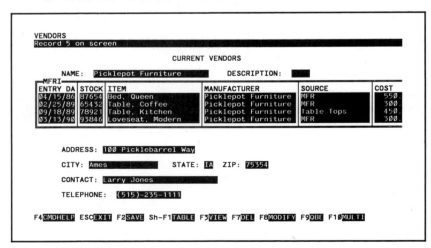

Figure 7.15: Table of Picklepot records

3. In the NAME field, type **MFR**
4. Press **Alt-F10** and select **SRCI** from the list.

Impressed? Your form should display the records shown in Figure 7.16.

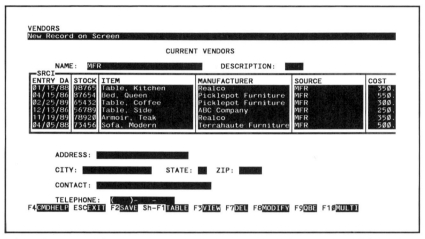

Figure 7.16: Multi-Form records from ITEMS showing MFR as SOURCE

Another reason to establish relationships is so that you can create a report which includes fields from more than one form.

CREATING REPORTS FROM RELATED FORMS

For your next report, you'll include records from both ITEMS and ORDERS. Since ITEMS will be the primary report form, you'll exit VENDORS and start from the Main Menu.

1. Press **Esc** twice and each time type **Y** to abandon the current record and return to the Main Menu.
2. Select **Query By Example–Quick Reports**

CH. 7

3. Select **Define List Fields** and select **ITEMS** from the list. The ITEMS form is now displayed. For this report, you'll provide columns for the STOCK#, ITEM, and QTY ONHAND fields, and the report will be sorted and grouped by STOCK#.

4. Select the fields in the order indicated below, selecting STOCK# as the grouped field:

   STOCK#   1 Group Order

   ITEM   2

   QTY ON HAND   3

5. Press **F10** and select **ORDERS** from the list.

6. Select the remaining fields from **ORDERS**, as indicated below:

   ORDER DATE   4

   ORDER#   5

   SOURCE   6

   AMOUNT ORDERED   7

7. Press **F2** to save the selections and return to the menu.

Next, define the format:

1. Press **Enter** to define the format.

2. Press **Enter** and type **Y** to include group headers and trailers.

> You can either retype STOCK#, as the steps below indicate, or cut and paste it using **F3** then **F6**.

You'll make several changes to the format to improve the appearance. First, you'll remove STOCK# as the header text and enter it as a column heading:

1. Move to the group header text STOCK# (Row 8, Column 1) and delete it.

2. Move to Row 3, Column 1 and type **STOCK#**.

Next, to avoid repeating ITEM and QTY ONHAND for every record, you'll move those fields to the group header area:

3. Move to Row 10, Column 10 and use **F3** to cut the fields to Row 10, Column 35.

4. Use **F6** to paste the fields at Row 8, Column 8.

After you moved ITEM and QTY ONHAND, the remaining fields in the .items area moved over, so you'll move them back under their column headings:

5. At Row 10, Column 11, press **Ins** and use the **Spacebar** to move the fields beginning with DATEORD to Column 38.

Now it's just a matter of editing the column headings:

6. Using Figure 7.17 as a guide, change the field headings.

7. Press **F7** to delete the extra row in the column heading area.

Take a look at your report, pictured in Figure 7.18. For each record in ITEMS, there may be several matching records displayed from ORDERS.

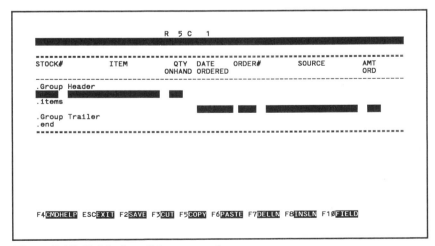

Figure 7.17: Guide for editing report format

206 MASTERING DATAEASE

CH. 7

```
                                        Running report
 SPACE or PgDn : More  EXIT : Abort PgUp Home LEFT RIGHT Arrows: Scroll
 ===========================================================================
 STOCK#         ITEM          QTY  DATE     ORDER#      SOURCE          AMT
                             ONHAND ORDERED                             ORD
 ---------------------------------------------------------------------------
 12345   Bed, Water, King      2
                                   02/23/91 0006  Country Cousins        1
 13456   Table, Side           2

 23456   Table, Bedside        1
                                   01/15/91 0001  Beds 'n Things         3
                                   02/05/91 0004  Beds 'n Things         1

 45234   Chair, Rocker         2
                                   02/23/91 0006  Country Cousins        2
                                   03/05/91 0008  Country Cousins        1
 45678   Chair, Lounge         4
                                   03/20/91 0011  Carver's Chairs        1
                                   03/30/91 0012  Carver's Chairs        1
 56123   Sofa, Modern          1
                                   01/17/91 0002  Realco                 3
                                   02/01/91 0003  Realco                 1
 56789   Table, Side           5
 F4 CMDHELP ESC EXIT C:\DEASE\SYBEX\          INVENTORY       02/25/91  12 29 pm
```

Figure 7.18: Completed report from ITEMS and ORDERS

8. Save the report as **ITEMORD**

You can see how easy it is to create a Quick Report from multiple forms; however, if the report includes *more* than two related forms, you should use the Data Query Language to create the report. This topic is covered in Chapter 12.

Relationships are the cornerstone of DataEase. Without them, you must work with flat files and build one-dimensional reports. As you learn more about working with your database, you will continue to use relationships to access the power of DataEase.

In the next chapter, you'll learn some new formulas that will increase the accuracy and speed of data entry. You'll also use relationships to automatically copy information already entered in another form.

SECURITY NOTES

You must have a high security level to create or modify a relationship.

CHAPTER EIGHT

Advanced Form Design

Fast Track

To enter the current date in a field,   210

press **F10** from the Form Definition screen to place or modify the field that will display the date. Make sure the field type is Date. Move to the Derivation Formula field. Then, to enter a date that does not change if the field is modified, enter ??/??/??. To enter a date that will automatically update when the record is modified, enter **LOOKUP CURRENT DATE**. Press **F2** to save the definition.

To automatically look up and copy values   212

from a field in a related form, press **F10** from the Form Definition screen to place or modify the field that will display the copied value. Move to the Derivation Formula field and enter **LOOKUP ("FORM NAME") ("FIELD NAME")**. (Quotes are necessary if the name is two or more words.) Save the field definition.

To use the IF function   213

to determine a field value, press **F10** from the Form Definition screen to place or modify the field that will use the IF function. Move to the Derivation Formula field and enter **IF(CONDITION,TRUE VALUE,FALSE VALUE)**. The TRUE VALUE tells DataEase what to display if the condition is true; the FALSE VALUE tells DataEase what to display if the condition is not true.

To convert text entries to UPPER, lower or Proper case,   219

press **F10** from the Form Definition screen to place or modify the field that will use the text conversion function. Move to the Derivation Formula field and enter one of these functions: **UPPER(field name)** to convert the text entered in the current field to UPPER case; **LOWER(field name)** to convert the field text to lower case; **PROPER(field name)** to convert the field text to Proper case.

To sequence a text or numeric string field, 220

press **F10** from the Form Definition screen to place or modify the field that you want to sequence. Move to the Derivation Formula field and enter the formula **SEQUENCE FROM** followed by the first text or numeric string character; then enter a field length that will accommodate the number of characters. For example, **SEQUENCE FROM 1** with a field length of 5 will sequence from 22301.

To reverse the order of a text entry, 223

press **F10** from the Form Definition screen to place or modify the field that will contain the values you want displayed in reverse. Move to the Derivation Formula field and enter the function **LASTFIRST(FIELD NAME)**. A value entered as John Smith will display as Smith, John.

To create a choice field, 228

press **F10** from the Form Definition screen to place or modify the field that will display the choices. Move to Field Type and select Choice. Move to the Optional Choice Type Name field and press **F1**. Enter each choice on a separate line (alphabetically if you want to sort by this field in a report).

To add fields to the Dictionary form, 235

select Form Definition and Relationships from the Main Menu. Select View or Modify a form from the Form Definition menu, then select Dictionary from the list of form names. Add, delete, or modify fields just as you would with any of your own forms.

To change the pitch of a report, 240

load or create your report from the Quick Reports menu. Select Define Print Style and move to the Characters Per Inch field. Enter **12** for 12 pitch (elite) or **15** for 15 pitch (condensed print). If necessary, move to the width field and change the width to accommodate more characters per line.

210

CHAPTER 8

WHEN YOU ARE DEFINING FORMS AND ENTERING records, it may appear that much of the work is repetitive. For example, fields such as STOCK#, ITEM, and SOURCE are defined in more than one form. In this chapter, you will learn how to use the DataEase DICTIONARY form to store predefined fields that you can copy into any form.

In addition, many field values for ITEM, STOCK#, and SOURCE are in both the ITEMS and the ORDERS forms. In previous chapters, you used derivation formulas to perform simple calculations and establish field defaults to save yourself some typing. In this chapter, you'll use the LOOKUP formula, which not only eliminates most repetitive typing, but avoids the errors that are often a consequence. In addition, you'll use the SEQUENCE formula to increment values automatically in text or numeric string fields.

To start, you'll modify the ORDERS form to include some new formulas. Let's begin with two shortcuts for entering dates.

1. From the Main Menu select **Form Definition**

2. Select **View or Modify Form**, and then select the ORDERS form.

ENTERING DATES

In Chapter 6, you placed a CURRENT DATE field in your report, and DataEase filled it with the current system date. You can also ask DataEase to enter the current date in a form using one of the following two methods:

- Enter ??/??/?? in the Derivation Formula field. DataEase will automatically enter the current system date. This date will not change when the record is modified.

- Enter LOOKUP CURRENT DATE in the Derivation Formula field. DataEase will automatically enter the current system date. However, this date will change each time the record is modified.

If you want the date field to reflect the last modification date, you should use the second method. But in the ORDERS form, you want the date of the original order to be retained:

1. Move the cursor to the ORDER DATE field; press **F10**
2. Move the cursor to the Derivation Formula field.
3. Type ??/??/??

In this case, you will not prevent data entry, so that you have the option to accept the current date or enter another. Figure 8.1 shows the completed form.

4. Press **F2** to save the definition.

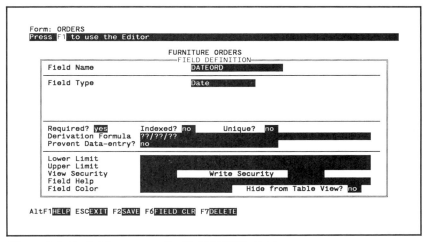

Figure 8.1: Definition screen for DATEORD field

212 MASTERING DATAEASE

CH. 8

LOOKING UP
FIELD VALUES IN ANOTHER FORM

After entering a stock number in the ORDERS form, you enter the item name, another field also found in the ITEMS form. Wouldn't it be nice if DataEase could retrieve that data for you, based on the STOCK#? The LOOKUP formula looks up and copies information from the matching record in another form based on a common field value. In this case the common field value is STOCK#. The format of the formula is:

LOOKUP (FORM NAME) (FIELD NAME)

For example,

LOOKUP ITEMS ITEM

would look up the STOCK# in the ITEMS form and copy the value of the ITEM field. The key is the STOCK#, which provides the link between the two forms. So before you can use a LOOKUP you must first establish the relationship. In this case you already have: ORDERS is related to ITEMS by STOCK#.

1. Move the cursor to the ITEM field and press **F10**

2. Move the cursor to the Derivation Formula field.

3. Type **LOOKUP ITEMS ITEM**

4. Move to Prevent Data-Entry? and select **Yes**

Figure 8.2 shows the completed definition for ITEM.

From now on, each time you enter a stock number in ORDERS, DataEase will find the record in ITEMS with that same stock number and copy the name in the ITEM field.

LOOKUP is also a form of verification. If you enter an incorrect stock number, DataEase tells you by copying either the wrong item or no item at all. If you enter a stock number that is correct but has not been entered into the ITEMS form, you can press F10 (Multi-View), select ITEMS, and enter a new record on the spot, without losing your place!

ADVANCED FORM DESIGN   213

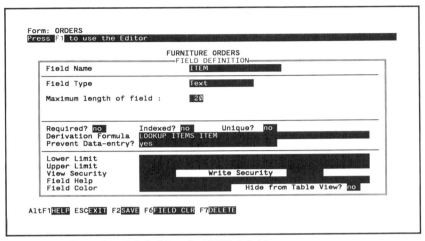

Figure 8.2: Completed definition for ITEM field

If either the field name or the file name is more than one word, you must enter quotes around the entire name. For example:

LOOKUP "ITEM LIST" "ITEM NAME"

5. Press **F2** to save the definition.

USING THE IF FUNCTION TO MAKE DECISIONS

The DataEase IF command is one of 58 built-in functions that calculate and manipulate text. In addition to IF, there are eight other types of functions: DATE, SPELL, TIME, TEXT, FINANCIAL, SCIENTIFIC, TRIG, and MATH. Any of the functions can be used in a derivation formula and you will learn about more of them later.

The IF function decides upon one of two field values, based on whether a condition (or argument) is true or false. The structure of the IF function is:

IF(CONDITION,TRUE VALUE,FALSE VALUE)

214 **MASTERING DATAEASE**

CH. 8

If the condition is true, DataEase displays the TRUE VALUE; otherwise, it displays the FALSE VALUE. For example, if the non-profit status of a company determines whether it is taxed or not, you would enter the following derivation formula as part of the TAX% field definition:

IF NON-PROFIT = "Y",0,.06

This tells DataEase if the value of the NON-PROFIT field is Y, then enter a 0 in the current field; otherwise, enter .06.

USING THE IF FUNCTION TO DETERMINE THE AMOUNT BACK-ORDERED

In the ORDERS form, you'll notice that the AMOUNT BACK-ORDERED (AMTBACK) field always displays the difference between the AMTREC and the AMTORD fields even if the shipment has not yet been received. Furniture Palace does not consider a shipment back-ordered unless only part of it has arrived, or a notification has been sent. So until the partial shipment or a notification has been received, the BACKORD field should display 0. The DATEREC field is likewise filled when either the shipment or a notice of the back order has been received. Therefore, if DATEREC is blank, then the BACKORD value should be 0.

1. Move the cursor to the AMOUNT BACKORDERED (AMTBACK) field and press **F10**

2. Move to the Derivation Formula field, press **F6** to clear the field and type:

IF(DATEREC = BLANK,0,AMTORD-AMTREC)

Figure 8.3 displays the corrected form.

When selecting records for reports, you used comparison symbols with values. Blank is a keyword used with = or not = to represent a null or empty field. Although you could have used >00/00/00, blank is more accurate especially in date or character fields.

3. Press **F2** to save the definition.

ADVANCED FORM DESIGN

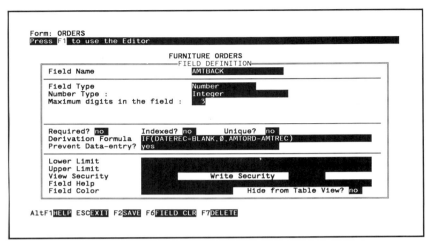

Figure 8.3: Definition for AMTBACK field

COMBINING IF AND LOOKUP IN A DERIVATION FORMULA

> The SOURCE field in ITEMS contains the actual name only if it is *not* the manufacturer. Otherwise, MFR is the default value of the SOURCE field.

You can increase the power of a formula by combining two or more functions in one formula. Let's go back and take a look at the SOURCE field. What you want to display in this field is the *name* of the source. So, how can you get DataEase to always retrieve that name?

Let's work this out logically. If the value of the SOURCE field in the matching record in ITEMS is MFR, what field contains the name? The MANUFACTURER field. Therefore, you want to tell DataEase if the value of the SOURCE field in ITEMS is MFR, then look up the MANUFACTURER field and copy the value; otherwise, copy the value of the SOURCE field. Let's try it:

1. Move the cursor to the SOURCE field and press **F10**

2. Type:

   IF((LOOKUP ITEMS SOURCE) = "MFR",LOOKUP ITEMS MANUFACTURER,LOOKUP ITEMS SOURCE)

When your formula exceeds the space allowed, DataEase automatically switches to full screen edit. Your formula, pictured in Figure 8.4, needs the extra set of parentheses around the first LOOKUP to tell DataEase to check and see if the result of the LOOKUP is

MFR, and if so, to copy the information from the MANUFACTURER field; but if not, to copy the information from the SOURCE field.

3. Press **F2** to save the formula.

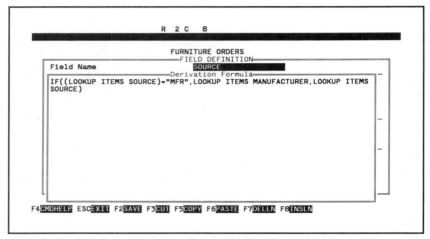

Figure 8.4: Completed definition for SOURCE field

4. Move to Prevent Data-entry? and select **Yes**
5. Press **F2** to save the definition.

There are more functions and data entry shortcuts to cover in this chapter, but first let's test the formulas and functions you have entered so far. Let's return to Record Entry to see how everything works:

1. Press **F2** to save the definition.
2. Type **N** to save the form under the same name.
3. Press **Esc** to return to the Main Menu.

ENTERING RECORDS WITH THE HELP OF FORMULAS AND FUNCTIONS

Because of the modifications you have made to the ORDERS form, you can now skip the ITEM, SOURCE, and sometimes the

ADVANCED FORM DESIGN   *217*

DATEORD fields. Let's open ORDERS and enter a few more records.

1. Select **Record Entry**
2. Select **ORDERS** from the list.

The cursor stops at ORDER DATE.

1. Press **Enter** to accept the current date.
2. Type **14** as the ORDER#.
3. Type **87654** as the STOCK#.

ITEM and SOURCE are automatically filled in and the cursor moves to AMTORD.

4. Type **2** for the amount.

Your order is now complete. That was so simple, let's add a few more records just to see the magic work. This time, you'll type dates as well.

1. Enter just the DATEORD, ORDER#, STOCK# and AMTORD for the records shown in Table 8.1 (use **Shift-F6** when repeating field values):

Table 8.1: Aditional Records for ORDERS.

DATE	ORDER#	STOCK#	ITEM	SOURCE	AMT-ORD
041091	0015	13456	Table, Side	ABC Company	2
041091	0015	56789	Table, Side	ABC Company	1
041591	0016	73456	Sofa, Modern	Terrahaute	2
041591	0016	78928	Table, Coffee	Terrahaute	2
042091	0017	78920	Armoire, Teak	Realco	1

You should now have 20 records in your ORDERS form.

2. Save the last record and return to the Main Menu.

CREATING A SALESPERSON FORM

The next form will contain information about the salespeople, and their sales volume and commissions.

1. Select **Form Definitions and Relationships** from the Main Menu.
2. Select **Define a Form**
3. Enter **SP** as the form name.
4. Use Figure 8.5 as a guide to place the form text and field prompts.

For those who have trouble finding the Shift key or Caps Lock, the next section is for you.

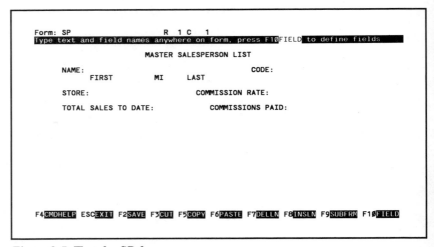

Figure 8.5: Text for SP form

ADVANCED FORM DESIGN **219**

USING FUNCTIONS
TO CONTROL CASE AND ORDER

In Chapter 3, you learned about the importance of consistency when entering data either in Proper Case, UPPERCASE, or lowercase. If, like the rest of us, you find it annoying to constantly switch cases, DataEase has three text manipulation functions, PROPER, UPPER, and LOWER that you can use to convert all character entries to the appropriate case. You'll love it. Like the other formulas you have learned, these functions are placed in the Derivation Formula field.

USING THE PROPER FUNCTION

The PROPER function automatically capitalizes the first letter of each word in the field. The format of the function is:

PROPER(FIELD NAME)

In the SP form, the name will include FNAME and LNAME. To automatically convert the values for the FNAME field to proper case, you would enter:

PROPER(FNAME)

⊙ Use the PROPER function with discretion. It will capitalize the first letter of every word, which may not always be appropriate for words such as *the, a, an, and*, etc.

in the Derivation Formula field. If you enter sandra, in the FNAME field, DataEase converts it to Sandra. And of course, when you type the functions you can use either proper, upper, or lower case.

In the SP form, you'll use the PROPER function to convert values entered for the FNAME, LNAME, and STORE fields.

1. Use the information below to define FNAME, LNAME, and STORE:

NAME	TYPE	LEN.	IND?	DERIV. FORM.
FNAME	Text	12	no	PROPER(FNAME)
LNAME	Text	15	yes	PROPER(LNAME)
STORE	Text	15	yes	PROPER(STORE)

USING THE UPPER FUNCTION

The UPPER function converts the text you type into uppercase. The format of the function is:

UPPER(FIELD NAME)

For example, to convert states to uppercase, you would enter:

UPPER(STATE)

as the derivation formula of the STATE field and after you type oh as the field value, DataEase converts it to OH.

In the SP form, you'll use the UPPER function to convert the salesperson's middle initial (in the MI field) to UPPERCASE.

1. Use the information below to define the MI field.

NAME	TYPE	LEN.	DERIV. FORM.
MI	Text	2	UPPER(MI)

2. Use the information below to define the remaining fields.

NAME	TYPE	LEN.	PREVENT DATA-ENTRY?
COMMRATE	Number, Fixed Point	0 to left, 2 to right	
TOTSALES	Dollar	5 (to left of decimal)	yes
COMMPAID	Dollar	4 (to left of decimal)	yes, and do not save (virtual)

USING SEQUENCE TO INCREMENT FIELD VALUES

If you use a numbering system to organize invoices or customers, you know how important it is to know the next number in sequence

ADVANCED FORM DESIGN **221**

and not repeat a number. The DataEase SEQUENCE formula will automatically increment text or numeric strings for you:

SEQUENCE FROM (TEXT OR NUMERIC STRING VALUE)

For example, SEQUENCE FROM 100 begins with 100 and increments subsequent values by one: 101, 102, 103, etc. DataEase fills remaining spaces with leading zeros; for example, if the field length is 5 and the formula is SEQUENCE FROM 1, the first number will be 00001. If the SEQUENCE formula begins with a single letter and the field length is greater than 1, DataEase will add a ; (semicolon) following the character. For example, if the formula is SEQUENCE FROM A and the field length is greater than 1, the first value will be A;.

In the SP form, you'll use the SEQUENCE formula to assign number codes for each salesperson. Let's define CODE and add the new derivation formula beginning with the first CODE, which will start at SP100.

1. Move the cursor next to the CODE prompt and press **F10**

2. Use the information below to begin the definition:

NAME	*TYPE*	*LEN.*	*REQ?*	*IND?*	*UNI?*
SPCODE	Text	5	yes	yes	yes

3. Move the cursor to the Derivation Formula field and type **SEQUENCE FROM SP100**

4. Select **Y** at Prevent Data-entry?.

5. Press **F2** to save the definition.

The completed definition is shown in Figure 8.6.

Remember, sequencing begins with the last character. Refer to Table 8.2 for some examples.

Your SP form is now complete, so let's save it and return to the Main Menu.

You may allow operator entry; however, if you enter text or a number out of sequence, DataEase will change the field value to the next in sequence when you save the record. The only way to enter a value out of sequence is to change it *after* you save the record, then *update* the record.

CH. 8

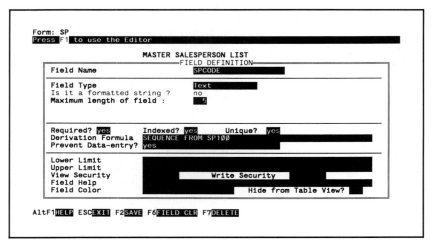

Figure 8.6: Completed definition for SPCODE field

Table 8.2: SEQUENCE FROM Examples

SEQUENCE FROM:			
AAAA	AA1A	AAA1	1234
AAAB	AA1B	AAA2	1235
AAAC	AA1C	AAA3	1236
AAAD	AA1D	AAA4	1237
AAAE	AA1E	AAA5	1238
AAAF	AA1F	AAA6	1239
AAAG	AA1G	AAA7	1240
AAAH	AA1H	AAA8	1241
AAAI	AA1I	AAA9	1242
AAAJ	AA1J	AAB0	1243

1. Press **F2** to save the form.
2. Type **n** to save it under the same name.
3. When the Form Definition menu displays, press **Esc** to return to the Main Menu.

ADVANCED FORM DESIGN 223

DATA ENTRY WITH
TEXT CONVERSION AND SEQUENCING

Now you're ready to enter some data and test your conversion and sequence formulas. Let's begin by opening SP:

1. From the Main Menu select **Record Entry**

2. Select **SP** from the list.

Before you start, make sure your Caps Lock is *off*. Enter everything in lowercase. The text will not convert until you have pressed Enter.

3. Enter the first record:

FNAME:	john ↵
MI:	h.
LNAME:	clifford ↵
STORE:	cleveland ↵
COMMRATE:	.13

The field values for your first SP record, shown in Figure 8.7, have all been converted to proper case, with the exception of MI, which was converted to uppercase.

4. Enter the remaining records from Table 8.3.

5. When the last record is saved, return to the Main Menu.

It would be a good idea (and good practice!) to print a report listing all your salespeople.

USING THE LASTFIRST FUNCTION

One reason you separate first and last names into two fields is to be able to sort easily by last name. However, if you want the name in a single field, and still want to sort by last name, you must remember to enter the last name first:

Smith, Frank

CH. 8

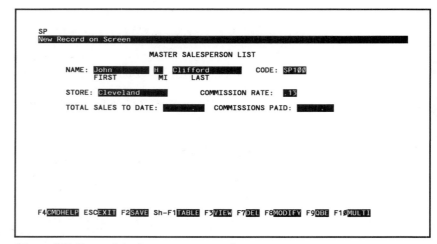

Figure 8.7: Record 1 after entry conversions

Table 8.3: Additional Records for SP.

FNAME	MI	LNAME	SPCODE	STORE	COMM-RATE
John	H.	Clifford	SP100	Cleveland	.13
Laura	M.	Engel	SP101	Cleveland	.10
Joyce	E.	Baker	SP102	Toledo	.15
Gail	C.	Fuller	SP103	Detroit	.14
Phil	F.	Roman	SP104	Milwaukee	.12
Beth	A.	Winters	SP105	Chicago	.12
Gordon	R.	Brown	SP106	Milwaukee	.13
George	T.	Johnson	SP107	Chicago	.10
Tom	R.	Green	SP108	Detroit	.10
Bob	C.	Fitch	SP109	Detroit	.14
Mark	P.	Mitchell	SP110	Indianapolis	.12
Frank	E.	Snow	SP111	Indianapolis	.10

The LASTFIRST function allows you to enter values in the regular manner, after which DataEase reverses the order. The format of the function is:

LASTFIRST(FIELD NAME)

For example, if you used the LASTFIRST function to reverse the order in the NAME field, you would enter:

LASTFIRST(NAME)

as the derivation formula of the NAME field. When you type the value Richard Smith, DataEase will convert it to Smith, Richard.

In the ITEMS form, you entered the furniture items in reverse. Now you can enter them in the normal manner. Let's use the LASTFIRST function to simplify entering the item names:

1. Modify the form **ITEMS**

2. Use **F10** to modify the field definition of the ITEM field.

3. Move the cursor to the Derivation Formula field and type **LASTFIRST(ITEM)**

COMBINING TEXT CONVERSION FUNCTIONS

You can also combine conversion functions in a derivation formula. For example, in this case you want not only to reverse the order of the item and description, but also to convert the entry to proper case with the PROPER function.

LASTFIRST(PROPER(ITEM))

or

PROPER(FIRSTLAST(ITEM))

1. Move the cursor to the beginning of the function, as shown below:

LASTFIRST(ITEM

2. Press **Ins**

3. Type **PROPER(**
4. Move the cursor to the end of the function.
5. Type **)** to end the function.

Let's clear the Field Help entry:

6. Move to the Field Help field and press **F6** to clear the entry.

> Now that you are using the LAST-FIRST function to reverse the entry, you no longer need the Field Help.

Your definition should look like the one pictured in Figure 8.8.

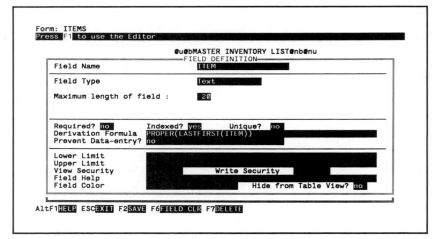

Figure 8.8: Completed definition for ITEM field

7. Save the field definition.

Before you test this new function, let's redefine three more fields using functions you learned in the previous exercises:

- Derive ENTRY DATE from the system date.
- Sequence the STOCK# field.
- Use the PROPER function in the MFR field.

First, have DataEase look up the current date for the ENTRY DATE field:

1. Move to the ENTRY DATE field and press **F10**
2. Move to the derivation formula field and type **??/??/??**
3. Move to Prevent Data-entry and select **Y**
4. Save the definition.

Next, sequence the STOCK# field:

1. Move to the STOCK# field and press **F10**
2. Move to the Derivation Formula field and type **SEQUENCE FROM 12345**
3. Select **Y** at Prevent Data-entry?.
4. Save the definition.

Finally, add the PROPER function to the field definition for MANUFACTURER:

1. Move to the MANUFACTURER field and press **F10**
2. Move to the Formula Derivation field and type **PROPER-(MANUFACTURER)**
3. Save the field definition.
4. Save the form definition under the same name and return to the Main Menu.

TESTING THE FIRSTLAST FUNCTION

Let's test this combination of functions by adding another item record.

1. Open ITEMS for record entry.

Today's date is filled in, the next STOCK# in the sequence is filled in, and the cursor moves to ITEM.

2. Type **modern loveseat** ↵

MASTERING DATAEASE

CH. 8

The entry is displayed in proper case and in reverse order:

Loveseat, Modern

3. Fill in the remaining fields:

MANUFACTURER: picklepot furniture

COST: 300

MARKUP%:   2

QTY ONHAND: 1

Do you still think there is too much typing involved when entering records? Then let's take a look at one more shortcut that you may like.

4. Save the record and return to the Main Menu.

CREATING CHOICE FIELDS

In some cases, you may want to limit the acceptable field values to a few selections. For example, a TAX field may accept only EXEMPT or NON-EXEMPT; in the marital status of an employee record, you may want to limit the entries to MARRIED, SINGLE, DIVORCED, WIDOWED. In a Choice field, only choices from a predefined numbered list are allowed. This eliminates typing errors and guarantees consistency.

In the VENDOR form, the field called DESCRIPTION defines each vendor as either a manufacturer (MFR) or distributor (DIST). Let's modify the VENDOR form and change the field type to Choice:

1. Display the form definition for VENDORS.

2. Move to the DESCRIPTION field and press **F10**

3. Move to the TYPE field and press **F1** to display the complete list of field types.

4. Select **Choice**

The cursor moves to the Optional Choice Type Name field and the prompt area displays the message:

Press F1 to see list of choices

The Optional Choice Type Name field will be explained shortly.

1. Press **F1** to display the full screen editor.
2. Type **MFR** ←
3. Type **DIST** ←

Your Choice list is pictured in Figure 8.9.

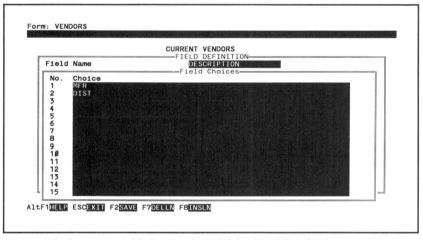

Figure 8.9: Completed Choice list for DESCRIPTION field

4. Press **F2** to save the choices.

Besides saving time and ensuring accurate data entry, Choice fields also save disk space since DataEase stores the selection number with the field, not the entire text.

Although you can index on a Choice field and search in Record Entry, you cannot display a Choice field in index order, since the * character is not accepted. You can, however, sort or group Choice fields for a Quick Report.

▬ The only character you can type into a choice field is the number or first character of a selection.

230 **MASTERING DATAEASE**

CH. 8

If you want to use the same choices in another field within the same form, you can enter an Optional Choice Type Name. Then when defining another Choice field, you enter only the Optional Choice Type Name. The choices you entered under that name are automatically included as the choices for the current field.

1. Save the field definition.

2. Type **N** to save it under the same name.

Next DataEase asks the question:

Do Choice field changes require Choice Numbers in records to be updated? (Y/N)

This question will be explained shortly and is irrelevant in this situation, so for now:

3. Type **n**

4. Return to the Main Menu.

USING CHOICE FIELDS IN DATA ENTRY

Now that you have defined DESCRIPTION as a Choice field, you can add that information to each of your VENDOR records:

1. Select **Record Entry** from the Main Menu and then select **VENDORS**

2. Display Record 1 and move to the DESCRIPTION field.

The numbered list of choices is displayed in the prompt area, as shown in Figure 8.10.

3. Select **MFR**

4. Press **F8** to update the record.

5. Press **F3** to display the next record.

ADVANCED FORM DESIGN   231

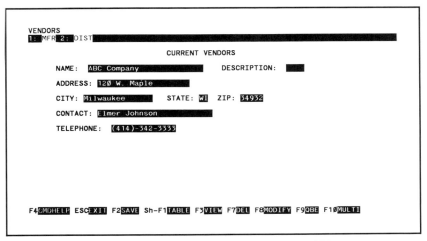

Figure 8.10: Choices for DESCRIPTION field in Record Entry

6. Use the list below to enter DESCRIPTION values for the remaining record:

VENDOR	*DESCRIPTION*
Carver's Chairs	DIST
Realco	MFR
Table Tops	DIST
Picklepot	MFR
Real Furniture	MFR
Beds 'n Things	DIST
Terrahaute	MFR
Country Cousins	DIST

7. When all records are updated, return to the Main Menu.

MODIFYING A CHOICE FIELD

When modifying a Choice field, you can change the text description and add or delete choices from the list. However, you must be

232 MASTERING DATAEASE

CH. 8

cautious or you can risk losing data. Whenever you save a form modification that involves a Choice field, DataEase will ask you the question you encountered earlier:

Do Choice field changes require Choice Numbers in records to be updated? (Y/N)

Remember, DataEase stores the Choice *Numbers* with the data, not the actual text of the choice.

When you make modifications to the Choice field, DataEase wants to know if these changes will affect the number assignments. The answer you give determines whether DataEase retains your current data. Always keep in mind the following rules when modifying a Choice field:

- If you are redefining a field as Choice and you have entered records, your data will be retained if your choices include data already entered. Any field values not included in the list of choices will be lost. This is the case regardless of whether you answer **Y** or **N** to the question regarding Choice Numbers.

- If you add choices to the end of the list, you can answer **N** since no Choice Numbers have been changed.

- If you change the value or description of a choice, for example from MFR to MANUF, then you should answer **N** to the question since the numbers have not been reassigned.

- If you change the *order* or delete choices, then you should answer **Y** since this would affect the number assignments.

- If you want to *insert* a new choice in its alphabetical position, you must modify the Choice field in two steps. First, add the choice to the end and save the form definition, answering **N**. Then modify the field to reorder the choices, and answer **Y** to the question.

- Do *not* reorder *and* change choice text in one operation, since they require *different* answers to the modification question.

- If you are changing a Choice field to another field type, DataEase will try to retain the data. If you change it to a Text field, DataEase replaces the Choice Number with the text description assigned to that number.

Another type of VENDOR is the importer. To understand the proper way to modify your Choice field, let's add IMP to your list and alphabetize it:

1. Modify the VENDORS form, move the cursor to the DESCRIPTION field and press **F10**
2. Move the cursor to the Optional Choice Type Name field and press **F1**
3. Press ↓ twice to move to the third row.
4. Type **IMP** and press **F2** to update the Choice list.
5. Press **F2** twice to update the field and form definitions.
6. Type **N** and save the form under the same name.
7. Type **N** so that you do *not* change the Choice Numbers on the disk.
8. Repeat steps 1 and 2 above.
9. Reenter the choice text as it appears in Figure 8.11.
10. Save the definition and the form.
11. Answer **Y** to change the choices in the disk.

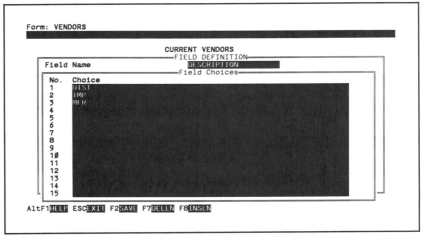

Figure 8.11: Modified choice text order for DESCRIPTION

234 *MASTERING DATAEASE*

CH. 8

With the change you made, choice 2 (DIST) is now choice 1, MFR becomes choice 3 and DataEase is making the appropriate changes to the records already saved. Let's make sure all your data is intact.

1. When the Form Definition menu appears, press **Esc** to return to the Main Menu and select **Record Entry**

2. Select **VENDORS** and use **F3** to display each record.

All the original entries are still there.

1. Move to the DESCRIPTION field and see that the list of choices now includes IMP and that the choices are alphabetized.

2. Return to the Main Menu.

CHOICE FIELDS AND REPORTS

As we've noted, DataEase sorts by the Choice Numbers. So if you want to sort a quick report by a Choice field, enter your choices alphabetically.

If you have changed a field type from Text to Choice, you must also change any Quick Reports that include that field or DataEase will omit all the data in the Choice field, even though it appears in Record Entry. You can update your Quick Report specification without redefining the format:

- Load the Report and select **Modify List Fields**

- Save the field list selection with **F2**

- Modify and keep the old format.

- Move to the Choice field.

- Press **F10** to modify and **F7** to delete the original field.

- Press **F10** and place the field again.

So far you've learned a number of formulas, functions, and features which eliminate quite a bit of typing. Next, let's look at a feature that saves you time when defining forms.

THE DATAEASE DICTIONARY FORM

The DICTIONARY form is a special form included with the DataEase program. It contains a number of predefined commonly used fields that you can copy into any form. You can also add, delete, or change fields in the DICTIONARY form. Let's take a look at it:

1. From the Main Menu select **Form Definition**
2. Select **View or Modify a Form**

You may have already noticed that the first form on the list is the DICTIONARY form.

3. Select **Dictionary**

The DICTIONARY form, pictured in Figure 8.12, contains fields typically used in forms.

Let's take a look at some of the field definitions:

1. Move the cursor to the Soc.Sec.No. field and press **F10**

This field is a numeric string and is required, indexed, and unique—all of the attributes usually associated with a Social Security number.

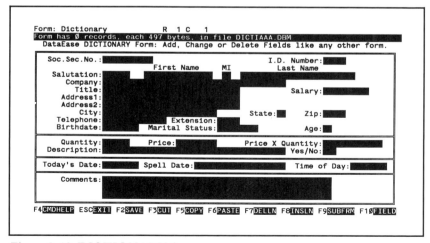

Figure 8.12: DICTIONARY form

236 *MASTERING DATAEASE*

CH. 8

2. Press **Esc** to clear the screen, move the cursor to the City field, and press **F10**

This field includes the PROPER function as the derivation formula.

3. Press **Esc** to clear the screen, move the cursor to the Salary field, and press **F10**

The Salary field includes a high and low range that you can change if necessary. Let's take a look at one more field:

4. Press **Esc** to clear the screen, move the cursor to the State field, and press **F10**

State is a Choice field. Move the cursor to the Optional Choice Type Name field and press **F1**. Notice that all of the states are listed in alphabetical order. That was quite a project for someone; however, it guarantees that the proper state abbreviations are used. The only drawback to defining State as a Choice field is that you cannot display records in index order by state in Record Entry. You can change the type to a text field if you prefer.

In the next section, you'll copy some of the fields in this form to create a customer form.

5. Press **Esc** to clear the screen.

It's a good idea to have a printed copy of the DICTIONARY form definition to help you choose which fields to copy. If you have a printer available:

6. Press **Shift-F9** to print the definition.

When the printout is complete, or if you do not have a printer:

7. Press **Esc** to return to the Form Definition menu.

COPYING FIELDS FROM THE DICTIONARY FORM

The next form is called CUST and will contain a list of Furniture Palace's current customers. Most of the fields for CUST can be found in the DICTIONARY form, so you'll save time by copying fields from the DICTIONARY and modifying them when necessary. When you copy fields from the DICTIONARY form, you are actually inserting the field, and any text following it will be moved aside, so you won't be entering all the prompts in advance this time. Since you'll be entering the promts and fields one at a time, the instructions will include row and column designations for each prompt and field. However, you can refer to Figure 8.13 as a guide and place fields and prompts wherever you like. Let's begin:

1. Select **Define a Form** from the menu and enter **CUST** as the form name.

2. Move to Row 2, Column 25 and type **MASTER CUSTOMER LIST**

3. Move to Row 4, Column 7 and type **CUST#:**

Next, you'll copy the I.D. Number field from the DICTIONARY form.

4. Move to Row 4, Column 14, and press **F5**

DataEase asks what you want to copy:

> 0:None 1:Block 2:Form 3:Dictionary Field
> Copy a Block, a Form or a Dictionary Field?

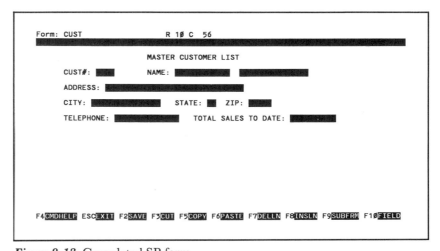

Figure 8.13: Completed SP form

238 MASTERING DATAEASE

CH. 8

> If you selected **Form**, DataEase would display the list of forms you have already created. Copying a form can save you time if many of the fields in the new form are similar to those in an existing form.

5. Select **Dictionary Field**

DataEase displays the list of fields from the DICTIONARY form, as shown in Figure 8.14.

6. Select **I.D. Number**
7. Press **F10**

The field name has been changed to CUST#, and it is a sequenced field.

8. Change the field length to 4 and press **F2** to save the change.

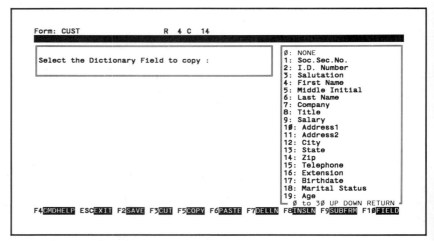

Figure 8.14: DICTIONARY form field list in Record Entry

Next, you'll place the fields for FNAME and LNAME:

1. Move the cursor to Row 4, Column 25, and type **NAME:**
2. At Row 4, Column 31, press **F5** and select **Dictionary**
3. Select **First Name** from the list.
4. Press **F10** and change the field name to **FNAME**, the field length to **12**, and the derivation formula to **PROPER(FNAME)**

ADVANCED FORM DESIGN 239

5. Follow the steps above to copy Last Name to Row 4, Column 45.

6. Press **F10** and change the name to **LNAME**, the length to **15**, and the derivation formula to **PROPER(LNAME)**

7. Save the definition.

Follow the steps below to copy the next remaining fields from the DICTIONARY form:

1. At Row 6, Column 7, type **ADDRESS:**

2. AT Row 6, Column 16 copy the Address1 field, change the name to **ADDRESS** and the derivation formula to **PROPER(ADDRESS)**

3. At Row 8, Column 7 type **CITY:**

4. At Row 8, Column 13 copy the City field and change the length to 15.

5. At Row 8, Column 31 type **STATE:**

6. At Row 8, Column 38 copy the State field, change the type to **text** and the derivation formula to **PROPER(STATE)**

7. At Row 8, Column 47 type **ZIP:**

8. At Row 8, Column 56 copy the Zip code field.

9. At Row 10, Column 7 type **TELEPHONE:**

10. At Row 10, Column 18 copy the Telephone field

11. At Row 10, Column 35 type **TOTAL SALES TO DATE:** and use the information below to define the field:

NAME	*TYPE*	*LENGTH*	*PREVENT DATA-ENTRY?*
TOTSALES	Dollar	6	yes, and do not save (virtual)

In Chapter 9, you'll learn about a special formula that will calculate the total sales for each customer. Your completed form, as you've seen, is pictured in Figure 8.13.

240 MASTERING DATAEASE

CH. 8

Next, let's enter a few records:

1. Save the form definition and proceed to Record Entry to enter the records shown in Table 8.4.

Before moving on, print a list of your customers.

CHANGING THE PITCH FOR A REPORT

If you do not have a printer available, this exercise may not be relevant at the moment. However, you should read it over, since it does contain information that you may find useful later.

1. Press **F9** from Record Entry to begin Quick Reports.

2. Select **Define List Fields**, select all fields in LNAME order, and save the selections.

3. Select **Define Print Style**

4. Select **Printer** from the list.

5. Press **F3** to display your default printer.

The TYPE STYLE area at the bottom of the Print Style Specification screen contains the characters per inch, also referred to as pitch.

```
TYPE STYLE
      Characters Per Inch 10       Lines Per Inch
      Highlights 1        2        3
```

The default is set to 10 characters per inch (*pica*), or approximately 80 characters per line. If your printer supports various pitch settings, you may prefer *elite* (12 characters to the inch). We will use the pitch setting of 15 characters per inch, which prints 120 characters per line and is referred to as *condensed print*.

1. Move the cursor to the Characters Per Inch field.

2. Press **F6** to clear the screen and type **15**

Table 8.4: Records to be Entered

CUST #	FNAME	LNAME	ADDRESS	CITY	STATE	ZIP	PHONE
0001	Linda	Enis	10 W. 55th St.	Milwaukee	WI	40932	(313) 434-2324
0002	William	Smith	20 E. Elm	Chicago	IL	60602	(312) 453-4223
0003	Peter	Grey	200 E. Euclid	Cleveland	OH	43430	(216) 233-4222
0005	Marti	Heida	890 Porter	Detroit	MI	54394	(313) 293-7282
0006	Marie	Edwards	500 Carver	Carmel	IL	53209	(317) 217-2654
0007	Clara	Clark	80 E. 15th St.	Milwaukee	WI	42353	(313) 271-6222
0008	Henry	Green	492 Madison	Chicago	IL	63934	(312) 523-5432
0009	Don	Martin	250 Filbert	Milwaukee	WI	46534	(313) 242-3256
0011	Paul	Jones	500 Indian Hollow	Cleveland	OH	44323	(216) 275-5322
0014	Jim	Porter	423 N. Maple	Toledo	OH	42354	(216) 275-3327

CH. 8

You may need to change one more setting in order to fit more information on each line. The Width field in the center of the page tells DataEase how wide your paper is. It is currently set at 8.5.

> PAGE SIZE AND POSITION ON CARRIAGE (in inches)
> Length   Width   Starting position

DataEase uses this value to determine how many characters to print on a line and normally that limit is 85 (10 characters per inch multiplied by 8.5 inches). Since you have changed the pitch to 15 (condensed print), you can fit up to 127 characters on a line (15 characters per inch multiplied by 8.5 inches). However, if your report is longer than 127 characters wide, you'll need to change the width. To be on the safe side, for this report you'll change the width to 12 inches, which will accommodate up to 180 characters per line (15 characters per inch multiplied by 12 inches).

3. Move the cursor to the Width field.
4. Press **F6** to clear the field and type **12**

With the possible exception of the printer type, your screen should now look like the one in Figure 8.15.

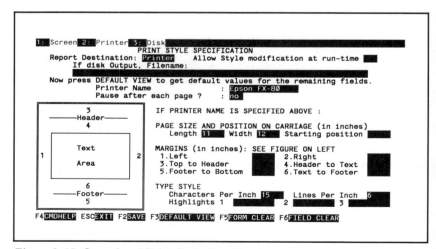

Figure 8.15: Completed Print Style Specification screen

5. Press **F2** to save the definition and print the report.

6. When the report is completed, save it again under the name **CUST**

7. Press **Esc** to return to the Form Relationship screen.

8. Return to the Form Definition screen.

In Chapter 7, you learned how to work with multiple forms, including Multi-Form, which displayed a temporary subform table of records. In the next chapter, you will learn how to create a sales invoice using subforms.

CHAPTER NINE

Keeping
Track of Sales

Fast Track

To hide a field from Table View,   252

move to the field you want to hide in the Form Definition screen. Press **F10** to define or modify the field. Press **End** to move to the last field in the Field Definition screen, and answer Y to this prompt. Press **F2** to save the definition.

To total records in a related form,   252

press **F10** from the Form Definition screen to place or modify the field that will display the total. Move to the Derivation Formula field and type **SUM OF (FORM NAME) (FIELD NAME)**, where FORM NAME represents the form that contains the field you want to total and FIELD NAME the name of the numeric field you want to total. Save the field and form definitions. You can create a relationship between the two forms based on a common field value.

To combine the subform with the main form,   259

move the cursor within the Form Definition screen of the main form to the row where you want the subform to begin. Press **F9** and select the form name from the list of related forms. Enter the minimum and maximum number of rows to display. Select the view: Automatic Table, Automatic Form, or Custom Form. Modify the subform if necessary.

To print a report on both the main form and the subform   267

using the Record Entry format, select Define List Fields from the Quick Reports menu, and select the fields from both the main form, and the subform. Save the field selection. Select Define Format then Record Entry. The format will display all fields except those from the subform. Use **F10** to place each field from the subform. Save the format and run the report.

CHAPTER 9

UP TO THIS POINT YOU HAVE CREATED FIVE FORMS for Furniture Palace: ITEMS, VENDORS, ORDERS, SP, and CUST. Along the way you have learned a number of techniques and skills to enhance the process of defining forms, working with records, and creating reports.

Now you're going to get down to the business of building some applications that will start to automate Furniture Palace's invoicing, receivables, and inventory.

In this chapter you'll create an invoice that copies fields from ITEMS, SP, and CUST. In addition, you'll create a formula to keep track of total sales dollars for customers and salespeople, as well as quantities sold for each item in inventory.

DESIGNING THE INVOICE FORM

First, let's talk about the invoice form. An invoice is used to show the purchaser's name, the items they purchased, and the total cost of their purchase. An invoice form, like the one shown in Figure 9.1 actually consists of three parts. The top half contains mostly customer information: name, address, date of sale, etc., and an identifying invoice number. The second part lists the products purchased, often referred to as the line items. And the last part consists of the invoice subtotal, tax, and grand total.

The number of fields in the customer and invoice total information is constant. However, the number of fields in the line item section depends upon how many items a customer purchases. The fields in the line item section would include STOCK#, ITEM, QTY PURCHASED, PRICE and TOTAL; you will need one row of these fields for each product purchased. Since the number of products purchased will vary with each invoice, there is no way of knowing in advance how many rows you'll need. And it would be a needless

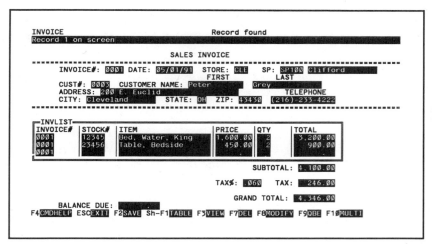

Figure 9.1: Sample invoice

waste of space to create, for example, ten rows of fields to accommodate the possibility of a large purchase.

Subforms provide the solution to this dilemma. You can store each line item as a separate record in the subform. The invoice form acts as the main form and consists of the customer information, subtotal, tax, and grand total. Each line item is stored as a different record in the related form, which acts as the subform when combined with the main invoice form. You will not include the customer information in the record for each line item, since it would be redundant and cost a great deal of disk space to do so. Therefore, you need a *link*, a common field that connects each record in the subform to the main invoice form. In this case, the link would be the INVOICE#. Although the products purchased are stored separately, DataEase displays them all together in one form by matching the INVOICE# values.

Unlike the ad hoc (temporary) subforms you created in Record Entry with Alt-F10 (Multi-Form), this subform always displays with the primary form even though the records are stored separately. All entries, modifications, and deletions are made through the primary form.

KEEPING TRACK OF SALES **249**

Before you begin creating your forms, and so you know exactly where you are headed, take a look at the general procedure for creating this main form with a subform:

- Create the subform.
- Create the primary form.
- Establish a relationship between the primary and subforms based on a common field.
- Modify the primary form and use F9 to combine the two forms.

DEFINING THE SUBFORM

You'll create the subform first because the main form will contain a formula which references the subform. The subform is a very simple form, containing only fields for invoice number, stock number, item, price, quantity purchased, and total.

> The format of the subform is generally not important since it is usually viewed only as a table in the primary form.

1. Create a new form called INVLIST.
2. Use the form in Figure 9.2 as a guide to place the form text and field prompts.

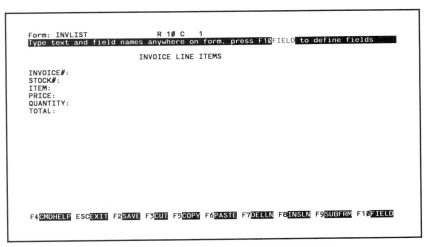

Figure 9.2: Text for INVLIST form

250 **MASTERING DATAEASE**

CH. 9

You'll need to enter information into only two of these fields: STOCK# and QUANTITY. The others will be entered for you automatically from LOOKUP formulas and other derivation formulas.

INVOICE# will be referenced from the primary form. ITEM and PRICE will be derived from the LOOKUP formula by matching STOCK# and copying the field values in ITEM and PRICE. The TOTAL field will be derived from a formula based on PRICE * QTY.

3. Use the information in Table 9.1 to define each of the fields:

Table 9.1: Field Definition for INVLIST

NAME	TYPE	LENGTH	REQ?	IND?	DERIV. FORMULA	PREVENT DATA-ENTRY?
INVOICE#	Numeric String	4		yes		yes
STOCK#	Numeric String	5	yes	yes		
ITEM	Text	20	yes		LOOKUP ITEMS PRICE	yes
PRICE	Dollar	4			LOOKUP ITEMS PRICE	
QTY	Number, Integer	3				
TOTAL	Dollar	5			PRICE * QTY	yes

4. Save the form and return to the Main Menu.

DEFINING THE MAIN FORM

Next, you'll define the main form, which includes the invoice header and invoice total fields.

1. Create a new form called INVOICE.
2. Use the form in Figure 9.3 as a guide to place the form text and field prompts.

You will enter information into three of the 13 fields in the top part of the form: DATE, SP(SPCODE), and CUST#. Although a default DATE will be derived from the system date, in most of the exercises, you will enter the dates.

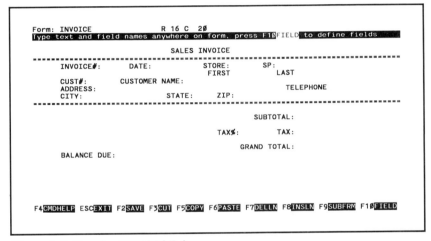

Figure 9.3: Text for INVOICE form

The other fields will be derived from SEQUENCE, Choice, or LOOKUP formulas. The INVOICE# will of course be sequenced and STORE will be selected from a list of choices.

Most of the information in the INVOICE form is contained in other forms. The CUST#, CUSTOMER NAME, ADDRESS, CITY, STATE, and ZIP are in the CUST form. When you type the CUST#, DataEase looks up the CUST# and copies the other fields from the matching record. And in this case you will allow entry, so the salesperson can enter an invoice for a new customer or correct an address for an existing one. The values for SPCODE and SPLNAME are in the SP form. When you type the SPCODE, DataEase will look up the SPCODE and copy the LNAME from the matching record.

Finally, the SUBTOTAL, TAX, and GRAND TOTAL fields will be derived from the subtotal of the subform records, using a new formula you will learn about in this chapter.

HIDING FIELDS FROM TABLE VIEW

The last field in the Field Definition screen is Hide From Table View?. If there are fields you do not need to see in Table View, you can omit them by answering Y to this prompt. This feature is especially helpful if you want to use the current form as a subform and include only some of the fields. In fact, in the next chapter, you will create a form in which INVOICE will act as a subform.

1. Use the information in Table 9.2 to define the fields for the top half of INVOICE. Use the choices listed in Table 9.3 to define STORE, a choice field.

USING SUM OF TO TOTAL RECORDS IN A RELATED FORM

SUM OF is one of several relational statistical operators that can be used in forms, reports, and procedures to perform arithmetic operations on records in related forms. Others include:

HIGHEST OF	Largest number.
LOWEST OF	Smallest number.
MEAN OF	Average number.
COUNT OF	Number of records.

The format is:

SUM OF FORM NAME FIELD NAME

For example,

SUM OF INVLIST TOTAL

entered as the derivation formula of the SUBTOT field calculates the sum of the TOTAL fields for all records in INVLIST. To total only

Table 9.2: Field Definition for INVOICE

NAME	TYPE	LENGTH	REQ?	IND?	UNI?	DERIVATION FORMULA	PREVENT DATA-ENTRY?	HIDE FROM TABLE VIEW?
INVOICE#	Numeric String	4	yes	yes	yes	SEQUENCE FROM 1001	yes	
DATE	Date		yes	ycs		??/??/??		
STORE	Choice			yes				
SPLCODE	Text	5		yes			yes	yes
SPLNAME	Text	15				LOOKUP SPLNAME	no	yes
CUST#	Numeric String	4	no	yes				
FNAME	Text	12				LOOKUP CUST FNAME	no	yes
LNAME	Text	15				LOOKUP CUST LNAME	no	yes
CITY	Text	15				LOOKUP CUST CITY	no	yes
STATE	Text	2				LOOKUP CUST STATE	no	yes
ZIP	Numeric String	5				LOOKUP CUST ZIP	no	yes
TELEPHONE	Numeric String	14				LOOKUP CUST TELEPHONE	no	yes

254 MASTERING DATAEASE

CH. 9

Table 9.3: Choices for STORE

NAME	TYPE

STORE	Choice
	    1: CHI
	    2: CLE
	    3: DET
	    4: IND
	    5: MIL
	    6: TOL

invoices with matching invoice numbers, you'll create a relationship between INVOICE and INVLIST based on INVOICE#. Let's start by defining the SUBTOT field:

1. Move the cursor one space after the SUBTOTAL prompt and press **F10**

2. Use the information in Table 9.4 to define the field.

Your completed definition should match Figure 9.4.

Table 9.4: Field Definition for SUBTOT.

NAME	TYPE	LENGTH	DERIV. FORM	PREVENT DATA-ENTRY?	HIDE FROM TABLE VIEW?
SUBTOTAL	Dollar	4	SUM OF INVLIST TOTAL	yes	yes

3. Use the information in Table 9.5 to define the remaining fields.

KEEPING TRACK OF SALES 255

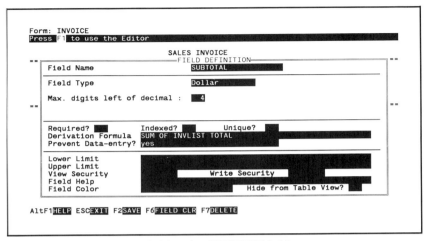

Figure 9.4: Completed definition for SUBTOT field

Table 9.5: Remaining Field Definitions.

NAME	TYPE	LENGTH	DERIV. FORM.	PREVENT DATA-ENTRY?	HIDE FROM TABLE VIEW?
TAX%	Fixed Point	0, 3			yes
TAX	Dollar	4	SUB TOTAL * TAX%	yes	yes
GRTOTAL	Dollar	5	SUB TOTAL + TAX	yes	
BALDUE	Dollar	5		yes	yes, and do not save (virtual)

You'll learn about the formula for the BALDUE field in the next chapter. Your completed form is pictured in Figure 9.5.

The next step is to define the relationships.

4. Save the form and return to the Form Definition menu.

CH. 9

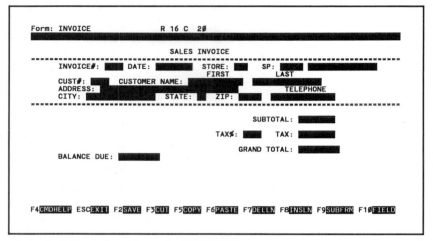

Figure 9.5: Completed form for INVOICE

CREATING THE RELATIONSHIPS

To perform the lookups in the INVOICE form, you must relate INVOICE to SP and CUST; for the lookups in INVLIST, you must relate INVLIST to ITEMS; and to link the subform and the main form, you must relate INVOICE and INVLIST.

Let's begin by defining the first three relationships.

- From the Form Definition menu, select **Define Relationships.**
- Select **INVOICE** from the list.
- Press **Tab** to skip this field.
- Select **CUST** from the list.
- Press **Tab** to skip this field.
- Select **CUST#** from the list.
- Select **CUST#** from the list.
- Press **F2** to save the record and **F5** to clear the form.

Follow the steps above to define the next two relationships:

Form 1	Form 2	Field 1	Field 2
INVOICE	SP	SPCODE	SPCODE
INVLIST	ITEMS	STOCK#	STOCK#

The last relationship, between INVOICE and INVLIST, will include information that affects how changes made to the common field in the primary form can affect the matching record in the subform. This feature is new to DataEase version 4.2. If you have an earlier version, you will be instructed to skip these steps. Regardless of your DataEase version, you'll begin with the steps below to create the relationship record.

1. If necessary, press **F5** to clear the form.

2. Select **INVOICE** from the list of form names for Form 1.

3. Press **Enter** to skip this field.

4. Select **INVLIST** from the list of form names for Form 2.

If you are using a version earlier than 4.2, skip to step 6. If you are using DataEase version 4.2, you'll notice the following menu that appears in the prompt line:

1:Cascade (Update) 2:Null (Blank) 3: Restrict (Don't Update)

The value selected for this field controls whether modifications made to the related field in the main form are also made to the matching field in the subform.

For example: the main form is VENDORS, the subform is ITEMS, and the related field is SOURCE. If a vendor changes its name, you will of course change the name in the VENDOR record. You would also want to change the value of the SOURCE field in ITEMS where that vendor's name appears.

If you select Cascade for the ITEMS form in the relationship record between ITEMS and VENDORS, then any changes made to the NAME field in VENDORS would also be made to the

Cascade only affects changes in a subform or multiform environment.

SOURCE field in ITEMS, but only when ITEMS is acting as a subform. If no subform is displayed, no changes are made.

In most instances, you would want the Restrict (Don't Update) selection, which is the default. For example, if ITEMS were the main form and VENDORS were the subform, you would *not* want a change made to the SOURCE field in ITEMS to also be made to the NAME field in the related VENDORS record.

The Null selection cancels any links between the records if the field in the primary form is changed.

In this case, you will select Cascade for INVLIST so that if, for some reason, you change the INVOICE# in INVOICE, that change would be cascaded to the matching INVOICE# in INVLIST.

5. Select Cascade from the list.
6. Select INVOICE# from the list of fields from Form 1.
7. Select INVOICE# from the list of fields from Form 2.

Your form relationship record should now match the one pictured in Figure 9.6.

8. Save the record and clear the screen.

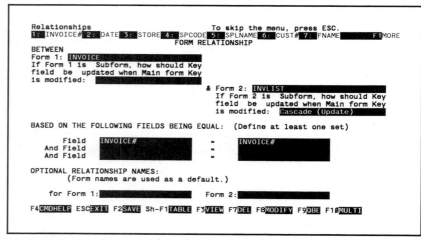

Figure 9.6: Completed INVOICE-INVLIST relationship record

KEEPING TRACK OF SALES   *259*

Now that you have created your forms and established your relationships, you are ready to add INVLIST to INVOICE as the subform.

9. Return to the Form Definition menu.

ADDING THE SUBFORM
TO COMPLETE THE INVOICE—F9

The final step in this process is to modify the INVOICE form and create the subform:

1. Select **View or Modify Form** and select **INVOICE** from the list of forms.

2. When the form is displayed, move the cursor to Row 10, Column 1 and press **F9** to begin the subform definition.

The Subform Definition screen is displayed in the middle of the form area, as pictured in Figure 9.7. The list of relationships is displayed in the prompt area of the screen.

3. Select INVLIST

You can scroll through the records if more than five records match.

```
Form: INVOICE                           To skip the menu, press ESC.
1: CUST  2: SP  3: INVLIST

                              SALES INVOICE
========================================================================
        INVOICE
        CUST#:              Subform Definition
        ADDRESS
        CITY:
                     Relationship Name
                     No. of Rows Minimum      Maximum
                     Define Subform as


     BALANCE DUE:



AltF1 HELP  ESC EXIT  F2 SAVE  F6 FIELD CLR  F7 DELETE
```

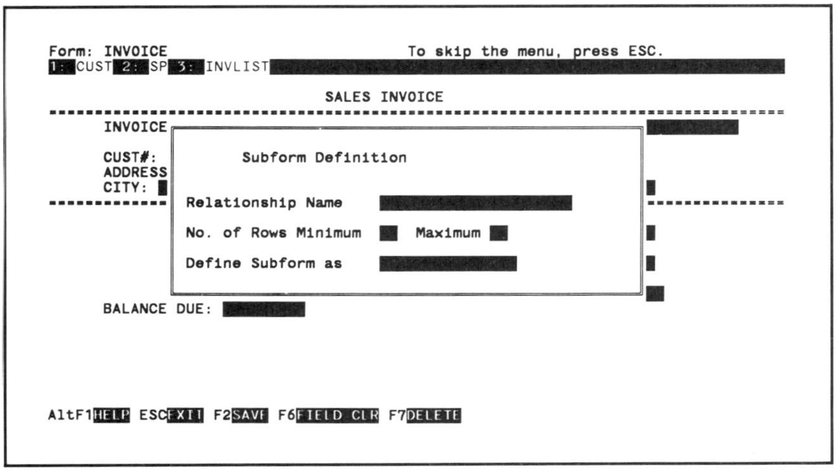

Figure 9.7: Subform Definition screen in INVOICE

Next, DataEase asks for the minimum and maximum number of rows displayed in the subform. For example, if you enter 3 (minimum) and 5 (maximum), at least three rows and no more than five rows will be displayed at a time. The number of rows you choose to display depends on how much space you want the subform to occupy as well as the average number of records you expect to have. In this case, since the INVOICE form takes up quite a bit of space, you'll select 3 and 3.

4. Type 3 for minimum and 3 for maximum.

Finally, DataEase wants to know how you want the subform to be displayed and offers a new menu:

1:Automatic Table 2:Automatic Form 3:Custom Form

Automatic Table displays the records in Table View; Automatic Form displays each record in Form View; Custom Form allows you to create a Form View of your design. Since the last two can take up quite a bit of space on the screen, the most commonly selected option is Automatic Table.

5. Select **Automatic Table**

6. Press **F2** to accept the subform definition.

The INVLIST is inserted into your main form, as pictured in Figure 9.8.

The width of each field in the subform is determined by the maximum length in its definition. The field names are used for column headings and may appear truncated if the field length is not long enough. Editing a subform is as easy as modifying any form. Before you make any changes, you'll need to erase the border around the subform:

1. Move the cursor to the top left corner of the border, Row 11, Column 10 and press **Alt-F10**

2. Select **Erase Border** from the menu.

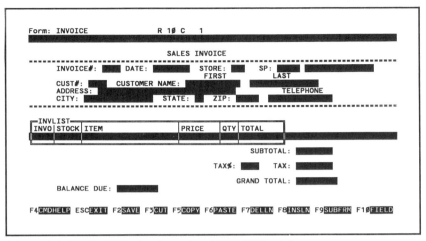

Figure 9.8: INVOICE after inserting INVLIST subform

3. Move the cursor to the bottom right corner of the border, Row 14, Column 57.

4. Press **Alt-F10**

Each field is separated by a vertical bar character, which you can remove if you like.

You can insert and delete, move and place subform fields anywhere on the screen. Let's begin by inserting more column heading text and inserting more spaces between fields:

> You can add a vertical bar by selecting number 55 in the Borders (Alt-F10) menu.

1. Move the cursor to Row 12, Column 6 under the vertical bar and press **Ins**

   INVO⌐

2. Type **ICE#** and press the **Spacebar** to complete the field prompt.

> You'll need to cancel Insert mode in order to see the Row and Column indicators again.

3. Move to Row 13, Column 6 and insert five spaces to line up the vertical bars.

4. Move to Row 12, Column 17 under the vertical bar:

   STOCK⌐

5. Type # and press the **Spacebar** to complete the STOCK# field prompt.

6. Move to Row 13, Column 17 and insert two spaces to line up the vertical bars.

7. Insert five spaces at Row 12, Column 53 and at Row 13, Column 53 to line up TOTAL with SUBTOTAL.

8. Move to Row 19, Column 43 and press **Del** to move the GRAND TOTAL field over.

When you have completed the editing, your form should look like the one in Figure 9.9.

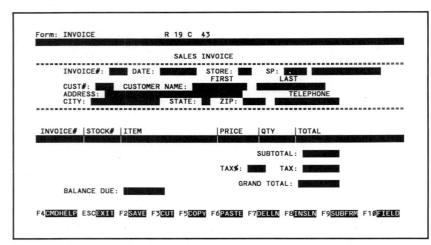

Figure 9.9: INVOICE subform after edit

1. Redraw the border from Row 11, Column 1 to Row 14, Column 68.

2. Move to Row 11, Column C3, make sure **Ins** is *off* and type **INVLIST**

The completed form is pictured in Figure 9.10.

Although you can move, place, and delete subform fields within the main form, if you want to change the definition of any of the subform fields, you must do that by modifying the form itself, in this case INVLIST.

Any changes you make to the field definitions will automatically be reflected in the subform as it appears in the primary form.

KEEPING TRACK OF SALES **263**

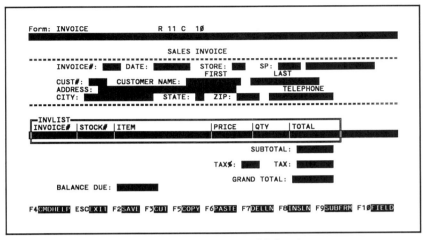

Figure 9.10: Completed INVOICE subform with borders

If you add or delete fields in the subform, the next time you open the main form, DataEase will warn you that a subform field was deleted or added. You can then easily delete or place a new field from the subform into the main form.

3. Save the form definition and return to the Main Menu.

ENTERING RECORDS INTO THE SUBFORM

Now for the fun part: entering records. With all the lookups and calculations, the typing will be minimal.

1. Select **Record Entry** and select **INVOICE** from the list.

The INVOICE form and accompanying subform are displayed, and the cursor stops at the DATE field. It will display the current date if you press Enter; however, you'll use another date instead.

1. Type **050191**
2. Select **CLE** from the list of stores.

264 MASTERING DATAEASE

CH. 9

3. Type **SP100** in SPCODE.

4. Type **3** in CUST#.

All the customer information is filled in automatically.

Remember, if you are using version 4.2, use Ctrl-PgDn to move to the subform; if using an earlier version, use ↓.

5. Move to the STOCK# field in the INVLIST subform and type **12345**

The ITEM and PRICE fields are copied from the ITEMS form and the cursor moves to QUANTITY.

6. Type **2** ◄┘

The TOTAL, SUBTOTAL, and GRTOT fields are calculated and the cursor moves to the STOCK# field in the next subform row.

7. Enter two more subform records:

STOCK#	QTY
23456	2 ◄┘
78923	2 ◄┘

The TOTAL is calculated, and SUBTOT and GRTOT are recomputed.

When you need to enter more records than the subform displays, press the End key (as you do in Table View) to display more blank rows:

1. Move the cursor to the STOCK# field at the beginning of the row.

2. Press **End**, then **Enter**

3. Enter the last two records:

STOCK#	QTY
73456	1
78928	1

4. Press ↓ to move to the TAX% field and type **.06** ◄┘

KEEPING TRACK OF SALES 265

The TAX is calculated and the GRTOT field is updated. The completed record is pictured in Figure 9.11. Now that the amount of typing has been greatly reduced, record entry is a breeze.

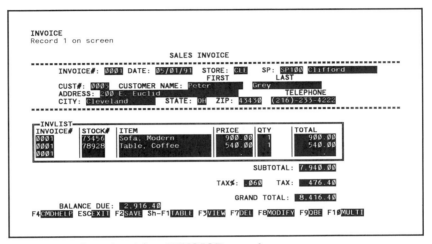

Figure 9.11: Completed first INVOICE record

5. Save the record and clear the screen.
6. Enter the records shown in Table 9.6.

Table 9.6: Records to Be Entered

INVOICE#	DATE	STORE	SPCODE	CUST#	STOCK#	QTY	TAX%
0001	05/01/91	CLE	SP100	0003	12345	2	.060
	05/01/91	CLE	SP100	0003	23456	2	.060
	05/01/91	CLE	SP100	0003	78923	2	.060
	05/01/91	CLE	SP100	0003	73456	1	.060
	05/01/91	CLE	SP100	0003	78928	1	.060
0002	05/02/91	DET	SP108	0005	45678	2	.065
	05/02/91	DET	SP108	0005	73456	3	.065
	05/02/91	DET	SP108	0005	78921	2	.065

MASTERING DATAEASE

CH. 9

Table 9.6: Records to Be Entered (continued)

INVOICE#	DATE	STORE	SPCODE	CUST#	STOCK#	QTY	TAX%
0003	05/10/91	CHI	SP105	0002	98765	1	.065
	05/10/91	CHI	SP105	0002	78928	2	.065
	05/10/91	CHI	SP105	0002	78923	2	.065
0004	05/15/91	MIL	SP106	0001	56789	4	.060
	05/15/91	MIL	SP106	0001	56123	2	.060
0005	05/16/91	TOL	SP102	0008	73456	2	.055
	05/16/91	TOL	SP102	0008	93845	1	.055
	05/16/91	TOL	SP102	0008	65432	3	.055
0006	05/22/91	CLE	SP101	0003	56123	1	.060
	05/22/91	CLE	SP101	0003	65789	2	.060
	05/22/91	CLE	SP101	0003	45234	3	.060
	05/22/91	CLE	SP101	0003	67891	2	.060
0007	05/23/91	DET	SP103	0005	12345	2	.055
	05/23/91	DET	SP103	0005	13456	4	.055
0008	05/23/91	MIL	SP104	0007	78920	3	.065
	05/23/91	MIL	SP104	0007	93845	1	.065
0009	05/24/91	IND	SP110	0006	45678	2	.055
	05/24/91	IND	SP110	0006	78920	1	.055
	05/24/91	IND	SP110	0006	56123	2	.055
	05/24/91	IND	SP110	0006	65432	1	.055
0010	05/26/91	CHI	SP107	0008	78923	2	.066
	05/26/91	CHI	SP107	0008	78928	1	.066
	05/26/91	CHI	SP107	0008	93846	2	.066
	05/26/91	CHI	SP107	0008	23456	2	.066
0011	06/01/91	CLE	SP101	0011	45678	2	.060
	06/01/91	CLE	SP101	0011	87654	2	.060
	06/01/91	CLE	SP101	0011	93847	2	.060

KEEPING TRACK OF SALES 267

Table 9.6: Records to Be Entered (continued)

INVOICE#	DATE	STORE	SPCODE	CUST#	STOCK#	QTY	TAX%
0012	06/02/91	MIL	SP104	0001	78920	1	.065
	06/02/91	MIL	SP104	0001	45678	2	.065
	06/02/91	MIL	SP104	0001	13456	2	.065
0013	06/05/91	CHI	SP105	0002	78921	3	.060
	06/05/91	CHI	SP105	0002	93845	2	.060
	06/05/91	CHI	SP105	0002	56123	2	.060
0014	06/07/91	IND	SP110	0006	73456	1	.060
	06/07/91	IND	SP110	0006	78928	2	.060
0015	06/09/91	TOL	SP102	0014	23456	6	.065
	06/09/91	TOL	SP102	0014	12345	3	.065
	06/09/91	TOL	SP102	0014	98765	1	.065

Since you have worked with subforms before, you know how easy it is to search for matching records:

1. Clear the screen with **Alt-F5** and enter **DET** in the STORE field.

2. Press **F3** to display the first matching record.

3. Press **Alt-F3** until all matching records are displayed.

4. Display all the records for salesperson Engel, SP101 (you should find 2).

Next, let's make use of those TOTSALES (total sales to date) fields you entered in the SP and CUST forms and TOTSOLD (total sold to date) in ITEMS.

PRINTING YOUR INVOICE

So far you have printed reports in a columnar format. You can print invoice information in a columnar format as well. However, you can also select the Record Entry format, which prints records exactly as they appear in record entry. This format is more appropriate for printing individual invoices.

1. Press **F9** to begin a Quick Report.
2. Select **Define List Fields** and select all fields, *except* BALDUE, as pictured in Figure 9.12.
3. Select **Define Format**
4. Select **Record Entry** from the list of format types.

Notice the report format begins with:

.items nosplit

The nosplit option tells DataEase not to split a record between two pages.

Your record entry format includes all the fields, *except* those in the subform. You'll add those fields:

1. Use **Alt-F10** to erase the subform border.

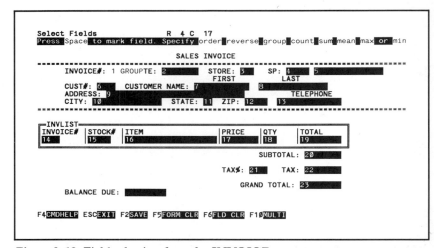

Figure 9.12: Field selection form for INVOICE report

KEEPING TRACK OF SALES **269**

2. Use **F10** to place the following fields below the subform column headings:

INVOICE#
STOCK#
ITEM
PRICE
QTY
TOTAL

In order to include *all* INVLIST subrecords, these fields must be in the .items area. The header information will become the group header (grouped by INVOICE#) and the invoice total fields will become the group trailer for each invoice.

1. Move to Row 14, Column 1 and press **F8** to insert a row and type . (period).

2. Select **items** from the menu.

3. Move to Row 1, Column 1 and delete the .items format command.

4. Type . (period) and select **group header**

5. Move to Row 16, Column 1 and press **F8** to insert a row.

6. Type . (period) and select **group trailer**

7. Delete the line with the BALDUE field prompt.

Finally, so that each invoice is printed on a separate page, you'll include a .page command at the end of the report:

1. Move to Row 22 under the .end command.

2. Press **F8** to insert a row.

3. Type . (period) and select page from the list.

The completed format is pictured in Figure 9.13.

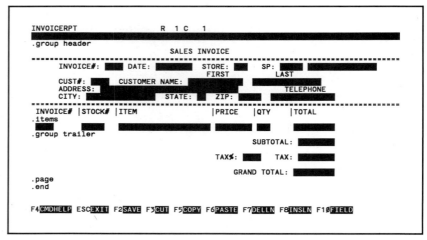

Figure 9.13: Completed INVOICE report format

1. Save the format.
2. If you have a printer, select Define Print Style and select your printer.
3. Run the report.

The first invoice, pictured in Figure 9.14, is displayed (or printed) for the customer Grey.

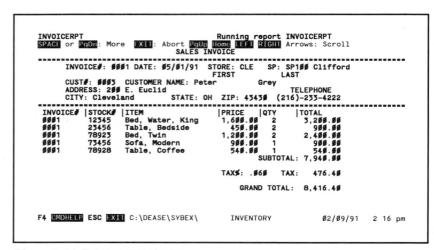

Figure 9.14: Printed INVOICE

KEEPING TRACK OF SALES **271**

1. If you are displaying the report on the screen, press **PgDn** several times to see that each invoice is displayed on a separate screen.

2. If you are printing the report, each invoice should print on a separate page.

3. After printing or displaying a few invoices, press **Esc** to clear the screen and save the report under the name **INVOICE**

If you plan to print invoices on a preprinted form or customer letterhead stationary, you may need to adjust some of the spacing in the INVOICE format.

In Chapter 15, you'll create an application that you can use to enter, then print, individual invoices.

USING SUM OF TO KEEP TRACK OF SALES

The SUM OF operator, which totals the INVLIST records to display the INVOICE grand total, can also be used to keep track of total sales for each customer, each salesperson, and each item. Let's modify the CUST, SP, and ITEMS forms, and add the derivation formula.

1. Return to the Main Menu and modify the CUST form.

2. When the form appears on the screen, move to the TOTAL SALES TO DATE (TOTSALES) field and press **F10**

3. Move to the Derivation Formula field and type **SUM OF INVOICE GRTOT**

Since you have already related INVOICE to CUST by CUST#, DataEase will add up all the GRTOT fields for each customer. The completed definition is displayed in Figure 9.15.

4. Save the field and form definitions and return to the Form Definition menu.

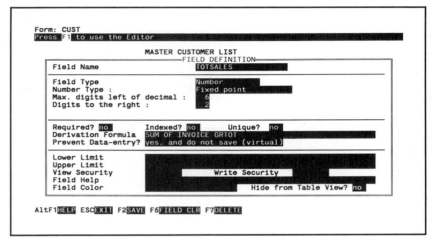

Figure 9.15: Completed definition for TOTSALES field

Next, you'll enter the derivation formula in SP:

1. Modify the SP form.
2. When the form appears on the screen, move to the TOTAL SALES TO DATE field and press **F10**
3. Move to Derivation Formula and type **SUM OF INVOICE SUBTOTAL**

This time you want DataEase to total the SUBTOT field, since gross sales for each salesperson should not include TAX. Since you have already related SP and INVOICE based on CUST#, you can also skip that step. The completed definition is displayed in Figure 9.16.

4. Save the field and form definitions and return to the Form Definition menu.

Finally, you'll add the formula to keep track of quantity sales for each item.

1. Modify the ITEMS form.
2. When the form appears on the screen, move to the TOTAL SOLD TO DATE (TOTSOLD) field and press **F10**

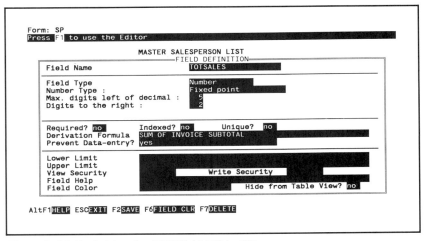

Figure 9.16: Definition for TOTSALES in SP

3. Move to Derivation Formula and type **SUM OF INVLIST QTY**

This formula asks DataEase to total the QTY field (from the INVLIST form) for each item. The completed definition is shown in Figure 9.17.

The relationship between INVLIST and ITEMS based on STOCK# was created in the last chapter.

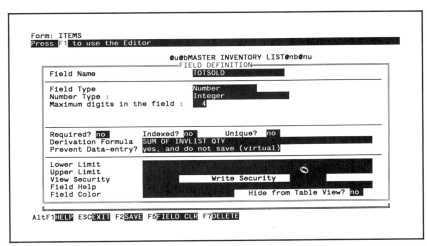

Figure 9.17: Completed definition for TOTSOLD in ITEMS

274   **MASTERING DATAEASE**

CH. 9

4. Save the field and form definitions and return to the Main Menu.

Now, let's see which customers and salespeople have generated the most sales.

1. Select **Record Entry** for CUST.

2. When the form is displayed, press **F3** and display each record.

Notice that the TOTSALES is automatically calculated. Want to check its accuracy?

1. Press **F3** until Record 1 (Enis) is displayed.

2. Press **Alt-F10**

The invoices for Enis are displayed.

3. Press **Tab** to move to the SUBTOT field and compare the numbers.

4. Continue to press **F3** and compare totals for each customer with sales.

5. Press **Esc** twice to exit to the Records menu.

USING CTRL-F9 TO RECALCULATE FORMULAS

Now let's check the SP records and see how Furniture Palace is doing in sales.

1. Select **SP** from the list of forms.

2. Press **F3** to display the first record.

What happened to our TOTSALES? The field value is still 0. The automatic calculation of the SUM formula is controlled by the Prevent Data-entry? field. If you select yes, and do not save (virtual)

KEEPING TRACK OF SALES **275**

(which does *not* store the data with the record) as you did in CUST and ITEMS, field values are automatically derived from related forms. However, if you select no or yes, then you must force DataEase to recalculate each record in one of two ways:

- Press **Enter** to move *past* the field, causing DataEase to recalculate, and press **F8** to update, or

- Press **Ctrl-F9** to automatically recalculate each derived field, then press **F8** to update.

In this case, you'll use Ctrl-F9 to calculate the formula.

1. Press **Ctrl-F9**

2. Press **F8** to update the record.

> Beware of Ctrl-F9. It recalculates *all* derived fields including LASTFIRST, and that will reverse the values *again* and place an extra comma in the field.

There is no reason in this case to save the calculation with the record, since this statistic is easily derived in a report. Let's redefine Prevent Data-entry? for this field.

1. Return to Form Definition and select **SP**

2. Modify the TOTSALES field and change the response to Prevent Data-entry? to **yes, and do not save (virtual)**

3. Save the definition and return to Record Entry for SP.

4. Press **F3** to display each record and see that the totals are now automatically calculated.

You have one more form to check: ITEMS.

1. Press **Esc** to exit SP and select **ITEMS** from the Record Entry menu.

2. Press **F3** to display each record and see that the TOTAL SOLD TO DATE field has been computed.

3. If you like, use **Alt-F10** to display the INVOICE data to check for accuracy.

276 *MASTERING DATAEASE*

CH. 9

4. When you are finished, return to the Main Menu.

Now that you have some salespeople, some customers, and finally some sales, we'll create a form to handle the payments, and wait for those checks to roll in.

CHAPTER TEN

Keeping
Track of Payments

Fast Track

To place fields next to each other in a columnar report,   293

select Modify Format from the Quick Reports menu. Move the cursor to the location at which you want the first field, and place it by pressing **F10.** Move to the next field and select **yes** at **Suppress Spaces?.** Place the second field with **F10.** If there is a third field, suppress trailing spaces on the second field. Save the definition.

To change margins in a report,   297

select Define or Modify Print Style from the Quick Reports menu. Under the MARGINS sections are fields for changing the margin settings. Enter the new settings in inches.

To add a field to a report,   298

from the Quick Reports menu, select Modify List Fields and select the additional fields for the report. Save the selection and select Modify Format. You can retain the old format or start over again. If you retain the old format, use **F10** to place the additional fields. If you have selected a field from a secondary form that has the same name as a field selected from the primary form, you must also delete the field from the primary form and use **F10** to place it again.

279

CHAPTER **10**

PERHAPS AS IMPORTANT AS SELLING YOUR PRODUCT is managing the receivables: applying payments and keeping track of current and not so current balances.

In this chapter, you'll create two new forms and apply payments to customer balances. PAYMENTS will keep information about customer payments and balances. It will contain a subform called PAYLIST to store the actual payment record, just as INVLIST keeps records of products purchased. In addition, you will also include part of the INVOICE form as a subform in PAYMENTS to keep track of the balance due for individual invoices.

CREATING THE PAYMENTS FORM WITH MULTIPLE SUBFORMS

Take a look at the typical CUSTOMER PAYMENTS record pictured in Figure 10.1. This is what one of your PAYMENTS records will look like when you complete all the steps. Notice that it includes *two* subform tables: INVLIST keeps track of payments; your INVOICE form shows only the fields that were *not* hidden from Table View, including the BALDUE field. The last two fields in the PAYMENTS form show the total payments made by a customer and the outstanding balance due for all invoices. As payments are received, you can keep track of open invoices and apply the payments accordingly.

Outlined below is the procedure you will follow to create your PAYMENTS form with subforms:

- Create PAYLIST.
- Create the primary form PAYMENTS.
- Modify INVOICE and add the derivation formula to the BALDUE field.

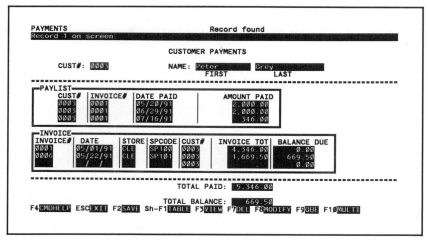

Figure 10.1: CUSTOMER PAYMENTS Form

- Create relationship records linking PAYMENTS to CUST; PAYMENTS to INVOICE; PAYMENTS to PAYLIST; and INVOICE to PAYLIST.

- Modify PAYMENTS and include PAYLIST and INVOICE as subforms.

Let's start by creating the form that will act as the subform.

CREATING THE PAYLIST FORM

PAYLIST is a simple form that includes only four fields: the customer number, invoice number, date of payment, and amount paid. Create this new form using the following steps:

1. When the Form Definition screen is displayed, use Figure 10.2 as a guide to place the form text and field prompts.

KEEPING TRACK OF PAYMENTS 281

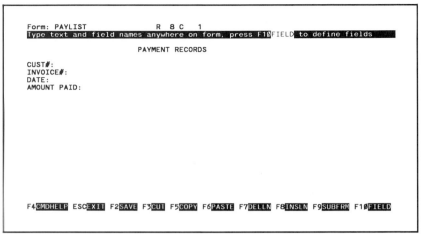

Figure 10.2: Text for PAYLIST form

2. Use the information below to place and define each field:

NAME	TYPE	WIDTH	IND?	PREVENT DATA-ENTRY?
CUST#	Numeric String	4	yes	yes
INVOICE#	Numeric String	4	yes	no
DATE	Date		yes	no
AMOUNT PAID	Dollar	4		no

3. Save the form definition and return to the Form Definition menu.

CREATING THE PAYMENTS FORM

PAYMENTS is also a simple form, which includes only five fields: the customer number, first and last names, total payments made,

CH. 10

and total balance due for all invoices. Create this new form using the following steps:

1. When the Form Definition screen is displayed, use Figure 10.3 as a guide to place the form text and field prompts.

```
Form: PAYMENTS              R  4  C  14
Type text and field names anywhere on form, press F10FIELD to define fields

                        CUSTOMER PAYMENTS

        CUST#:              NAME:
                                      FIRST       LAST
------------------------------------------------------------------------

------------------------------------------------------------------------
                        TOTAL PAID:

                        TOTAL BALANCE:




    F4CMDHELP ESCEXIT F2SAVE F3CUT F5COPY F6PASTE F7DELLN F8INSLN F9SUBFRM F10FIELD
```

Figure 10.3: Text for PAYMENTS form

2. Use the information in Table 10.1 to define the fields.

3. Save the form definition and return to the Form Definition menu.

CALCULATING BALANCE DUE FOR EACH INVOICE

When you defined the INVOICE form, you included a calculated field called BALANCE DUE (BALDUE). You'll now enter the derivation formula for that field, which will subtract the total payments applied to that invoice from the invoice total. In other words, the derivation formula will represent the GRTOT field minus the SUM OF the AMTPD fields in the PAYLIST form applied to the current invoice.

Table 10.1: Field Definition for PAYMENTS.

NAME	TYPE	WIDTH	IND?	DERIV. FORM.	PREVENT DATA-ENTRY?
CUST#	Numeric String	4	yes		no
FNAME	Text	12	no	LOOKUP CUST FNAME	yes
LNAME	Text	15	no	LOOKUP CUST LNAME	yes
TOTPD	Dollar	5	no	SUM OF PAYLIST AMTPD	yes, and do not save (virtual)
TOTBAL	Dollar	5	no	SUM OF INVOICE GRTOT TOTPD	yes, and do not save (virtual)

1. Modify the INVOICE form.

2. When the form appears on the screen, move your cursor to the BALANCE DUE field.

3. Modify the field and move the cursor to Derivation Formula.

4. Type **GRTOT-SUM OF PAYLIST AMTPD**. Your form should look like the one in Figure 10.4.

5. Save the field and form definitions and return to the Form Definition menu.

CREATING THE RELATIONSHIPS

Before you can enter any records, you'll need to create the relationships to make the formulas work by linking PAYLIST and INVOICE.

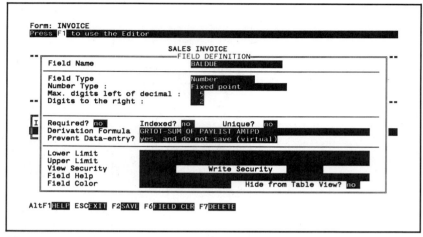

Figure 10.4: Completed field definition for BALDUE

1. From the Form Definition menu, select **Define Relationships**

2. Enter and save four new relationship records using the information below:

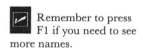 Remember to press F1 if you need to see more names.

FORM 1	FORM 2	FIELD 1	FIELD 2
PAYMENTS	CUST	CUST#	CUST#
PAYMENTS	PAYLIST	CUST#	CUST#
PAYMENTS	INVOICE	CUST#	CUST#
INVOICE	PAYLIST	INVOICE#	INVOICE#

3. Save the last record, but do not exit Define Relationships.

INCLUDING THE SUBFORMS WITH THE PAYMENTS FORM

The final step is to modify the PAYMENTS form and use F9 to include PAYLIST and INVOICE as subforms, starting with PAYLIST.

> If you have version 4.2, you might also select Cascade under PAYLIST in the PAYMENTS-PAYLIST relationship record. That way, if you correct a CUST# field value in PAYMENTS, the value will also be corrected in the matching PAYLIST record.

1. Modify the PAYMENTS form.
2. When the form appears on the screen, move the cursor to Row 7, Column 1 and press **F9**
3. Select **PAYLIST**
4. Type **3** as the minimum and **3** as the maximum.
5. Select **Automatic Table**
6. Press **F2** to confirm.

The PAYLIST form appears as a subform, also pictured in Figure 10.5. Next, you'll improve the appearance of the subform by making modifications, as you did for the INVLIST subform.

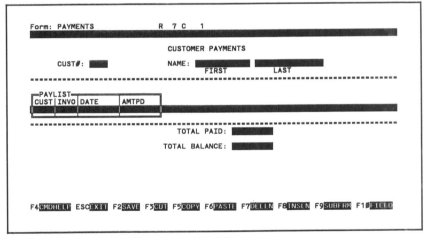

Figure 10.5: PAYMENTS with PAYLIST subform

1. Use **Alt-F10** to erase the borders of the subform.
2. Press **Ins** and using Figure 10.6 as a guide, modify the field widths and headings.
3. Redraw the border and type **PAYLIST** at the top left of the form border.

286 MASTERING DATAEASE

CH. 10

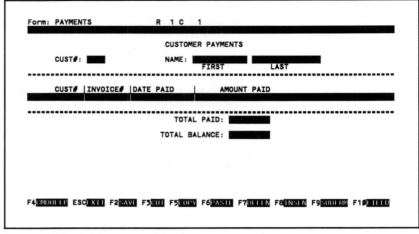

Figure 10.6: Guide to modifying PAYLIST subform

Next, you'll include INVOICE as a subform:

1. Move to Row 11, Column 1 and press **F9** to begin the subform definition.

2. Select **INVOICE** and enter **3** for both the minimum and the maximum number of rows.

3. Select **Automatic Table** and press **F2** to confirm.

Figure 10.7 shows PAYMENTS with the INVOICE subform added. Next, you'll follow the steps below to modify the INVOICE subform:

1. Use **Alt-F10** to erase the border.

2. Using Figure 10.8 as a guide, insert the additional characters for the INVOICE#, STORE, and CUST# column headings.

3. Change the GRTOT column heading to INVOICE TOT.

4. Again, using Figure 10.8 as a guide, insert spaces to align the INVOICE TOT and TOTAL PAID fields.

5. Use **Alt-F10** to redraw your border, and then type **INVOICE** in the top left corner, as shown in Figure 10.8.

> You can use Cut and Paste to change the order of the fields. This will not affect the original form.

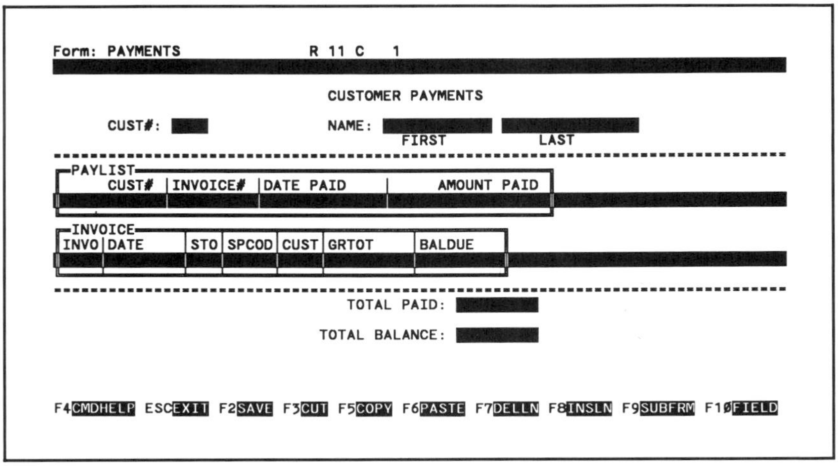

KEEPING TRACK OF PAYMENTS 287

Figure 10.7: PAYMENTS with INVOICE subform

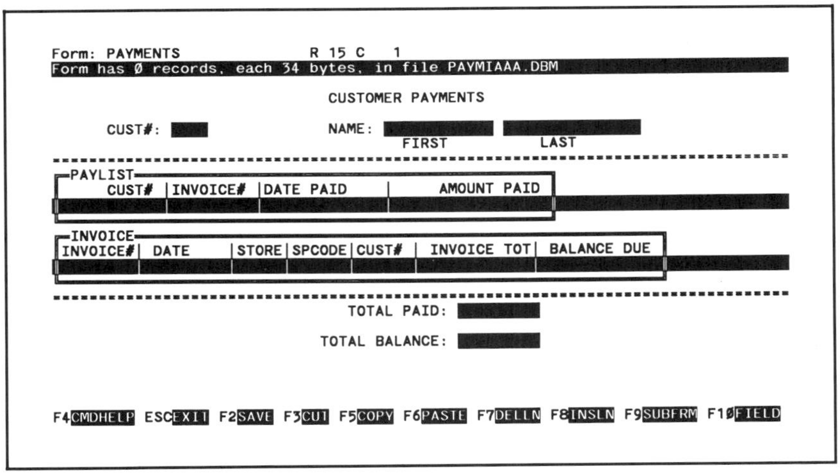

Figure 10.8: Guide to modifying INVOICE subform

There! You have created your PAYMENTS form, complete with subforms. However, you won't appreciate how efficient you've become until you enter some records.

6. Press **F2** to save the definition and return to the Main Menu.

288 MASTERING DATAEASE

CH. 10

ENTERING PAYMENT RECORDS

Furniture Palace has been receiving customer payments. You'll enter the first group and see how these subforms help you keep track of account balances.

1. Select **Record Entry** from the Main Menu.

2. Select **PAYMENTS** from the list.

3. When the form appears on the screen, enter your first record from the information below:

CUST#	3
INVOICE#	1
DATE:	052091
AMTPD:	2000

Your new record shows that the fields for TOTPD and TOTBAL are automatically updated with the new information.

However, BALDUE in the INVOICE subform has not been updated. Why not? Remember, BALDUE subtracts SUM OF TOTPD from GRTOT. TOTPD is stored on the disk in the PAYLIST form and doesn't yet include this latest payment. Therefore, before BALDUE can be updated, you must update PAYLIST with the new TOTPD. Since this is the first payment received from this customer, you'll save the record. But the next time you receive a payment from this customer, you'll *update* their record.

1. Press **F2** to save the record in PAYMENTS *and* the records in PAYLIST.

Now the BALDUE for this invoice is reduced. Perhaps the greatest usefulness of the INVOICE subform is that it helps you ensure that certain invoices don't get overlooked by the customer. For example, if a customer sends a check in payment for a recent invoice, and an older invoice still has an outstanding balance, you'll see that right away and apply the payment correctly. In Chapter 14, you'll learn how to send a letter to customers who get behind in their payments.

KEEPING TRACK OF PAYMENTS 289

But for now, you have a few more payments to enter:

2. Use the information below to enter the next few records.

CUST#	INVOICE#	DATE	AMTPD
5	2	052591	2500
2	3	061591	1000
1	4	061591	2000
6	9	062091	1500
7	8	063091	1200
11	11	063091	2000
8	5	063091	2200
14	15	071091	3000

Remember, these are first-time payments from these customers, so press F2 to save the records.

Time has passed and some of these customers have sent in their second payments. This time when you apply their payments, you'll update their records. Start with the first one.

1. Press **F5** to clear the screen if necessary.

2. Type **3** as the CUST#.

3. Complete the payment record with the following information:

INVOICE#	DATE	AMTPD
1	062991	2000

Since this customer has already made a payment, the payment record appears.

4. Press **F8** to update the record.

5. Clear the screen and enter the remaining payment records:

CUST#	INVOICE#	DATE	AMTPD
5	2	063091	1500
6	9	071091	193.28
11	11	071091	1500
8	5	071591	2368.15
5	2	071591	1463.45

CH. 10

CUST#	INVOICE#	DATE	AMTPD
5	7	071591	2000
1	12	071591	1500
3	1	071691	500
2	3	072091	500
1	4	072091	2134
1	12	072091	1000
7	8	073091	250
11	11	073091	1248.80
6	9	081591	1000
14	15	081591	2000
8	10	081591	2500
3	1	081691	1000
2	3	081591	3000
14	15	091591	3000

When you have saved the last record:

6. Press **Esc** twice to return to the Main Menu.

The accounting department would like a list of invoices and payments made. You can create a quick report called PAYMENTS using the information from both INVOICE and PAYLIST.

CREATING A REPORT WITH MULTIPLE GROUPS

In order for Accounting to ascertain the current status of each customer, you'll group this report by customer. And since some customers have more than one invoice, you'll subgroup each customer by invoice number.

1. From the Main Menu, select **Quick Reports**

2. From the Quick Reports menu select **Define List Fields**

KEEPING TRACK OF PAYMENTS **291**

3. Select **INVOICE** from the list of forms.

4. Follow the information below to select the fields from INVOICE:

FIELD	*ORDER*
CUST#	1 Group Order
INVOICE#	2 Group Order
LNAME	3
GRTOT	4
BALDUE	5

5. After you have selected the fields from INVOICE, press **F10** and select **PAYLIST** from the list of relationships.

6. Select **DATE** and **AMTPD**

7. Press **F2** to end the selection.

8. Press **Enter** at Define Format.

9. Press **Enter** to accept columnar.

10. Type **Y** for headers and trailers.

If you had a third group (a group within the subgroup), its header would be the third in the list and its trailer would be third from the end.

The report format, pictured in Figure 10.9, includes *two* group headers and trailers, one for CUST# and one for INVOICE#. Group headers and trailers are paired from the outside in. In other words, the first group header goes with the second group trailer, and the second group header goes with the first group trailer.

Some changes should be made to improve the appearance of the report. For one thing, since LNAME is the same for each record in a customer group, you'll move that field to the group header for CUST#. And since GRTOT and BALDUE are the same for each invoice repeated in an invoice group, these fields should be moved to the group header for INVOICE#.

1. Move to Row 10, Column 11 and use **F3** (Cut) and **F6** (Paste) to move LNAME to Row 6, Column 12 after the CUST# field.

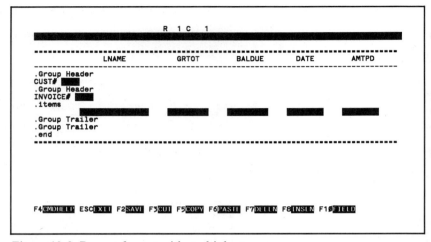

Figure 10.9: Report format with multiple groups

2. Move to Row 10, Column 15 and use **F3** to cut GRTOT (Row 10, Column 15) and BALDUE (Row 10, Column 37) and use **F6** to paste the fields at Row 8, Column 30 under their headings.

3. Insert spaces in front of the DATE and AMTPD fields (beginning at Row 10, Column 18) in the .items area until the fields are aligned again with their headings (at Row 10, Column 57).

4. Use the form in Figure 10.10 as a guide and edit the column headings.

5. Use **F8** to insert two rows beginning at Row 1 to create the header shown in Figure 10.10, and include the current date. If you need help with the header and date fields, turn to Chapter 5 for a refresher.

Finally, let's add the STORE field to the group header for CUST#, right next to LNAME.

1. Move your cursor to Row 10, Column 16 and press **F10**

2. Press **Enter** to enter a new field, and type **STORE**

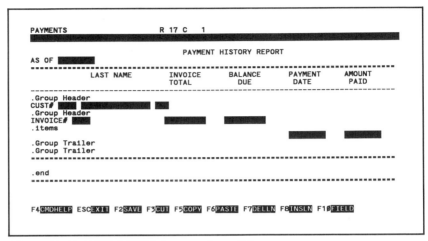

Figure 10.10: PAYMENTS format after editing

3. Press **F2**

To make the report easier to read, let's add an extra line between CUST groupings.

1. Move the cursor to Row 15 and press **F8** twice to insert two lines.
2. Use **F3** and **F6** to move the double line at the end of the report to Row 16.
3. Save the format.
4. Save the report under the name PAYMENTS.
5. If you have a printer available, print the report as well.

> If you printed the last report in condensed print, you'll need first to reset the printer or turn it off for a few seconds to clear the condensed-print command from the printer buffer.

SUPPRESSING FIELD SPACES

As you view your report, pictured in Figure 10.11, the STORE names are displayed in a separate column, instead of right next to each name. The LNAME field was assigned a width of 25 characters and the field is always allotted that space even if the values are shorter. These additional spaces are called *trailing spaces*. We can eliminate those by modifying the format.

> Normally, you should not remove trailing spaces for the field in the .items area, or you will lose your columnar format.

294 MASTERING DATAEASE

CH. 10

```
                                        PAYMENT HISTORY REPORT
                 AS OF
                 =========================================================================
                             LNAME          GRTOT        BALDUE      DATE       AMTPD
                 -------------------------------------------------------------------------
                 CUST# 0001 Enis          MIL
                 INVOICE# 0004                4,134.00        0.00
                                                                      06/15/91    2,000.00
                                                                      07/20/91    2,134.00
                 INVOICE# 0012                2,907.45      407.45
                                                                      07/15/91    1,500.00
                                                                      07/20/91    1,000.00
                 INVOICE# 0016                3,200.00    3,200.00

                 =========================================================================

                 CUST# 0002 Smith         CHI
                 INVOICE# 0003                5,032.13      532.13
                                                                      06/15/91    1,000.00
                                                                      07/20/91      500.00
                                                                      08/15/91    3,000.00
                 INVOICE# 0013                6,810.50    6,810.50

                 INVOICE# 0017                5,790.00    5,790.00

                 =========================================================================

                 CUST# 0003 Grey          CLE
                 INVOICE# 0001                8,798.00    3,298.00
                                                                      05/20/91    2,000.00
                                                                      06/29/91    2,000.00
                                                                      07/16/91      500.00
                                                                      08/16/91    1,000.00
                 INVOICE# 0006                5,194.00    5,194.00

                 INVOICE# 0018                1,600.00    1,600.00


                 =========================================================================

                 CUST# 0005 Heida         DET
                 INVOICE# 0002                5,463.45        0.00
                                                                      05/25/91    2,500.00
                                                                      06/30/91    1,500.00
                                                                      07/15/91    1,463.45
                 INVOICE# 0007                5,749.75    3,749.75
                                                                      07/15/91    2,000.00
                 =========================================================================

                 CUST# 0006 Edwards       IND
                 INVOICE# 0009                4,763.33    2,070.05
                                                                      06/20/91    1,500.00
                                                                      07/10/91      193.28
                                                                      08/15/91    1,000.00
                 INVOICE# 0014                2,862.00    2,862.00

                 =========================================================================

                 CUST# 0007 Clark         MIL
                 INVOICE# 0008                2,742.38    1,292.38
                                                                      06/30/91    1,200.00
                                                                      07/30/91      250.00
                 =========================================================================

                 CUST# 0008 Green         TOL
                 INVOICE# 0005                4,568.15        0.00
                                                                      06/30/91    2,200.00
                                                                      07/15/91    2,368.15
                 INVOICE# 0010                5,852.34    3,352.34
                                                                      08/15/91    2,500.00
                 INVOICE# 0019                3,206.50    3,206.50
```

Figure 10.11: Completed PAYMENTS report

KEEPING TRACK OF PAYMENTS **295**

```
================================================================================
CUST# 0011 Jones          CLE
INVOICE# 0011                4,748.80         0.00
                                                       06/30/91    2,000.00
                                                       07/10/91    1,500.00
                                                       07/30/91    1,248.80

================================================================================

CUST# 0014 Porter         TOL
INVOICE# 0015                8,546.63       546.63
                                                       07/10/91    3,000.00
                                                       08/15/91    2,000.00
                                                       09/15/91    3,000.00
================================================================================

================================================================================
```

Figure 10.11: Completed PAYMENTS report (continued)

1. Clear the screen.

2. Modify and keep the old format.

3. Move the cursor to the LNAME field and press **F10**

The last field in the Report Field Definition box is Suppress Spaces?. Though the value is normally no, if you change it to yes, those extra spaces will be eliminated in the report.

1. Press **End** to move to the last field and type **Y**

2. Save the definition and run the report again.

Your new report, also shown in Figure 10.12, displays STORE right next to LNAME.

```
                          PAYMENT HISTORY REPORT
AS OF
================================================================================
            LNAME           GPTOT         BALDUE       DATE         AMTPD
--------------------------------------------------------------------------------
CUST# 0001 Enis MIL
INVOICE# 0004                4,134.00         0.00
                                                       06/15/91    2,000.00
                                                       07/20/91    2,134.00
INVOICE# 0012                2,907.45       407.45
                                                       07/15/91    1,500.00
                                                       07/20/91    1,000.00
INVOICE# 0016                3,200.00     3,200.00
```

Figure 10.12: Report after trailing spaces removed

```
===============================================================
CUST# 0002 Smith CHI
INVOICE# 0003              5,032.13       532.13
                                                    06/15/91    1,000.00
                                                    07/20/91      500.00
                                                    08/15/91    3,000.00
INVOICE# 0013              6,810.50     6,810.50

INVOICE# 0017              5,790.00     5,790.00

===============================================================
CUST# 0003 Grey CLE
INVOICE# 0001              8,798.00     3,298.00
                                                    05/20/91    2,000.00
                                                    06/29/91    2,000.00
                                                    07/16/91      500.00
                                                    08/16/91    1,000.00
INVOICE# 0006              5,194.00     5,194.00

INVOICE# 0018              1,600.00     1,600.00

===============================================================
CUST# 0005 Heida DET
INVOICE# 0002              5,463.45         0.00
                                                    05/25/91    2,500.00
                                                    06/30/91    1,500.00
                                                    07/15/91    1,463.45
INVOICE# 0007              5,749.75     3,749.75
                                                    07/15/91    2,000.00
===============================================================
CUST# 0006 Edwards IND
INVOICE# 0009              4,763.33     2,070.05
                                                    06/20/91    1,500.00
                                                    07/10/91      193.28
                                                    08/15/91    1,000.00
INVOICE# 0014              2,862.00     2,862.00

===============================================================
CUST# 0007 Clark MIL
INVOICE# 0008              2,742.38     1,292.38
                                                    06/30/91    1,200.00
                                                    07/30/91      250.00
===============================================================
CUST# 0008 Green TOL
INVOICE# 0005              4,568.15         0.00
                                                    06/30/91    2,200.00
                                                    07/15/91    2,368.15
INVOICE# 0010              5,852.34     3,352.34
                                                    08/15/91    2,500.00
INVOICE# 0019              3,206.50     3,206.50

===============================================================
CUST# 0011 Jones CLE
INVOICE# 0011              4,748.80         0.00
                                                    06/30/91    2,000.00
                                                    07/10/91    1,500.00
                                                    07/30/91    1,248.80

===============================================================
CUST# 0014 Porter TOL
INVOICE# 0015              8,546.63       546.63
                                                    07/10/91    3,000.00
                                                    08/15/91    2,000.00
                                                    09/15/91    3,000.00
===============================================================

===============================================================
```

Figure 10.12: Report after trailing spaces removed (continued)

CHANGING THE REPORT LAYOUT

If you printed your report, you'll notice another problem: this report is longer than just one page and there are no margins separating the two pages. You can change that by modifying the print style.

1. Clear the report and select **Modify Print Specifications**

2. If necessary, select **Printer** from the list.

3. Press **Tab** twice and press **F3** to display your default printer.

There are several fields in the Print Style Specification screen that you can change to control the layout of your report on the paper.

Refer to the page layout drawing to the left of the screen. To the right, under MARGINS, are the fields that correspond to the different areas of the layout.

1.Left	2.Right
3.Top to Header	4.Header to Text
5.Footer to Bottom	6.Text to Footer

The default margin settings are 0; however, you can enter new settings, in inches, to change the position of the report on the page.

Left and Right are the left and right margin settings, the space separating the report from the left and right edges of the paper. Header to Text and Text to Footer determine the space between the header and footer text and the body of the report, which begins with the column headings.

> In word processing, the lines between headers/footers and text are often called the header or footer margins.

Top to Header is the space from the top of the page to the first line of the report; Footer to Bottom is the space between the last line of the report and the end of the page. These are usually referred to as the top and bottom margins. You'll need to change the Footer to Bottom value to create space between pages in a multipage report.

1. Move the cursor to the **Footer to Bottom** field and type **1**

5.Footer to Bottom**1**	6.Text to Footer

2. Save the specification and run the report.

298 MASTERING DATAEASE

CH. 10

The printed report now has one inch of additional space at the bottom of the page. If you position your paper in the printer at the very top edge, you should also set a Top to Header margin. Otherwise, adjust your paper so that the printhead is positioned where you want to print your first line of text.

SELECTING RECORDS WITH A REFERENTIAL FORMULA

Now Accounting would like a report that includes only customers with outstanding balances more than 60 days old (30 days past due). The record selection for this report involves two conditions: the balance due must be greater than 0 and the payment date must be 60 days *after* the invoice date (invoice date + 60). The formula would be entered into the DATE field of PAYLIST but would *refer* to the DATE field in the INVOICE form.

1. If necessary, clear the screen to return to the Quick Reports menu.

2. Select **Define Record Selection**

3. Press the **End** key to move to the BALDUE field.

4. Type **>0**

5. Press **F10** and select **PAYLIST** from the list of forms.

6. Move to the DATE field and type > **INVOICE DATE** + **60**

7. Press **F2** to save the selection.

Remember, you can press Esc if you want to return to the primary form instead of the Quick Reports menu.

ADDING FIELDS TO THE FIELD SELECTION LIST

There is one more step to complete before running this report. You really should add the DATE field from the INVOICE form so that Accounting can tell exactly *how many* days past due the invoice payments are.

You know that you can modify the format and use F10 to enter the name of a field not originally selected. *However,* you already have a field called DATE from the PAYLIST form. Normally, if you type

KEEPING TRACK OF PAYMENTS   **299**

the field name in the Report Field Definition screen, DataEase assumes you are referring to a field in the primary form. However, if the report already contains a field of the same name from a related form, DataEase may print incorrect values for the two fields when you run the report. You can avoid this without redefining your report.

> Don't be concerned that the number assigned to the newly selected field is also assigned to another field.

1. Select Modify List Fields.
2. Move to the DATE field and press **Spacebar**
3. Press **F2** to save the selection.

Now you have two fields with the same name. Since one of them was selected after defining the format, you need to make two changes to your report format: use F10 to place the DATE field from INVOICE, and delete the DATE field from INVLIST and place it again with F10.

1. Select **Modify Format** and keep the old format.
2. Move to Row 10, Column 16 and press **F10**
3. Press **F1** to display all fields.
4. Select **DATE**
5. Press **F2** to confirm.
6. Move to Row 12, Column 57 (DATE field from INVLIST).
7. Press **F10** and press **F7** to delete the field.
8. Move back to Column 57 and press **F10** again.
9. Press **F1** and select **DATE**
10. Press **F2** to confirm.

When working with related forms you must be careful when adding fields with the same names. In the next chapter, you'll learn a method of creating reports from multiple forms that can avoid this confusion. For now, let's see the results of your changes.

1. Save the format and run the report.

Now you can compare the dates to see that only open invoices more than 60 days old are displayed.

2. Save the report under the same name.

3. Press **Esc** to return to the Main Menu.

In the last two chapters, you spent time creating forms that automate some aspects of sales and accounting. However, there is still some work to do in order to tie together the processing of sales orders and the maintenance of an adequate inventory supply. And the Accounting department is demanding more complex reports. You can accomplish all this and more with the DataEase Data Query Language. In the next chapter, you'll learn the basics of DQL.

CHAPTER ELEVEN

Creating
Reports with the
Data Query Language

Fast Track

To convert a quick report to a DQL procedure, 305

select DQL Advanced Processing from the Main Menu. From the DQL menu, select Load Procedure. Select the name of the quick report and type **y** to convert the report. When the query is displayed, make any changes necessary and save the query. Modify the format and place any fields that were not included during the conversion.

To create a report using the DQL, 307

select DQL from the Main Menu. From the DQL Menu, select Define Query. Using the interactive menus, select the primary form. Select **with** to make a record selction, or select **none**. Following the List Fields statement, select each field for the report, in groups if you wish. You can also include statistics for numeric fields. Select the ; (semicolon) from the menu to complete each field selection. Following the last field selection, select the . (period) from the menu. Define the format and print style as you would for any quick report.

To include fields from a related form in a DQL report, 314

follow the steps to create a simple DQL report. When the menu displays the field list from the primary form, press the **Tab** key twice and select the relational operator. Then, select the related form from the list. Press **Tab** again and select the field from the related form. Repeat these steps for each field from the related form. If you want to include a tertiary (third) related form, press **Tab** twice when the menu displays the list of fields from the secondary form; select a relational operator, and select a name from the list of related forms. Press **Tab** again and select the field from the related form.

To modify a query, 319

load the procedure if necessary, and select Modify Query from the DQL menu. Move the cursor to the place where you want to make the modification. If the modification may occupy more than the current line, press **F8** to insert additional lines. Press **F1** to select from the menu, or type your changes. Press **F2** to save the query. If you add new fields, make sure they are separated by the semicolon. The last field must be followed by the period.

To select records at run time for a DQL report, 330

select Define Data Entry Form from the DQL menu. Select **y** if you want to redisplay the form after the procedure is run. Create the form as you would any other form, including only those fields on which the selection will be made, or fields that are the result of lookups based on the selected fields. You may include explanatory or instructional text. Press **F2** to save the form. Select Define or Modify Query. Under the **for** statement that selects the form, include a **with** statement. Now, select the field on which the record selection is based. Select the operator, select **data-entry** from the list, then select the data entry field from the next list. If there are additional criteria, select **and** or **or** from the menu and repeat the steps for the next field.

CHAPTER 11

DATAEASE FORMS OFFER YOU A USER-FRIENDLY method of performing your daily database management tasks. However, to tap into the potential of DataEase, you should graduate from forms and utilize the power of the DataEase Data Query Language (DQL).

The DQL comprises a wide variety of words and phrases that you can organize into a series of statements, just like any other language. However, this language has been developed particularly for the purpose of extending your current report and record processing capabilities.

If you are already familiar with a programming language, you will find the DQL simple to learn. If not, the DataEase DQL provides an excellent opportunity to introduce yourself to the concepts and techniques of programming. DQL offers the simplicity required by novice users, as well as the tools needed by experienced programmers.

You have already created a number of reports using DataEase forms to select records and fields. These report specifications can be translated into the Data Query Language. However, if you use the DQL instead of the Quick Reports to create your reports, you can:

- Work more efficiently with related forms.

- Perform more sophisticated calculations.

- Create a special data entry form that allows you to select different records each time you run the report.

In this chapter, you will learn how to create reports using the DQL, starting with the most simple techniques and statements. In Chapter 12, you will learn how to create more complex reports with DQL. In Chapters 13–15 you will use DQL record processing techniques to modify your database and automate record entry, editing, and report processing.

To start, let's go to the DQL menu and see what a DQL report looks like:

1. Select **DQL Advanced Processing** from the Main Menu.

THE DQL MENU

The DQL menu, pictured in Figure 11.1, looks suspiciously like the Quick Reports menu. However, you'll notice that Procedure is used in place of Report in most menu selections. A report is actually just one of many procedures you can perform. In addition, the Define Data-entry Form selection appears in place of Define Record Selection, and Define Query appears in place of Define List Fields. The report format and print specification appear as they do in Quick Reports.

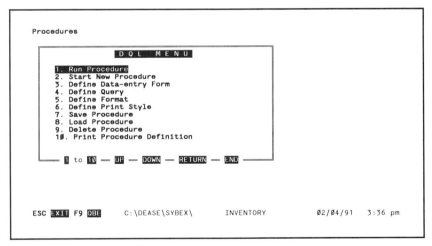

Figure 11.1: The DQL menu

CONVERTING A QUICK REPORT TO DQL

Any report created using Quick Reports can be converted to DQL. You can then use DQL to expand the report. Before you

306 MASTERING DATAEASE

CH. 11

create your first report with DQL, let's see what one looks like. Let's convert INVLIST, the first report you created:

1. Select **Load Procedure**
2. Select **INVLIST**

DataEase asks:

> 1:NO 1:Yes
> Convert this QBE (Quick Report) to a DQL Procedure?

3. Select **Y** to convert the report.

The statements listed below represent the query that creates the report. They combine the steps for both record and field selection.

```
for ITEMS
with ITEM = "table*" and
   COST <600 ;
list records
   STOCK# ;
   MANUFACTURER in order ;
   ITEM in order ;
   COST : item mean ;
   PRICE : item mean ;
   QTY ONHAND :  item sum mean count .
```

Let's look at some of these statements:

for ITEMS	The primary form you selected for this report.
with ITEM = "table*" and COST < 600 ;	Identifies the records you selected in the Define Record Selection form.
list records	Lists the fields and statistics you selected for the report. MANUFACTURER is first in order, ITEM second in order. COST, PRICE and QTY ONHAND include statistics.

CREATING REPORTS WITH THE DATA QUERY LANGUAGE 307

Notice that lists of fields are indented within the other statements. They are considered substatements of the list field statement. Indenting is a formatting technique used by programmers to group related statements and improve the legibility of the program. Indenting is recommended, but not required.

And that's all there is to it. However, every programming language has certain rules about the ways in which statements are organized within a program and phrases are organized within statements. These are referred to as syntax rules. Listed below are some syntax rules that you should note:

After converting from Quick Reports, modify the format from the DQL menu before running the report to make sure all fields are converted properly.

- The Report procedure begins with a **for** statement which selects the form.

- If no **with** statement is included, a ; (semicolon) is entered.

- The ; character follows each selected field.

- Field statistics are preceded by the : (colon) character.

- The . (period) follows the last selected field to indicate the end of the query.

In the next section, you will create a report similar to INVLIST, using the DQL. For now, you can abandon this procedure:

1. Press **Esc**

DataEase asks:

Normally, when you press Esc to abandon a query, the entire procedure is cleared from memory. In this case, since you just converted a quick report, the procedure was not cleared.

1:NO 2:Yes
Do you want to abandon the procedure?

2. Select **Y**

3. Select **Start new procedure**

CREATING A SINGLE FORM REPORT

Creating a DQL report is not unlike creating a Quick Report: you select records and fields, define the format and print style, and then run the procedure. The major difference is that you create a query to select both records and fields.

MASTERING DATAEASE

CH. 11

DEFINING QUERIES

A query is the list of statements that actually define and describe the procedure. The query statements select the form, records, and fields for a report. Statements are comprised of keywords, form or field names, and user-supplied values. Keywords are words or phrases that DataEase requires in a statement. These keywords, as well as the field or form names, can be selected from a menu, which you will learn how to use in this chapter. You may also be prompted to enter text or values to complete a statement.

DataEase offers two types of queries: low level and high level. The low level query is used to create simple reports, single or multiform. The INVLIST report is an example of a low level query.

You would use the high level query to include a variety of math operators in your report or to create sophisticated procedures such as adding or modifying records. You'll begin with low level queries.

1. Select **Define Query**

USING INTERACTIVE MENUS

The Query screen, pictured in Figure 11.2, begins with **for**, the first word of the statement that selects your form. Low level queries *always* begin with the keyword **for** followed by a form name. The list of form names is displayed at the top of the screen.

This is the first in a series of DQL menus from which you select the words, phrases, and form and field names to build your query. These menus take you step by step through entering each query statement, and can save you a considerable amount of typing. All query menus, required or optional, are displayed. You can skip an optional menu by pressing Tab or selecting the NONE option from the Menu. If you attempt to skip a required menu, DataEase will sound a beep and wait until you make a selection.

When DataEase displays the menus, it is in interactive mode. As you become more familiar with DQL you can switch to edit mode and type the statements without the help of the menus. The query screen mode is displayed at the bottom of the screen, along with the list of function keys.

Do not press Esc to clear a menu or DataEase will ask if you want to abandon the procedure; if you answer Y, the procedure will be cleared.

CREATING REPORTS WITH THE DATA QUERY LANGUAGE

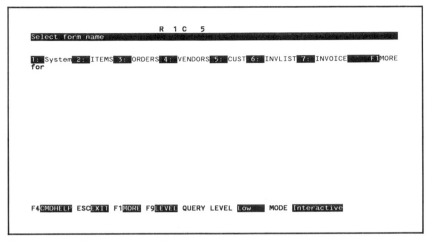

Figure 11.2: Query screen with menus

Interactive is always the default. To exit the menus, press ← or ↑; to return to interactive mode, press F1. DataEase will always display the correct menu.

The bottom line of your screen also displays the query level, currently set at low. For the time being, you will work with the low level. In the next chapter, you will use the high level menus to create more complex queries.

1. Select **ITEMS** from the menu.

The next menu,

    0: NONE 1:with

prompts you to begin (**with**) or skip (**NONE**) record selection. In the original INVLIST report, you selected tables that cost less than $600. For this report, you'll use the following query statement to include only records from ABC Company:

    with MANUFACTURER = "ABC Company";

1. Select **with**
2. Select **MANUFACTURER**
3. Select =

When entering a search string, follow the same methods as in Record Entry. Case is irrelevant.

Once you select the field name, you can type ; (semicolon) to bypass the remaining field options and select the next field or . (period) to save and exit the query.

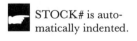
STOCK# is automatically indented.

DataEase prompts you to:

> Enter a text string, enclosed in "". To skip hit TAB

4. Type **"ABC Company"**

As soon as you type the second ", DataEase adds the semicolon and moves to the next menu:

> Any more criteria?
> 0:NONE 2:and 3:or

5. Press **Tab** to end the record selection.

So far, your query reads:

> for ITEMS
> with MANUFACTURER = "ABC Company";
> list records

In a low level query, DataEase always follows the form and record selection with the keywords **list records** and displays the field list from the selected form. In this case the list of fields from ITEMS is displayed.

1. Select **STOCK#**

The next menu:

> 0: NONE 1: in order 2: in reverse 3: in groups 4: in groups with group totals

should be somewhat familiar. These choices are similar to those displayed in the Define List Fields screen for a quick report. The last selection, **in groups with group totals** includes statistics for each group.

2. Select **in order**

CREATING REPORTS WITH THE DATA QUERY LANGUAGE 311

The next short menu offers only two options:

0: None 1: ;

If you select 0 (no more fields), DataEase enters a . (period) to end the query, and returns to the DQL menu. If you select ; (semicolon), DataEase redisplays the field list so you can select the next field.

> If you accidentally select NONE, DataEase will save the query and return to the DQL menu. If this happens, simply select Modify Query, position the cursor under the . (period) and press F1 to start the menus.

3. Select ;

4. Select **ITEM**

5. Type ;

DataEase skips the other menus and displays the field list again.

6. Select **COST**

7. Press **Tab** to skip the Group menu.

Next, DataEase asks you:

Any Statistics desired with this item?
0: None   1: :

8. Select :

9. Press **F1** to display more selections.

The Statistics menu, pictured in Figure 11.3, is always displayed after you select a numeric field. It offers the same choices found in Quick Reports with one addition: item. You must select item in order to include the selected field in the .items area of the report. However, if you select any of the other statistical operators, and you *don't* select the keyword **item**, the column heading will appear in the report, but the field itself will appear only as a statistic in the footer and/or at the end of the report.

1. Select **item** and **mean**

2. Type ;

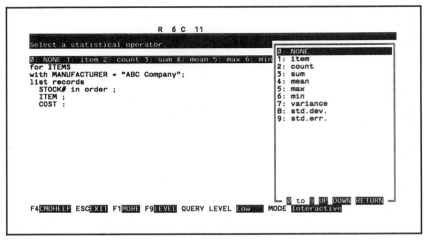

Figure 11.3: Statistics menu

Your query now reads:

for ITEMS
with MANUFACTURER = "ABC Company";
list records
   STOCK# in order ;
   ITEM ;
   COST : item mean ;

3. Press **F1** to display more selections and select **PRICE**

4. Type ;

5. Press **F1** and select **QTY ONHAND**

6. Type **:** and press **Spacebar** to display the Statistics menu.

7. Select **item sum mean count**

You have now completed the query and are ready to save it. Before you do, compare your screen with Figure 11.4.

8. Type **.** (period) to end the query.

The **.** (period) character always tells DataEase to end a low level query, save it, and return to the DQL menu. If you have made a mistake in one of your statements, DataEase will move the cursor to the

CREATING REPORTS WITH THE DATA QUERY LANGUAGE   313

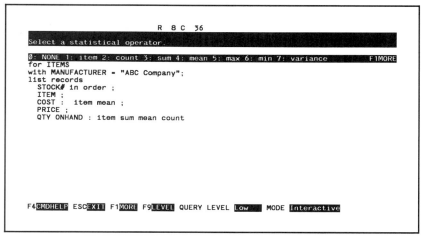

Figure 11.4: Completed query

mistake, and display a message and the correct menu. DataEase will *not* allow you to save a query that has been entered incorrectly.

1. Save the procedure as **INVLISTP**
2. Select **Run Procedure**

The complete report is pictured in Figure 11.5.

> In previous exercises, you have defined the format for each report. From now on, unless it is necessary to the procedure, you'll skip that step. However, if you want to take the time to edit the format, it would certainly be good practice.

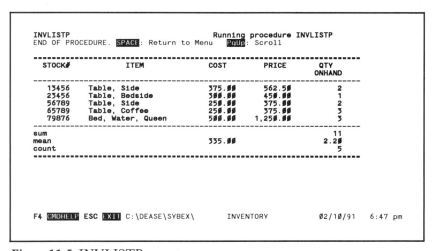

Figure 11.5: INVLISTP report

314 **MASTERING DATAEASE**

CH. 11

CREATING A DQL REPORT USING TWO RELATED FORMS

In Chapter 7, you created ITEMORD which included records from ITEMS (the primary form) and ORDERS (the related form). Let's convert the ITEMORD report and see what it looks like as a DQL procedure.

1. Press **Esc** to clear the report.

2. Select **Load Procedure**

3. Select **ITEMORD**

4. Type **Y** to convert the report.

The query statements listed below contain some familiar statements.

```
for ITEMS
;
list records
    STOCK# in groups with group-totals ;
    ITEM ;
    QTY ONHAND ;
    all ORDERS DATEORD ;
    all ORDERS ORDER# ;
    all ORDERS SOURCE ;
    all ORDERS AMTORD .
```

This is similar to the previous query; however, this report includes fields from a related form, ORDERS. Each of these fields is preceded by the phrase **all ORDERS**, which selects all records in ORDERS that contain matching values in the related field. **all** is one of several relational operators you can use to select records from the related form.

You'll create a similar report using the DQL. First, you can abandon this procedure:

1. Press **Esc**

2. Type **Y** to abandon the procedure.

3. Select **Start new procedure**

CREATING REPORTS WITH THE DATA QUERY LANGUAGE   *315*

Now you're ready to define the query for the new procedure. This time we'll group the report by MANUFACTURER and include statistics:

1. Select **Define Query**

2. Select **ITEMS**

3. Press **Tab** to skip record selection.

4. Select **MANUFACTURER**

5. Select **in groups with group-totals** and type ;

6. Select **STOCK#** from the list of fields.

7. Select **in groups**

8. Select ;

9. Select **ITEM in groups**

10. Type ;

The remaining fields are selected from ORDERS. To select a related form, you will skip some menus:

1. Press **Tab**

The next menu,

0: NONE 1:Current

allows you to select from the list of system-derived fields, such as date and page number. Skip this menu:

2. Press **Tab**

3. Press **F1** to display more selections.

> It is usually more practical to place these fields in headers or footers when defining your report format. Select them here if you want them to appear as columns in your report.

The next menu, pictured in Figure 11.6, is the list of relational operators. You must choose one of these when selecting fields from a related form. In this case, you want *all* records from ORDERS that contain matching STOCK# values. When you select fields from

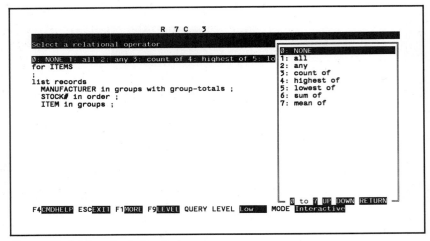

Figure 11.6: List of relational operators

related forms in Quick Reports, DataEase always selects all matching records. DQL offers the flexibility of six additional operators. You'll use those later in this chapter.

4. Select **all**

5. Select **ORDERS** from the menu of relationships.

The next menu:

    0 NONE 1: with

allows you to specify any record selection that should take place within the related form. This creates an ad hoc relationship that remains in effect only for the duration of this procedure. You'll learn more about this later.

6. Press **Tab** to skip the menu. Next, you'll select DATEORD.

7. Type **1** (for DATEORD).

At this point, DataEase displays the message

    Enter a Space or a Digit to Complete

CREATING REPORTS WITH THE DATA QUERY LANGUAGE   *317*

When numbered lists include double digits (more than nine selections), you may need to press **Spacebar** after some single digits to complete the selection. In this case, since there are ten fields, you must enter a space after selecting 1.

8. Press **Spacebar** to complete selection for **DATEORD**

9. Type **;** to select the next field.

10. **Tab** twice and select **all**

Once you have established the connection to the related form, with or without additional record selection, DataEase continues to select that form each time you select the **all** operator. If you select any other operator, DataEase will again display the list of related forms.

11. Select **ORDER#** and type **;**

The last two fields, SOURCE and AMTORD, are also selected from ORDERS. Let's leave the menus and type the last two statements:

DataEase displays form and field names in the case in which you typed them originally. When typing queries, case is not significant.

12. Press ← to leave the menu and then press **Spacebar** to move back to the previous position.

13. Type **all orders source; ←┘**

14. Type **all orders amtord: item sum**

Before you save your new query, compare it with the statements below to make sure it's complete.

```
for ITEMS
;
list records
    MANUFACTURER in groups with group-totals ;
    STOCK# IN GROUPS ;
    ITEM# IN GROUPS ;
    all ORDERS DATEORD ;
    all ORDERS ORDER# ;
    all ORDERS SOURCE ;
    all ORDERS AMTORD: item sum
```

318 MASTERING DATAEASE

CH. 11

> ✍ When you are working from the menus, type . (period) to end and save the query. When you are *not* working from the menus, you must type the . (period) *and* press **F2** to save the query.

15. Type . (period) and press **F2** to end the query, save it, and return to the DQL menu.

16. Select **Run Procedure**

Your report, pictured in Figure 11.7, shows no group headers or trailers since you didn't define the format. However, the values for grouped fields are only displayed once.

```
                                        Running procedure
    SPACE  or  PgDn : More   EXIT : Abort  PgUp   Home   LEFT   RIGHT   Arrows: Scroll
    ----------------------------------------------------------------------------------
      MANUFACTURER        STOCK         ITEM           all     all      all ORDERS
                            #                         ORDERS   ORDE       SOURCE
                                                     DATEORD    RS
                                                              ORDE
                                                               R#
    ----------------------------------------------------------------------------------
      ABC Company        13456 Table, Side           04/10/91 0015 ABC Company
                         23456 Table, Bedside        01/15/91 0001 Beds 'n Things
                         23456                        02/05/91 0004 Beds 'n Things
                         56789 Table, Side           04/10/91 0015 ABC Company
                         65789 Table, Coffee         03/01/91 0007 Table Tops
                         79876 Bed, Water, Queen     03/15/91 0009 ABC Company
    ----------------------------------------------------------------------------------
    sum
    ----------------------------------------------------------------------------------
      Picklepot Furniture 65432 Table, Coffee        03/29/90 0019 Picklepot Furnitu
                          78921 Table, Kitchen
                          87654 Bed, Queen           03/25/90 0014 Picklepot Furnitu
                          93846 Loveseat, Modern
    ----------------------------------------------------------------------------------
    F4  CMDHELP  ESC  EXIT  C:\DEASE\SYBEX\        INVENTORY        02/04/91   4:34 pm
```

Figure 11.7: Completed MANUFACTURER report

Your column headings, which always display the field name, include the field relationship as well. The field is not just AMTORD, it's **all ORDERS AMTORD**. You'll find that as your reports become more complex, so will your column headings. If you like you can take the time to edit them.

1. Press **Esc** to clear the form.

2. Select **Save Procedure**

Any time you save a procedure, and have *not* just saved the query, DataEase redisplays the query and waits for you to confirm.

3. Press **F2**

4. Type **MFRORD** for the procedure name.

CREATING REPORTS WITH THE DATA QUERY LANGUAGE   *319*

MODIFYING A PROCEDURE

The DQL menus are flexible and forgiving. If you make a mistake you can switch to edit mode, correct your mistake and switch back to the menus. If you omit an essential keyword or punctuation, Data-Ease will move your cursor to the error and display the appropriate menu.

Let's modify the INVLISTP procedure, add statistics for the PRICE field, and change the record selection to tables that cost less than $600.

1. Load the INVLISTP procedure.

2. Select **Modify Query**

3. Move the cursor right under the ; after PRICE, as follows:

   PRICE **;**

4. Press **F1**

5. Press **Tab** and select :

6. Select **mean**

7. Type ;

When adding a query statement that may take more than one line, insert extra lines to make room. Otherwise, it may write over existing text.

Next, you'll change the record selection to ITEM = "table*" and COST < 600, which will occupy two lines. (Please note that you are including the manufacturer's cost here, not the selling price, which you used earlier in Chapter 5 for your INVLIST report.) Therefore you'll be inserting additional lines for the statement.

1. Move to Row 2, Column 1 and press **F7** to delete the line.

2. Press **F8** to insert two additional lines.

3. Press **F1** to display the menus.

DataEase immediately displays the **with** option.

4. Select **with**

5. Select **ITEM**

6. Select =

> After typing a number in response to the Enter a number menu prompt, always press Spacebar to indicate the end of the number.

7. Type **"table*"**
8. Select **and**
9. Select **COST**
10. Select **<**
11. Type **600 ;**

The selection is completed and DataEase skips past **list records** to the first field and displays the list of fields. The modified query is pictured in Figure 11.8.

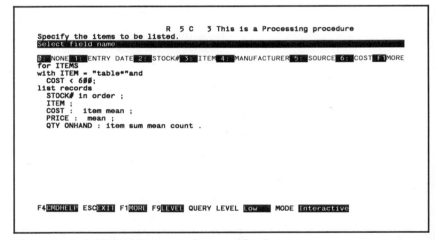

Figure 11.8: INVLISTP query after modification

This time, because you modified the query and added statistics to a field, you must also modify the format and include the new field. In this case, you will recreate the format.

1. Press **F2** to save the query and return to the DQL menu.
2. Modify the format and type **n** so that you do *not* keep the existing format.
3. Accept columnar and when the format displays, press **F2** to save the format.
4. Run the procedure.

CREATING REPORTS WITH THE DATA QUERY LANGUAGE 321

The report, pictured in Figure 11.9, is missing the values in the PRICE column. Since you selected a statistic, but did not include **item**, PRICE was included only in the report totals. Let's correct that:

1. Press **Esc** to clear the report.
2. Select **Modify Query**

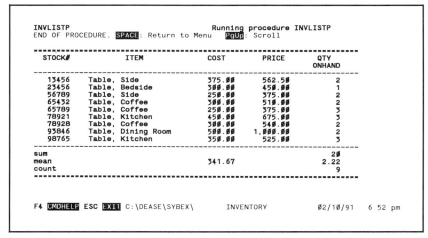

Figure 11.9: Completed INVLISTP report

3. Move the cursor under the "m" in mean for PRICE:

   PRICE : *m*ean

4. Press **Ins**, type **item**, and press **Spacebar** to change the statement to:

   PRICE : item mean ;

5. Press **F2** to save the query.
6. Select **Modify Format** and do not use the existing format.
7. Press **F2** to save the format, and run the procedure again.

Remember, you must modify the format since you added an item.

Compare the new report with Figure 11.10 and notice that now the PRICE field is included in the .items area and at the end of the report.

322 MASTERING DATAEASE

CH. 11

```
INVLISTP                                 Running procedure INVLISTP
END OF PROCEDURE.  SPACE : Return to Menu     PgUp : Scroll
==============================================================================
   STOCK#          ITEM              COST          PRICE        QTY
                                                                ONHAND
------------------------------------------------------------------------------
   13456     Table, Side            375.00        562.50          2
   23456     Table, Bedside         300.00        450.00          1
   56789     Table, Side            250.00        375.00          2
   65432     Table, Coffee          300.00        510.00          2
   65789     Table, Coffee          250.00        375.00          3
   78921     Table, Kitchen         450.00        675.00          3
   78928     Table, Coffee          300.00        540.00          2
   93846     Table, Dining Room     500.00      1,000.00          2
   98765     Table, Kitchen         350.00        525.00          3
------------------------------------------------------------------------------
 sum                                                             20
 mean                               341.67        556.94          2.22
 count                                                            9
==============================================================================


 F4  CMDHELP  ESC  EXIT  C:\DEASE\SYBEX\        INVENTORY      02/10/91   7:29 pm
```

Figure 11.10: INVLISTP report with PRICE field

8. Clear the screen and save the procedure under the same name.

USING OTHER RELATIONAL OPERATORS IN REPORTS

Up to now, you have been using the **all** operator to select all matching records in the related form. However, you have six other operators you can use when selecting records:

- **any** selects the first record that contains a matching value in the related field.

- **count of** counts the number of matching records in the related form for each record processed in the primary form.

- **highest of** selects the highest value in the selected field from each group of matching records.

- **lowest of** selects the lowest value in the selected field from each group of matching records.

- **sum of** totals the value in the selected field from each group of matching records.

CREATING REPORTS WITH THE DATA QUERY LANGUAGE *323*

- **mean of** averages the values of the selected field from each group of matching records.

In Quick Reports, you can select count, max, min, mean, and sum for numeric fields. These statistics are included in your group trailers and/or at the end of the report. However, in DQL these operators can be useful when you want to include summary fields in your .items area.

To demonstrate this, let's prepare a report for the Operations department that lists the total, average, highest, lowest, and count of orders placed for each item in inventory.

The query will include three fields for products ordered. ITEM (from ITEMS), and AMTORD and SOURCE (from ORDERS). Let's begin with the form and record selection. The primary form is ITEMS, since you want all items listed; however, record selection is based on the AMTORD field in ORDERS.

1. Select **Start new procedure**

2. Select **Define Query**

3. Select **ITEMS**

4. Select **with**

5. Press **Tab** twice and select **any**

6. Select **ORDERS** from the list of predefined relationships.

7. Press **Tab** and select **AMTORD**

8. Select **>** and type **0;**

Next, you'll select the fields, beginning with ITEM:

1. Select **ITEM**

2. Select **in order** and type **;**

> You won't select SOURCE from ITEMS, since some SOURCE fields contain the MFR value.

Next, you will include SOURCE from the ORDERS form. However, you do not want *all* records with matching sources; you want DataEase to select the SOURCE from the first matching record.

1. Press **Tab** twice and select **any**

324 MASTERING DATAEASE

CH. 11

This time ORDERS appears in a menu by itself and DataEase prompts:

Select relationship already used in the Query?

DataEase always displays a separate menu of relationships you have used previously in the current query. If you bypass this menu, DataEase displays a list of all relationships. The difference between these two menus will be significant later on when you learn about ad hoc relationships. For now, it doesn't matter.

2. Select **ORDERS**

3. Press **Tab** and select **SOURCE**

4. Type ;

Next, you will select the AMTORD field for each statistic, beginning with **count of**:

> Each time you select a relational operator other than **all**, DataEase prompts you for the form name.

1. Press **Tab** twice and select **count of**

2. Select **ORDERS** and type ;

3. **Tab** twice and select **sum of**

4. Select **ORDERS**

5. Select **AMTORD** and type ;

6. **Tab** twice and select **highest of**

7. Select **ORDERS**

8. Select **AMTORD** and type ;

9. Either use the menus or press ← to leave the menus and type the last two field selections:

   lowest of orders amtord;
   mean of orders amtord

The completed query is listed below:

   for ITEMS
   with any ORDERS AMTORD > 0 ;

CREATING REPORTS WITH THE DATA QUERY LANGUAGE   325

```
list records
   ITEM in order ;
   any ORDERS SOURCE ;
   count of ORDERS ;
   sum of ORDERS AMTORD ;
   highest of ORDERS AMTORD ;
   lowest of ORDERS AMTORD ;
   mean of ORDERS AMTORD
```

10. Type . (period) to save the query and return to the Main
    Menu.

11. Save the procedure as **ORDSTAT**

12. Run the procedure.

As you can see from your report, pictured in Figure 11.11, these
relational operators provide summary information about your
records.

You may want to take the time to edit the format, and if you like,
you can use the example in Figure 11.12 as a guide. The new report
with the modified format is pictured in Figure 11.13.

```
ORDSTAT                              Running procedure ORDSTAT
END OF PROCEDURE. SPACE: Return to Menu    PgUp Home LEFT RIGHT Arrows: Scroll

---------------------------------------------------------------------------------
         ITEM              any ORDERS      count  sum of  highest lowest  mean
                            SOURCE           of   ORDERS    of     of     of
                                           ORDERS AMTORD  ORDERS ORDERS ORDERS
                                                           AMTORD AMTORD AMTORD
---------------------------------------------------------------------------------
   Armoire, Teak          Realco            3      3       1      1      1
   Bed, Queen             Picklepot Furniture 1    2       2      2      2
   Bed, Queen             Real Furniture    1      1       1      1      1
   Bed, Water, King       Country Cousins   1      1       1      1      1
   Bed, Water, Queen      ABC Company       1      1       1      1      1
   Chair, Lounge          Carver's Chairs   2      2       1      1      1
   Chair, Rocker          Country Cousins   2      3       2      1      1
   Sofa, Modern           Terrahaute Furniture 1   2       2      2      2
   Sofa, Modern           Realco            2      4       3      1      2
   Table, Bedside         Beds 'n Things    2      4       3      1      2
   Table, Coffee          Terrahaute Furniture 1   2       2      2      2
   Table, Coffee          Table Tops        1      2       2      2      2
   Table, Dining Room     Real Furniture    1      1       1      1      1
---------------------------------------------------------------------------------

F4 CMDHELP ESC EXIT C:\DEASE\SYBEX\       INVENTORY        02/10/91    7:57 pm
```

Figure 11.11: Completed statistical report

Figure 11.12: Guide for modifying report format

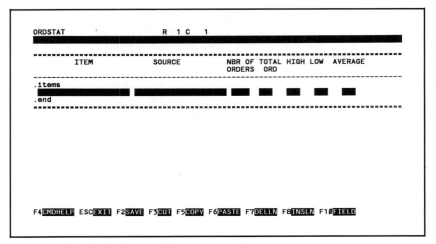

Figure 11.13: Modified ORDSTAT report

CREATING A DQL REPORT USING THREE RELATED FORMS

The Sales department requests a list of all customers and their recent sales and payment history. Since all customers, even inactive

CREATING REPORTS WITH THE DATA QUERY LANGUAGE   327

ones, must be included, CUST will be the primary form. Records matching the CUST# will be selected from INVOICE, the secondary form; records matching the INVOICE# will be selected from the tertiary (third) form, PAYLIST.

Since each record from CUST may have several INVOICE records and each INVOICE record may have several PAYLIST records, to avoid repeating data, you'll group all fields from CUST and INVOICE.

1. Select **Start New Procedure** and select **Define Query**

2. Select **CUST** from the list of forms and type ; to indicate no record selection.

3. Select **CUST# in groups** ;

4. Select **LNAME in groups** ;

Now you are ready to select the fields from INVOICE:

1. Press **Tab** twice to skip to the relational operator menu.

2. Select **all**

3. Select **INVOICE** from the list of predefined relationships.

4. Press **Tab** to skip the **with**

5. Type **1**, then press the **Spacebar** to select **INVOICE#** from the list of fields.

6. Select **in groups** and type ;

7. Press **Tab** twice again and select **all**

8. Select **DATE in groups** and type ;

9. Repeat steps 6 and 7 to select **all INVOICE GRTOT in groups** and type ; to complete the field.

So far, your query includes the following statements:

Remember, since your field list includes ten or more field names, you must enter a space after selecting field 1 to end the selection.

```
for CUST
;
list records
   CUST# in groups ;
   LNAME in groups ;
```

328 MASTERING DATAEASE

CH. 11

> all INVOICE INVOICE# in groups ;
> all INVOICE DATE in groups ;
> all INVOICE GRTOT in groups ;

and DataEase displays the list of fields from the CUST form.

The next few fields, DATE and AMTPD, are from PAYLIST, a tertiary form directly related to INVOICE.

1. **Tab** twice and select **all**

2. Select **PAYLIST** from the menu.

3. Press **Tab** and select **DATE** from the field list. Type ;

4. **Tab** twice and select **all**

5. **Tab** twice and select **all** again.

6. Select **AMTPD** and type ;

Since you already established the link, this time DataEase automatically selects PAYLIST.

So far, your query reads:

```
for CUST
;
list records
    CUST# in groups ;
    LNAME in groups ;
    all INVOICE INVOICE# in groups ;
    all INVOICE DATE in groups ;
    all INVOICE GRTOT in groups ;
    all INVOICE all PAYLIST DATE ;
    all INVOICE all PAYLIST AMTPD ;
```

Using DQL to create reports avoids the problems caused by duplicate field names.

This report also includes two fields called DATE, from two different forms. However, the form names are also included to distinguish each field.

You have one more field to select. The last column in the report should display the BALANCE DUE for each invoice.

7. **Tab** twice and select **all**

8. Select **BALDUE in groups**

CREATING REPORTS WITH THE DATA QUERY LANGUAGE   329

Your completed query should now include the following statements:

```
for CUST
;
list records
    CUST# in groups ;
    LNAME in groups ;
    all INVOICE INVOICE# in groups ;
    all INVOICE DATE in groups ;
    all INVOICE GRTOT in groups ;
    all INVOICE all PAYLIST DATE ;
    all INVOICE all PAYLIST AMTPD ;
    all INVOICE BALDUE in groups
```

9. Type . (period) to end and save the query.

10. Run the procedure.

Like your last report, this report, (shown in Figure 11.14) doesn't include headers and trailers; however, the duplicate values are not repeated. This style is useful when you need to include multiple groups, but want to avoid the clutter of multiple headers and trailers.

Figure 11.14: Completed customer invoice report

330 MASTERING DATAEASE

CH. 11

11. Clear the screen and save the procedure under the name **CUSTINV**

When building a report procedure with more than two related forms, remember the following rules:

- Select as primary the form that contains all the records you want to include. The secondary form must be directly related to the primary form. The tertiary form must be directly related to the secondary form.

- If you use the **all** operator to select matching records from the secondary form, you cannot then select *another* secondary form as your third form. You must choose either the secondary form again or select one of the tertiary forms directly related to the secondary form.

- If you select a fourth form, using the **all** operator, it must be directly related to the third form, and so on.

- If you select any of the other operators, DataEase will then allow you to select from any of the direct or indirect relationships established with the primary form.

USING THE DATA ENTRY FORM TO SELECT RECORDS

The report you just created is very handy if you want to see all the customers. However, what if you wanted to see information on only one customer? You could modify the query each time and enter a different record selection, which seems like a lot of extra trouble. And what if the person running the report doesn't know how to modify the query, or shouldn't do so?

DataEase procedures can include a *data entry form*. This form is designed by you and contains only the fields you want to use for selecting records. For example, you may want to use date fields to select invoices entered during a certain period of time. Then, each time you run your procedure you enter the selection dates.

CREATING REPORTS WITH THE DATA QUERY LANGUAGE **331**

The general steps for creating and using a data entry form are listed below:

- Create the form as you would any other form, including the fields you want to use as selection criteria and any form text that would be helpful to the person filling in the form.

- If you include a lookup in one of the fields, you must create a relationship between the data entry form and the lookup form. The name of the relationship is the name of the procedure.

- Modify the query and include a **with** statement to select records: with <fieldname> = data entry <fieldname>

For this procedure, you'll create a data entry form with two fields: the CUST# field and the LNAME field.

> Though it is not part of the selection, the LNAME value can be displayed, since it is a lookup field based on the value of CUST#.

1. Select **Define Data Entry Form**

DataEase asks:

After running the procedure, display data-entry form again?

If you often run reports on several customers, you'll want to redisplay the form after running each report.

2. Type **Y** to redisplay the form.

This form definition will also contain special instructions for selecting customers.

> The wild card characters * and ? can be used in the Record Entry form to select multiple records.

3. Use the information below to enter the form text.

<pre>
                                        FIRST RECORD IN GROUP
ENTER CUSTOMER#:

OR:
ENTER ???? FOR ALL CUSTOMERS
ENTER 000? FOR CUSTOMERS 1-9
ENTER ??1? FOR CUSTOMER 10-19
ENTER ??2? FOR CUSTOMER'S 20-29 ETC.
</pre>

332 MASTERING DATAEASE

CH. 11

4. Use the information below to define the fields:

NAME	TYPE	LENGTH	REQ?	DERIV. FORM.
CUST#	Numeric String	4	yes	
LNAME	Text	15		LOOKUP CUST LNAME

If the wild card characters are used, DataEase will look up and display the LNAME of the first record in that selected group.

Information in a data entry form is stored temporarily during the processing of the procedure. Therefore, you cannot define fields as indexed, unique, sequenced, or virtual, or with security level options. You also cannot include subforms.

Next, let's modify the query to include the record selection statement.

1. Press **F2** to save the form.

2. Select **Modify Query**

3. Move the cursor to Row 2, Column 1 under the ;

4. Press **F1** and select **with**

5. Select **CUST#**, and select = . The data entry form you created is now included as part of the query menus.

6. Select **data entry**

7. Select **CUST#** and type **;** to end the record selection.

The additional query statement:

```
for CUST
with CUST# = data-entry CUST# ;
```

tells DataEase to select only records that match the CUST# in the data entry form.

8. Press **F2** to save the query.

9. Save the procedure under a new name, CUSTQRY.

CREATING REPORTS WITH THE DATA QUERY LANGUAGE   333

Next, to copy the LNAME from the CUST form, you must create the relationship between the data entry form, called CUSTQRY, and the CUST form:

1. Press **Esc** to exit to the Main Menu.
2. Select **Form Definition**
3. Select **Define Relationships**
4. Select **CUST**
5. **Tab** to the field for Form 2.

Data entry forms are not included in the list of form names displayed in the Form Relationship screen. To enter the data entry form name, you must clear the menu:

1. Press **Esc** to clear the menu.
2. Type **CUSTQRY** (the name of the procedure).
3. **Tab** twice and select **CUST#** from the field list.
4. Type **CUST#** as the related field from the data entry form. The completed relationship record is pictured in Figure 11.15.

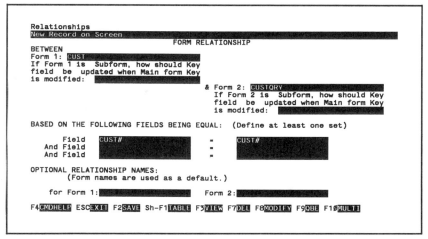

Figure 11.15: Completed relationship record for CUSTQRY

334 MASTERING DATAEASE

CH. 11

5. Save the record and return to the DQL menu.

Now you are ready to test your procedure.

1. Load the **CUSTQRY** procedure.
2. Run the procedure.
3. Enter **3** as the CUST# for Grey.
4. Press **F2** to save the record. Your report includes only records for Grey.
5. Press **Esc** to clear the report.

The data entry form redisplays and waits for you to make another selection. This time, display all records:

6. Type **????** and press **F2** to save. Now all records are displayed.

Try one more on your own. Display customers 10 through 19.

MODIFYING A DATA ENTRY FORM

You can modify a data entry form just as you modify any form. However, when you select Modify data-entry form, the first question DataEase asks is:

Delete data-entry form?

not

After running the procedure, display data-entry form again?

So don't get finger-happy and type Y, anticipating the wrong question. Type N unless you really want to delete it. Following that, DataEase will ask you if you want to display it again each time.

As you can see, using the DQL to create your reports offers greater flexibility and power. In the next chapter, you will increase your report capabilities with high level queries.

CREATING REPORTS WITH THE DATA QUERY LANGUAGE   *335*

SECURITY NOTES

If you have a low security level you can only run an existing procedure from a custom menu or from the DQL menu. You cannot run an existing procedure by pressing F9 to move between Record Entry, Quick Reports, and DQL.

If you have a low or medium security level, you can define and run procedures, but not save them.

DataEase checks your security level when you define a query. If you do not have view rights to a form for which you are currently processing a **list records**, the following message is displayed:

Not authorized to view this form

If you do not have view rights to a field you are including in a **list records**, the following message is displayed:

Not authorized to view this field

CHAPTER TWELVE

Creating
High Level Queries

Fast Track

To switch to the high level query menu,   339
press **F9** from the query screen.

To save a high level query menu,   344
type . (period) after the last statement. If you are using the menus, press **Tab** to
save and return to the DQL menu. If you are not using the menus, press **F2**,
then press **Tab** when the high level menu is displayed.

To create an ad hoc relationship in a query   346
using the menus, select the first form from the menu. Press **Tab** twice and select
the relational operator. Next, select the second form. Press **Tab** and select **with**.
Then select the criteria by which the records are to be selected.

To modify the print style   351
each time you run the procedure, select Define or Modify Print Style from the
DQL menu. Select Yes following the Allow Style Modification at Runtime?
prompt. Each time you run the procedure, the Print Style Specification screen
will display first.

To print your procedure specification,   353
select Print Procedure from the DQL menu.

CHAPTER 12

IN THE LAST CHAPTER, YOU CREATED SEVERAL LOW level report queries. Low level queries are adequate for creating simple multiform reports. However, if you use the high level query to create your report procedure, you can also:

- Create calculated fields and include them in report statistics.
- Use comparison operators to test fields.
- Use the blank comparison operator to select records with null field values.
- Calculate percentages on tested fields.

In this chapter, you will create report procedures that include calculated fields, comparison operators, and percentages.

THE HIGH LEVEL QUERY MENU

Since high level queries offer a wide variety of commands and features, there are a few points you should note when creating a high level query:

- Press **F9** to use the high level menus.
- A low level query always begins with a **for** statement; a high level query can begin with any of 35 commands.
- Each command is completed by typing . (period). A few, such as the **for** statement, must be followed by the **end** statement.
- When you complete a command, the high level query menu appears again. You may begin another command or press **Tab** to save the query and return to the DQL menu.

340 MASTERING DATAEASE

CH. 12

INCLUDING CALCULATED FIELDS IN A REPORT QUERY

In Chapter 5, you created a calculated field called INVEST that multiplied QTY ONHAND by COST. This field was not included in any group or report statistics. However, the high level query allows you to create calculated fields as part of the query and include them in the statistics.

The Accounting department needs a salesperson commission report organized by store. Since Furniture Palace pays commissions after they receive payment from the customer, this report must include both projected commissions (based on total sales to date) and commissions paid (based on payments received by customers).

The primary form will be SP; INVOICE and PAYLIST will act as secondary and tertiary forms, respectively.

1. Select **Start New Procedure**

2. Select **Define Query**

3. Press **F9**

4. Select **SP** and type ; to skip record selection.

5. Press **F1** to display all the choices.

The bottom of your screen shows that the query level, usually low, is now high.

Take a look at your screen and compare it to Figure 12.1. In a high level query, **list records** is the first selection in a menu that contains 35 different commands.

6. Use ↓ to move through the list to the end.

7. When finished press **Home** to return to the top of the list.

This menu contains three types of commands: processing, procedural, and control. You'll learn about the last two in later chapters. Processing commands are used to access records for selection, input, or output. You've already worked with two processing commands: **list records** and **for**. In the following chapters, you'll work with **modify records**, **delete records**, **enter a record**, and **input**. You'll continue to work with **list records** for the next two reports.

CREATING HIGH LEVEL QUERIES   341

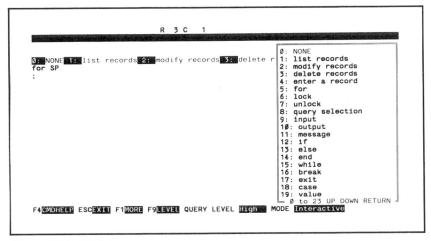

Figure 12.1: High level query menu

1. Select **list records**
2. Select **store**

Next, DataEase displays another high level menu of comparison operators. These operators allow you to test field values. Skip this menu for now.

3. Press **Tab**
4. Select **In groups with group-totals**

Next, DataEase asks for any statistics. Skip this menu.

5. Type ;
6. Select **LNAME** and type ;
7. Press **F1** to display all field names and select **TOTSALES**
8. Type :, press **Spacebar** and select **item sum**
9. Type ;

> You can include statistics on any field type. However, DataEase will not give statistics on grouped fields, even though the menu asks for statistics.

CH. 12

So far, you have:

```
for SP
;
list records
    STORE in groups with group-totals ;
    LNAME ;
    TOTSALES : item sum ;
```

The next two fields are calculated fields. Projected commissions are derived by multiplying COMMRATE by TOTSALES, fields that are both found in SP.

1. Select **COMMRATE**

2. Select *

3. Press **Tab** five times and select **TOTSALES**

4. Type :, press **Spacebar**, select **item sum** and type ;

The query statement reads:

```
COMMRATE * TOTSALES : item sum ;
```

COMPARING FIELD VALUES

Comparison operators can be used to test the contents of any field value, returning a yes/no result. For example, TOTAL>CREDIT LIMIT would return a yes result if the value in the TOTAL field were greater than the value in the CREDIT LIMIT field. The next field in your report is a test field.

Furniture Palace has a special club called the Over $10,000 Club for salespeople who have sold more than $10,000 in furniture during a quarter. DataEase will determine the value of TOTSALES for each record processed and if it is over $10,000, DataEase will display yes for that record; otherwise, it will display no.

1. Select **TOTSALES**, press **Tab** twice and select >

2. Type **10000** and press **Spacebar**

3. Type : and press **Spacebar**

CREATING HIGH LEVEL QUERIES **343**

Whenever you use a comparison operator in a field selection, Data-Ease includes **percent** in the Statistics menu.

4. select **item percent** and type ;

So far your query reads:

```
for SP
;
list records
    STORE in groups with group-totals ;
    LNAME ;
    TOTSALES : item sum ;
    COMMRATE * TOTSALES : item sum ;
    TOTSALES > 10000 : item percent ;
```

The last field contains the actual commissions paid to date, derived by multiplying the commission rate (COMMRATE) by the total payments (AMTPD) applied against invoices for each salesperson. Ready?

Remember, PAY-LIST, which contains AMTPD, is directly related to INVOICE.

You are selecting **sum of** because you cannot use **all of** or **any** as operators when creating a calculated field.

1. Press **Tab** two times and select **sum of**

2. Select **INVOICE** from the list of predefined relationships.

3. Press **Tab** four times and select **sum of**

4. Select **PAYLIST**

5. Press **Tab** two times and select **AMTPD**

6. Select *

7. Press **Tab** five times and select **COMMRATE**

8. Type :, press **Spacebar** and select **item sum**

This last statement,

```
sum of INVOICE sum of PAYLIST AMTPD * COMMRATE : item
    sum
```

tells DataEase to total the AMTPD values applied to invoices for each salesperson.

344 MASTERING DATAEASE

CH. 12

Your completed query is listed below:

```
for SP
;
list records
    STORE in groups with group-totals ;
    LNAME ;
    TOTSALES : item sum ;
    COMMRATE * TOTSALES : item sum ;
    TOTSALES > 10000 : item percent ;
    sum of INVOICE sum of PAYLIST AMTPD * COMMRATE : item
        sum
```

9. Type . (period) to end the query.

Each processing command in a high level query ends when you type a period. DataEase then redisplays the first high level menu, from which you can select another processing command. To save your query and return to the DQL menu, you must press Tab when this menu is displayed.

10. Press **Tab**

Before you edit the format, let's run the procedure and take a quick look at the results.

1. Select **Run Procedure**

The yes or no is always displayed in lowercase.

The report, displayed in Figure 12.2, displays **yes** or **no** in the test field for TOTSALES. Although the projected commissions are displayed, the COMMRATE * TOTSALES field shows no value. Let's modify the format and find out why that happened. Also, this report might look better with group headers and trailers.

2. Clear the screen.

To improve the looks of the percent field, you can change the type to integer and type % after the field.

3. Save the procedure as **SPCOMM**

4. Select **Define Format**, accept columnar, and include headers and trailers.

CREATING HIGH LEVEL QUERIES **345**

```
                              Running procedure
SPACE or PgDn: Continue procedure EXIT: Abort procedure PgUp: Scroll

===================================================================
        STORE           LNAME        TOTSALES   COMMRATE TOTSALES   sum of
                                                    *        >      INVOICE sum
                                                 TOTSALES  10000    of PAYLIST
                                                                     AMTPD *
                                                                     COMMRATE
-------------------------------------------------------------------
   Chicago           Winters        11,150.00     .00     yes        540.00
                     Johnson         5,490.00     .00     no         250.00
-------------------------------------------------------------------
   sum                              16,640.00 ,887.00                790.00
   percent                                             50.00
===================================================================
   Cleveland         Engel           9,380.00     .00     no         474.88
                     Clifford        8,300.00     .00     no         715.00
-------------------------------------------------------------------
   sum                              17,680.00 ,017.00              1,189.88
   percent                                          0.00
===================================================================
   Detroit           Green           5,130.00     .00     no         546.34
                     Fuller          5,450.00     .00     no         280.00
F4 CMDHELP ESC EXIT C:\DEASE\SYBEX\      INVENTORY      02/04/91   8 22 pm
```

Figure 12.2: Preliminary salesperson commission report

5. Move the cursor to the COMMRATE * TOTSALES field and press **F10**.

The maximum number of characters to the left of the decimal is 0, not enough to display a whole number. DataEase bases the type and length of a calculated field on those of the first field in the calculation, in this case COMMRATE. You can correct this by reversing the operands in the formula:

1. Change the number of digits to the left of the decimal to **5**

2. Press **F2** to save the change.

3. Delete and insert spaces as necessary to align the right edges of your number fields.

4. If you want to edit the report format, you can use Figure 12.3 as a guide to change the column and row headings.

5. When you are finished, save the format and run the procedure. The finished report with format modifications is displayed in Figure 12.4.

6. Save the procedure again under the same name.

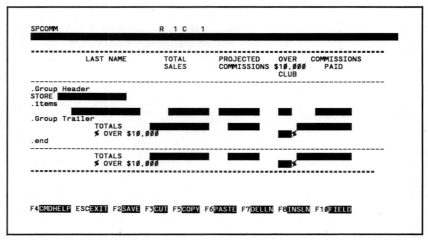

Figure 12.3: Completed format for salesperson report

Figure 12.4: Completed salesperson commission report

ADDING AN AD HOC RELATIONSHIP TO A PROCEDURE

Accounting wants a summary list of customer balances that includes invoice and balance due totals for each customer. That's easy. The invoice total can be found in the TOTSALES field for each

CREATING HIGH LEVEL QUERIES **347**

customer in the CUST form. The balance can be derived from SUM OF BALDUE in the related form, INVOICE.

In addition to current balances, Accounting wants information about customers who tend to take more than 60 days to complete payments. They want to know:

- How many payments were received after 60 days.

- The sum of payments received after 60 days.

- The percentage of payments received after 60 days.

To do this, you'll create an ad hoc relationship between INVOICE and PAYLIST. An ad hoc relationship is entered in a query to select records in a related form. This relationship is temporary and stays in effect only during the current procedure.

Let's begin with CUST as the primary form and select customers with values greater than 0 in TOTSALES.

1. Select **Start new Procedure**

2. Select **Define Query**

3. Press **F9** for high level.

4. Select **with**

5. Select **TOTSALES > 0;**

6. Select **list records**

7. Select **CUST#** and type ;

8. Select **LNAME** and type ;

9. Select **TOTSALES**, type :, press **Spacebar**, select **item sum max**, and type ;

> Remember, now that you have double digit selections, you cannot just type 1 to select **list records**; you must type 1, then press the Spacebar to complete the selection, otherwise DataEase waits for a second digit.

So far your query reads:

```
for CUST
with TOTSALES > 0 ;
list records
    CUST# ;
    LNAME ;
    TOTSALES : item sum max ;
```

348 *MASTERING DATAEASE*

CH. 12

The next field, total balances for each customer, is in the secondary form, INVOICE. This time you'll use more shortcuts to skip menus.

1. Press **Tab** twice and select **sum of**

2. Select **INVOICE**, press **Tab** twice and type **BALDUE:**

3. Press **Spacebar** and select **item sum max** and type ;

> Since you want summary, not itemized information, you won't use the **all** operator to select INVOICE.

The next field counts the number of payments made over 60 days after the invoice date. To select these records, you will need to create the ad hoc relationship between PAYLIST and INVOICE. Let's begin:

1. **Tab** twice and select **sum of**

2. Select **INVOICE** from the list of relationships already used in the query.

3. Press **Tab** twice and select **count of**

4. Select **PAYLIST**

5. Press **Tab** to skip the next menu and select **with**

6. Select **DATE**, press **Tab**, and select >

7. Select **INVOICE**

8. Select **DATE**

9. Select +

10. Press **Tab**, type **60**, press **Spacebar**, select), and type ;

> You used **sum of INVOICE** to access the secondary form, PAYLIST. **count of** only counts occurrences within the current form.

Now your query reads:

```
for CUST
with TOTSALES > 0 ;
list records
   CUST# ;
   LNAME ;
   TOTSALES : item sum max ;
   sum of INVOICE BALDUE : item sum max ;
   sum of INVOICE count of PAYLIST with ( DATE > INVOICE DATE +
        60 ) ;
```

CREATING HIGH LEVEL QUERIES **349**

The next field calculates the sum of the payments made after 60 days. This will be similar to the above statement; but since you want totals, not the number of occurrences, you will use **sum of** in place of **count of**. The ad hoc relationship is still in effect.

1. **Tab** twice and select **sum of**

2. Select **INVOICE**

3. Press **Tab** twice and select **sum of**

DataEase asks if you want to use the relationship previously created with PAYLIST in this query, referring to the ad hoc relationship you just defined.

4. Select **PAYLIST**

5. Select **AMTPD** and type **;**

DataEase skipped right to the field list, since you selected the ad hoc relationship PAYLIST.

The last field calculates the percentage of payments made after 60 days. This is actually a repeat of the above statement; however, you'll divide the results by the TOTSALES fields to get the percentage.

1. Use the menus, copy and edit, or type to enter the last statement:

   sum of INVOICE sum of PAYLIST AMTPD / TOTSALES

Your query is complete:

```
for CUST
with TOTSALES > 0 ;
list records
  CUST# ;
  LNAME ;
  TOTSALES : item sum max ;
  sum of INVOICE BALANCE : item sum max ;
sum of INVOICE count of PAYLIST with ( DATE > INVOICE DATE +
      60 ) ;
sum of INVOICE sum of PAYLIST AMT PD;
sum of INVOICE sum of PAYLIST AMTPD / TOTSALES
```

350 MASTERING DATAEASE

CH. 12

2. Enter . (period) to end the query.

3. If the menus are active, press **Tab** to save the query; if not, press **F2**, then **Tab** to save the query.

4. Save this procedure under **OVER60**

5. Run the procedure.

Let's compare this report, pictured in Figure 12.5, with your **CUSTQRY** report to verify that the information is correct. If you don't have a printout, refer to Figure 12.6.

```
OVER6Ø                                      Running procedure OVER6Ø
SPACE or PgDn: More   EXIT: Abort PgUp Home LEFT RIGHT Arrows: Scroll
========================================================================
CUST      LNAME       TOTSALES      sum of      sum of    sum of    sum of
  #                                 INVOICE     INVOICE   INVOICE   INVOICE
                                    BALDUE      count of  sum of    sum of
                                                PAYLIST   PAYLIST   PAYLIST
                                                with (    AMTPD     AMTPD /
                                                DATE >              TOTSALES
                                                INVOICE
                                                DATE + 6Ø
                                                )
------------------------------------------------------------------------
ØØØ1 Enis               1Ø,241.45   3,6Ø7.45 1            2,134.ØØ    Ø.21
ØØØ2 Smith              17,632.63  13,132.63 2            3,5ØØ.ØØ    Ø.2Ø
ØØØ3 Grey               15,592.ØØ  1Ø,Ø92.ØØ 2            1,5ØØ.ØØ    Ø.1Ø
ØØØ5 Heida              11,213.2Ø   3,749.75 1            1,463.45    Ø.13
ØØØ6 Edwards             7,625.33   4,932.Ø5 1            1,ØØØ.ØØ    Ø.13
ØØØ7 Clark               2,742.38   1,292.38 1              25Ø.ØØ    Ø.Ø9
ØØØ8 Green              13,626.99   6,558.84 1            2,5ØØ.ØØ    Ø.18
ØØ11 Jones               4,748.8Ø       Ø.ØØ Ø                Ø.ØØ    Ø.ØØ
ØØ14 Porter              8,546.63     546.63 2            5,ØØØ.ØØ    Ø.59
------------------------------------------------------------------------
F4 CMDHELP ESC EXIT C:\DEASE\SYBEX\        INVENTORY      Ø2/19/91   8 29 am
```

Figure 12.5: OVER60 report

For example, look at Grey's record and compare it with his record in CUSTPMT. As you can see, this customer made two payments 60 days after the invoice date, for a total of $1500, which represents approximately 11% of his total payments made so far.

If you want to improve the appearance of the column headings, you can use Figure 12.7 as a guide to making modifications. The completed report after modifications is picture in Figure 12.8.

```
CUSTQRY                                   Running procedure CUSTQRY
SPACE or PgDn: More  EXIT: Abort PgUp Home LEFT RIGHT Arrows: Scroll
============================================================================
  CUST#    LNAME        all      all       all      all       all      all
                       INVOICE  INVOICE   INVOICE  INVOICE   INVOICE  INVOICE
                       INVOICE#  DATE     GRTOT     all       all     BALDUE
                                                   PAYLIST   PAYLIST
                                                    DATE      AMTPD
----------------------------------------------------------------------------
  0001    Enis          0004    05/15/91  4,134.00 06/15/91  2,000.00   0.00
                                                   07/20/91  2,134.00
                        0012    06/02/91  2,907.45 07/15/91  1,500.00 407.45
                                                   07/20/91  1,000.00
  0002    Smith         0003    05/10/91  5,032.13 06/15/91  1,000.00 532.13
                                                   07/20/91    500.00
                                                   08/15/91  3,000.00
                        0013    06/05/91  6,810.50                    6,810.50
  0003    Grey          0001    05/01/91  8,798.00 05/20/91  2,000.00 3,298.00
                                                   06/29/91  2,000.00
                                                   07/16/91    500.00
                                                   08/16/91  1,000.00
                        0006    05/22/91  5,194.00                    5,194.00
  0004    Crawl
F4 CMDHELP ESC EXIT C:\DEASE\SYBEX\         INVENTORY       02/04/91  9 33 pm
```

Figure 12.6: CUSTQRY report

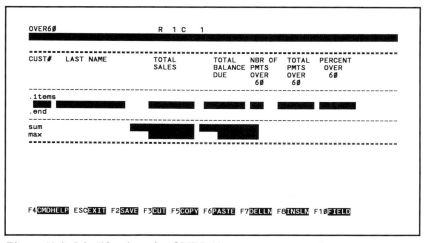

Figure 12.7: Modifications for OVER60 report

MODIFYING THE PRINT STYLE BEFORE RUNNING THE PROCEDURE

In past exercises, you may have stopped to modify the Print Style Specification screen when you wanted to change the destination or

352 MASTERING DATAEASE

CH. 12

```
OVER6Ø                               Running procedure OVER6Ø
END OF PROCEDURE. SPACE: Return to Menu  PgUp Home LEFT RIGHT Arrows: Scroll

=======================================================================
CUST#   LAST NAME         TOTAL      TOTAL   NBR OF  TOTAL   PERCENT
                          SALES      BALANCE PMTS    PMTS    OVER
                                     DUE     OVER    OVER    6Ø
                                             6Ø      6Ø
-----------------------------------------------------------------------
ØØØ1 Enis             1Ø,241.45    3,6Ø7.45 1    2,154.ØØ   Ø.21
ØØØ2 Smith            17,652.63   13,132.63 2    5,5ØØ.ØØ   Ø.2Ø
ØØØ3 Grey             15,592.ØØ   1Ø,Ø92.ØØ 2    1,5ØØ.ØØ   Ø.1Ø
ØØØ5 Heida            11,213.2Ø    3,749.75 1    1,465.45   Ø.13
ØØØ6 Edwards           7,625.33    4,932.Ø5 1    1,ØØØ.ØØ   Ø.13
ØØØ7 Clark             2,742.38    1,292.38 1      25Ø.ØØ   Ø.Ø9
ØØØ8 Green            13,626.99    6,558.84 1    2,5ØØ.ØØ   Ø.18
ØØ11 Jones             4,748.8Ø        Ø.ØØ Ø        Ø.ØØ   Ø.ØØ
ØØ14 Porter            8,546.63      546.63 2    5,ØØØ.ØØ   Ø.59
-----------------------------------------------------------------------
sum                   91,969.41   43,911.73
max                   17,652.63   13,132.63
=======================================================================

F4 CMDHELP ESC EXIT C:\DEASE\SYBEX\        INVENTORY       Ø2/19/91   8:5Ø am
```

Figure 12.8: OVER60 report after modifications

modify the report layout. If you make changes to this screen often, you can save yourself a step by asking DataEase to display this screen each time you run a report or procedure. The Print Style Specification screen includes the field Allow Style Modification at Runtime?. Select **yes** to display the screen each time you run the procedure.

1. Select **Define Print Style**

2. When the screen displays, press **Tab** to move to the field:

   Allow Style Modification at Runtime?

3. Select **yes** and save the modification. DataEase asks

   Do You Want to Complete Specification at Runtime?

4. Select **yes** and run the procedure again.

As you requested, DataEase displays the Print Style Specification screen.

5. Make any changes you like and then press **F2** to continue the procedure.

6. Save the report with this new change and use the same name.

You can also use the CURRENT DATE for comparisons. For example, you can include aged invoices by comparing the invoice date with the current date. For example,

(INVOICE DATE − CURRENT DATE) > 60 and BALDUE > 0

would select open invoices over 60 days old as of today.

PRINTING YOUR PROCEDURES

In Chapter 2, you printed your form definition. It is equally important to keep hard copy documentation about your reports and queries, especially as your queries become more complex. It can be difficult to retrace your steps after you have spent hours developing a query to perfection. So before continuing, let's get into the habit of printing each procedure by starting with this one.

1. Select **Print Procedure Definition**

The printed procedure includes the query statements and format. As you can see, you would have no trouble rebuilding from this information. The only step omitted is any relationship you might have created between forms. It would be a good idea to print each query you create from this book. That way, you have a quick reference if you need to recreate a similar query for your own applications.

You have gotten a small sampling of the wide variety of reports you can create with the high level DQL commands. Applied to your own work requirements, these concepts and commands should allow you to build powerful database applications. Next, you'll learn how to use the DQL to make changes to your database.

CHAPTER THIRTEEN

Modifying Your Database with High Level Queries

Fast Track

To modify selected records using a procedure, 357

select **modify records** from the high level query menu. Select the form name from the list, unless you have already selected the form with a **for** statement. Following the **modify records** statement, select the fields to be modified one at a time, along with their new values.

To add a record to a form using a procedure, 368

select **enter a record** from the high level query menu, then select the form name. One at a time, select the fields from the form and enter their new values.

To use a conditional if statement in a query, 369

select **if** from the high level query menu. Select the condition, followed by the statement that DataEase will execute if the condition is true. Follow this with an optional **else** statement that tells DataEase what to do if the statement is false. Complete the series of statements with **end**.

To select records for processing from a temporary input form, 375

select **input using** from the high level query menu. Select the name of the existing form from which you want to select records, and enter the name of the temporary input form. Next, select the form that contains the records you want to process. Select the criteria on which the records are selected (usually these are matching field values from both the selected form and the input form). Then select the command for processing the records, such as **list records**, **modify records**, or **enter a record**.

CHAPTER 13

IN THE LAST TWO CHAPTERS, YOU CONCENTRATED ON using the DQL to build more sophisticated reports. In addition to enhancing your report capabilities, you can use the DQL to:

- Add, modify, or delete records in related forms.
- Create custom applications for your inventory, accounts receivable, or sales.
- Link separate tasks such as record entry, processing records, and creating reports in one procedure.

The DQL can be used as a decision-making tool to select the appropriate records for processing, to select the appropriate report format, and even to select a custom-designed user menu.

What if the cost of all products from ABC company were increased by ten percent? In Chapter 4, you learned how to modify and delete individual records. It can be very time consuming to modify a large number of records. However, if you are updating records that have some values in common, you can process the modifications with a simple DQL query.

In this chapter, you will learn how to create DQL procedures to change and add information in existing records. In addition, you'll learn how to use a query to *add* records to your database.

USING A HIGH LEVEL QUERY TO MAKE GLOBAL CHANGES

ABC Company has indeed increased the cost of its products by ten percent. You can use **modify records**, one of the high level processing commands, to change field values in the primary form or a related form. The source of the field modifications can be either a list of

CH. 13

modified field values or another related form. The format of the command is:

```
modify records in (FORMNAME/RELATIONSHIP) [named
(UNIQUE RELATIONSHIP NAME] [with (selection criteria)]
    FIELDNAME : = MODIFIED VALUE
```

It may seem a little complicated, but let's look at an example:

```
modify records in ITEMS with (MFR = "ABC COMPANY");
    COST : = COST * 1.1 .
```

This example modifies records in a related form selected with the **in** statement.

Here is another example:

```
for ITEMS
with MFR = 'ABC COMPANY';
modify records
    COST : = COST * 1.1 .
end
```

The second example begins with a **for** statement and modifies records in the primary form. The **for** statement in a high level query is always completed with the **end** statement.

In both examples, the list of modified fields follows and the last item ends with the . (period).

In the next exercise, you'll modify the COST field in ITEMS, the primary form, and include **list records** to verify the modifications.

The query you'll create is listed below:

```
for ITEMS
with MANUFACTURER = "ABC Company";
list records
    STOCK# ;
    ITEM ;
    COST ;
    PRICE .
modify records
COST : = COST * 1.1 .
```

```
list records
    COST ;
    PRICE .
end
```

This query begins with a **list records** that will show COST and PRICE for each item *before* modification. DataEase does not display the results of any **list records** until after the query is completed. However, the *value* of the displayed fields is determined by any processing commands which precede the **list fields**. So in this case, the fields from the second **list records** will display the values *after* the modification. PRICE is included as well because it too will increase automatically as the COST changes.

Notice that each processing command is completed by . (period).

TYPING QUERY STATEMENTS WITH THE MENUS ACTIVE

As you know, whenever you move the cursor backwards, you exit the menus. However, as long as you move forward, whether you are typing or moving the cursor forward through existing query statements, the menus stay active, changing as you move from word to word.

So this time, you'll try something a little different and type the statements with the menus active. Watch how the menus change as you type the statements.

You can type your query in uppercase or lowercase.

Type slowly and keep an eye on your query as you type. For example, when you type ; or . (period) to end a field or command, DataEase returns you to the next line. If you make a typo, DataEase *will* beep at you; however, in most cases, you can backspace and correct your error. If the menus give you a hard time, "back out" of them, fix the mistake, and continue with the menus.

1. If necessary, select **Start new procedure**

2. Select **Define Query** and press **F9** to switch to high level.

360 MASTERING DATAEASE

CH. 13

3. Create the following query statements:

```
for items
with manufacturer = "abc company";
list records
   stock# ;
   item ;
   cost ;
   price .
modify records
```

When you type the field name and press Spacebar in the next statement, DataEase automatically enters the : = .

```
cost : = cost * 1.1 .
list records
   cost ;
   price .
end
```

If you make a mistake, DataEase sounds a beep and displays the appropriate menu selection. If you are a proficient typist, you can type the statements faster than you can make menu selections. However, if you make a mistake while typing, DataEase will catch it immediately. And if you are unsure of the next step, you can just let the menus take over.

> If you include other processing commands in the high level query along with **list records,** you *must* define the report format or no records will be listed.

1. When you have completed the query, press **Tab** to save it and return to the DQL menu.

2. Save the report under the name NEWCOST.

3. Select **Define Format** and accept all defaults.

4. When the format is displayed, save it and run the procedure.

> When you type the entire query in lowercase, as you did above, the column headings in your report will appear in lowercase.

The report, displayed in Figure 13.1, shows the COST and PRICE fields before and after modification.

Although this query only takes a few moments to build, if there are frequent cost changes, you might prefer to use a data entry form with

MODIFYING YOUR DATABASE WITH HIGH LEVEL QUERIES 361

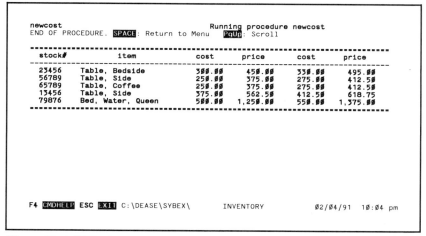

Figure 13.1: NEWCOST report showing COST and PRICE before and after modification

fields for the MANUFACTURER and the current COST (or PRICE). In that case, your query would be:

```
for ITEMS
with MANUFACTURER = data-entry MANUFACTURER ;
list records
   STOCK# ;
   ITEM ;
   MANUFACTURER ;
   COST .
modify records
COST : = data-entry COST * 1.1 .
list records
   COST .
end
```

You could also use this query to change the cost of items from various manufacturers. In that case, the data entry form would contain the STOCK#, ITEM, and a field for the new cost. However, since DataEase executes the entire procedure each time you enter another data entry record, you may want to omit the **list fields**. In Chapter 15, you will learn about control procedures, which allow you to run several different procedures automatically.

362 *MASTERING DATAEASE*

CH. 13

USING A HIGH LEVEL QUERY TO RECORD SHIPMENTS

When a shipment arrives from a vendor, two forms must be updated: ORDERS and ITEMS. For each STOCK# received, the DATEREC and AMTREC must be entered in ORDERS, and the QTY ONHAND field must be updated in ITEMS. A simple procedure with a data entry form will update *both* these forms for you automatically.

The data entry form will include the date the shipment was received, the stock number, the order number, and the amount received. It will also contain LOOKUP fields for the item name and quantity ordered. Let's begin by creating the data entry form.

1. Start a new procedure and define a data entry form.

2. Answer **Y** to redisplay the form.

3. Use the layout below as a guide to placing the form text:

SHIPMENTS RECEIVED

DATE: STOCK#:   ORDER#:

ITEM: AMTREC: AMTORD:

4. Use the information in Table 13.1 to define each field.

5. Save the form.

Next, you'll define the query. ORDERS will be the primary form and ITEMS the related form.

1. Define the query.

2. Press **F9** and type or select the following query statements:

```
for ORDERS
with (ORDER# = data-entry ORDER# and
stock# = data-entry stock#);
modify records
    DATEREC : = data-entry DATE ;
    AMTREC : = data-entry AMTREC .
```

The indents shown in the lines below will appear if you use the menus; if you type the statements, you are not required to add indents, though they will make the query easier to read.

> modify records in ITEMS with (STOCK# = data-entry
> STOCK#)
>   QTY ONHAND : = data-entry AMTREC + QTY ONHAND .
> end

3. Press **Tab** to save the query.

4. Save the procedure under the name **ORDREC**

Table 13.1: Field Definition for the Data Entry Form.

NAME	TYPE	LENGTH	REQ?	DERIV. FORM.	PREVENT DATA ENTRY?
DATE	Date			??/??/??	no
STOCK#	Numeric String	5	yes		
ORDER#	Numeric String	4	yes		
ITEM	Text	20		LOOKUP ORDERS ITEM	yes
AMTREC	Number	3	yes		
AMTORD	Number	3		LOOKUP ORDERS AMTORD	yes

CREATING A RELATIONSHIP BASED ON TWO FIELDS

In order to look up the ITEM and AMTORD in ORDERS, you must establish a relationship between ORDERS and the data entry form, ORDREC. Up to now the relationships you have established have been linked by only one field. However, the ORDERS form contains *two* fields that make each record unique and that must match the data entry form: STOCK# and ORDER#. To copy the correct ITEM and QTYORD, DataEase must find the record that matches both the ORDER# and STOCK# fields.

Let's return to the Form Definition menu and create this relationship:

1. Press **Esc** to return the Main Menu and select **Form Definition**
2. Select **Define Relationship**
3. When the Relationship form is displayed, select **ORDERS** as Form 1.
4. **Tab** to the Form 2 field and press **Esc** to clear the menu.
5. Type **ORDREC** for Form 2 and **Tab** twice to select the field from ORDERS.
6. Select **ORDER#**
7. Type **ORDER#** as the field for Form 2.
8. Press **Tab** and select **STOCK#** as the second match field from Form 1.
9. Type **STOCK#** as the second match field for Form 2.
10. Save the record and return to the DQL menu.

Remember that this menu does not display data-entry form names.

The completed record is pictured in Figure 13.2.

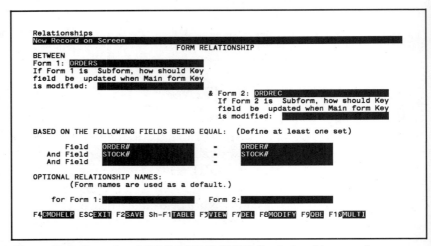

Figure 13.2: Completed ORDREC-ORDERS relationship record

MODIFYING YOUR DATABASE WITH HIGH LEVEL QUERIES   *365*

SWITCHING TO QUICK REPORTS

Before you run the report, let's create a quick report showing the current QTY ONHAND for each item. You can create the same report with the DQL, but this way is much faster; that's why they call it a quick report. You can switch to the Quick Reports menu from DQL by pressing F9.

Before you can use F9 to switch between DQL and Quick Reports, you must first clear any current report or procedure.

1. Press **F9**

The Quick Reports menu is displayed and you can begin:

2. Select **Define List Fields** and select **ITEMS**

3. Select the following fields:

STOCK#

ITEM

QTY ONHAND

4. Save the selection and print the report.

If you have no printer available, just skip to the next step. You can display this report later after processing your procedure.

5. Save the report as QTY.

Next, create a quick report from orders, which you'll print after running the procedure:

1. Select **Start New Report** to clear the report.

2. Select **Define List Fields** and select **ORDERS**

3. Select all fields *except* ITEM and SOURCE.

4. Return to the Quick Reports menu.

5. If you have a printer, select **Define Print Style** and select your printer.

6. Save the report as SHIPS.

366 *MASTERING DATAEASE*

CH. 13

7. Select **Start New Report** to clear the report.

8. Press **F9** to return to DQL.

From the DQL menu:

1. Select **Run Procedure**

2. Select **ORDREC**

3. Enter and save each record listed below:

DATEREC	STOCK#	ORDER#	AMTREC
021591	23456	1	2
022091	56123	2	1
022091	78920	2	1
031591	56123	3	1

4. Save the last record.

5. Press **Esc** to clear the form.

DataEase takes a few seconds processing these records, adding to ORDERS and modifying records in ITEMS. If DataEase has any problems while adding or modifying the records, it will display an error message.

Next, you'll print the QTY report again to compare the QTY ONHAND amounts. Then you'll print the SHIPS report to verify the modifications in the ORDERS form.

If you have no printer available, you can refer to Figures 13.3 and 13.4 and compare them to the outcome of your procedure.

1. Select **Start New Procedure** to clear the current procedure.

2. Select **Run Procedure** and select **QTY**

3. Repeat steps 1 and 2 above to run **SHIPS**

First, compare the QTY reports and see that STOCK# 23456 now shows three on hand, and that 56123 also shows three. Now look at the SHIPS report, shown in Figure 13.5, and see that the order

MODIFYING YOUR DATABASE WITH HIGH LEVEL QUERIES   **367**

```
    STOCK#              ITEM              QTY
------------------------------------------------
    98765      Table, Kitchen             3
    12345      Bed, Water, King           2
    87654      Bed, Queen                 3
    23456      Table, Bedside             1
    65432      Table, Coffee              2
    45678      Chair, Lounge              4
    56789      Table, Side                5
    78920      Armoire, Teak              2
    78921      Table, Kitchen             3
    78923      Bed, Twin                  4
    73456      Sofa, Modern               2
    78928      Table, Coffee              2
    65789      Table, Coffee              3
    13456      Table, Side                2
    79876      Bed, Water, Queen          3
    45234      Chair, Rocker              2
    56123      Sofa, Modern               1
    67891      Bed, Queen                 1
    93845      Table, Dining Room         2
    93847      Loveseat, Modern           1
================================================
```

Figure 13.3: QTY report before ORDREC

```
    STOCK#              ITEM              QTY
------------------------------------------------
    98765      Table, Kitchen             3
    12345      Bed, Water, King           2
    87654      Bed, Queen                 3
    23456      Table, Bedside             3
    65432      Table, Coffee              2
    45678      Chair, Lounge              4
    56789      Table, Side                5
    78920      Armoire, Teak              3
    78921      Table, Kitchen             3
    78923      Bed, Twin                  4
    73456      Sofa, Modern               2
    78928      Table, Coffee              2
    65789      Table, Coffee              3
    13456      Table, Side                2
    79876      Bed, Water, Queen          3
    45234      Chair, Rocker              2
    56123      Sofa, Modern               3
    67891      Bed, Queen                 1
    93845      Table, Dining Room         2
    93847      Loveseat, Modern           1
================================================
```

Figure 13.4: QTY report after ORDREC

records for these products have been modified with the new information about DATEREC, AMTREC, and AMTBACK.

You have learned how to modify records with DQL. Next, you'll
learn how to *add* records to a form with DQL.

MASTERING DATAEASE

CH. 13

```
        DATEORD  ORDER#  STOCK#  INVOICE#  AMTORD  DATEREC  AMTREC  AMTBACK
        --------------------------------------------------------------------
        01/15/91  0001    23456              3      02/15/91   2        1
        01/17/91  0002    56123              3      02/20/91   1        2
        01/17/91  0002    78920              1      02/20/91   1        0
        02/01/91  0003    56123              1      03/15/91   1        0
        02/05/91  0004    23456              1                          0
        02/22/91  0005    78920              1                          0
        02/23/91  0006    45234              2                          0
        02/23/91  0006    12345              1                          0
        03/01/91  0007    65789              2                          0
        03/05/91  0008    45234              1                          0
        03/15/91  0009    79876              1                          0
        03/17/91  0010    98765              2                          0
        03/20/91  0011    45678              2                          0
        03/30/91  0012    45678              1                          0
        04/06/91  0013    67891              1                          0
        04/06/91  0013    93845              1                          0
        03/25/90  0014    87654              2                          0
        04/10/91  0015    13456              2                          0
        04/10/91  0015    56789              1                          0
        04/15/91  0016    73456              2                          0
        04/15/91  0016    78928              2                          0
        04/20/91  0017    78920              1                          0
        ====================================================================
```

Figure 13.5: SHIPS report

USING A DQL
PROCEDURE TO PLACE ORDERS

At the end of each day, when sales orders are processed, the clerk at Furniture Palace checks the inventory for the quantity on hand and places orders with vendors, as necessary. This requires going back and forth between ITEMS and ORDERS. Even with multiforms this can be tedious. To help the clerk out, you can create a high level query to look up the information in ITEMS and enter a record in ORDERS if the inventory is low.

DataEase offers several processing commands which enter records. One of them, **enter a record,** adds a record to an existing form. The format is:

enter a record in (FORM NAME)

The source can be a list of fields or any related form. In this case there will be two sources: a data entry form and a list of field values. The data entry form will include the STOCK#, ITEM, QTY ONHAND, and QTY PURCHASED fields. You'll enter values for the STOCK# and QTY PURCHASED fields. ITEM and QTY ONHAND will be copied from the ITEMS form. The remaining fields in each new ORDER record will be derived.

MODIFYING YOUR DATABASE WITH HIGH LEVEL QUERIES 369

Let's begin by creating the form:

1. Select **Start New Procedure** and type **Y**

2. Select **Define data-entry form** and type **Y** to redisplay it each time.

3. Place the following form text:

   STOCK#:   ITEM:
   QTY ONHAND: QTY PURCHASED:
   PRESS F2 TO ENTER RECORD
   PRESS ESC WHEN FINISHED

4. Use the information in Table 13.2 to define each field:

Table 13.2: Field Definition for the Data Entry Form.

NAME	TYPE	LEN.	DERIV. FORM.	PREV. DATA-ENTRY?
STOCK#	Numeric String	5		
ITEM	TEXT	20	LOOKUP ITEMS ITEM	yes
QTY ONHAND	Number	3	LOOKUP ITEMS "QTY ONHAND"	yes
QTY PURCHASED	Number	3		

You must use the quotation marks in a LOOKUP when the field or file name is more than one word.

Next, you'll define the query that enters the orders.

USING AN *if* STATEMENT IN YOUR QUERY

Before you tell DataEase to enter a record in ORDERS, DataEase must know when to place an order. In this case, an order is placed only when the quantity purchased is equal to or greater than the current QTY ONHAND.

370 MASTERING DATAEASE

CH. 13

if is a procedural command that can make these decisions for you. The format of the **if** statement is:

```
if CONDITION then
    action1
    [action2
    ...

[else
    action1
    action1


    ...
end
```

For your query, the statement would read:

```
if data-entry QTYPURCH > = ITEMS QTY ONHAND then enter
    a record in ORDERS
```

The concept of the **if** command is similar to the concept of the **if** function. DataEase uses the result of a condition to determine the action to take. However, the **if** command does *not* require that you include the action that must be taken if the condition is false. In other words, the **else** statement is optional. In this case, the following **if** statement is sufficient. However, the **end** statement *is* required.

Now you're ready to put the query together.

1. Select **Define query**

2. Press **F9** to display the high level menus.

Each time you exit a query, DataEase returns to the low level menus. When you create or modify a high level query, always press F9 to check the menu level.

DataEase still displays the low level menus. If you want to begin your high level query with a statement other than **for**, you must exit the menu, then return again to "turn on" the high level menu. Since you are on the first line, Home will turn off the menus and position you in Column 1.

1. Press **Home** to return to Column 1.

2. Press **F1** to display the high level menu.

MODIFYING YOUR DATABASE WITH HIGH LEVEL QUERIES *371*

3. Press **F1** and select **if**

4. Select **data-entry**

5. Select **QTYPURCH** and type > =

6. Select **data-entry QTY ONHAND**

7. Press **Tab** three times.

8. Press **F1** and select **enter a record**

9. Select **ORDERS** and press.

The ITEM and SOURCE fields are automatically copied from the ITEMS form.

Next, you'll list the values for each field in the ORDERS form. The first field, DATEORD, will be derived from the system date.

1. Use the menus or type the next statement:

   DATEORD : = current date ;

Another field which must be filled is ORDER#. Since it is not a sequenced field, the problem is determining the next order number without looking it up. Since the last ORDER# entered is the highest number, you could add 1 to the last (**highest of**) ORDER# to increment the ORDER# automatically. You'll use the menus to enter this statement. This takes quite a bit of skipping around the menus, so be careful.

If you lose your place or get lost, move the cursor back to the beginning of the line, press F1, and begin the statement again.

2. Select **ORDER#**

3. Press **Tab** and type **1 +**

4. Press **Tab** six times and select **highest of**

5. Press **Tab** and select **ORDERS**

6. Press **Tab** seven times and select **ORDER#**

7. Type ;

The query statement should read:

   ORDER# : = 1 + highest of ORDERS ORDER# ;

The next two fields, STOCK# and AMTORD, are copied from the data entry form.

MASTERING DATAEASE

CH. 13

8. Add the next three statements:

```
STOCK# : = data-entry STOCK# ;
AMTORD : = data-entry QTYPURCH .
end
```

The last part of the query will update the ITEMS form by replacing the QTY ONHAND with the QTY ONHAND minus the amount of the data entry field, QTYPURCH. A negative result would indicate how many products are currently on backorder.

1. Add the following statements to the query:

```
for ITEMS
with STOCK# = data-entry STOCK# ;
modify records
QTY ONHAND : = QTY ONHAND − data-entry QTYPURCH .
end
```

The complete query should read:

```
if data-entry QTYPURCH > = data-entry QTY ONHAND then
enter record in ORDERS
DATEORD : = current date ;
ORDER# : = 1 + highest of ORDERS ORDER# ;
STOCK# : = data-entry STOCK# ;
AMTORD : = data-entry QTYPURCH .
end
for ITEMS
with STOCK# = data-entry STOCK# ;
modify records
QTY ONHAND : = QTY ONHAND − data-entry QTYPURCH .
end
```

2. Press **F2** (if necessary) to save the query, and **Tab** to return to the DQL menu.

3. Save the procedure under the name INVORD.

The final step is to create the relationships that will allow the lookups in the data entry form.

MODIFYING YOUR DATABASE WITH HIGH LEVEL QUERIES 373

1. Define the following relationship:

FORM 1	FORM 2	FIELD 1.1	FIELD 2.1
ITEMS	INVORD	STOCK#	STOCK#

2. Save the record and return to the DQL menu.

Remember, to enter INVORD as Form 2, you must first press Esc to clear the menu.

Now you can enter some records, after which you'll print the QTY report again and compare figures.

1. Load the INVORD procedure and run it.

2. Enter the following records.

STOCK#	QTYPURCH
12345	4
56789	3
65432	3

3. Press **Esc** after the last record is saved and the blank form is redisplayed.

4. Select **Start New Procedure** to clear the report.

5. Run the QTY report again.

6. Select **Start New Procedure** and run the SHIPS report again.

The new QTY report, shown in Figure 13.6, shows that the QTY ONHAND values in ITEMS for the ordered products have decreased and some show negative numbers indicating products on backorder. Look at the end of the SHIPS report, Figure 13.7, and notice that new orders were placed for all but STOCK# 56789, because the QTY ONHAND was *higher* than the QTYPURCH.

7. If you have a printer, load INVORD and print the definition.

The procedure definition also includes your data entry form.

374 MASTERING DATAEASE

CH. 13

```
QTY                                     Running report QTY
SPACE or PgDn: Continue report  EXIT: Abort report  PgUp: Scroll

-----------------------------------------------------------------
    STOCK#           ITEM                QTY
                                         ONHAND
-----------------------------------------------------------------
    98765       Table, Kitchen            3
    12345       Bed, Water, King         -2
    87654       Bed, Queen                3
    23456       Table, Bedside            3
    65432       Table, Coffee            -1
    45678       Chair, Lounge             4
    56789       Table, Side               2
    78920       Armoire, Teak             3
    78921       Table, Kitchen            3
    78923       Bed, Twin                 4
    73456       Sofa, Modern              2
    78928       Table, Coffee             2
    65789       Table, Coffee             3
    13456       Table, Side               2
    79876       Bed, Water, Queen         3
    45234       Chair, Rocker             2
    56123       Sofa, Modern              1
 F4 CMDHELP  ESC EXIT  C:\DEASE\SYBEX\       INVENTORY     02/16/91   6 23 pm
```

Figure 13.6: New QTY report after INVORD

```
  DATEORD   ORDER#   STOCK#  INVOICE#  AMTORD  DATEREC  AMTREC  AMTBACK
-----------------------------------------------------------------------
  01/15/91   0001    23456              3     12/15/91   2        1
  01/17/91   0002    56123              3     02/20/91   1        2
  01/17/91   0002    78920              1     02/20/91   1        0
  02/01/91   0003    56123              1     03/15/91   1        0
  02/05/91   0004    23456              1                         0
  02/22/91   0005    78920              1                         0
  02/23/91   0006    45234              2                         0
  02/23/91   0006    12345              1                         0
  03/01/91   0007    65789              2                         0
  03/05/91   0008    45234              1                         0
  03/15/91   0009    79876              1                         0
  03/17/91   0010    98765              2                         0
  03/20/91   0011    45678              2                         0
  03/30/91   0012    45678              1                         0
  04/06/91   0013    67891              1                         0
  04/06/91   0013    93845              1                         0
  03/25/90   0014    87654              2                         0
  04/10/91   0015    13456              2                         0
  04/10/91   0015    56789              1                         0
  04/15/91   0016    73456              2                         0
  04/15/91   0016    78928              2                         0
  04/20/91   0017    78920              1                         0
  04/19/90   0018    12345              4                         0
  04/19/90   0019    65432              3                         0
=======================================================================
```

Figure 13.7: New SHIPS report after INVORD

MODIFYING YOUR DATABASE WITH HIGH LEVEL QUERIES   375

USING input TO SELECT RECORDS FOR A REPORT

Each method has its limitations. The **with** statement requires that you alter the query to change the record selection. And the data entry form only displays selected information.

So far you have learned two methods for selecting records in a report in a high level procedure:

- Include a **with** statement in the query when selecting the form.

- Create a data entry form to select records before the query is run.

Suppose that the Sales Manager of Furniture Palace would like to use the CUST form to select customers for a report on invoice totals, balances, and payments. DataEase's **input** command allows you to accomplish this task, using the Record Entry form to select records for processing. The format of the command is:

input using FORM NAME into "TEMPFORM"

The FORM NAME is the form you want to use for the record selection. "TEMPFORM" names the temporary form that holds the record you select. In this case, the commands

input using CUST into CUSTFORM .
for INVOICE
with CUST# = CUSTFORM CUST# ;

would display the Record Entry form for CUST. Since all the Record Entry commands are available, you can use an input form to select individual records, search for selected records, enter a new record, or delete an existing one in the designated form. When you press F2, the selected record is copied into memory and processed.

The **for** statement selects the primary database, in this case INVOICE, and is followed by a **with** statement to select the record that matches the one stored in the "TEMPFORM". The next command you select tells DataEase whether you want to add, delete,

376 *MASTERING DATAEASE*

CH. 13

modify, or report on the selected record. For this query, you'll process records for a **list records**.

1. **Start New Procedure** and select **Define Query**
2. Press **Home** to clear the low level menu.
3. Press **F9** to switch to high level.
4. Press **F1** to return to the menus.
5. Press **F1** to display further selections, and select **input**
6. Select **CUST**
7. Type **"CUSTFORM"**
8. Type **for INVOICE**
9. Select **with**
10. Select **CUST# = CUSTFORM CUST#**

> Notice that now CUSTFORM is included in the list of form names.

This last statement tells DataEase to process the record that matches the value of the CUST# field.

The next step is the **list records** command. You'll include fields from INVOICE (the primary form) and PAYLIST.

1. Continue using the menus or type the following statements:

```
list records
    LNAME in groups ;
    CUST# in groups ;
    INVOICE# in groups ;
    DATE in groups ;
    GRTOT in groups ;
    BALDUE in groups ;
    all PAYLIST DATE ;
    all PAYLIST AMTPD .
end
```

The complete query is listed below:

```
input using CUST into "CUSTFORM".
for INVOICE
with CUST# = CUSTFORM CUST# ;
```

MODIFYING YOUR DATABASE WITH HIGH LEVEL QUERIES 377

```
list records
    LNAME in groups ;
    CUST# in groups ;
    INVOICE# in groups ;
    DATE in groups ;
    GRTOT in groups ;
    BALDUE in groups ;
    all PAYLIST DATE ;
    all PAYLIST AMTPD .
end
```

2. When you are finished, press **Tab** to save the query and return to the DQL menu.

3. Run the procedure.

DataEase immediately displays the Record Entry form for CUST. First, let's see the listing for a single customer.

1. Press **F3** to display the first record for Enis.

2. Press **F2** to store the record in memory.

DataEase displays the report, shown in Figure 13.8, for the selected customer.

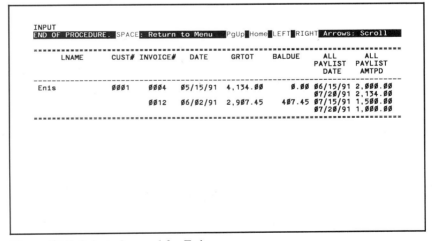

Figure 13.8: Selected record for Enis

378 MASTERING DATAEASE

CH. 13

Although DataEase can hold only one record in memory, you *can* include multiple records in the report by using a wild card search in the selected field. Remember, DataEase processes records that match the selection field (in this case STOCK#) in the record stored in memory. If you use a wild card, DataEase will process all records that match.

1. Press **Esc** to clear the screen.

2. Select **Run procedure**

3. Press **Alt-F5** to clear the screen unchecked.

4. In the CUST# field, type **000?** DataEase selects records with CUST#s from 0001 to 0009 for the report.

5. Press **F2** to store the record.

6. Save the procedure as **INVPMTS**

So far, you have created reports primarily in a columnar format. However, you can also use DataEase to create other types of documents. In the next chapter, you'll create statements and form letters.

SECURITY NOTES

If you do not have a high enough security level to access a form and you attempt to modify or add records in that form, one of the following messages will appear:

Not authorized to modify this form
Not authorized to enter in this form

If you do not have modification or entry rights to a particular field that you are including in a **modify records** or **enter a record** statement, the following message will appear:

Not authorized to modify this field

CHAPTER FOURTEEN

Creating Customer Statements and Form Letters

Fast Track

To create a form letter,   382

select Define Query from the DQL menu, and use **list records** to select the fields you want to include in your letter. Include the optional **with** statement to make any record selections.

After saving the query, select Define Format and select Custom as the format type. Create a .group header area that includes the date, name, and address information. Create an .items area that includes the body of the letter. Use **F10** to place the fields that represent the variables. You can place the fields anywhere you like, even in the middle of a sentence (in this case, suppress trailing spaces). Create a .group trailer area that includes the sign-off. Save the format, define the print style, and save and run the procedure.

To create mailing labels,   396

select Define Query from the DQL menu, and use **list records** to select the address fields. Include the **with** statement if you want to select records for the mailing. Save the query.

Select Define Format and select Mailing Labels as the format type. Enter the number of labels across, and the number of columns in the longest line in the label. Each field will be displayed on a separate line in the Format screen. Move any fields that need to be on the same line as other fields, such as city, state, and zip. Save the format, select the print style, and save and run the procedure.

CHAPTER *14*

THE PREPARATION OF CUSTOMER STATEMENTS IS AN important accounting procedure. On the fifteenth of each month, Furniture Palace sends a statement, like the one pictured in Figure 14.1, to each active customer. As you can see, it lists the balance for each invoice and at the bottom includes the total balance due, any portion of the balance which has aged 120 days, and applicable finance charges for those overdue balances.

```
                              CUSTOMER STATEMENT
    AS OF: SEPTEMBER 15, 1991

    CUSTOMER NUMBER: 0002
    William Smith
    20 E. Elm
    Chicago IL  60602

    INVOICE#     INVOICE          INVOICE        BALANCE
                 DATE             TOTAL          DUE
    --------------------------------------------------------
    0003         05/10/91         5,032.13          532.13
    0013         06/05/91         6,810.50        6,810.50
                                                 ==========
    TOTAL BALANCE DUE                             7,342.63

    BALANCE OVER 120 DAYS                           532.13

    PENALTY                                          26.61

    TOTAL DUE                                     7,369.24
```

Figure 14.1: Sample customer statement

If you haven't already guessed, in this chapter you'll produce this special report using a high level query. Because of the report design, you'll use a custom format instead of columnar.

Customers with outstanding balances over 120 days old will get special treatment. In addition to the statement, Furniture Palace would like to send a letter reminding delinquent customers of the past due portion of their balance. Until now, they never had the time to research the information and type each letter. To help Furniture Palace out, you'll use DataEase to create and print the personalized form letter.

382 MASTERING DATAEASE

CH. 14

CREATING THE QUERY

The closing date for the statement you'll prepare for Furniture Palace is 9/15/91. Since all customers receive a statement, CUST will be the primary form; since the summary totals come from INVOICE, that will be the secondary form. Let's begin:

1. Select **Start New Procedure**

2. Select **Define Query** and press **F9** to switch to high level.

3. Either use the menus or type the following statements:

> Even if you plan to type the statements rather than use the menus, it's a good idea to switch to high level menus. If DataEase catches a mistake when you save, it needs to know which level menu to display.

```
for CUST
;
list records
   CUST# in groups ;
   FNAME ;
   LNAME ;
   ADDRESS ;
   CITY ;
   STATE ;
   ZIP ;
```

The above fields make up the header information of the statement. The next four fields summarize the invoice balances and come from INVOICE.

4. Add the next four statements to your query:

```
all INVOICE INVOICE# ;
all INVOICE DATE ;
all INVOICE GRTOT ;
all INVOICE BALDUE ;
```

> You might wonder why we don't simply include statistics in the INVOICE BALDUE statement. However, since we are not using the standard custom format, field statistics are not applicable. Each statistic must be created as a separate field.

The last four fields comprise the footer part of the statement and include current and overdue balance totals as well as penalty charges. The next field is the sum of BALDUE.

5. Add the following statement to the query:

```
sum of INVOICE BALDUE ;
```

NAMING AD HOC RELATIONSHIPS

You have used the **with** statement to create an ad hoc relationship in the primary form as well as in the secondary and tertiary forms. If you need to refer to an ad hoc relationship again later in the query, you can assign a name that will be added to the menu of relationships. This is especially handy if you require several different record selections for the same form.

For example, the previous field, sum of INVOICE BALDUE, sums all open invoices for each customer; the next two fields you'll create with calculate totals and penalties for invoices with open balances aged over 120 days. The last field totals both current open balances *and* penalties for those aged 120 days. In the next statements, you will name and create an ad hoc relationship that selects records with open balances aged over 120 days as of the statement date.

1. Use the menus to create the statement. (Press **F9** to switch to high level and **F1** to return to the menus if necessary.)

2. Press **Tab** twice and select **sum of**

The following menu appears:

> **Select a Relationship defined earlier in this query?**
> **0: None 1:INVOICE**

To select INVOICE with no record selection, just as you did for the previous, field you'll skip this menu.

3. Press **Tab**

The next menu appears as follows:

> **Select pre-defined relationship>**
> **0: None 1:INVOICE 2:PAYMENTS**

You've seen this menu before. It displays the relationships you have created between CUST and the forms listed. Here, you'll select **INVOICE** from the current menu.

You can create an ad hoc relationship in addition to the pre-defined relationship. If you press Tab again, DataEase displays all forms and you can create an ad hoc relationship based on any form in the database.

384 *MASTERING DATAEASE*

CH. 14

4. Select **INVOICE**

Next, you'll create an ad hoc relationship called **OVER120** which selects open invoices with dates occurring more than 120 days prior to the statement date. First, you'll name the relationship:

1. Select **Named**

2. Type **"OVER120"**

Next, you will define this ad hoc relationship: DATE + 120 < 09/15/91 and BALDUE > 0 (open invoices).

3. Select **with**

4. Select **DATE**

5. Select + and press **Tab**

6. Type **120** and press **Spacebar** to complete the number.

7. Press **Tab** twice and select <

8. Press **Tab**; type **09/15/91** then press the **Spacebar**

9. Press **Tab** and select **and**

10. Select **BALDUE**

11. Press **Tab** twice and select >

12. Press **Tab**; type **0** then press the **Spacebar**

13. **Tab** three times; select **BALDUE** then type ;

Always press the Spacebar after typing numbers.

The statement you just created,

> sum of INVOICE NAMED "OVER120" with (Date + 120 < 09/15/91 and BALDUE > 0) BALDUE ;

tells DataEase to sum the BALDUE fields for all INVOICE records that match an ad hoc relationship called "OVER120" that selects records with open balances and dates more than 120 days prior to 09/15/91. More importantly, you have created an ad hoc relationship that you can use again, just by selecting OVER120 from the relationship menu.

CREATING CUSTOMER STATEMENTS AND FORM LETTERS   *385*

The next field will calculate the penalty on records having open invoices aged over 120 days by multiplying the balance by five percent. Because you have already established the relationship that selects records over 120 days old, you will not have to do a lot of typing. Let's continue to use the menus:

1. Press **Tab** twice and select **sum of**

Do you remember this menu?

> Select a Relationship defined earlier in this query?
> 0: None 1:OVER120 2:INVOICE

Now it also includes **OVER120**.

2. Select **OVER120**

3. Select **BALDUE**

4. Select * and type **0.05 ;**

This new statement:

> sum of OVER120 BALDUE * 0.05

tells DataEase to multiply the sum of the invoices selected by the ad hoc relationship OVER120 by five percent.

The next (and last) statement combines both relationships defined in this query for INVOICE. It asks DataEase to add the penalty payment (if any) to the sum of the balance due, to arrive at the total due for each customer:

1. Press **Tab** twice and select **sum of**

2. Select **INVOICE**

3. Select **BALDUE** and press **Tab**

4. Select + and press **Tab** six times.

5. Select **sum of**

6. Select **OVER120** and press **Tab** five times.

386   MASTERING DATAEASE

CH. 14

7. Select **BALDUE** and type *** 0.05** .

8. Type **end**

Take a look at the entire query, shown in Figure 14.2.

The menus can be quite helpful as they guide you through creating and using your ad hoc and predefined relationships.

1. Press F2 to save the query.

2. Press **Tab** to return to the DQL menu.

3. Save the procedure under the name **STATEMENT**

```
for CUST
;
list records
  CUST# in groups ;
  FNAME ;
  LNAME ;
  ADDRESS ;
  CITY ;
  STATE ;
  ZIP ;
  all INVOICE INVOICE# ;
  all INVOICE DATE ;
  all INVOICE GRTOT ;
  all INVOICE BALDUE ;
  sum of INVOICE BALDUE ;
  sum of INVOICE NAMED "OVER120" with ( Date + 120 <
     09/15/91 and BALDUE > 0 ) BALDUE ;
  sum of OVER120 BALDUE * 0.05 ;
  sum of INVOICE BALDUE + sum of OVER120 BALDUE * 0.05 .
end
```

Figure 14.2: Completed query for the statement

───── *DESIGNING A CUSTOM FORMAT* ─────

Now that you have defined all the fields you'll use for your statement, let's design the custom format.

1. Select **Define Format**

2. Press **F1** and select **Custom**

The custom format provides you with a blank screen on which you can place text and fields from your query anywhere you like. Like any format, it must include one .items command and one .end command. Other than that, you are free to design your report from scratch.

Refer back to Figure 14.1, which pictures a sample statement, and note the three separate areas of this format. Since you grouped this report by CUST#, the title, date, customer address, and column headings are all part of the .group header area, and will appear only once at the top of each statement group. The invoice summary fields, which will vary in length for each customer, are in the .items area. The total due information is in the .group trailer area. The format will end with a .page command so that each statement is printed on a separate page.

Let's begin by defining the .group header area. The following instructions include row and column designations. You can use these or refer to Figure 14.3 as a guide and place the text where you like.

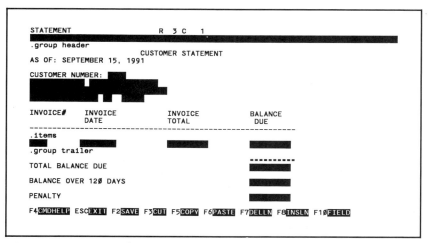

Figure 14.3: Completed format

1. At Row 1, Column 1 type . (period) and select **group header**
2. Use the information below to enter the text:

   .group header
      CUSTOMER STATEMENT
   AS OF: SEPTEMBER 15, 1991
   CUSTOMER NUMBER:

388 MASTERING DATAEASE

CH. 14

Next, you'll place the name and address fields for the header area:

1. At Row 5, Column 18 press **F10**, select **CUST#**, and press **F2**
2. At Row 6, Column 1 use **F10** to place **FNAME**
3. Suppress spaces.
4. On the same line after FNAME, place **LNAME**
5. At Row 7, Column 1 place **ADDRESS**
6. At Row 8, Column 1 place **CITY** and suppress the spaces.
7. Next to CITY, place **STATE**
8. Next to STATE, place **ZIP**

Remember, you need to suppress trailing spaces for the first field when you want two fields placed right next to each other.

Place the field headings below in Row 11:

INVOICE#	INVOICE DATE	INVOICE TOTAL	BALANCE DUE

Now you are ready to place the fields in the .items area:

1. At Row 13, Column 1 type **.** (period) and select **items**
2. Beginning at Row 14, Column 1, place the following fields:

COLUMN	*FIELD NAME*
1	all INVOICE INVOICE#
12	all INVOICE DATE
31	all INVOICE GRTOT
49	all INVOICE BALDUE

Finally, you'll create the .group trailer area and place the total fields.

1. At Row 15, Column 1 type **.** (period) and select **group trailer**
2. Use the information below to enter the text, starting at Row 16.

.group trailer

TOTAL BALANCE DUE
= = = = = = = = = =

BALANCE OVER 120 DAYS

PENALTY

TOTAL DUE

3. Beginning at Row 17, Column 49, place the following fields:

ROW	FIELD NAME
17	sum of INVOICE BALDUE
19	sum of INVOICE NAMED "OVER120" with etc.
21	sum of OVER120 BALDUE * 0.05
23	sum of INVOICE BALDUE + sum of OVER120 etc.

4. At Row 24, Column 1, type . (period) and select **page**

5. At Row 25, Column 1, type . (period) and select **end**

Your completed format is pictured in Figure 14.3.

6. Save the format.

7. Save the procedure again under the same name.

8. Run the procedure.

9. Press **PgDn** to display the second statement, for customer Smith.

This statement, pictured in Figure 14.4, shows the balance over 120 days late, plus the five percent penalty at the bottom, along with the total due. As you proceed to display each invoice, you'll see that your query summarizes and calculates each customer's account balance accurately.

Now you can prepare the letter to send to those two delinquent customers.

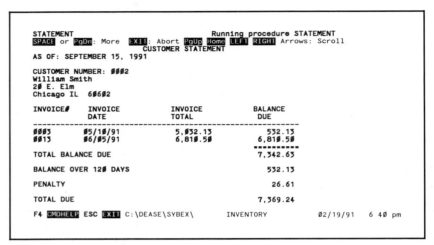

Figure 14.4: Completed statement for Smith

CREATING A FORM LETTER

The form letter you'll create, pictured in Figure 14.5, includes a .header area similar to the one in your customer statement. The body of the letter, which is the .items area, includes both text and fields. The .group trailer area is the closing that appears at the bottom of each letter.

The query will contain some of the same fields you used in your customer statement, and will also include a record selection. To simplify the process, you'll edit the STATEMENT query, create a new format, and save it under a different name. Let's begin:

1. Select **Modify Query** from the DQL menu.

You'll keep the **for** statement and the header fields from the CUST form. However, you'll begin by adding a record selection statement. This query must select customers with an open balance 120 or more days old in INVOICE.

2. Press **F9** to switch to high level and move to Row 2, Column 1 under the ;

The **with** statement must select customers with open balances aged over 120 days. Since the OVER120 relationship was not created until

```
                                                      September 15, 1991

          CUSTOMER NUMBER: 0002
          William Smith
          20 E. Elm
          Chicago IL  60602

          Our records show that you have an outstanding balance of 532.13
          which is more than 120 days past due.  A 5% penalty of 26.61
          has been added bringing the total past due to 558.74.

          Please submit a check to bring your account up to date.

          Sincerely yours,


          Jane Moneypenney
                                                      September 15, 1991

          CUSTOMER NUMBER: 0003
          Peter Grey
          200 E. Euclid
          Cleveland OH  43430

          Our records show that you have an outstanding balance of 3,298.00
          which is more than 120 days past due.  A 5% penalty of 164.90
          has been added bringing the total past due to 3,462.90.

          Please submit a check to bring your account up to date.

          Sincerely yours,


          Jane Moneypenney
```

Figure 14.5: Sample form letter

later in this query, it won't appear in any menus. Therefore, you'll need to define it again for this procedure.

3. Press **F8** twice to insert two rows.

4. Use the menus or type the following selection statement:

   with any INVOICE named "OVER120"with (DATE + 120 < 09/15/91) BALDUE > 0 ;

The next seven rows stay the same.

The next four statments select fields from the INVOICE form that are not needed in the form letter, so you'll delete them.

5. Move to Row 12 and press **F7** four times to delete the next four rows.

6. The next field calculates the total balance due that is over 120 days old. Modify the next row to read:

   sum of OVER120 BALDUE ;

392 MASTERING DATAEASE

CH. 14

7. The next statement, which occupies two rows, is also unnecessary since it basically repeats the statement you just created. Press **F7** twice to delete the next two rows.

The next statement remains, since it calculates the penalty for the overdue balance and will be included in the letter. The last field adds the sum of OVER120 BALDUE to the penalty calculated in the previous field.

8. Edit or retype the last statement to read:

   sum of OVER120 BALDUE + sum of OVER120 BALDUE *
   0.05 .

9. Complete the query by typing **end** on the next row.

The completed query is listed below:

```
for CUST
with any INVOICE named "OVER120"with ( DATE + 120 <
      09/15/91 ) BALDUE > 0 ;
list records
   CUST# in groups ;
   FNAME ;
   LNAME ;
   ADDRESS ;
   CITY ;
   STATE ;
   ZIP ;
   sum of OVER120 BALDUE ;
   sum of OVER120 BALDUE * 0.05 ;
   sum of OVER120 BALDUE + sum of OVER120 BALDUE *
         0.05 .
end
```

Now that you have completed the query, you're ready to modify the format.

1. Save the query and return to the DQL menu.

2. Save the procedure under the name **OVER120LET**

CREATING CUSTOMER STATEMENTS AND FORM LETTERS   *393*

Next, to save time, you'll simply modify the STATEMENT format to create your letter.

3. Select **Modify Format**

4. Select **y** to keep the original format.

The heading area is the same except for the title. The name and address fields will remain.

5. Use the information below to edit the .header area.

    .group header

    September 15, 1991

    CUSTOMER NUMBER:

> When placing fields of fixed length into a body of text, you should suppress the spaces to avoid gaps in the middle of lines.

The body of the text will be placed in the .items area. Although you can enter paragraphs of text, DataEase has no word wrap feature found in most word processing programs, so you must press Enter to end each line. You'll place the last three fields of the query in the body of the letter.

1. Delete the remainder of the customer statement format.

2. At Row 9, Column 1 type . (period) and select **items**

3. Beginning on the next row, type the following text:

    Our records show that you have an outstanding balance of

4. Press **F10** and select **sum of OVER120 BALDUE**

5. Enter **y** in the last field to suppress the spaces, and press **F2** to confirm.

6. Press **Enter** to move to the next line and type:

    which is more than 120 days past due. A 5% penalty of

7. Press **F10** and select the next field, **sum of OVER120 BAL-DUE * 0.05**

8. Suppress the spaces, and press **F2**

9. Type the following text on the next line to complete the sentence:

    has been added bringing the total past due to

10. Press **F10** and place the last field, **sum of OVER120 BALDUE + sum of OVER120 BALDUE * 0.05**, and suppress the spaces.

11. Enter the information below to complete the format:

    Please submit a check to bring your account up to date.

    .group trailer
    Sincerely yours,

    Jane Moneypenny
    .page
    .end

Your completed format is pictured in Figure 14.6.

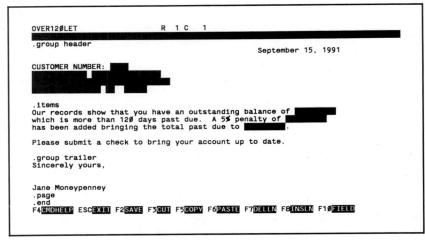

Figure 14.6: Completed format for OVER120LET

CREATING CUSTOMER STATEMENTS AND FORM LETTERS 395

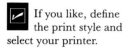
If you like, define the print style and select your printer.

Now you are ready to print your letters.

1. Press **F2** to save your format.
2. Save the procedure again.
3. Run the procedure.

The first letter is pictured in Figure 14.7.

```
OVER120LET
SPACE or PgDn: More  EXIT: Abort  PgUp Home LEFT RIGHT Arrows: Scroll
                                                September 15, 1991
CUSTOMER NUMBER: 002
William Smith
20 E. Elm
Chicago IL  60602

Our records show that you have an outstanding balance of 532.13
which is more than 120 days past due.  A 5% penalty of 26.61
has been added bringing the total past due to 558.74.

Please submit a check to bring your account up to date.

Sincerely yours,

Jane Moneypenney



F4 CMDHELP ESC EXIT  C:\DEASE\SYBEX\        INVENTORY        02/19/91   4 27 pm
```

Figure 14.7: Completed OVER120LET

PRINTING TO A DISK FILE

If you prefer to print the form letters using your word processing program, simply change two settings in the Define Print Style screen.

1. Press **Esc** to clear the screen.
2. Select **Define Print Style**
3. In the first field, select **disk** as the report destination.
4. Enter **y** to allow style modification at run time.

The next field asks for the disk output file name. If you want to print to the disk, you must enter the name of a destination file. This is

396   MASTERING DATAEASE

CH. 14

a DOS file, so the name must conform to the DOS file naming conventions, which require eight characters with an optional three-character extension. All characters are allowed with the exception of spaces, commas, question marks, asterisks, and periods (except for the one preceding the extension). The file that DataEase creates is a simple ASCII file that can be read by just about any word processing program. You can consult your word processing manual for instructions on reading ASCII files.

5. Type **AGE120.LET**

6. Press **F2** to save, and run the procedure again.

The file name should be one that is read or easily converted by your word processing program. Some of them have special rules about the use of extensions.

This file was saved in the \dataease\sybex directory; however, you can save the file in any directory by simply preceding the file name with the directory path.

7. Save the procedure again under the same name.

CREATING MAILING LABELS

If you send mailings to customers on a regular basis, using labels to address the envelopes is a great timesaver. You can create a custom format for your labels or select Mailing Labels from the list of format types. Let's take a look at the mailing label format. We'll save time by modifying the current query.

1. Select **Modify Query**

2. Delete all lines except for the address lines, so that your query looks like the one below:

```
for CUST
;
list records
   CUST# ;
   FNAME ;
   LNAME ;
   ADDRESS ;
   CITY ;
```

STATE ;
ZIP .
end

3. Save the query.

4. Save the procedure under the name **LABELS**

Next, you'll change to the mailing label format.

1. Select **Modify Format**

2. Type **n** to clear the current format.

3. Press **F1** and select **Mailing Label**

The first question DataEase asks is:

How many labels across?   2

Most label sheets have two labels across, as indicated by the default.

1. Press **Enter** to accept the default.

The next question,

How many columns per label   40

requires you to enter the width of your longest field. The longest field in this case is the address, which is only thirty columns.

2. Press **Enter** to accept the default.

The label format, pictured in Figure 14.8, includes a variation of the .items format command: .items across 2 wide 40. DataEase automatically enters this command, based on how you answered the two previous questions. You can change it on this screen if necessary.

Also, each field is entered on a separate line. You'll need to move some of the fields. (DataEase has automatically suppressed spaces for FNAME and CITY.)

1. Move LNAME from Row 4 next to FNAME in Row 3.

2. Use F7 to delete the blank row.

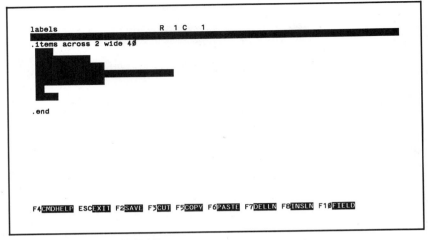

Figure 14.8: Mailing label format

  3. Move STATE next to CITY and ZIP next to STATE.

 Another aspect to consider is the number of lines between labels. Measured in inches, there are six lines to the inch. If your labels are one inch in length and your addresses have three lines of text, then you'll want three lines to separate each label, or three lines between the last label line and the .end command. Since you moved STATE and ZIP up to Row 5, you now have a total of seven rows between the beginning of the label and the .end statement. (Remember, the first line of the label is on Row 2). Assuming you are printing on one-inch labels, you have one additional row that you don't need.

  4. Use **F7** to delete the blank Row 6.

Your completed format is pictured in Figure 14.9.

  5. Save the format.

  6. Save the procedure again under the same name.

  7. Run the procedure.

The labels, pictured in Figure 14.10, include all names from the CUST form.

CREATING CUSTOMER STATEMENTS AND FORM LETTERS   399

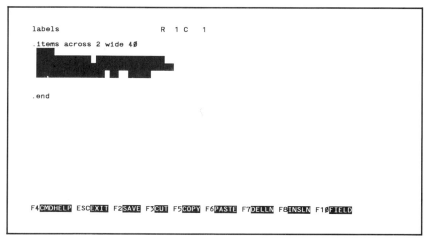

Figure 14.9: Completed LABELS format

Figure 14.10: Completed labels

You have now created reports using four types of report formats: columnar, record entry, custom, and mailing label. Other formats, including GrafTalk, CrossView, and export are all used to send the data to other programs. GrafTalk is discussed in Appendix C of this book. For information on other formats, refer to Volume 3 of your DataEase documentation.

CH. 14

In the last few chapters, you used the DQL to automate many of Furniture Palace's inventory, sales, and accounting functions. You have processed information in your database with **modify records, list records,** and **enter a record**. Further, you have controlled the sequence of operations in a query with the **if** procedural command. In the next chapter, you'll learn additional procedural commands, as well as control commands that link procedures and perform special database maintenance functions.

CHAPTER FIFTEEN

Automating
Sales and Order Entry

Fast Track

To use the case command in a query,   **405**

select **case** from the High Level Query menu, and within parentheses select or enter the expression that will be compared to a list of values. If you are not working with the menus, enter the keyword **value** on the next line. Following that, enter the first value to be compared. On the following line, enter the action DataEase should take if the value equals that of the expression. Continue entering on separate lines the possible values and the actions to be taken if the values are equivalent. You can complete the series of **case** statements with an **others** statement followed by the action to be taken if none of the values equal that of the expression.

To copy data from another form in a query   **408**

using the High Level Query menu, after you have entered or selected **modify records** or **enter a record**, enter **copy all from** on the next line and select or enter the form name. The form can be a form you created or a temporary input form. DataEase will copy values from all fields with matching names.

To display a message in a query,   **409**

move the cursor to the point in the query where you want the message to be displayed. From the High Level Query menu, select **message**. Within the double quotes, enter the message you want displayed, up to 40 characters. Select **window** if you want to temporarily clear the query and display the message in the center of the screen.

To use a variable in a query,   **412**

define the variable by entering or selecting the keyword **define** from the High Level Query menu. Select the variable type (temp or global), and enter the variable name, the type of data it will store, and the maximium length of the value. This is usually entered at the beginning of the query. When you are ready to give the variable a value, enter or select **assign** and then enter or select the value.

To create a loop in a query   414

with the **while** keyword, select the keyword **while** from the High Level Query menu and enter the condition. If you are not working with the menus, follow the condition with the keyword **do.** On the next line, enter the series of commands DataEase should execute if the condition is true. Complete the series of statements with the keyword **end.**

To create a control procedure,   419

select **Define Query** from the DQL menu. From the High Level Query menu, enter or select the control or procedural commands you want to execute. Save the query and run it.

CHAPTER 15

SO FAR, THE PEOPLE AT FURNITURE PALACE ARE quite pleased with the applications you have developed for them under DataEase. However, they have requested some revisions to the procedure for entering sales and placing orders:

- First, the salespeople want to know upon entering the invoice if the item is in stock. At the same time, DataEase should enter any necessary orders to save the clerical staff time at the end of each day.

- Accounting would like DataEase to add the records of new customers to CUST and to add the customer numbers to the invoices.

- If the salespeople modify an invoice or address information, DataEase should modify the INVOICE and/or CUST form accordingly.

- Accounting does *not* want salespeople deleting invoices.

This may seem like a very tall order, but actually it's quite simple. You will use some familiar processing and procedural commands and learn some new ones. In this chapter, you will learn how to use:

- **case**, a procedural command used when you have a multiple **if** situation.

- **while**, a procedural command that repeats a set of query statements as long as a condition is true.

- **copy all from**, a command used to copy fields from another form.

- **define** and **assign**, which create variables that act as temporary storage places for information.

AUTOMATING SALES AND ORDER ENTRY **405**

> • **message**, which displays user-defined text or variable information in the message area.

In addition, you will learn later on about control commands that chain together multiple procedures.

To begin, you'll create the procedure (to be named INVENTRY) that the salespeople will use to enter and modify invoices.

> 1. Select **Start New Procedure**
>
> 2. Select **Define Query**

Since the **input** command offers all the features of Record Entry, it is a convenient way to process records. In the last chapter, you used it to select records for a **list records**. In this procedure, the salesperson will use the temporary form to enter a new invoice, or view or modify an existing one.

> 1. Press **F9** to switch to high level.
>
> 2. Press **Home** to clear the low level menu and press **Home** to move to the top of the screen.
>
> 3. Type **input using INVOICE into "INVTEMP"**
>
> 4. Press Enter.

Although your form and fields names were created in uppercase, it is not necessary to use uppercase when typing a query. We have used uppercase to distinguish field and form names more easily. However, you may use whatever case you prefer.

USING THE case COMMAND FOR MULTIPLE CONDITIONS

When DataEase displays the "INVTEMP" form, salespeople can enter a new invoice, view and/or modify an invoice, or press Esc to do nothing and clear the screen. **case** is a procedural command that selects an action based on one of several expressions. In this case, the action depends on the keys pressed by the salespeople. If the salespeople press F2 to save a new invoice, you want DataEase to enter a record; if they press F8, you want DataEase to modify the invoice; if they press F7, you want DataEase to tell them they can't delete records. If the salespeople press Esc, you want DataEase to stop displaying the input form.

The format of the **case** command is:

```
CASE (EXPRESSION)
    value COMPARISON 1 :
        ACTION SERIES 2
    [value COMPARISON 2 :
        ACTION SERIES 2]
    [value COMPARISON 3 :
        ACTION SERIES 3]

    .. etc..

    [others :
        OTHER ACTION SERIES]
end
```

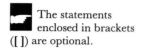

The statements enclosed in brackets ([ ]) are optional.

The EXPRESSION can be one of the system variables, such as the current date or a field in one of your forms. You can also use one of DataEase's 56 functions, such as LASTFIRST, which you learned about in Chapter 8. The value of the expression determines the action that DataEase will take. Each COMPARISON is a possible value for the expression and the ACTION is the command you want DataEase to execute if the value of the expression is equal to the comparison value. For example, if the value of the expression is equal to the value of COMPARISON 1, then DataEase will execute ACTION SERIES 1. If not, then DataEase will compare the value of COMPARISON 2 to ACTION SERIES 2, and so on. The **others** keyword is added at the end if there is an action you want DataEase to take if none of the comparison values are equal to the value in the expression. Without **others**, if none of the values are equal, DataEase will do nothing.

USING CURRENT STATUS

Whenever you press Esc, F2, F8, or F7, DataEase stores the value of that key in a system variable called the *current status*. DataEase uses

AUTOMATING SALES AND ORDER ENTRY   *407*

the following values for these keys:

KEY	VALUE
Esc	1
F2	2
F8	3
F7	4

You can determine the last key pressed by checking the value of the current status. The following statement uses the current status with the **if** command:

```
if current status = 1 then
    exit
```

and tells DataEase, "If the user presses Esc, exit the procedure."

In our example, you would ask DataEase to take certain actions, depending on the value of the current status:

```
CASE (current status)
    value 1: exit
    value 2: enter a record in INVOICE
    value 3: modify records in INVOICE
    value 4: message ""
```

The above statements tell DataEase that if the value of the current status is 1 (Esc), then exit the procedure; if the value is 2 (F2), enter a record in INVOICE; if the value of the current status is 3 (F8), modify records in INVOICE; if the value is 4 (F7), display a message.

Of course, this is a simplified version of the query. But let's start with the basics, using the menus:

1. Press **F1** to display the high level menus.

2. Press **F1** and type **c** to highlight **case**

3. Press **Enter** to accept **case**

4. Select **current**

To make a selection from a vertical list, you can simply type the first character. DataEase will highlight the first (and only the first) word that begins with that character. This shortcut is helpful when selecting from a long list.

408 MASTERING DATAEASE

CH. 15

5. Press F1 and select **status**

6. Press **Tab** twice.

DataEase returns to the next line, automatically adds the word **value**, and waits for you to enter the value to compare with the contents of the current status.

7. Press **Tab** three times and type **1** and press **Spacebar**

8. Press **Tab** three times and select **exit**

9. Press **Enter** to move to the next line.

DataEase will not return to the next line automatically after you select **exit** from the menu. Step 9 is necessary only so that the query will look properly formatted.

COPYING DATA FROM ANOTHER FORM

If the user presses F2 (Save), you'll want DataEase to enter a new record in INVOICE. This time, instead of entering a list of field values, as you did in Chapter 13, you'll use the **copy all from** command, which copies all fields from the input form. **copy all from** is an option only with the **modify records** and **enter a record** commands. It copies all fields with matching field names from any related form, including the input form.

1. Press **F1**

2. Type **v** and press **Enter** to select **value**

3. Press **Tab** three times and type **2** and press **Spacebar**

4. Press **Tab** three times and select **enter a record**

5. Select **INVOICE**

6. Press **Tab** and select **copy all from**

7. Select **INVTEMP** and press **Tab**

So far your query reads:

```
input using invoice into "INVTEMP" .
case ( current status )
value 1:
    exit
```

AUTOMATING SALES AND ORDER ENTRY **409**

```
value 2:
  enter a record in INVOICE
copy all from INVTEMP .
```

Just in case the salesperson made any changes to the customer heading information, you'll add a **modify records** command to copy all fields to the matching record in the CUST form.

1. Use the menus or type the following statements:

```
modify records in CUST with (CUST# = INVTEMP CUST# )
copy all from INVTEMP
```

Next, if the value is 3, you want DataEase to modify the matching record in INVOICE. Since you won't know which fields were modified, you'll copy all of them into the temporary INVOICE form. And in case a change was made to a customer address, you also want CUST modified.

1. Either use the menus or type the following command statements:

```
value 3:
  modify records in INVOICE with ( INVOICE# = INVTEMP
INVOICE# )
copy all from INVTEMP
  modify records in CUST with ( CUST# = INVTEMP CUST# )
copy all from INVTEMP .
```

DISPLAYING MESSAGES

The **message** command displays information at the designated point in the query. The message, up to 40 characters in length, appears in the message area of the next screen. You can create your own message or ask DataEase to display the value of any of the system variables, such as the date, time, or current status.

If the message is important, or longer than 40 characters, you can select the *window* option, which clears the screen and displays the message until the user presses any key to continue. Using the window

410   *MASTERING DATAEASE*

CH. 15

guarantees that the user will "get the message." You can include as many messages as necessary. In this case, you'll display a warning message if the user presses F7 to delete the current invoice.

1. Press **F1** to redisplay the menus if necessary.
2. Press **F1** and select **value**
3. Tab three times and type **4** :
4. Select **message**
5. Press **Tab** and type **"YOU ARE NOT AUTHORIZED TO DELETE INVOICES"**
6. Select **window**
7. Select **End** to terminate the **case** command.

Your query should look like the one displayed in Figure 15.1.

```
input using invoice into "INVTEMP" .
case ( current status )
value 1:
  exit
value 2:
  enter a record in INVOICE
copy all from INVTEMP .
modify records in CUST with (CUST# = INVTEMP CUST# )
copy all from INVTEMP
value 3:
  modify records in INVOICE with ( INVOICE# = INVTEMP
    INVOICE# )
copy all from INVTEMP .
modify records in CUST with ( CUST# = INVTEMP CUST# )
copy all from INVTEMP .
value 4:
  message"YOU ARE NOT AUTHORIZED TO DELETE INVOICES"window .
end
```

Figure 15.1: Query with **message** command

ADDING A NEW CUSTOMER

There are a few more actions to add before the value 2 case is complete. If the customer is new, he or she will have no record in the CUST form, so the salesperson must type in the name and address. That information should then be entered as a new record in CUST. DataEase will know that the customer is new if the CUST# field in the INVTEMP form is blank. You used the **if** statement in the last chapter, and it will also work well in this situation.

Remember, the **copy all from** command copies all matching fields from the input form into the designated form. The operative word is "matching": only fields found in both forms will be copied. In this case, only name and address information will be copied into the new record in CUST. The CUST# is sequenced, so DataEase will add that automatically.

1. Move to Row 10, Column 1 and press **F8** five times to insert rows.

2. Either use the menus or type the following statements:

   ```
   if INVTEMP CUST# = blank then
       enter a record in CUST
       copy all from INVTEMP .
   message "ADDING NEW CUSTOMER TO DATABASE" .
   end
   ```

Remember, an **if** statement requires an accompanying **end** statement.

The query, as it reads so far, is displayed in Figure 15.2.

```
    input using invoice into "INVTEMP" .
    case ( current status )
    value 1:
       exit
    value 2:
       enter a record in INVOICE
    copy all from INVTEMP .
    modify records in CUST with (CUST# = INVTEMP CUST# )
        copy all from INVTEMP
    if INVTEMP CUST# = blank then
       enter a record in CUST
       copy all from INVTEMP .
       message "ADDING NEW CUSTOMER TO DATABASE" .
    end
    value 3:
       modify records in INVOICE with ( INVOICE = INVTEMP
          INVOICE# )
    copy all from INVTEMP .
    modify records in CUST with ( CUST# = INVTEMP CUST# )
    copy all from INVTEMP
    value 4:
       message"YOU ARE NOT AUTHORIZED TO DELETE INVOICES"window .
    end
```

Figure 15.2: Query with **if** and **end** statements

412 MASTERING DATAEASE

CH. 15

> When creating lengthy queries such as this one, it is a good idea to save the query from time to time.

3. Press **F2** to save the query.

The CUST# field in INVOICE also needs to be filled. Without going into the CUST form, the salesperson now has no idea what that number is. You can use a variable to pass that information between the CUST and INVOICE forms.

USING VARIABLES TO ENTER DATA

A variable is a temporary storage place that holds information. For example, DataEase comes with system variables that store the date, time, and current status, all of which change continually. You can create your own variables to store information that is used during a procedure.

There are two steps to using variables. First, you must define a variable with a name, data type, and length, just as you define a field in a form. You must also define it as global or temp. Information in a *global* variable can be passed between procedures, while information in a *temp* variable is available only within the current procedure. Variables are usually defined at the beginning of the procedure.

The last step is to assign a value to the variable. You might think of a variable as a temporary field, which is not part of any form. By assigning a value, you are simply telling DataEase what that field contains.

In this case, you will use a variable to hold the CUST# assigned to the new record in the INVOICE form. That information will then be copied into the CUST# field of the current invoice. Since the CUST# field is sequenced, the variable will contain **highest of CUST#** in the CUST form.

You will start by defining the variable at the beginning of the procedure.

1. Press **Home** to move to the top of the procedure.

2. Press **F8** to insert a blank row.

3. Press **F1** to display the menus.

4. Press **F1** again and select **define**

5. Select **Temp** and type **"CUSTNBR"**
6. Select **numeric string** and type **4**

You have now created an empty variable called "CUSTNBR." As part of case 2, DataEase will fill that variable with the last CUST# entered. Your menus should still be active.

1. Move the cursor to Row 15, Column 1 and press **F8** three times to insert three blank rows after the first **message** statement.

2. With the menu still active, press **F1** and select **assign**

3. Select **temp** and type **highest of CUST CUST#**

Next, you must modify the INVOICE record and copy the value of the CUSTNBR variable into the CUST# field.

1. Either use the menus or type the following statements:

    modify records in INVOICE with (CUST# = blank)
    CUST# : = temp CUSTNBR .

The query you should have up to this point appears in Figure 15.3.

```
define temp "CUSTNBR"numeric string 4 .
input using invoice into "INVTEMP" .
case ( current status )
value 1:
   exit
value 2:
  enter a record in INVOICE
copy all from INVTEMP .
modify records in CUST with (CUST# = INVTEMP CUST# )
copy all from INVTEMP
if INVTEMP CUST# = blank then
  enter a record in CUST
  copy all from INVTEMP .
  message "ADDING NEW CUSTOMER TO DATABASE" .
assign temp CUSTNBR := highest of CUST CUST# .
modify records in INVOICE with ( CUST# = blank )
CUST# := temp CUST# .
end
value 3:
   modify records in INVOICE with ( INVOICE = INVTEMP
     INVOICE# )
copy all from INVTEMP .
modify records in CUST with ( CUST# = INVTEMP CUST# )
copy all from INVTEMP
value 4:
   message"YOU ARE NOT AUTHORIZED TO DELETE INVOICES"window .
```

Figure 15.3: Query with INVOICE modification

414 *MASTERING DATAEASE*

CH. 15

If the current status value is 2 (user presses **F2**), DataEase will add the record to INVOICE. If the CUST# is blank, DataEase will also add a new customer record in CUST and copy the new customer number to the CUST# field in the matching INVOICE record.

USING *while* TO REPEAT QUERY STATEMENTS

Your query is almost complete. It needs one very important statement. If you leave the query as it is, DataEase will stop the procedure after one record has been processed. In other words, as soon as the user presses a key, DataEase will process the appropriate action and then return to the DQL menu. However, the salesperson may have other Record Entry tasks to perform, so you want to tell DataEase to redisplay the input form until the user presses Esc.

while is a procedural command that creates what is known in programming as a "loop." A programming loop continuously repeats a series of statements as long as the specified condition is true. This eliminates a lot of repetitive typing. The format of the command is:

```
while CONDITION do
    ACTION 1
    ACTION 2

    ..ETC
end
```

When DataEase encounters a **while** statement, it processes the following actions until it encounters the accompanying **end** statement. Then, as long as the condition is true, it returns to the **while** statement and repeats the following actions again. In this case, DataEase will repeat the **case** commands until the value of the current status is 1 (user presses Esc).

1. Move to Row 2, Column 1, just above the **input using** statement, and press **F1** to display the menus.

2. Press **F8** to insert a row.

3. Press **F1** again and select **while**

AUTOMATING SALES AND ORDER ENTRY   *415*

4. Select **current**

5. Press **F1** and select **status**

6. Press **Tab** twice and select **not**

7. Select **=**

8. Press **Tab**; type **1** then press **Spacebar**

9. Press **Tab** three times. DataEase automatically adds the keyword **do**; the completed statement is:

while current status no = 1 do

And finally, **while** also requires an accompanying **end** statement:

1. Move to the first blank row after the last statement of the query.

2. Type **end** to close the **while** command.

Take a look at your entire query, shown in Figure 15.4.

```
define temp "CUSTNBR"numeric string 4 .
while current status not = 1 do
input using invoice into "INVTEMP" .
case ( current status )
value 1:
  exit
value 2:
  enter a record in INVOICE
copy all from INVTEMP .
modify records in CUST with (CUST# = INVTEMP CUSTNBR )
copy all from INVTEMP
if INVTEMP CUSTNBR = blank then
  enter a record in CUST
  copy all from INVTEMP .
  message "ADDING NEW CUSTOMER TO DATABASE" .
assign temp CUSTNBR := highest of CUST CUST# .
modify records in INVOICE with ( CUST# = blank )
CUST# := temp CUST# .
end
value 3:
  modify records in INVOICE with ( INVOICE = INVTEMP
    INVOICE# )
copy all from INVTEMP .
modify records in CUST with ( CUST# = INVTEMP CUST# )
copy all from INVTEMP
value 4:
  message"YOU ARE NOT AUTHORIZED TO DELETE INVOICES"windov
end
end
```

Figure 15.4: Completed INVENTRY query

416 *MASTERING DATAEASE*

CH. 15

To paraphrase this query, you are asking DataEase to:

1. Create a temporary variable called CUSTNBR, which is currently empty.

2. Display (until the user presses Esc) a temporary input form called INVTEMP which allows the user to enter, view, or modify a record from INVOICE.

3. Depending upon which key the user presses, execute one of the following actions:

   - Exit the procedure if the user presses **Esc**.

   - Enter a record into INVOICE if the user presses **F2**.

   - If the CUST# is blank, also enter a new record into the CUST form.

   - Modify records in INVOICE and CUST if the user presses **F8**.

   - Tell the user he or she can't delete invoices if they press **F7**.

Another command word, **break**, also halts execution of the **while** actions. However, instead of stopping the procedure, it executes the statements appearing after the **while** command's matching **end**. If the query ends after the **while** actions, **break** causes DataEase to exit the procedure.

When the condition in a **while** statement is no longer true, DataEase continues processing, beginning with the statements that appear after the **while** command's accompanying **end** command. In this case, it is also the end of the procedure, so DataEase will return to the DQL menu.

Let's save this query and the procedure.

1. Press **F2** to save the query and return to the DQL menu.

2. Save the procedure under the name **INVENTRY**

You are no doubt ready to test this procedure. However, this procedure does not stand alone. Along with entering invoice information, the salesperson must first run the INVORD procedure to check the status of the current items purchased and to place any necessary orders. And after the invoices are entered, the salesperson will want to print each one. INVORD is complete; however, before proceeding you must convert and modify the INVOICE quick report you created earlier.

PREPARING AND RUNNING
A CONVERTED PROCEDURE

You created INVOICE as a quick report. To run it as a procedure (named INVPRINT), you must first convert it and make some other changes.

1. Load the **INVOICE** report and type **y** to convert it.

All of the statements were converted; however, you'll need to make a few changes to the query.

First, DataEase translated the INVOICE field to include **in groups with group totals**. Since the last four fields, SUBTOTAL, TAX%, TAX, and GRTOT, were placed in the .group trailer area and will display the invoice totals, you do not need to include the **with group totals** phrase.

2. Move to Row 4 and delete the phrase **with group totals**

Next, each salesperson will want to select the invoice(s) to print. An **input using** command is just what they need.

3. Press **Home** to move to the top if necessary.

4. Press **F8** twice to insert two rows and add the following statements:

```
while current status not = 1 do
input using invoice into "INVTEMP" .
```

5. Move to Row 4 under the ; (semicolon) and add the following statement:

```
with ( INVOICE# = INVTEMP INVOICE# ) ;
```

6. Press **End** to move to the end of the query and type **end** to close the **while** statement.

Finally, you'll enter a message telling the user what keys to press to display invoices or to print. This message must be placed in the query so that it appears in the message area of INVOICE.

418 MASTERING DATAEASE

CH. 15

7. Move to Row 2, Column 1, press **F8** to insert a row, and enter the following statement:

message "PRESS SHIFT-F3 TO SEE INVOICE; F2 TO PRINT" .

The modified query appears in Figure 15.5.

```
while current status not = 1 do
MESSAGE "PRESS SHIFT-F3 TO SEE INVOICE; F2 TO PRINT" .
input using INVOICE into "INVTEMP" .
for INVOICE
with ( INVOICE# = INVTEMP INVOICE# ) ;
list records
  INVOICE# in groups ;
  DATE ;
  STORE ;
  SPCODE ;
  SPLNAME ;
  CUST# ;
  FNAME ;
  LNAME ;
  ADDRESS ;
  CITY ;
  STATE ;
  ZIP ;
  TELEPHONE ;
  all INVLIST INVOICE# ;
  all INVLIST STOCK# ;
  all INVLIST ITEM ;
  all INVLIST PRICE ;
  all INVLIST QTY ;
  all INVLIST TOTAL ;
  SUBTOTAL ;
  TAX% ;
  TAX ;
  GRTOT .
end
```

Figure 15.5: INVPRINT query

8. Save the query, and then save the procedure under the name **INVPRINT**

When quick reports are converted to procedures, DataEase may drop some of the fields from the format; so always modify the format and replace any fields that were lost. In this case, some of the line item fields are missing.

1. Select **Modify Format** and type **y** to retain the old format.

As you can see, STOCK#, ITEM, PRICE, QTY, and TOTAL are missing from the .items area. You'll need to place them again.

AUTOMATING SALES AND ORDER ENTRY **419**

2. Use **F10** to place these five fields in Row 12 under their column headings. You can use the column positions suggested below:

COLUMN *FIELD*

12	all INVLIST STOCK#
20	all INVLIST ITEM
41	all INVLIST PRICE
50	all INVLIST QTY
58	all INVLIST TOTAL

3. Save the format, and save the procedure under the same name.

Each of these three procedures, INVORD, INVENTRY, and INVPRINT, may be run separately by the salesperson. However, it would be much more efficient if the salesperson could use one procedure that would run all three. That one procedure is called a control procedure.

USING CONTROL PROCEDURES TO RUN MULTIPLE PROCEDURES

A *control procedure* is a parent procedure from which you can run (or call) processing procedures, other control procedures, user defined menus, and many other database operations, including record entry. A control procedure can include control and procedural commands, but *not* processing commands.

Control commands are executed on forms and files, not records, and perform primarily maintenance functions. You will learn about the database maintenance commands in Chapter 17. One of the procedural commands is **run**, which is used to execute, or call, any procedure you have already created. After the procedure is run, DataEase returns to the ''calling'' control procedure and executes the next statement. By including several **run** statements you can execute several procedures without interruption.

420 *MASTERING DATAEASE*

CH. 15

The control procedure you will create consists of only three statements:

```
run INVORD
run INVENTRY
run INVPRINT
```

Let's create the control procedure:

1. Select **Start New Procedure**

2. Select **Define Query**

3. Press **Home** to clear the menus.

4. Press **F9** and press **F1** to redisplay the menus.

5. Press **F1** and select **Run Procedure**

6. Press **F1** and select **"INVORD"** from the list of procedures.

7. Use the menus or type the last two statements:

```
run procedure "INVENTRY"
run procedure "INVPRINT"
```

8. Press **F2** to save the query.

9. Save the procedure under the name **INVPROC**

RUNNING A CONTROL PROCEDURE

Now you can test your new procedure:

1. Select **Load Procedure** then select **INVPROC**

2. Select **Run Procedure**

3. Enter the following values:

STOCK#	QTYPURCH
12345	2
23456	4

AUTOMATING SALES AND ORDER ENTRY **421**

4. When the data entry form appears again, press **Esc**

Next, the input form for INVOICE is displayed and DataEase displays the message:

Running procedure INVENTRY

1. Enter an invoice containing the values shown in Table 15.1.

Table 15.1: Values for the Invoice

DATE	STORE	SP	CUST#	STOCK#	QTY	TAX
081591	MIL	SP104	9	12345	2	.06
081591	MIL	SP104	9	23456	4	.06

2. Save the record.

3. When the invoice form displays again, press **Esc**

Finally, DataEase takes a few seconds to complete processing the query and displays the input screen from INVPRINT along with the message:

Running procedure INVPRINT

followed by your message:

"PRESS SHIFT-F3 TO SEE INVOICE; F2 TO PRINT" .

1. Press **Shift-F3** to display the last invoice, then press **F2**

2. When the invoice has been printed and the form redisplays, press **Esc**

There you have it, your completed order entry procedure, which enters invoices, checks inventory supplies, places orders, and finally prints the invoices.

3. Press **Esc** to return to the Main Menu.

CONSOLIDATING THE ORDERS

Since orders are placed each time INVORD is run, several orders may be placed throughout the day for the same product. These orders are easily consolidated into one order form at the end of the day.

Listed below is the query that would select the fields for each order:

```
for ORDERS
with DATEORD = CURRENT DATE ;
list records
   ORDER# ;
   STOCK# ;
   ITEM ;
   AMTORD ;
   any VENDORS NAME in groups ;
   any VENDORS ADDRESS ;
   any VENDORS CITY ;
   any VENDORS STATE ;
   any VENDORS ZIP .
```

This query produces a report that can be used as the order form. The report is organized by VENDOR NAME and selects records of orders placed on the current day.

The suggested format, pictured in Figure 15.6, is a custom format that places the VENDOR ADDRESS information at the top of the

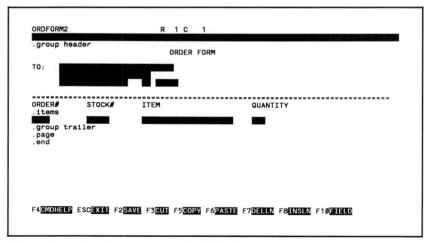

Figure 15.6: Custom format for ORDERS

form and lists below the orders placed for products purchased from that vendor.

AN OPTIONAL METHOD FOR ENTERING ORDERS

Instead of entering multiple orders for the same product, you can easily consolidate daily multiple orders for the same product into a single record in the ORDERS form. This will require you to create a new form and modify the INVORD procedure. The steps are listed below:

- Create a new form called ORDPLACED, which contains only STOCK#, ITEM (a lookup field), and QTYPURCH.

- Modify INVORD procedure and change the **enter a record in ORDERS** to **enter a record in ORDPLACED**. The modified query is listed below:

```
if data-entry QTYPURCH GT= data-entry QTY ONHAND then
     enter a record in ORDPLACED
   STOCK# : = data-entry STOCK# ;
   QTYPURCH : = data-entry QTYPURCH .
end
for ITEMS
with STOCK# = data-entry STOCK# ;
MODIFY RECORDS
   QTY ONHAND : = QTYONHAND − data-entry QTYPURCH .
end
```

- Create a procedure called SUMORD which, run daily, would print the list of records in ORDPLACED, then enter a record in ORDERS for each different STOCK# in ORDPLACED. The AMTORD field for each record would be the sum of QTYPURCH for each STOCK# in the ORDPLACED form. Finally, the procedure would delete all records in ORD-PLACED. This procedure is listed in Figure 15.7.

You are not quite ready to turn Furniture Palace loose with their new procedures. The staff needs very specific directions for using

424 MASTERING DATAEASE

CH. 15

```
define TEMP "ORDTOT"number
for ORDPLACED
;
list records
  STOCK# in groups ;
  ITEM ;
  QTYPURCH ;
end
for ITEMS
with STOCK# = any ORDPLACED STOCK# ;
assign temp ORDTOT := sum of ORDPLACED QTYPURCH .
enter a record in ORDERS
DATEORD := current date ;
ORDER# := 1 + highest of ORDERS ORDER# ;
STOCK# := ITEMS STOCK# ;
AMTORD := temp ORDTOT .
end
for ORDPLACED
delete records .
end
```

Figure 15.7: SUMORD procedure

these procedures. These directions can be cleverly mapped out in the form of custom menus, which is the subject for the next chapter.

SECURITY NOTES

You must have a high security level to perform the **copy all from** command. If you attempt to use this command without the appropriate security level, the following message will be displayed:

You do not have access to this action

CHAPTER SIXTEEN

Creating
Your Own Menus

Fast Track

To create a custom menu,   **429**

select Menu Definition from the Main Menu. Enter the name of the menu and the minimum security level required to use the menu. Enter the menu title that you want to appear at the top of the menu. For each menu choice, enter the description, which will appear when the menu is displayed; the type of function that DataEase will execute when that selection is made; and the function name (the name of the procedure, report, or form) that will be used with each selection.

To load a menu   **433**

when it is first created, you must exit and reload the DataEase program so that DataEase recognizes the menu. After that, each time you load the program your custom menu is automatically loaded into memory.

To call a menu from a procedure,   **433**

select Define or Modify Query from the DQL menu. Enter the command **call menu** followed by the name of the menu in quotes. Run the procedure.

To call a menu from a custom menu,   **436**

from the Menu Definition form, enter the choice description that the user will select to call the custom menu. Select **user menu** as the function type and enter the name (not the title) of the menu as the function name. Save or update the menu.

To create a chain menu,   **438**

from the Menu Definition form, enter **chain** as the menu title. Enter the choice description, function type, and function name for each menu, procedure, or function that will be run from the chain menu. Save or update the menu record.

To select a custom menu as the start-up menu,   **441**

create or modify a user information record and enter the name of the custom menu in the Start-up Menu field. Save or update the menu record. Exit DataEase and sign on under the name whose record you modified to include the custom start-up menu.

To print the user menus,   **443**

select Quick Reports from the Main Menu. Select Define Format, then select System from the list of form names. Select Menus from the list of system forms; select Record Entry as the format type. Delete any rows of text or fields you don't want to include. Save the format. Define the print style and select Printer as the destination. Save the print style and run the report.

CHAPTER 16

THOUGH YOU HAVE AUTOMATED SALES, ACCOUNTS receivable, and order entry through the procedures you have created, the employees at Furniture Palace are still required to know their way around the DataEase menus to perform their tasks. You can make it easier for anyone to use DataEase by creating *custom menus*. With custom menus, you can:

- Make common tasks accessible to the novice user.
- Save the experienced user time and keystrokes.
- Include only the tasks you want to make available to users.

Figure 16.1 shows a sample of a custom menu. As you can see, it includes the major tasks performed by salespeople and clerical staff. It does *not* include access to form, report, or procedure definition. Later in this chapter, you'll create this menu and learn how the user sign-on name can determine the first menu displayed.

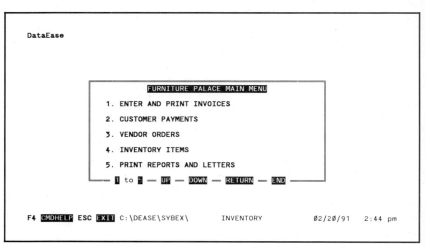

Figure 16.1: Furniture Palace MAIN MENU

There are four types of menus you can use in any menu system:

- The *start-up menu,* used in place of the Main Menu when a designated user signs on.
- *User menus,* which are called by other menus, such as the start-up menu. A user menu can in turn call another menu.
- *Chain menus,* or special user menus that perform multiple tasks without displaying the menus.
- *DataEase menus,* any of which can be called from within a custom menu.

Let's start out by creating a simple user menu.

CREATING A MENU FOR INVOICE ENTRY

A salesperson may want to perform one of three tasks: to enter and print one or more invoices; just to print or modify an invoice; or just to check stock. The salesperson would need to be familiar with the names of all the procedures that perform these tasks. Wouldn't it be simpler if he or she could select these tasks from one menu?

The SALES menu pictured in Figure 16.2 includes a selection for

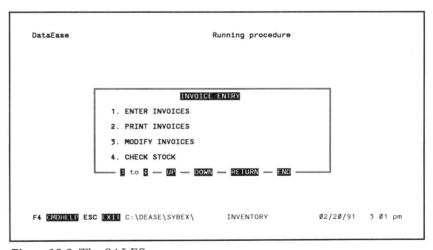

Figure 16.2: The SALES menu

each type of task. A control procedure can be used to call the menu. Let's start by creating the menu:

1. Select **Menu Definition**

Figure 16.3 shows the MENU DEFINITION form. DataEase uses the information you enter in the following fields to design the form:

- The first field is MENU NAME. Here, you will enter the name you'll use when referring to this menu. It will appear in all DataEase lists of menu names.

- The value of the second field, SECURITY LEVEL, determines the minimum security level a user must have in order to work with this menu.

- The MENU TITLE field contains the text that will appear at the top of the menu when it is displayed.

- The CHOICE DESCRIPTION field holds the text you want to display for each menu selection. Each menu can have up to nine selections.

- The FUNCTION TYPE you select is the task that the menu selection performs, such as record entry, execution of a procedure or query, or calling another menu.

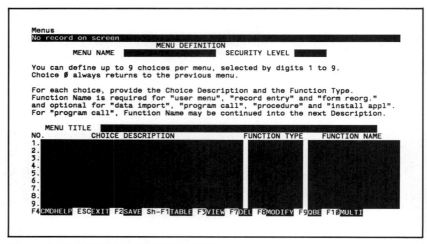

Figure 16.3: MENU DEFINITION form

CREATING YOUR OWN MENUS   431

- The FUNCTION NAME field contains the form or procedure name associated with the task.

Follow the steps below to enter the field values:

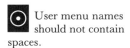
User menu names should not contain spaces.

1. Enter **SALES** at MENU NAME.
2. Press **Tab** and select medium 3 at SECURITY LEVEL.
3. Enter **INVOICE ENTRY** at MENU TITLE.
4. Tab to CHOICE DESCRIPTION No. 1 and type **ENTER AND PRINT INVOICES**
5. Tab to FUNCTION TYPE and press **F1** to display more selections.

The list of function types, shown in Figure 16.4, displays the different DataEase tasks. The function type tells DataEase which menu or screen to display when the user chooses that menu selection. This first menu selection for the SALES menu will call the control procedure named INVPROC that runs INVORD, INVENTRY, and INVPRINT.

6. Select **procedure**
7. Type **INVPROC** at FUNCTION NAME.

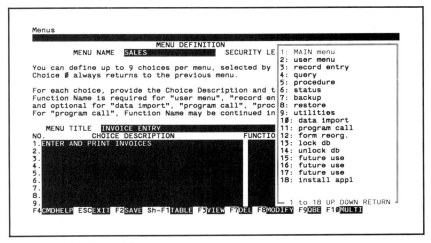

Figure 16.4: Menu of function types

CH. 16

8. Use the information below to enter the last three menu selections:

CHOICE DESCRIPTION	FUNCTION/ TYPE	FUNCTION NAME
PRINT INVOICES	procedure	INVPRINT
MODIFY INVOICES	procedure	INVENTRY
CHECK STOCK	procedure	INVORD

Your completed form is shown in Figure 16.5.

9. Press **F2** to save the record.
10. Press **Esc** to return to the Main Menu.

Before you can use your custom menu, you must load it into the computer's memory.

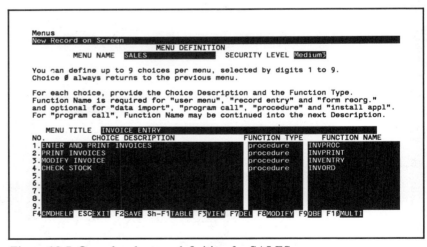

Figure 16.5: Completed menu definition for SALES

LOADING THE MENUS

In order for DataEase to recognize your menu, it must reside in the computer's memory. DataEase loads all menus into the computer's memory each time you start the program. So after you create a menu, you must exit DataEase and reenter so that DataEase recognizes your custom menu.

1. From the Main Menu, press **Esc** and type **y**
2. At the DOS prompt, if necessary type **cd\dease** to move to the DEASE subdirectory.
3. Type **dease sybex** ⏎
4. Select **INVENTORY**
5. Sign on under your name and skip the password.

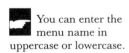
You must select or create a database each time you sign on.

Now your menu is loaded into memory. The next step is to create the control procedure that calls this menu.

CALLING A MENU

The control command **call menu** is used in a control procedure to display the designated menu. The format of the command is

    call menu *"MENU-NAME"*

You can enter the menu name in uppercase or lowercase.

This menu can be one you created, or any DataEase menu. For example,

    call menu *"SALES"*

would display the menu you created called SALES, while

    call menu *"MAIN"*

would display the DataEase Main Menu. Refer to Table 16.1 for a list of DataEase system menu titles.

CH. 16

Table 16.1: DataEase System Menu Titles.

TITLE	DATAEASE MENU
MAIN	Main Menu
FORMS	Form Definition menu
RECORDS	Record Entry menu
QUICK REPORTS	Query By Example–Quick Reports menu
DQL	Data Query Language menu
PROCEDURES	
MAINTENANCE	Maintenance menu
UTILITIES	Utilities menu
ADMINISTRATION	Administration menu

You can include the DataEase Utilities menu and Main Menu in a custom menu by selecting MAIN menu or utilities from the list of function types. To include the Administration menu in your custom menu, select user menu as the function type and enter $ADMIN as the function name.

System menus can be displayed only by calling them from a control procedure. However, you can select a control procedure as one of your function types. For example, if you wanted to include Quick Reports in a user menu, you would follow these steps:

- Create a control procedure that contains the statement:

  call menu "QUICK REPORTS"

- Enter a choice description in your custom menu for Quick Reports.

- Define the function type as **procedure** and enter the name of the control procedure as the function name.

Let's create the control procedure that calls your SALES menu.

1. From the Main Menu, select **DQL**
2. Select **Define Query**

3. Press **Home** to clear the screen and type the following statement:

    call menu "SALES" .

4. Save the query and return to the DQL menu.

5. Save the procedure under the name **SALES**

6. Run the procedure.

The menu you have created, pictured in Figure 16.6, displays only the menu title you entered and the choice description text for each selection. Let's try it out:

1. Select **CHECK STOCK**

DataEase runs the procedure called INVORD and displays the data entry screen.

2. Press **Esc** to return to your menu and try out each of the other selections.

3. When you are finished, press **Esc** until you return to the Main Menu.

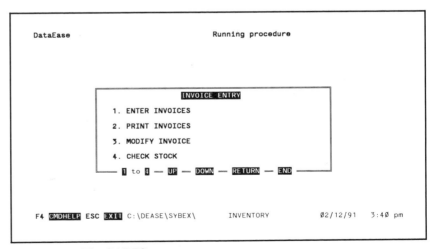

Figure 16.6: The SALES menu

CALLING ONE MENU FROM ANOTHER

Custom menus can do more than just run procedures. They can also be used to select forms for record entry and to call other menus. What Furniture Palace really needs is a custom menu that all of the staff can use. For that purpose, you'll create the menu pictured in Figure 16.7.

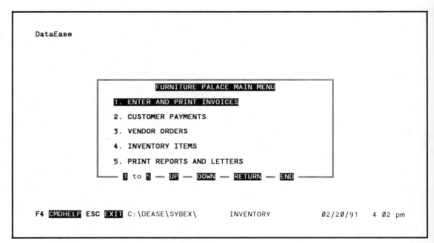

Figure 16.7: Furniture Palace MAIN MENU

Selections 1 and 5 from this menu will each call a different user menu. You've already created one called SALES. Before creating the MAIN MENU for Furniture Palace, let's create the second user menu called PRINT.

1. Return to the Main Menu and select Menu Definition.

2. Use the information in Figure 16.8 to complete the menu definition.

3. Save the record and clear the screen.

Now that you have your two user menus defined, let's create the MAIN MENU for Furniture Palace.

1. Use the information in Figure 16.9 to create Furniture Palace's MAIN MENU.
2. Save the record and return to the DataEase Main Menu.

Next, you must exit DataEase and sign on again, so that DataEase will recognize your new menu.

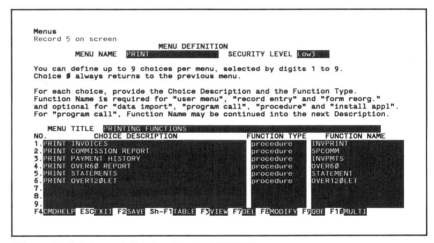

Figure 16.8: Menu definition for the PRINT menu

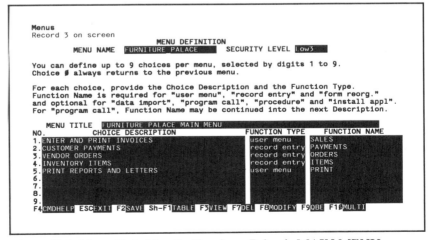

Figure 16.9: Menu Definition for Furniture Palace's MAIN MENU

438 *MASTERING DATAEASE*

CH. 16

1. Exit DataEase.

2. Load the program and sign on again.

3. Select **DQL** and create a procedure with the following query statement:

   `call menu "FURNITURE_PALACE" .`

4. Save the query and save the procedure under the name **MAIN**

5. Run the procedure.

> The underscore character is used here because spaces are often not allowed in menu names.

Your Furniture Palace MAIN MENU is displayed with the five choice descriptions.

1. Select **ENTER AND PRINT INVOICES**; the INVOICES menu you created earlier is displayed.

2. Press **Esc** to clear the menu and select **CUSTOMER PAYMENTS**; this time, DataEase displays the Record Entry form for PAYMENTS.

3. Press **Esc** to return to the Furniture Palace MAIN MENU.

Go ahead and take a few moments to test your other menu selections. Print some reports and display some invoices. You'll see that these menus that take only moments to create can save all users a great deal of time.

CREATING CHAIN MENUS

A chain menu is a special menu that allows you to perform multiple tasks from a single menu selection. When a user selects a choice that calls a chain menu, all actions listed are automatically run without a display of the menu.

A chain menu can help Furniture Palace carry out its operations. Every quarter, Furniture Palace prints the OVER60 payment report, produces statements, sends the OVER120 delinquency letters, and prints the commission reports. Let's create a chain menu for these tasks and add it to the Main Menu. You'll also include a Record Entry function so that any new payments can be entered.

To define a menu as a chain menu, simply enter **chain** at the MENU TITLE prompt.

1. Return to the Main Menu and select **Menu Definition**
2. Use the information in Figure 16.10 to create the menu.
3. Save the record and press **F3** to display the Furniture Palace MAIN MENU.
4. Add the following menu selection:

   6. QUARTERLIES   user menu   QUARTERLY

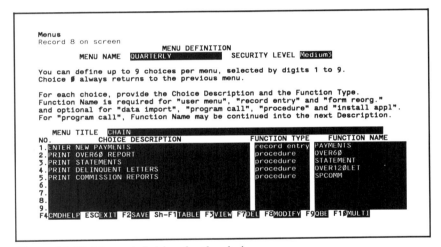

Figure 16.10: Menu definition for the chain menu

When you change an existing menu, you must again exit and reenter DataEase so that DataEase recognizes the modification:

1. Modify the record and return to the DataEase Main Menu.
2. Exit, then load DataEase and sign on again.
3. From the DataEase Main Menu, select **DQL**
4. From the DQL menu, select **Run Procedure**, then select **MAIN**

Your modified menu now includes the chain menu selection, pictured in Figure 16.11.

1. Select **Quarterlies**
2. When the Record Entry screen displays, press Esc to skip entering payments, then run the reports.

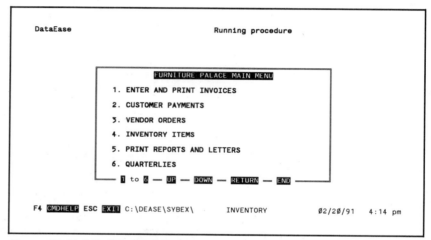

Figure 16.11: Modified Furniture Palace MAIN MENU

The first report, OVER60, is displayed on the screen. One at a time, DataEase runs the reports listed in the chain menu. Each time a report is displayed on the screen, you must press Esc to clear the report and continue with the next one.

3. Press **Esc** to clear the screen.

Before processing the next report, DataEase asks:

>   Do you want to abort the chain?

4. Type **n**

Continue displaying each report. When the chain is complete, DataEase will return to the Furniture Palace MAIN MENU.

The next step is to eliminate the necessity of running the procedure to start the menu. You can do that by selecting FURNITURE_PALACE as a start-up menu.

CHANGING THE START-UP MENU

Ordinarily, after you sign on, DataEase always displays the Main Menu. In Chapter 2, you learned that if you enter a name the first time you sign on to DataEase, a user information record is automatically created for you. By making a change to a user information record, you can display another menu at start up. Let's take a look at your record. User information records are defined and modified from the System Administration menu:

1. Return to the Main Menu, and select **System Administration**
2. Select **Define Users**

The USER INFORMATION form, displayed in Figure 16.12, begins with the Name and Password fields. Here, you can add a password for a user if he or she did not originally enter one when signing on for the first time. The Level assigns the security level which, along with Screen Style, is covered more thoroughly in the

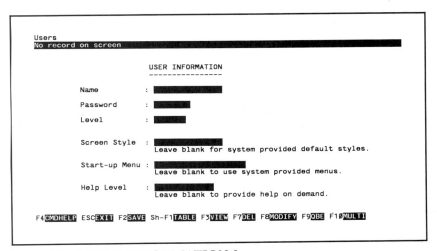

Figure 16.12: USER INFORMATION form

442 MASTERING DATAEASE

CH. 16

next chapter. The Start-up Menu field asks for the name of the start-up menu, and defaults to the DataEase Main Menu.

3. Press **F3** to display your user information record.

Let's create two more user information records: one called SALES (just for sales staff), and one called FP (for all Furniture Palace staff). When you sign on as SALES, DataEase will automatically display the SALES menu; when you sign on as FP, DataEase will display the Furniture Palace MAIN MENU.

1. Press **F5** to clear the form.

2. Enter **SALES** as the user name.

3. Enter **SALES** as the password.

4. Skip to the Start-up Menu field and select **SALES**

The completed form is displayed in Figure 16.13. Next, you'll create an information record for all Furniture Palace staff.

1. Press **F2** to save the record and **F5** to clear the screen.

2. Enter FP as the user name.

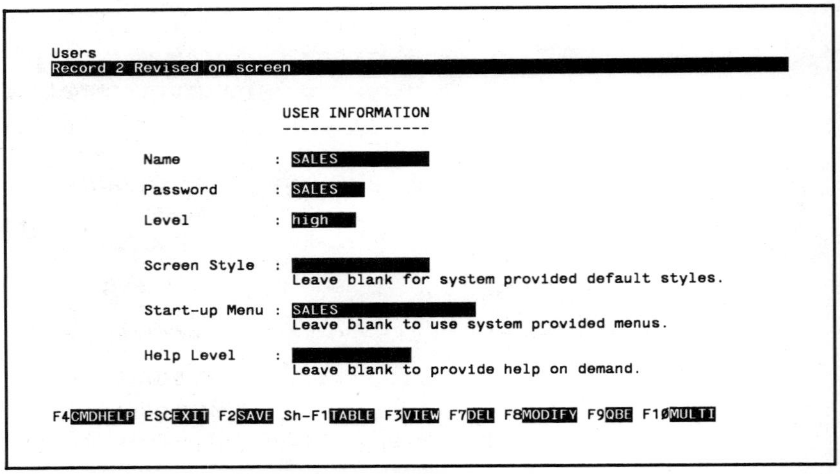

> ◉ If you assign no security level, the high level is automatically assigned. In this case it doesn't matter, since the SALES user is restricted by the selections in the start-up menu.

Figure 16.13: Completed SALES information record

CREATING YOUR OWN MENUS   **443**

3. Enter FP as the password.

4. Skip to the Start-up Menu field and select **FURNITURE_-PALACE**

5. Save the record and return to the DataEase Main Menu.

Now you are ready to test your new users, starting with SALES. Only a high level user can change user definition.

1. Press **Esc** and type **y** to leave DataEase.

2. At the DOS prompt, type **dease sybex**

3. Select **INVENTORY**

4. When prompted for the name, type **sales** ◄─┛

5. When prompted for the password, type **sales** ◄─┛

DataEase automatically displays the SALES menu. This is now the Main Menu, and the only tasks you can access are the ones listed on this menu. And, of course, you will exit the program from this menu, just as you otherwise would exit from the DataEase Main Menu.

Next, let's sign on as FP to test the Furniture Palace MAIN MENU.

1. Press **Esc** and type **y** to exit DataEase.

2. Load DataEase again, and this time sign on with **fp** as the name and as the password.

This time, DataEase displays the Furniture Palace MAIN MENU.

3. Press **Esc** to exit DataEase, then return again under your own user name.

PRINTING YOUR CUSTOM MENUS

As you know, documenting your forms, reports, and queries is an important part of your database tasks. It's also a good idea to print your menus. The record entry format is a good style in which to print menus.

> You should always assign at least one user a high security level so he or she has access to the Main Menu or System Administration menu. If you make any major mistakes when defining users, you can sign on under that user's name to make modifications.

444 MASTERING DATAEASE
CH. 16

> If you want to include all fields in a report, you can skip field selection and proceed to define the format.

1. From the Main Menu, select **Quick Reports**
2. Select **Define Format**

The forms that come with the DataEase program are called system forms and include those that you use to create user, relationship, and menu records. You can print reports on any of the system forms from Quick Reports by selecting **System** from the list of forms.

3. Select **System**

DataEase displays the list of system forms, pictured in Figure 16.14.

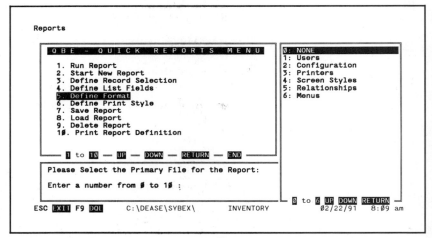

Figure 16.14: Menu of system forms

4. Select **Menus**
5. Select **Record Entry** as the format.

The record entry format is displayed, including the **items nosplit** formatting command that tells DataEase not to break up a record between two pages. Since only the fields are necessary, you can remove most of the text.

6. Delete the rows of explanatory text. The completed format is pictured in Figure 16.15.

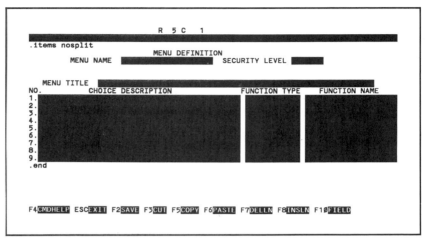

Figure 16.15: Completed format for menus report

7. Save the format.

8. If you have a printer, select **Define Print Style** and select your printer.

9. Save the style and run the report. Each menu is printed on (or displayed as) a separate page.

OPTIONAL MENU CONFIGURATIONS

You may prefer that the same menu always appear at start up for everyone. In that case, you may want to include generic selections, such as:

1. DATA ENTRY
2. REPORTS
3. MAINTENANCE

These are just a few of the possible custom menu configurations you can create for yourself and other users. For example, the DATA ENTRY selection would run a control procedure that allows the user

CH. 16

name to determine the next menu displayed. The control procedure would include the following sample **case** statement.

```
case (current user name)
value "SALES"
call menu "SALES"
value "STAFF"
call menu "STAFF"
value "ADMIN"
call menu "ADMIN"
```

The current user name is the system variable that contains the sign-on name of the current user. Therefore, if the user signs on as STAFF and selects DATA ENTRY from the start-up menu, DataEase would automatically display the menu with data entry selections for staff only.

A menu selection often omitted from custom menus is MAINTE-NANCE. Sometimes referred to as "housekeeping," maintenance tasks are usually reserved for the systems administrator (or yourself, if you are a single user).

Up to now you have learned the ropes of manipulating records. In the next chapter, you'll learn how to manage your database files.

SECURITY NOTES

Only users with a high security level can create or define custom menus.

CHAPTER SEVENTEEN

Maintaining
Your Database

Fast Track

To make a duplicate of a form,   450
> select Form Definition and Relationships from the Main Menu, then select View or Modify a Form. Select the form you want to copy from the list. Make a change that does not permanently affect the form. Save the form and respond with **y** when prompted to save the form under another name; enter the new name. If you want to copy the records as well, respond with **y** when prompted.

To delete a group of records in a query,   452
> select DQL from the Main Menu, then select Define Query. To delete all records, enter the command **delete records** and select the form name. To delete selected records, select the keyword **with** and enter the selection criteria. Save the query and run the procedure.

To copy field values in a query   453
> from one form to another, select Define Query from the DQL menu. Following the **for** statement, select the form you want to copy from, and include a **with** statement if you want to copy fields from selected records. On the next line, enter the command **enter a record in** and select the name of the form you want to copy to. On the next line, enter the command **copy all from** and select the name of the form you want to copy from. Only fields with matching names in each form are copied.

To copy records between two forms,   456
> select System Administration from the Main Menu, then select DataBase Utilities. Select Transfer Data and select the name of the source form. Next, select the name of the destination form.

To copy a DataEase Form, report, or procedure between two databases,   **457**

sign on to the database into which you're copying. From the Database Utilities menu, select Install form to copy a form, or Install procedure to copy a report or procedure. Enter a name, then the DOS file name for the form (.DBA) or report or procedure (.DBR). To copy the data from the form, enter the DOS file name for the data (.DBM); if copying a report or procedure, type **y** to copy the data entry form, **n** not to copy.

To copy multiple files between two database,   **462**

copy or create an installation command file in the directory that contains the files you want to install; and enter the list of commands to install the files. Sign on to the database in which you want to install the file. From the Main Menu, select System Administration; then select Database Utilities. Select Install/ Convert Application and then select Install DataEase Application. Enter the name of the command file, including the extensions.

To back up a database,   **465**

select Database Maintenance from the Main Menu and then select Backup Database. Specify the disk and/or directory path in which you want to create the backup. Select the action to be taken by DataEase if it encounters any errors.

To restore your database,   **467**

sign on under the database you want to restore. Select Database Maintenance from the Main Menu and then select Restore Database. Enter the source drive and/or directory. Select the action to be taken by DataEase if it encounters errors. If you are restoring from a floppy disk, insert the source diskette and press Enter.

CHAPTER 17

WHETHER YOU USE DATAEASE ON YOUR OWN, SHARE your computer with others, or are a systems administrator managing many users on a local area network, you need to develop good "housekeeping" habits to maintain your database efficiently.

Database maintenance involves such tasks as backing up your database, deleting selected groups of records, copying and reorganizing forms, copying data between forms, deleting forms, and copying files between databases.

Most of these functions are found under one of three Main Menu selections: Form Definition and Relationships, Systems Administration, and Database Maintenance.

COPYING FORMS AND RECORDS

When you save a form after any modification, DataEase always asks if you want to save the form under a new name. Normally, you answer **n**. However, if you want to create a new form that is similar to an existing form, you can save time if you modify the existing form and save the changes under a new name. DataEase also copies any relationship records under the new name. If the relationships don't apply to the new form, you may want to delete them. Your original form and relationships will stay intact.

You can use the following method to make a duplicate of a form and its records:

- Modify the form and *appear* to make a change—for example, by deleting and then reinserting a blank line.

- After you enter the new name, answer **y** to transfer the data as well.

This can be an excellent safety net. If you have made modifications you are not sure will work or if you are about to test a query on your

MAINTAINING YOUR DATABASE **451**

form, making an extra copy is a good way to prevent accidental loss of data.

At the end of the last chapter, you looked at a modified version of the INVORD query that enters orders in a new form called ORD-PLACED. This form contains only STOCK#, ITEM, and QTY-PURCH. As a shortcut you can modify either ITEMS or ORDERS, since they both contain two of the fields. However, the ITEM field in ORDERS has a lookup formula that you'll need. So let's modify ORDERS. Although this new form would normally have no records until you ran the query, let's copy the data anyway.

1. Modify the ORDERS form.

2. Use **F7** (Delete Row) to delete all rows *except* those containing ITEM and STOCK#.

3. Use **F3** to cut fields and text in front of STOCK#.

4. Press **Esc** to cancel **F3** after the data is cut.

5. Move ITEM to the same row as STOCK# and delete SOURCE.

6. Add the last field:

> *NAME*   *TYPE*   *LENGTH*
>
> QTYPURCH   NUMBER 3

The completed form is pictured in Figure 17.1.

Next, you'll save this form under the name ORDPLACED and copy the data as well.

1. Press **F2** and type **y** to save under a new name.

2. Type **ORDPLACED** as the new form name.

3. Type **y** to transfer the data.

DataEase saves the new form, transfers the data, copies relationships, and updates the indices. Remember, all field attributes, including indices, are copied as well.

> If you delete the wrong text or fields, you can always press Esc, return to the menu without saving changes, and start over again.

452 MASTERING DATAEASE
CH. 17

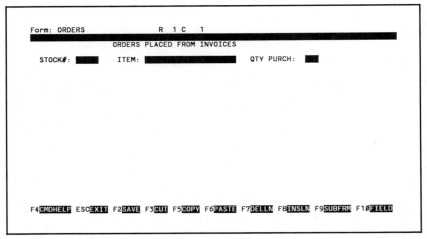

Figure 17.1: Completed modification of ORDERS

Next, let's take a look at the new relationships:

1. Select **Define Relationships**
2. When the relationship form displays, press **Shift-F1** to display the Table View.
3. Press **End** to move to the bottom of the list.

You can see the new relationship records between ORDPLACED and ITEMS, and between VENDORS and ORDREC. Next, let's verify that the records were copied:

1. Press **Esc** twice to return to the Definition menu.
2. Press **Esc** to return to the Main Menu.
3. Select **Record Entry** for **ORDPLACED**
4. Press **F3** to see that all the records were duplicated.

> Keeping a duplicate form is one way to prevent losing data in case you delete the wrong records.

DELETING GROUPS OF RECORDS WITH DQL

In Chapter 4, you learned how to delete individual records with F7. If you need to delete a large group of records or all of your records in a form, it is more efficient to use a DQL procedure.

MAINTAINING YOUR DATABASE **453**

The command **delete records** is a processing command that deletes records in the designated form. The format is similar to the one used for **modify records**:

delete record in (FORMNAME/RELATIONSHIP) [named
("UNIQUE RELATIONSHIP NAME")][with (selection criteria)]

The Sales Manager of Furniture Palace would like to remove from the CUST form all customers with a zero balance in the TOT-SALES field. However, before you delete any records from a form, it is a good idea to archive the records you want to delete in a separate form—you never know when you will need those records again. And of course the IRS always appreciates historical information. So let's begin by making a copy of the CUST form with no record transfer:

1. Return to the Main Menu and select **Form Definition and Relationships**

2. Modify the **CUST** form.

3. Move to any completely blank row and press **F7** to delete the row and then **F8** to insert it again. (This is just to make a modification to the form.)

4. Press **F2** and type **y** to save under a new name.

5. Type **CUSTDEL** ◄─┘ and **n** to choose *not* to transfer the data.

6. Return to the Main Menu and select **DQL**

Now you'll create a query that copies the records with a zero balance to the new form CUSTDEL and then deletes those records from CUST.

COPYING FIELDS
FROM ANOTHER FORM

Remember, the **copy all from** command is only used following a **modify records** or **enter a record** command.

In a previous query, you used **copy all from** to copy fields from a temporary input form. You can also use it to copy fields from an existing form. In this case, the **copy all from** command copies all fields from each record with a 0 in the TOTSALES field.

454 *MASTERING DATAEASE*

CH. 17

1. Select **Define Query** and enter the following statements:

```
for CUST
with TOTSALES = 0 ;
    enter a record in CUSTDEL
    copy all from CUST .
end
delete records in CUST with ( TOTSALES = 0 ) .
```

Since the **for** statement was completed with **end**, you need to repeat the record selection criteria with the **delete** command; otherwise you would have deleted all records in CUST.

2. Save the query.

3. Save the procedure under **DELCUST**

4. Run the procedure.

5. When the procedure is complete, return to the Main Menu and select **Record Entry** for CUST.

6. Display your records.

Before you run this procedure, you might want to create a duplicate of the CUST form, just in case.

As you can see, all customers with a zero balance have been deleted. However, as you press F3, DataEase skips those customers' record numbers, so their numbers are still in use.

1. Return to the Record Entry menu and select **CUSTDEL**

2. Press **F3** to see that the form contains the five deleted records and then return to the Main Menu.

You can continue to add records to this form with the **enter a record** command each time you delete records from the CUST form.

FORM REORGANIZATION

When you delete records from your database they are no longer displayed with other records or included in your reports. However, they still remain in your database, taking up space on the disk. In Chapter 4, you were able to access deleted records with Ctrl-F3

MAINTAINING YOUR DATABASE 455

The reorganization takes only a few seconds, since there are just a few records in this form. If you have a large number of records, reorganization could take considerably longer.

(View Record Number) because their record numbers were still in use. In order to remove the deleted records from the database and reassign record numbers, you must reorganize your forms.

Let's reorganize CUST.

1. Select **Form Definition and Relationships**

2. Select **Reorganize a form**

3. Select **CUST**

4. When the reorganization is complete, return to Record Entry and select **CUST**

5. Press **F3** to display each record.

As you can see, the record numbers have been reassigned and the deleted records are gone for good.

When you use F7 or **delete records**, you can still retrieve the deleted records with Ctrl-F3 until you reorganize your forms. However, this is not the case if you delete *all* your records in a given form. For example:

- If you delete *all* your records using **F7**, once you press **Esc** to exit Record Entry, you will lose all your records. You cannot return to Record Entry for that form and use **Ctrl-F3** to access records.

- If you use **delete records** to delete *all* your records in a form, they are also gone for good. You cannot retrieve them with **Ctrl-F3**.

To prove this point, let's delete the records in ORDPLACED.

1. Press **Esc** to leave Record Entry and return to the Main Menu.

2. Select **DQL**

3. Create the following query:

   delete records in ordplaced .

4. Save the query.

456 MASTERING DATAEASE

CH. 17

5. Save the procedure under the name **DELORD** and run the procedure.

6. When the procedure is complete, leave DQL and return to Record Entry; you will see that the records in ORD-PLACED have been deleted.

7. Press **Ctrl-F3** and type **1**

DataEase displays:

no more records

indicating that all records have gone to "data heaven" (even without form reorganization).

DELETING AND RESEQUENCING

When you reorganize a form, the record numbers are resequenced. However, the values in sequenced fields are not changed. If you display records in your CUST form, you'll notice that there are still gaps in customer numbers, since you removed records. That is as it should be, since you certainly don't want DataEase to reassign customer numbers.

However (there's always a "however"), if you should happen to delete the last record (or last few records), form reorganization *will* affect the next number or character in sequence. For example, if you delete INVOICE# 15 and 16, and haven't yet reorganized your form, the next INVOICE# will be 17, since 15 and 16 are still on the disk. However, *after* you reorganize, and permanently remove, INVOICE# 15 and 16, DataEase will change the next available INVOICE# to 15.

As you've seen, making a duplicate form is one way of copying data. You can also use a duplicate form to transfer data between forms.

COPYING RECORDS BETWEEN FORMS

The Transfer Data command copies data between two existing forms. All records are copied; all field values in the first form are copied to fields in the second form with matching names.

MAINTAINING YOUR DATABASE **457**

For example, if you accidentally delete all your records in a form, *and* you have created a duplicate, you can transfer the data from the duplicate form. If you are testing a new query that deletes *any* of the records in a form, it is a good idea to make a duplicate before running the query. Let's see how this works. Earlier in this chapter you created a form called ORDPLACED by modifying orders and copying all the data. Later, you deleted all the records in ORDPLACED. Now you'll use the Transfer Data command to copy records from ORDERS back into ORDPLACED.

The Transfer Data command is a database utility under System Administration.

1. Return to the Main Menu and select **System Administration**

2. Select **DataBase Utilities**

3. Select **Transfer Data**

DataEase prompts:

Please select source form:

4. Select **ORDERS**

Next, DataEase prompts:

Please select destination form:

5. Select **ORDPLACED**

When the transfer is complete:

Transfer Data does not look for duplicate records. All records from the source are copied and added to the destination form.

6. Return to **Record Entry**

7. Select **ORDPLACED** and press **F3** to see that all the records are there.

COPYING DATAEASE FILES BETWEEN DATABASES

You have seen how easy it is to copy forms within the current database. But what if you want to copy a form or procedure from another database? Copying files between databases is called *installing*. The **install form** or **install procedure** command installs a single form, procedure, or report. The **install application** command allows you to install multiple forms and procedures with one command.

DETERMINING DATAEASE DOS FILE NAMES

Before you can install any file, you must know the DataEase DOS file names for each form and procedure you want to copy. A simple method for finding these names is to use Database Status. Database Status allows you to print or display each form and procedure in the current database, along with its DOS name.

Follow the steps below either to print or to display the status of forms and procedures.

1. From the Main Menu, select **Database Maintenance**
2. Select **Database Status**

The Database Status screen, pictured in Figure 17.2, allows you to display or print the status of forms or procedures. For now, you will print (or display, if you don't have a printer) the forms and procedures.

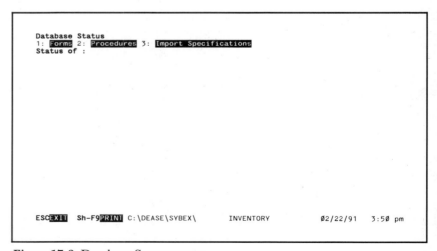

Figure 17.2: Database Status screen

MAINTAINING YOUR DATABASE 459

1. Select **Forms**

2. Press **Shift-F3** to display or **Shift-F9** to print the names.

3. Press **PgDn** at the end of each screen to continue.

4. Press **Esc** at the end of the report.

5. Select **Procedures** and repeat steps 2–6 above to print or display the procedures.

6. Return to the Main Menu when you are finished.

If you did not print your status report, refer to Figures 17.3 and 17.4 for a partial list of forms and procedures.

Let's take a look at forms first. Every form has at least two files, each of which is identified by its unique extension:

.DBA   The form definition file stores form definition information.

.DBM   The form data file stores records.

.I*nn*   Index files store information on key fields. (The unique two-digit numbers following the I are significant only to DataEase.)

> The first four characters of a DOS file name are taken from the first four letters of the form, report, or procedure name. The fifth character is the letter originally assigned to the database. The last three characters are assigned by DataEase to make the name unique.

```
Database Status
SPACE or PgDn: Continue report  EXIT: Abort report  PgUp: Scroll
         Form Definition File              C:VENDIAAA.DBA        503
    9.  INVLIST              48        12  C:INVLIAAA.DBM       3000
         Index File                         C:INVLIAAA.I01      2048
         Index File                         C:INVLIAAA.I02      2048
         Form Definition File               C:INVLIAAA.DBA       475
   10.  SP                   12         0  C:SPAAIAAB.DBM        672
         Index File                         C:SPAAIAAB.I04      1024
         Form Definition File               C:SPAAIAAB.DBA       746
   11.  PAYMENTS              9         0  C:PAYMIAAA.DBM        306
         Index File                         C:PAYMIAAA.I01      1024
         Form Definition File               C:PAYMIAAA.DBA      1443
   12.  PAYLIST              29         0  C:PAYLIAAB.DBM        725
         Index File                         C:PAYLIAAB.I01      1556
         Index File                         C:PAYLIAAB.I02      1556
         Form Definition File               C:PAYLIAAB.DBA       291
   13.  ITEMS                20         1  C:ITEMIAAB.DBM       4872
         Index File                         C:ITEMIAAB.I02      1024
         Index File                         C:ITEMIAAB.I03      1556
         Index File                         C:ITEMIAAB.I04      1556
         Form Definition File               C:ITEMIAAB.DBA      2178
   14.  ORDERS               26        24  C:ORDEIAAA.DBM       3750
         Index File                         C:ORDEIAAA.I02      1556
ESC EXIT   Sh-F9 PRINT  C:\DEASE\SYBEX\       INVENTORY     02/22/91   3 50 pm
```

Figure 17.3: Sample screen from Form Status

460 MASTERING DATAEASE

CH. 17

```
Database Status
SPACE or PgDn: Continue report EXIT: Abort report PgUp: Scroll

No of procedures 26
No.    PROCEDURE NAME      DISK FILE NAME      FILE SIZE Bytes
---  ------------------    ----------------    ---------------
 1.  INVLIST              C:INVLIAAA.DBR            1686
 2.  INVMFR               C:INVMIAAA.DBR            1486
 3.  ITEMORD              C:ITEMIAAA.DBR            1420
 4.  INVOICE              C:INVOIAAA.DBR            3171
 5.  PAYMENTS             C:PAYMIAAA.DBR            2244
 6.  INVLISTP             C:INVLIAAB.DBR            1507
 7.  MFRORD               C:MFROIAAA.DBR            1953
 8.  ORDSTAT              C:ORDSIAAA.DBR            1613
 9.  CUSTINV              C:CUSTIAAA.DBR            1896
10.  CUSTQRY              C:CUSTIAAB.DBR            1954
     Data-entry Form      C:CUSTIAAB.DBF             450
11.  SPCOMM               C:SPCOIAAA.DBR            2089
12.  OVER60               C:OVERIAAA.DBR            2266
13.  NEWCOST              C:NEWCIAAA.DBR            1324
14.  ORDREC               C:ORDRIAAA.DBR             937
     Data-entry Form      C:ORDRIAAA.DBF             490
15.  QTY                  C:QTYAIAAA.DBR             712
16.  SHIPS                C:SHIPIAAA.DBR            1058
ESC EXIT  Sh-F9 PRINT  C:\DEASE\SYBEX\     INVENTORY      02/22/91   3:50 pm
```

Figure 17.4: Sample screen from Procedure Status

.E*nn*   Exception files capture any error messages while
           processing forms or records. These are
           DOS-readable files that can be deleted. (The unique
           two-digit numbers following the E are significant
           only to DataEase.)

When you install a form, you must copy the first three file types for
each form. DataEase will ask you only for the names of the .DBA and
.DBM files. Index files are copied automatically.

The procedure file names are much simpler. Each procedure or
quick report has only one name with a .DBR extension, so it is easily
recognizable.

INSTALLING A SINGLE FORM OR PROCEDURE

To see how easy it is to copy forms and procedures, you'll copy the
ITEMS form and the INVLIST report you created at the beginning
of this book. The procedure for installing a form is as follows:

> Before installing a
> report or form,
> print the definition. After
> installing, compare the
> definition with the newly
> installed form or report to
> make sure that field
> definitions for the form or
> field match record selec-
> tions for the report.

- Sign on to the database in which you want to install the files.

- Select **Systems Administration**

- Select **Database Utilities**

- Select **Install form**

MAINTAINING YOUR DATABASE   461

- Enter a name for the new form.
- Enter the DOS file name for the form (.DBA).
- If you want to copy the data, enter the DOS file name for the data (.DBM).

To install a procedure:

- Follow the first two steps above.
- Select **Install procedure**
- Enter a name for the new procedure.
- Enter the DOS file name of the report or procedure (.DBR).
- Type **y** to copy or **n** not to copy the data entry form.

Your first step will be to create another database.

1. From the Main Menu, press **Esc** to exit.
2. From the DOS prompt, type **dease sybex** ◄━┛
3. From the Sign On screen, select **NONE**
4. At the prompt, type **INVENT2** as the new database name.

You have created a new database called INVENT2 and you're ready to install the form ITEMS. You'll call the new form ITEMS also, although you could assign any name you liked.

1. From the Main Menu, select **System Administration**
2. Select **Database Utilities**
3. Select **Install form**. DataEase will ask you to:

   Please enter the new form name to be defined

4. Type **ITEMS** ◄━┛. DataEase now asks you to:

   Please enter the Form (DBA) filename:

5. Type **ITEMIAAB.DBA**. Next, DataEase asks you to:

   Please enter any data (DBM) filename:

6. Type **ITEMIAAB.DBM**

If the file you are copying is in a different directory, precede the file name with the DOS directory path.

462 MASTERING DATAEASE

CH. 17

DataEase copies only the individual form and *not* any of the relationships. If you have other forms that are dependent on this form or vice versa, you will need to create the relationships separately.

After a few seconds, DataEase displays the message,

Form Installed

and returns you to the Utilities menu.

DataEase copies only the main form. If there are subforms connected to the installed form, they must be copied separately.

Next, install the INVLIST report:

1. Select **Install Procedure**

2. Type **INVLIST** as the name of the new report.

3. Type **INVLIAAA.DBR** as the DOS procedure file name.

4. Type **n** to indicate no data entry form.

Let's take a look at your new files. After the procedure is installed and the Utilities menu is displayed,

1. Return to the Main Menu and select **Record Entry**

2. Select **ITEMS**

3. Press **F3** to display the first record.

The TOTSOLD field is blank, since it depends upon the missing relationship with INVLIST. Since no relationship records have been established and INVLIST is not in this directory, DataEase displays:

Unknown relationship INVLIST

4. Press **F3** again to see that all records were copied.

5. When you are finished, return to the Main Menu and select **Quick Reports**

6. Select **Run Report**, then select **INVLIST**

7. The report is displayed on the screen.

8. Press **Esc** to clear the screen and return to the Main Menu.

INSTALLING APPLICATIONS

When you need to install multiple forms or procedures, it is more practical to install them as an application. To do that you must create

MAINTAINING YOUR DATABASE   **463**

an *installation command file* that contains commands for each form and procedure you want to install, using the guidelines below:

- Create the installation command file with any word processing program or editor that can produce an ASCII file. (See below for a list of commands.)

- Copy or create this file in the same directory that contains the files you want to install.

- Select **System Administration** from the Main Menu.

- Select **Database Utilities**

- Select **Install/Convert Application**

- Select **Install DataEase Application**

- Enter the name of the command file, including the extension. If no extension is included, DataEase assumes a default extension of .DIN.

Remember to precede DOS file names with the directory path if the installed files are in a different directory.

Listed below are the commands that you can include in the installation command file.

command: install form FORMNAME from:<DOS filename>.DBA ;

example: install form ITEMS from:ITEMIAAB.DBA ;

Installs a new form without data into the current database.

command: install form FORMNAME from:<DOS filename>.DBA

data:<DOS filename>.DBM ;

example: install form ITEMS from ITEMIAAB.DBA

data:ITEMIAAB.DBM ;

Installs a new form with data into the current database.

command: install form FORMNAME from:<DOS filename>.DBM ;

example: install form ITEMS from:ITEMIAAB.DBM ;

Installs new data into an existing form in the current database.

464 *MASTERING DATAEASE*

CH. 17

command: replace form FORMNAME from:<DOS filename>.DBA ;

example: replace form ITEMS from ITEMIAAB.DBA ;

Replaces an existing form in the current database with an updated version from another database.

command: install procedure PROCEDURENAME from:<DOS filename>.DBR

example: install procedure INVLIST from INVLIAAA.DBR ;

Installs a new procedure into the current database.

command: replace procedure PROCEDURENAME from:<DOS filename>.DBR

example: replace procedure ORDREC from ORDRIAAA.DBR ;

Replaces an existing procedure in the current database with the updated file from another database.

command: install report REPORTNAME from:<DOS filename>.DBR

example: install report INVLIST from INVLIAAA.DBR ;

Replaces an existing report in the current database with the updated file from another database.

command: replace report REPORTNAME from:<DOS filename>.DBR

example: replace report INVLIST from INVLIAAA.DBR ;

Replaces an existing report in the current database with the updated file from another database.

The Install/Convert Application menu contains selections for converting dBase, Lotus, and Paradox files. That topic is covered in Appendix B.

You now have the necessary tools to copy files within the current database as well as from another database. Before you move on, you'll need to exit from this database and return to INVENTORY:

1. Press **Esc** and type **y** to exit to DOS.

MAINTAINING YOUR DATABASE   **465**

2. Type **cd/dease** to return to the DEASE directory if necessary.

3. Type **dease sybex**

4. Select INVENTORY and sign on to move to the Main Menu.

There is one more type of copy you should perform regularly that makes a backup copy of all your files.

BACKING UP YOUR DATABASE

It is best to back up your files onto a floppy disk, rather than your current hard disk, in case the entire hard disk becomes unusable.

The DataEase Backup command makes a duplicate of the entire database, including all forms, records, reports, queries, and relationships. This backup is your insurance against disk damage or user mishaps that can cost you all your database files.

You may have used the DOS copy or backup command to copy files from other programs. However, there are several advantages to using the DataEase Backup command:

- It backs up only database files, ignoring program files.

- It erases any files from a previous backup on the target disk only if you select **y** at the prompt.

- It ignores, and does not erase, any other files in the target directory.

- It checks for errors.

If DataEase runs out of room on the target disk, you are prompted to insert another disk, and the backup continues.

If the database you are restoring *to* has a different name, any existing DataEase files in the target database will be erased.

The DataEase Restore command restores files backed up with the DataEase Backup command on the designated directory to a database with the same or different name.

The procedure for backing up your database is as follows:

- Sign on under the database you want to back up.

- If you are backing up to a floppy disk, insert a formatted disk into your floppy disk drive.

- From the Main Menu, select **Database Maintenance**

466 MASTERING DATAEASE

CH. 17

- Select **Backup Database**
- Enter the drive and/or directory path you want to use for the backup.
- From the menu, select the action you want DataEase to take if it encounters an error.
- At this point, you will be instructed to insert your disk and press ⏎.
- If the backup requires more than one disk, you will be instructed to remove the first disk, label it, and insert another.

This would be a good time to back up the files you have created during the exercises.

1. If you have a floppy disk drive, insert an empty, formatted diskette.

2. From the Main Menu, select **Database Maintenance**

3. Select **Backup Database**

DataEase requests you to:

Specify the path name to use for Backup and press RETURN

4. Type **A:** ⏎

Next, DataEase asks:

1:Ignore Error and Continue   2:Cancel   3:Decide upon Error
If a backup Error occurs, what do you want to do?

If DataEase does encounter an error, it may mean that the file is unusable. One way to prevent errors is to reorganize your forms before backing them up.

If you do not want to stay at your computer during the backup, select either Cancel or Ignore Error and Continue, depending upon whether you want an error-free backup.

If you select Decide upon Error, you must be present during the backup to make the decision.

5. Select **Ignore Error and Continue**

MAINTAINING YOUR DATABASE   **467**

DataEase displays the message:

> STARTING BACKUP
> PLEASE INSERT FIRST BACKUP DISK IN DRIVE A:
> PRESS 'RETURN' WHEN READY OR 'ESC' TO ABORT

As the backup progresses, DataEase lists each file type as it copies. These files should fit on a single disk. When the backup is complete, DataEase prompts you with the following message:

> BACKUP COMPLETE: PLEASE REMOVE DISK AND LABEL IT:
> BACKUP DISK NUMBER:1
> DATABASE NAME: INVENTORY
> DATE:<CURRENT DATE> TIME: <CURRENT TIME>
> PRESS 'RETURN' WHEN READY

If your files require more than one diskette, DataEase displays the message:

> PLEASE REMOVE DISK FROM DRIVE A AND LABEL IT:
> BACKUP DISK NUMBER:n
> DATABASE NAME:<database name>
> DATE: TIME:
> INSERT NEW DISK IN DRIVE A: AND PRESS 'RETURN' WHEN
>   READY

RESTORING YOUR DATABASE

The DataEase Restore command restores only files that you backed up with the DataEase Backup command. It works exactly like the Backup command, only in reverse; you follow these steps:

- Sign on under the database you want to restore.

- From the DataBase Maintenance menu, select **Restore Database**.

- Enter the source drive and directory.

- Select the action to be taken if errors are encountered.

- Insert the source diskette into the designated drive and press **Enter**.

468 MASTERING DATAEASE

CH. 17

One great feature of the Restore command is that you can restore files that were backed up from a different database. This is one way to transfer an entire database to another. However, any information in the existing database will be written over by the data that is being restored. So if you need to copy individual files, use Install.

How often should you back up your database? That depends on how much you use it. You should back up at least weekly, and daily during heavy work sessions.

PERFORMING DOS FUNCTIONS

DataEase has many file management utilities built into the program; you can perform a CHKDSK, Format, DOS Backup, or DOS Restore from the DOS Functions menu:

1. Select **Database Maintenance** from the Main Menu.

2. Select **DOS Functions**

3. Select the DOS command to be performed.

In addition, if you need to return to DOS to check directories, or use another program to, for example, create an installation command file, you can do so without actually exiting DataEase.

4. Select **Other**

You should *not* load any memory resident program, as it could cause problems with your data.

DataEase removes or "swaps" itself out of conventional memory into your EMS (expanded) memory (if you have any) or onto the disk, leaving you up to 500K of conventional computer memory. You are free to load another program or perform any DOS function. To return to DataEase, simply type **exit**.

5. Type **exit**; DataEase returns you to the DOS menu.

6. Press **Esc** twice to return to the Main Menu.

DataEase provides you with all the features you need to maintain your records *and* your files. For more information on importing files from other programs, see Appendix B.

SECURITY NOTES

Any user can back up a database or view the database status. Only users with a high security or medium security level can transfer data. All other Maintenance or Utility functions and all System Administration functions require a high security level.

If you attempt to transfer data and you do not have a security level that allows you to enter data into the target form, the following message will be displayed:

Not authorized to enter this form

If you attempt to transfer data and you do not have a security level that allows you to view data in the source form, the following message will be displayed:

Not authorized to view this form

During data transfer, the data will be transferred only *to* fields for which you have Write access and *from* fields for which you have View access. No messages are displayed in either case.

LAN NOTES

If you attempt to back up or restore a shared database, and other users are signed on, DataEase displays the following message:

Not allowed — other users active

When a database is being backed up or restored, DataEase automatically locks it. If you attempt to sign on to a database while Backup or Restore is in progress, DataEase displays the following message:

Access not allowed — Database locked

CHAPTER EIGHTEEN

System Configuration and Administration

Fast Track

To change the default video display, 475

select Define Configuration from the System Configuration menu. If you have a color graphics monitor, select Color; if your monitor supports neither color nor graphics, select Monochrome; if your monitor supports graphics but not color, select Color card–Mono screen.

To maintain or modify compatibility between files 478

created with different versions of DataEase, select Define Configuration from the System Configuration menu. Press **PgDn** to move to page 4 of the form and make the appropriate changes.

To modify the DataEase locking rules, 479

select Define Configuration from the System Configuration menu. Press **PgDn** to move to page 5 of the form and make the appropriate changes. For more information, consult Volume 2 of your DataEase documentation.

To create a custom printer definition, 479

select Define Printer from the System Configuration menu. Refer to the chapter on system administration in Volume 2 of your DataEase documentation for specifics on defining your printer.

To define a custom screen style, 480

select Define Screen Style from the System Administration menu. Select Color for a color display, Monochrome for a black and white display, and Color card–Mono screen if your monitor supports graphics but not color. Select the background and foreground color combinations for the different screen areas.

To modify Record Entry security requirements for a particular field,   **485**
select Form Definition from the Main Menu. Select View or Modify Form. Move to the field where you want to change the security requirement and press **F10**. Move to the View Security field and select the security level. Move to the Write Security field and select the security level. Press **F2** to save the modification.

To change the Record Entry security requirements,   **485**
select Form Definition from the Main Menu. Select View or Modify Form. Press **Shift-F10** to display the Form Properties screen. Select the security level for each record entry function. If you do not want records to be read by another database, select **yes** to encrypt records.

To change the default view to Table,   **486**
select Form Definition from the Main Menu. Select View or Modify Form. Press **Shift-F10** to display the Form Properties screen. Change the value of the field labeled **Default view of this Form** to Table.

To clear a record after entering and saving,   **486**
select Form Definition from the Main Menu. Select View or Modify Form. Press **Shift-F10** to display the Form Properties screen. Change the value of the field labeled **Clear Form after entering a record?** to **yes**.

To suppress the automatic tab when filling a field,   **486**
select Form Definition from the Main Menu. Select View or Modify Form. Press **Shift-F10** to display the Form Properties screen. Change the value of the field labeled **Suppress automatic TAB when a field fills?** to **yes**.

CHAPTER 18

SYSTEM ADMINISTRATION IS THE MANAGEMENT OF DataEase files and users. Administrative tasks will vary depending on whether you use DataEase alone on your computer, share your computer with other DataEase users, or manage a number of users in a local area network environment. Initially, you may use System Administration to make changes to the DataEase system defaults to suit your work environment. For example, in Chapter 2 you learned how to change the default printer. In Chapter 16, you added user information records.

In this chapter, you will learn how to modify other program defaults. This chapter also discusses security restrictions that affect users in a multiuser environment, whether those users share one computer or operate DataEase in a LAN environment. And finally, you'll learn how you can avoid the problem of losing user passwords.

THE SYSTEM ADMINISTRATION MENU

From the Main Menu:

1. Select **System Administration**

The Administration menu, pictured in Figure 18.1, should be familiar. You used selections from this menu when you selected your default printer, added new users, and installed applications.

If you are the systems administrator in a multiuser environment, you will use this menu to identify all the users, select your printer, change system defaults, establish network locking rules, and convert files (from other programs) that you want to use with DataEase. Most of these tasks are performed when you first start to use DataEase. However, system administration is an ongoing process, because users come and go and hardware configurations change.

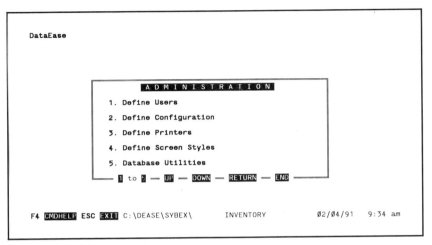

Figure 18.1: Administration menu

If you are a single user, you will not be concerned about establishing user information records or defining locking rules for the network environment. However, there are other possible changes to your system configuration in this chapter that you may find helpful.

DEFINING YOUR SYSTEM CONFIGURATION

The System Configuration form is five pages long and contains fields that allow you to specify your hardware environment, network locking rules, country and language, and other defaults that control file handling. Let's take a look at these default settings and consider why you might want to change some of them. First, bring up the form:

1. Select **Define Configuration**

The first screen (page 1 of 5), pictured in Figure 18.2, is primarily concerned with printer information, particularly in a network environment where you may have multiple printers.

The first field, SCREEN STYLE, allows you to change the type of video display. The selections include color and monochrome, offered

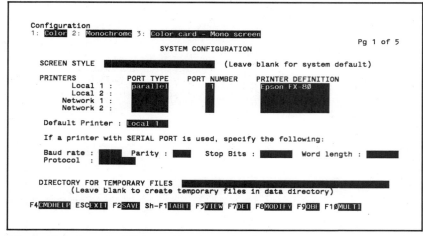

Figure 18.2: Page 1 of System Configuration form

when you first installed DataEase, and one other choice: color card with mono screen. Color video screens support color and graphics; monochrome screens display no colors and no graphics; and color cards with mono screens have graphics but no color capabilities. Later in this chapter, you will learn how to create a custom screen style.

The last field specifies the directory in which DataEase stores temporary (buffer) files created during tasks such as sorting. If you have a limited amount of disk space on the current disk, you may prefer to specify a floppy disk or another part of your hard disk.

2. Press **PgDn** to move to the next page.

Page 2, pictured in Figure 18.3, configures DataEase for a country other than the United States, and controls the language, date format, and currency.

3. Press **PgDn** to move to the third page.

Page 3, pictured in Figure 18.4, contains a number of fields you might want to change, starting with the BEEP field. Normally, DataEase sounds a beep when it encounters an error. However, if you find the sound annoying or are operating in a room that contains

If you have a 40 megabyte hard disk which has been segmented into drives C (which contains DataEase) and D, and you have more room on D, you may want to change this field value.

SYSTEM CONFIGURATION AND ADMINISTRATION

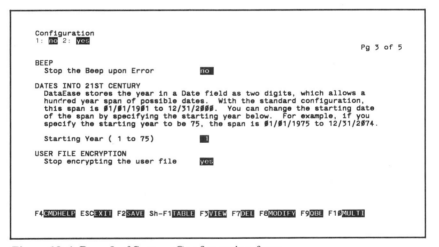

Figure 18.3: Page 2 of System Configuration form

Figure 18.4: Page 3 of System Configuration form

many computers making similar noises, you can change the selection to **yes** to stop the beep.

The second field, DATES INTO 21ST CENTURY, is particularly relevant as we approach the end of this century. DataEase returns date values over a 100 year period, beginning with the value of the Starting Year field. The default is set to year 1 of this century, which means this span will end in the year 2000.

You may want to change the default to a year closer to the present, depending on how many years you may need to back-date your date fields. Your Starting Year entry can range from 1 to 75.

The last field, USER FILE ENCRYPTION, is covered later in this chapter.

4. Press **PgDn** to move to the fourth page.

The fourth page of the form, pictured in Figure 18.5, is important *only* if you need to maintain compatibility with files created with versions of DataEase earlier than version 4.0 and no earlier than version 2.12. As you know, DataEase automatically checks the Unique?, Required?, and Lower/Upper Limit fields. These checks are handled differently in files created from versions prior to 4.0. If you want these earlier files to be compatible with 4.0 and above, select **yes** to suppress automatic checks and derivations.

Versions of DataEase prior to 2.5 do *not* insert leading zeros in numeric string fields; versions after 2.5 do insert the zeros to the left of the number. If you want to be compatible with files from a version earlier than 2.5, *or* with other programs that insert trailing spaces instead of leading zeros, answer **yes** to this prompt.

5. Press **PgDn** to move to the last page of the form.

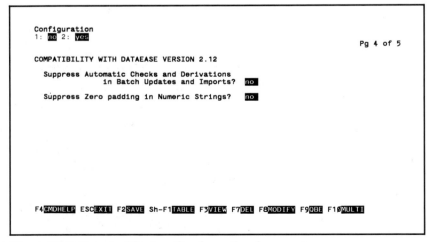

Figure 18.5: Page 4 of System Configuration form

SYSTEM CONFIGURATION AND ADMINISTRATION   479

The last screen, pictured in Figure 18.6, is relevant only if you are a systems administrator operating DataEase in a LAN environment. If you need more information about this topic, refer to Volume 2 of your DataEase documentation.

6. Press **Esc** to return to the Configuration menu.

CREATING A CUSTOM PRINTER DEFINITION

If your printer is *not* included in this list, you can create a record for your printer using the Printer Definition form.

DataEase comes with 190 predefined printer definition records. The names of these records are displayed in the PRINTER DEFINITION field on the first page of the System Configuration form. If you need to change the default printer, select your printer from this list.

1. Select **Define Printers**

The Printer Definition form, page 1 of which is pictured in Figure 18.7, is a two-page form.

2. Press **F3** several times to display records from the predefined printers.

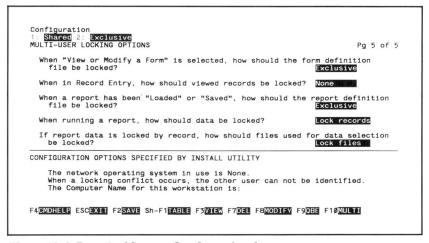

Figure 18.6: Page 5 of System Configuration form

CH. 18

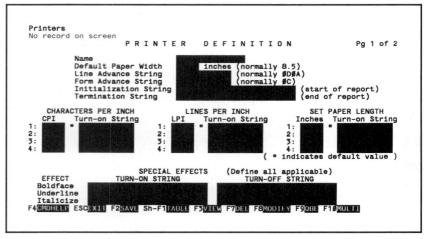

Figure 18.7: Page 1 of Printer Definition form

> For details on creating a printer record, refer to the chapter on system administration in Volume 2 of your DataEase documentation, and/or consult with a technical expert in your department.

The fields in this form contain the character strings that control the operation of each printer. This information can be found in the documentation that comes with your printer. DataEase allows up to 2000 printer definition records.

3. Press **Esc** to return to the Administration menu.

DEFINING A CUSTOM SCREEN STYLE

If you have a color monitor, you may be interested in changing screen colors. Define Screen Style is used to select color combinations for the different areas of your screen. Let's take a look at the current defaults:

1. From the Administration menu, select **Define Screen Style**

The Screen Style form, pictured in Figure 18.8, contains fields that display the foreground and background colors for the major text areas of the screen. This form already includes records for the three types of video displays that DataEase supports: Color, Monochrome, and Color card–Mono screen. You can modify these or create new ones of your own.

SYSTEM CONFIGURATION AND ADMINISTRATION   481

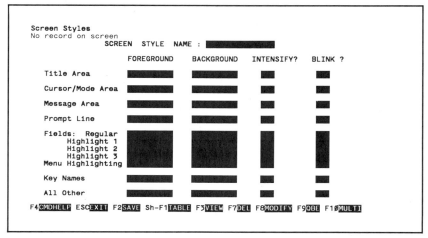

Figure 18.8: The Screen Style form

2. Press **F3** to see each record and stop when the record for color is displayed.

The first field of the color record, pictured in Figure 18.9, is SCREEN STYLE NAME. You can assign a screen style to any user by entering the screen style name in the user information record.

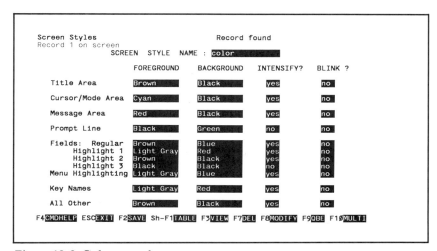

Figure 18.9: Color record

482 *MASTERING DATAEASE*

CH. 18

Let's create a screen style for a new user called Frank. Normally, you might create the screen style first. However, since you're unfamiliar with the appearance of some of these color combinations, you'll create the user information record first, sign on under that user name, and then create the style. You'll be able to see the results immediately.

1. Press **Esc** to return to the Configuration menu.

2. Select **Define Users**

3. Use the information below to create the new user information record.

Name:	Frank
Level:	High
Screen Style:	Frank

Now you'll exit DataEase and sign on as Frank.

4. Press **F2** to save the record.

5. Press **Esc** twice to return to the Main Menu and exit DataEase.

6. Load the program again and sign on under the name of Frank.

Next, you'll create the screen style called Frank and watch the colors change when you save (or update) the record.

1. From the Main Menu, select **System Administration**

2. Select **Define Screen Style**

3. Press **F3** until the color record is displayed.

You'll modify this record, changing only some of the colors.

4. In the SCREEN STYLE NAME field, press **F6** to clear the field and type **frank**

Only users with a high security level can define screen styles. Since you want to create this style after you sign on as Frank, he must have a high security level.

You should keep the original screen style records and assign at least one of them to an existing user with a high security level. That way you can return to them if you accidentally create an illegible screen style. If you do modify an original record, save it under another screen style name, as you did in this exercise.

SYSTEM CONFIGURATION AND ADMINISTRATION **483**

5. Move to the FOREGROUND field of the Title Area and select **Cyan** from the menu.
6. Press **F2** to save the record.

Notice that the Title Area color changes automatically. When you change a color in the screen style assigned to the current user, the colors change immediately.

7. Change the FOREGROUND color of the Cursor/Mode Area to **Light Grey**, and press **F8** to update the record and change the color.
8. Use the information below to change two more screen areas:

	FOREGROUND	*BACKGROUND*
Message Area	Magenta	Blue
Key Names	Green	Red

The completed record for frank is pictured in Figure 18.10.

9. Press **F8** to update the record.
10. Return to the Main Menu.

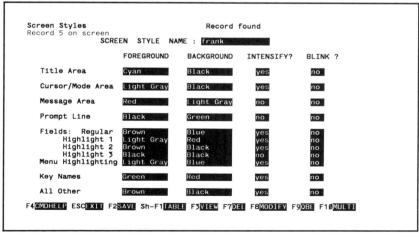

Figure 18.10: Completed record for Frank

484 MASTERING DATAEASE

CH. 18

If you select **yes** for INTENSIFY?, it lightens and brightens the foreground color. This works well with a light color, such as brown, against a darker color, such as blue or black. However, a combination such as red against light gray looks better if it is not intensified.

If you select **yes** at BLINK?, the foreground text will blink on and off like the cursor. This can work well as an attention-getting device in the message area. Take some time to experiment with other combinations.

1. When you are finished, save the record and return to the Main Menu.

2. You can remain signed on under Frank or exit and sign on under your own name.

When creating a new screen style record, be sure to fill in all the fields, even if they do not differ from the default colors. If you leave one blank, the text that should appear in that color will not display on your screen.

ASSIGNING USER SECURITY LEVELS

As you know, when you create each user information record you can enter a security level to restrict the user's access to database tasks or information. Chapters 3–7 in Volume 2 of your DataEase documentation contain a table of minimum security levels required to perform basic tasks. In summary, the restrictions are as follows:

- Only users with a high security level can create, save, and modify forms, reports, menus, relationships, and procedures.

- All Maintenance and Utility functions, with the exception of Transfer, Import, Backup, and View Status, are reserved for those with a high security level.

- Only the first page of the System Configuration form is available to medium security users.

- Low level users cannot access any of the options on the Administration menu.

- Anyone can view a record; however, only users with a medium security level or higher can modify, enter, or delete records.

The first four security level rules cannot be modified. However, you can modify the Record Entry security restrictions.

MODIFYING RECORD ENTRY SECURITY REQUIREMENTS

The minimum security level required to enter, view, modify, or delete data in Record Entry can vary from form to form. You can set these levels by modifying the form properties. Let's take a look at this:

1. From the Main Menu, select **Form Definition**
2. Select **View or Modify Form**
3. Select **ITEMS**
4. Press **F4** and select the **Tools** menu.
5. Press **Shift-F10** to select **Form Properties**

The first page of Form Properties, pictured in Figure 18.11, displays the default minimum security level for each Record Entry function. You can change these to suit your own security requirements.

Encrypted records are specially coded so that they can only be read by the current database, and therefore cannot be transferred to another database with the **install** command. The default setting does *not* encrypt records. If security is an issue, you may want to change the setting to **yes**.

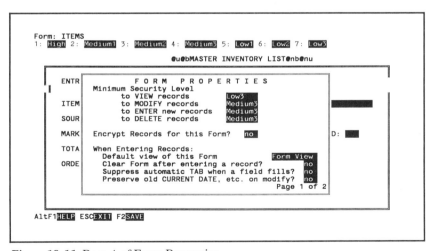

Figure 18.11: Page 1 of Form Properties

486 *MASTERING DATAEASE*

CH. 18

The remaining form properties control how DataEase performs during Record Entry:

Default view of this form	You can change the default view from Form to Table. Since you can hide fields from Table View, this is helpful if you do not want certain fields displayed, such as derived fields.
Clear form after entering a record?	To save yourself an extra keystroke, you can have DataEase automatically clear the form after saving each record.
Suppress automatic TAB when a field fills?	The automatic TAB feature automatically moves the cursor to the next field when you fill up the field. This can be distracting if you are not watching the screen as you enter records, and aren't aware that you've completed a field. If you want the consistency of pressing Tab each time you complete a field, change this field value to **yes**.
Preserve old CURRENT DATE, etc. on modify?	In Chapter 8, you learned about the two methods of entering dates: ??/??/??, which always retains the original date value, and LOOKUP CURRENT DATE, which changes to the current system date when the record is modified. If you change this setting to **yes**, CURRENT DATE will retain the original entry date.

In Chapter 2, you created field help. You can also create help for the form that is displayed when you press Alt-F1. To display form or field help automatically, change the Help Level field in the user information record to Automatic. To activate automatic help you must update the record, exit DataEase, and sign on again under that user name.

SYSTEM CONFIGURATION AND ADMINISTRATION   *487*

1. Press **PgDn** to move to the second page of the form.

2. Press **Esc** to return to the ITEMS form.

ESTABLISHING FIELD SECURITY LEVELS

Within each form you may have fields that contain sensitive information, such as salaries or employee review ratings. The definition screen for each field includes a View Security and a Write Security field in which you can enter the minimum security level required to display or enter data.

For example, if you assign a high View Security level, only users with high security can see the information in that field; it will appear blank to all other users. If you assign a high Write Security level, the data will display, but only users with high security will be able to enter information. If these fields contain no entry, all users are permitted access to the data.

Let's place some security restrictions on the MARKUP% field, so that certain users don't get creative.

1. Move to the MARKUP% field.

2. Press **F10** to modify the field.

3. Move to the View Security field and select **Medium 1**

4. Move to the Write Security field and select **High**

The completed definition is displayed in Figure 18.12.

1. Press **F2** to save the field.

2. Save the form and return to the Main Menu.

Users who sign on under FP have a medium security level, which means that they can see the MARKUP% value, but can't change it. Let's test that:

1. Exit the program and sign on under **fp**

2. Select **INVENTORY ITEMS**, then select **ITEMS**

3. Press **F3** to display the first record and press **Tab** to move to each field.

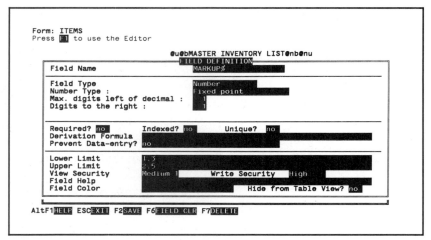

Figure 18.12: Revised definition for MARKUP%

The cursor skips the MARKUP% field since the security level for FP is not high enough to change the value of that field.

4. Return to the Main Menu.
5. Exit DataEase.
6. To return to the DataEase Main Menu, load the program again and sign on under your name.

In summary, there are a number of ways to protect your data:

- Modify Form Properties to require minimum security levels to perform certain Record Entry tasks.
- Modify the View and Write Security fields to protect individual fields in a form.
- Change the default view to Table and hide sensitive fields from Table View.

If you are operating DataEase on a local area network, DataEase uses locking rules, which provide additional restrictions on accessing data. For detailed information on locking rules, see the chapter on LAN system administration in Volume 2 of your DataEase documentation.

USER PASSWORDS

Chapter 2 discussed the necessity of caution when assigning user passwords, since once they are assigned, the user *must* enter the password in order to sign on.

If a user forgets his or her password, another user with a high security level can sign on and check that user's record. However, what if the systems administrator leaves suddenly, and no one can find his or her password? This problem can be solved in one of two ways. First, you can create a user record with no name and no password, with a high security level. This can be risky, since it would allow anyone who can load the program to get into the database.

However, there is another method that allows you to access names and passwords *without* loading the DataEase program. The USER FILE ENCRYPTION field in the System Configuration form controls the readability of the user information records from DOS. These records are stored in a DOS file called USER*d*AAA.DBM. (The letter *d* represents your assigned database letter. In this case, the file is USERIAAA.DBM.) Normally, these records are encrypted and if you use the **type** command

```
type useriaaa.dbm
```

from DOS, you will see only graphic characters.

If you change this field to **yes**, then DataEase will cease encrypting user information records and DOS will display the name and password for each record. To change existing user information records, you must display each record and press F8 to modify. Let's try changing the encryption default to see how this works:

1. From the Main Menu select **DataBase Maintenance**

2. Select **DOS functions**

3. Select **Other**

> You may need to substitute your drive or directory path in this command.

4. From the DOS prompt, type **type c:\dease\sybex\user-iaaa.dbmCR**

What you see is a graphic character, since DOS cannot interpret the DataEase encrypted coding.

490 *MASTERING DATAEASE*

CH. 18

5. Type **exit** to return to DataEase.

6. Return to the Main Menu and select **System Administration** and then **Define Configuration**

7. Press **PgDn** twice to return to page 3 and change the last field to **yes**

8. Press **F2** to update the configuration record and press **Esc** to return to the Configuration menu.

Next, you must update your user information records.

9. Select **Define User**

10. One at a time, display each record and press **F8** to update.

11. When you are finished, press **Esc** twice to return to the Main Menu.

12. Repeat steps 1–4 to display the contents of the USER-IAAA.DBM file, and see that DOS displays the user name and password for each record.

Congratulations! You now have all the skills necessary to become a productive user of DataEase. If you haven't already started to build your own database yet, you certainly can now. The next and final chapter contains some helpful hints and shortcuts that you might find useful now or later as you become more proficient with DataEase.

CHAPTER NINETEEN

Tips and Shortcuts

CHAPTER 19

DO YOU HAVE A CATCH-ALL DRAWER IN YOUR kitchen? If so, you'll understand exactly what this chapter is about. It contains tidbits of information that didn't find a place in any of the other chapters, but are extremely handy. Let's start with a shortcut for loading DataEase.

SIGNING ON FROM DOS

You can include all the sign on information when you load DataEase from DOS:

```
dease \<directory> <database> <user name> <password>
```

If you were using the FP sign on, for example, you would enter:

```
dease \dease\sybex inventory fp fp
```

If you include no password and/or user name, DataEase will stop at those prompts anyway.

COPYING QUERIES

Normally, you use F5 to copy text or fields within a form, procedure, or report. However, you can also copy a query from one procedure to a new or existing procedure by using the steps below:

- Use **F5** to mark the beginning and end of the query statements you want to copy.

- Press **Esc** instead of **F6** to begin the process of pasting to another query.

- Type **y** to abandon the current query.

- Type **y** to confirm that you want to paste to another query.
- Either start a new procedure or load the procedure to which you want to paste.
- Select **Modify or Define Query**.
- Position the cursor and press **F6** to paste the query.

SORTING YOUR DATABASE

You know how to display your records sorted by an indexed field. You also know how to sort your records for a report. However, these are only temporary reorderings, and the display always returns to Record Number order after the last record in sequence is displayed.

However, you can physically sort your records by any field so that they are permanently ordered by that field. To do that, you must create a second identical form with no records and create a procedure that includes a **list fields** and copies sorted records to the new forms. Using the CUST form as an example, the following steps create a new form called CUST2 with records ordered by LNAME:

- Modify the CUST form and insert and delete a blank row, just to make a change.
- Save the "modified" form under a new name, such as CUST2, and *do not* copy the data records.
- Create the following query:

```
for CUST
;
list records
   LNAME in order ;
enter a record in CUST2
   copy all from CUST .
end
```

You needn't include all the fields in your **list fields** statement—only those that need to be sorted. Your new form, CUST2, will contain all the records from CUST; however, they will always display in LNAME order.

494 MASTERING DATAEASE

CH. 19

MULTIPLE HEADERS AND FOOTERS IN REPORTS

The .header and .footer format commands print the following text at the top and bottom of each page of your report, beginning with the first page. If you need to print different text on the second or third pages, you can specify that in your .header command. For example,

.header 2 Prints the text following the command at the top of page 2 and all subsequent pages.

.header 3 Prints the text following the command at the top of page 3 and all subsequent pages.

All headers are placed at the beginning of your report.

APPENDIX A

Installing DataEase

496

APPENDIX *A*

THIS APPENDIX HAS INSTRUCTIONS FOR INSTALLING DataEase on a single computer. For detailed information about installing DataEase on a LAN, you should consult your DataEase Installation and Upgrade Guide that accompanies the documentation. However, before you proceed, read the section below entitled, "General Installation Guidelines."

If you are upgrading from version 4.0 or 4.1, refer to the section in this appendix on "Upgrading from Version 4.1 or 4.0." If you are upgrading from version 2.53 or earlier, refer to the section entitled "Upgrading from Version 2.5 or Lower." If you are upgrading your LAN version, refer to the Installation and New Features Guide that comes with the DataEase documentation.

After you complete the installation or upgrade, you will be ready to begin learning how to use DataEase. If you are new to database management, you should start with Chapter 1, which includes information about database concepts and terminology, as well as concepts and terminology unique to DataEase. Then you can proceed to Chapter 2, which begins with starting the DataEase program.

HARDWARE AND SOFTWARE REQUIREMENTS

In order to use DataEase on a stand-alone system, you must have the following hardware:

- An IBM PC, XT, AT, 3270 PC, or PS/2, or a system compatible with these models. Your computer must come equipped with a hard disk drive that contains at least 1.4 megabytes of space for the DataEase system and data files.

- A minimum of 640K random access memory (RAM).

- A color or monochrome monitor.

In addition, you must have DOS version 3.1 or higher as your operating system.

For information on hardware and software requirements for LAN use, as well as on installing DataEase on a LAN, refer to Chapter 2 of your DataEase Installation and New Features Guide.

GENERAL INSTALLATION GUIDELINES

You should observe the general installation guidelines below:

- DataEase provides a special program called **install** that copies all the system files to your hard disk in the designated directory. These files were compressed to fit on floppy disks, and the **install** program "decompresses" them back to their normal size as it copies. Therefore, you should not copy the DataEase system files onto your hard disk; use the **install** procedure described in the next section.

Your target disk does not have to be formatted, since Diskcopy formats as it copies.

- Use the Diskcopy command to make a backup of your original disks. Copy them onto 360K floppy disks only, since **install** will not work from a high density diskette. You must have a copy of the DOS file diskcopy.com and two floppy disk drives to perform this command. If you do, insert the disk labeled Disk 1 (the source disk) in drive A and insert a blank disk (the target disk) in drive B. Type **diskcopy a: b:** and press any key when prompted to begin the operation. When DOS asks you if you want to copy another, type **y** and follow the prompts to insert Disk 2 in drive A and another blank disk in drive B. Follow these steps for each of the five disks. Use your working copies to install the program and put your originals in a safe place.

You can load DataEase from any directory if you edit your autoexec.bat file and include the DEASE subdirectory as part of the path command. Ask someone for help if you are not familiar with modifying your autoexec-.bat file.

- Modify the config.sys file and add the following statement to it:

```
Files = 60
Buffers = 2
```

498 MASTERING DATAEASE

APP. A

To modify this file you can use any word processing program that creates or edits ASCII files. You can also use the DOS Edlin command if you are familiar with it. If you are unsure of how to create or modify this file, please seek technical assistance.

- If you are installing on a LAN, the config.sys file for each workstation must also include the above statements.

INSTALLING DATAEASE ON A SINGLE COMPUTER

Installing DataEase is quite simple and requires no technical skill. Follow the steps below to install DataEase:

1. Create a subdirectory for the DataEase program files. The default name is c:\dease; however, you may use whatever directory name you like. To create the directory, type **md\dease**◄┘

2. Insert the DataEase disk labeled Disk 1 in drive A and type **a:install**◄┘ (or if you are using drive B, type **b:install**◄┘). DataEase asks:

    Is your computer's screen Color [C] or Monochrome [M]

3. Type **c** for color or **m** for monochrome.

Next, DataEase displays the Installation Program menu, pictured in Figure A.1.

4. Select **Install DataEase**

DataEase displays the Software Version menu, pictured in Figure A.2.

As you can see, DataEase has two versions of the program: 640K and 16M. The 16M version is for users who have at least 1Mb of extended memory and want to take advantage of it. By using your extended memory you can build bigger and more powerful applications.

Aside from its ability to address extended memory, the 16M version of the program operates in exactly the same way as the 640K

You need at least 384K of extended memory to run the 16M version. With that limited configuration, the 16M version will run very slowly. You need at least 700K of extended memory to run DataEase at normal speed. With 2Mb of extended memory, you will notice an increase in the speed of the program; beyond 2Mb you will notice no difference.

INSTALLING DATAEASE 499

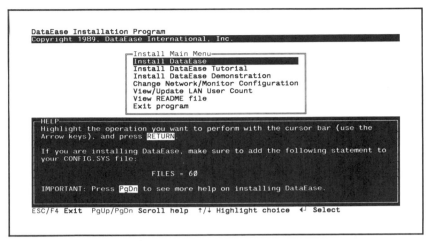

Figure A.1: Installation Program menu

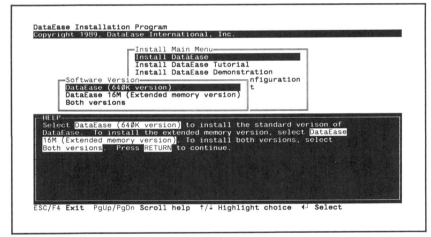

> You should choose the Both versions selection only if you are installing DataEase on a LAN that contains workstations with and without extended memory. For more detailed information on the 16M version, see the DataEase Installation and New Features Guide that comes with your DataEase documentation.

Figure A.2: Software Version menu

version. From the Software Version menu, you should select either 640K or 16M.

5. Select either **640K** or **16M**

DataEase then asks for:

   Floppy drive for master disks

500 MASTERING DATAEASE

APP. A

6. Enter the drive letter that contains DataEase Disk 1.

Next, DataEase asks for the

DataEase System directory   C:\DEASE

7. Enter the directory you created for the DataEase program files or press **Enter** to accept the default.

8. Press **F2** to begin installing the program.

DataEase will prompt you to insert the program disks one at a time until all have been copied. When installation is complete, the Installation Program menu is displayed again. If you wish, you can also install the DataEase Tutorial and Demonstration disks.

The last menu selection, View README file, displays the contents of the README.txt file that accompanies the DataEase program. README.txt is an ASCII text file that can be displayed on the monitor or printed. This is an important file that contains information that does not appear in the documentation. However, it is a rather lengthy file and it's recommended that you print it. To print your README file, follow the steps below:

> The printout is easier to read if you use the DOS print program to print. In that case, type **print readme.txt**. If the DOS directory is not included in your autoexec path statement, you will need to precede the print command with the name of the directory that contains the print.com program.

1. If you have completed the installation, select **EXIT program**

2. Type **cd\dease↵** to change to your DataEase program directory.

3. Make sure your printer is on and type **readme.txt > prn**

Now you are ready to proceed to Chapter 1 to begin learning about DataEase.

UPGRADING FROM VERSION 4.1 OR 4.0

If you have received an upgrade version of DataEase, the disks will be clearly marked as such. Before you begin upgrading, read the following guidelines:

- The upgrade diskettes do not contain your serial number, and you must get this information from your current version.

Therefore, do not erase your current version of DataEase before upgrading.

- Because the serial number from your current version must be written onto the upgrade diskettes, update from the *original* upgrade diskettes, not a copy. You can use Diskcopy to make a copy afterwards.

- The new version of DataEase will be able to read all your data files. However, it is always recommended that you back up your database before making any changes that affect your disks.

Follow the steps below to upgrade your version of DataEase:

1. Insert Disk 1 in your floppy drive.

2. From your hard disk, type either **a:install←** or **b:install←**

3. Enter **c** for color monitor or **m** for monochrome.

4. When the Upgrade Main menu displays, select **Upgrade DataEase**

5. When prompted for the system directory, enter the directory that contains your current version of DataEase.

6. After the upgrade is complete, exit the **install** program and load DataEase again to verify that the serial number was copied from your old version.

7. Refer to the Installation and New Features Guide for more detailed information on upgrading, as well as on the new features in version 4.2

UPGRADING FROM VERSION 2.5 OR LOWER

If you are upgrading from Version 2.5 or lower, the steps for upgrading the product are the same as for upgrading from version 4.0 or 4.1 (see previous section). However, before you upgrade,

502 MASTERING DATAEASE

APP. A

you must back up your data files and then restore them to your new version. To do that, follow the steps below:

1. Back up your data files. For instructions, see the section on backing up your database in Chapter 17.

2. Follow the steps in the previous section to upgrade your program.

3. After upgrading, use your new version to create a new database in a different directory.

4. Restore your database files to your new database.

You can restore your backed up database to its original database and directory; however, you must erase all the old files before restoring. It is much safer to create a new database.

APPENDIX B

Converting Files from Other Programs

APPENDIX *B*

IF YOU HAVE FILES FROM LOTUS, SYMPHONY, dBASE, or Paradox that you would like to use with DataEase, you can convert them with Install/Convert Application. In the conversion process, DataEase creates a form for the file and transfers the data. This appendix summarizes steps required for file conversion, as well as the preliminary steps. For more detailed information, refer to Chapter 5 in Volume 2 of the DataEase documentation.

TRANSFERRING FROM LOTUS OR SYMPHONY

Before beginning the conversion for Lotus 1-2-3 or Symphony files, take note of the following:

- You must name the range(s) you are converting, even if you are converting the entire worksheet.

- DataEase uses the data in the first row of each range for the field names. Each column must begin with a field name, even if the column is blank.

- Field values can begin with any label prefix character. However, field values cannot contain an embedded caret (^) character, since DataEase uses this character as a field separator for importing.

- Macros are converted as text fields.

To convert your Lotus or Symphony files:

1. Select **System Administration** from the DataEase Main Menu.

2. Select **Database Utilities**

3. Select **Install/Convert Application**

CONVERTING FILES FROM OTHER PROGRAMS   505

4. Select **Convert and Install Lotus Files** or **Convert and Install Symphony files**

5. At the prompt, enter the name of the directory that contains the source files.

6. Select each file you want to convert from the list of files displayed.

7. Press **F2** to confirm.

The next screen DataEase displays contains the list of ranges under each worksheet you selected to convert.

8. Select the ranges you want to convert for each worksheet and press **F2** to confirm.

At this point, DataEase briefly displays the Conversion Progress screen, followed by a series of messages telling you that it is transferring the data. When the conversion is complete, the Utilities menu is displayed again. Now you can use Record Entry to view, modify, or add more records, or use the Modify Form command to make any changes.

The name of your new form consists of the name of the worksheet followed by the name of the range that was converted.

CONVERTING DBASE FILES

You can convert files from dBase III, dBase III Plus, or dBase IV. Before beginning your dBase file conversion, take note of the following:

- dBase files are converted to DataEase forms, using the field and file names of the dBase files you are converting.

- DataEase will also convert any index (with the extension .NDX) or screen format (with the extension .FMT) with the same name as the database file.

- You should convert any memo fields to character fields before converting.

506 MASTERING DATAEASE

APP. B

To convert your dBase files:

1. Select **System Administration** from the DataEase Main Menu.
2. Select **Database Utilities**
3. Select **Install/Convert Application**
4. Select **Convert dBase Files**
5. At the prompt, enter the name of the directory that contains the source files.
6. Select each file you want to convert from the list of files displayed.
7. Press **F2** to confirm.

At this point, DataEase briefly displays the Conversion Progress screen, followed by a series of messages telling you that it is creating the form and screen files and transferring the data. When the conversion is complete, the Utilities Menu is displayed again. Now you can use Record Entry to view, modify, or add more records, or Modify Form to make any changes.

CONVERTING PARADOX FILES

You can convert files from Paradox, Paradox 1, or Paradox 3. Before beginning your Paradox file conversion, take note of the following:

- Before any files are converted, you must specify the directory path that contains the paradox.exe file.
- This directory must be included in the path command of your autoexec.bat file, or the data will not transfer. If you add this to your path, don't forget to reboot so that DOS can read the changes.
- You must delete any password tables in the files you want to convert before beginning the conversion process.

CONVERTING FILES FROM OTHER PROGRAMS   *507*

To convert your Paradox files:

1. Select **System Administration** from the DataEase Main Menu.
2. Select **Database Utilities**
3. Select **Install/Convert Application**
4. Select **Convert Paradox Files**
5. At the prompt, enter the name of the directory that contains the paradox.exe file.
6. At the prompt, enter the name of the directory that contains the Paradox files you want to convert.
7. Select each file you want to convert from the list of files displayed.
8. Press **F2** to confirm.

At this point, DataEase briefly displays the Conversion Progress screen followed by a series of messages telling you that it is creating the form and screen files and transferring the data. When the conversion is complete, the Utilities Menu is displayed again. Now you can use Record Entry to view, modify, or add more records, or Modify Form to make any changes.

APPENDIX C

Exporting
to GrafTalk

APPENDIX *C*

YOU CAN EXPORT RECORDS FROM DATAEASE directly into GrafTalk by selecting one of two special formats from Quick Reports: the GrafTalk export format and the GrafTalk chart format.

THE GRAFTALK EXPORT FORMAT

So far, you have used the columnar, Record Entry, and custom report formats. The export format is another possible format, which exports data in a format compatible with one of many different programs, including MultiMate, WordPerfect, Lotus, WordStar, and GrafTalk. When you select GrafTalk, DataEase creates a special file that can then be read by GrafTalk.

To export DataEase data into the GrafTalk export format, begin from the DataEase Quick Reports menu:

- Select the numeric fields you want to chart. The first field can be a text field to use for labels for your graph.

- Select **Define Format** and select **Export**.

- Select **GrafTalk** from the list.

- Select **y** if you want to use the DataEase field names as GrafTalk column names; if not, select **n**.

- If the first field is a text field, remove the field name if you included one. Only the column headings for the numeric fields should remain.

- GrafTalk uses only the first eight characters as the field names for the graph legends, so you might want to change your column headings. Field names in column headings must be separated by at least two spaces.

EXPORTING TO GRAFTALK **511**

> You can exit from the Main Menu, or you can use the shortcut exit by selecting Other from the DOS Functions menu and then load GrafTalk when the DOS prompt is displayed. After you exit GrafTalk, you need only type **exit** to return to DataEase.

- Save the format and select **Define Print Style.**

- Select **Disk** as the destination and enter a DOS file name, using DOS file-naming conventions. It's a good idea to precede the file name with the name of the directory where your GrafTalk files are stored.

- Save the print style and run the report.

- Save the report if you want to use it again, then exit DataEase.

- Load GrafTalk.

CREATING A GRAPH FROM DATAEASE DATA

You are no doubt familiar with creating graphs with GrafTalk using the conventional method. The steps below describe how to create, enter, and select DataEase data for your graphs:

- Load GrafTalk.

- From the GrafTalk Main Menu, select **Design Chart** and select the style of graph.

- Select **Enter Data** from the next menu, and then select **DataEase Data.**

The Data from DataEase or ASCII File form, pictured in Figure C.1, asks you for information about your data file:

- At the first prompt, enter the name of the export file you created in DataEase. If it is not in the current directory, include the directory path.

- If you included column names (field names) in your report, select **y** in response to the following prompt:

  Are there names in the file for the columns ?

512 MASTERING DATAEASE

APP. C

```
     Data from DataEase or ASCII File
    Enter a String

    ┌ Data from DataEase or ASCII File ──────────────
     Disk file name

     Are there names in the file for the columns ? no
     Are there names in the file for the rows    ? no

     Characters to be ignored $%.

     Do you want the entire file read ? yes




                   Press F3 to read the file.


    F1▌Draw  F3▌Read  F1▌Help  F7▌Status  Ret▌Enter  F4▌Exit  F2▌Edit  F6▌Clear      ...F1
```

Figure C.1: Data from DataEase or ASCII File form

- If you included a text column for row headings, answer **y** to the following prompt:

    Are there names in the file for rows   ?

- If there are characters in the numeric columns that you want to ignore, enter them in response to the next prompt:

    Characters to be ignored

- If you want to specify certain rows and columns to be read, answer **n** to the next prompt:

    Do you want the entire file read ?

    GrafTalk will prompt you to specify which columns and rows to include.

- Press **F3** to read the file.

- Press **F4** to return to the Main Menu.

Once you have read the file, you must then select the data. This allows you to identify whether you want the numbers to be graphed by rows or columns. Then you must specify which columns (or rows) you want to include:

- Select **Data**

The Data Selection screen, pictured in Figure C.2, uses a pie chart as an example. Notice that since the style is a pie, GrafTalk will allow you to select only one column or row.

- Select either Rows or Columns for plotting in response to the following prompt:

  Select data for plotting as

> If you did not include row and/or column names in your export format, DataEase will assign numbers.

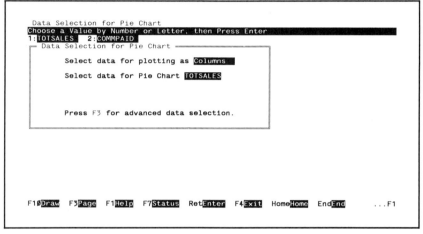

Figure C.2: Data Selection screen

- Select the columns or rows you want to include in response to the next prompt:

  Select data for Pie Chart

- Return to the Main Menu.

> If you included a text column and forgot to remove the field name for that column, GrafTalk will use that name for the first numeric column in the list and omit the name of the last numeric column you selected, preventing you from selecting that column for your graph.

If you want to include legends for your graph, you must specify that from a separate screen, and how you do that will, of course, depend on the style of graph you selected. For more information on defining your graphs, consult your GrafTalk documentation.

THE GRAFTALK CHART FORMAT

The GrafTalk chart format performs a dual purpose. Like the GrafTalk export format, it converts your DataEase report data into a

DOS file that can be read by GrafTalk. However, after you have run the report, it temporarily exits DataEase, loads GrafTalk, and displays the GrafTalk Main menu, prompting you to select a style. If you have already designed and saved the style for this data, GrafTalk automatically draws the graph for you and, after you press any key, returns you to DataEase.

You begin from the Quick Reports menu in DataEase, just as if you were using the export format:

- Select the numeric fields you want to chart. The first field can be text and can be used for row labels for your graph.
- Select **Define Format** and select **Export**.
- Select **GrafTalk** from the list.

The report format shown in Figure C.3, using the SP form as an example, is slightly different from the export report format. First of all, it automatically includes the field names. The format also adds a **.call** statement that calls the GrafTalk program. This statement includes several important parameters:

- The /D tells GrafTalk to draw the chart if the style has been defined.

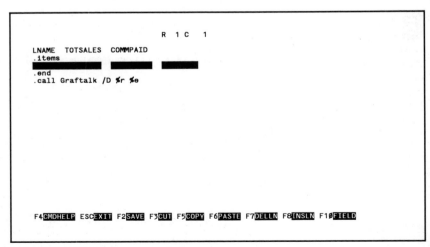

Figure C.3: Chart format

EXPORTING TO GRAFTALK   515

- The %r is a variable that represents the name of the chart file with a .DBG extension.
- The %e is a variable that represents the name of the DataEase file with a .DAT extension.

Next, you can make any changes to the format you want, using the following guidelines:

- If you included field names, and the first is a text field, remove the field name. Only the column headings for the numeric fields should remain.
- GrafTalk uses only the first eight characters as the field names for the graph legends, so you might want to change your column headings. Field names must be separated by at least two spaces.
- Save the format.
- Save the report.

In the example shown in Figure C.3, LNAME, the name of the text field, must be removed before the format is saved.

DataEase will automatically select Disk as the destination for the format and the destination file will use the first four characters of the report name.

The next step is to run the report and design the graph style:

You must clear the memory before running a report with a chart format.

- Select **Start New Report** and select the report you just saved.
- When the GrafTalk menu appears, design your report. If you need help, refer to the earlier section, "Creating a Graph from DataEase Data."
- Remember to save your graph, or the next time you run this report, you will need to design it again.
- After you exit GrafTalk, you will return to DataEase.

The next time you run this report, if you saved your graph, GrafTalk will automatically draw the graph, and then return you to DataEase. If you need to make any changes to this graph, you'll need to exit DataEase, load GrafTalk, and restore this graph.

516 MASTERING DATAEASE

APP. C

You must remember the name of the graph, since no directory of graph names is available from GrafTalk. Either assign a name that is easy to remember, or write down the complete name assigned to it by GrafTalk. If you can't remember the name, display a directory listing of the .DBG file name from DOS. You can use the following command:

```
dir *.dbg
```

INDEX

Note: Page numbers followed by *n* indicate that the entry can be found in the magin note on that page.

A

ad hoc relationships, 346–351, 383–386
addition, 41
administration. *See* system administration
Administration menu, 434, 474–475
all relational operator, 314, 317, 330
Allow Style Modification at Runtime? option, 352
and operator, 119
any relational operator, 322, 325
applications, installing, 462–465
arithmetic operators, 41
arrow keys
    for Form Definition screen, 30
    for menu selection, 15
    for record entry, 55
    in subforms, 192
    for Table View, 88
ascending sorts, 72, 102
ASCII format, saving reports in, 118, 396
asterisks (*)
    with data entry forms, 331n
    for multiplication, 41
    in searches, 80–82
attributes
    field, 36–44, 57–59
    print, 163–164
autoexec.bat file, 497n
Automatic Form subform option, 260
Automatic Table subform option, 260
automatic tabs, 486
averages in reports, 102, 252, 323, 325

B

background color, 158, 161–162
backing up
    databases, 465–468
    program disks, 497
backorders, determining, 214
Backspace key with record entry, 55
Backup command (DataEase), 465
Backup command (DOS), 468
balances
    calculating, 282–283
    updating, 288–289
beeps
    for query errors, 360
    setting for, 476–477
between operator, 119–120, 124n
BLANK keyword, 214
blink setting, 484
blocks, copying, 149
bold attribute, 163–164
borders for forms, 159–161
    erasing, 260
    printing, 167
bottom margins, 297
break command, 416n
buffer files, 476, 497
building databases, 8–9

C

calculated fields
    creating, 40–42
    in queries, 340–346
    in reports, 134–136
    width of, 345

518 MASTERING DATAEASE

call menu command, 433
calling menus, 433–438
canceling editing changes, 85
capitalization with PROPER, 219
Cascade modification option, 257–258
case (alphabetic)
    with exact matches, 78
    functions for, 219–220
    in queries, 317n
case command, 405–408
chain command, 439
chain menus, 429, 438–441
characters, numbers as, 36
chart format, GrafTalk, 513–516
CHKDSK command (DOS), 468
choice fields, 29, 228–230
    in data entry, 230–231
    modifying, 231–234
    and reports, 234
City field, 236
clearing screen and forms, 53–54, 486
colons (:) with DQL, 307, 311
Color menu, 158
colors, 158–159, 161–162, 476, 480–484
column headings, 318
columnar reports, 99, 105
Command Help menu, 23–27, 190–191
commas (,)
    in dollar fields, 38
    in numbers, 29
comment fields, 147–150, 166
common fields, 178
    copying values of, 196–198
    for subforms, 248
comparisons
    case, 406
    of field values, 342–346
compatibility between versions, 478
compressed files, 497
condensed print, 240, 242
conditions
    in forms, 213–218
    multiple, case for, 405–408
    in queries, 369–374
    for record selection, 119–124

config.sys file, 497–498
Configuration form, 16
configurations
    menu, 445–446
    system, 475–484
control procedures, 419–421
converting
    case, 219–220
    dBASE files, 505–506
    INVOICE report to procedure, 417–419
    Lotus 1-2-3 and Symphony files, 504–505
    Paradox files, 506–507
    Quick Reports to DQL, 305–307, 314
    text, 223–228
copy all from command, 408–409, 411, 453
Copy command
    help screen for, 26
    with reports, 132–133
copying
    blocks, 149
    fields and field values, 180, 196–198, 212–213,
        408–409, 411, 453–454
    files, 457–465
    forms, 450–452
    queries, 492–493
    records, 450–452, 456–457
    report format data, 132–133
COUNT OF operator, 252
count statistic for reports, 102
counting operators, 102, 252, 322–323, 325
country settings, 476
criteria, selection, 76, 79–80
    numeric, 120, 123–124
    text, 119–123
Ctrl key in Table View, 88
currency setting, 476
current date
    displaying, 10
    on forms, setting for, 210–211, 486
    in headers, 113–115
CURRENT DATE Definition form, 115
CURRENT DATE system field, 114–115, 210–211
CURRENT PAGE NUMBER Definition form, 116
current status (system variable), 406–407
current time, displaying, 10

current user name (system variable), 446
cursor movement keys
  for data entry, 55
  for Field Definition screen, 34
  for field selection, 104
  for Form Definition screen, 30
CUST form, 236–240
  adding records to, 410–414
  DQL with, 327–330
  relating, to INVOICE, 256
  totals for, 271–272
CUSTINV procedure, 330
Custom Form subform option, 260
custom formats for statements, 386–390
custom menus, 428
  calling, 433–438
  chain, 438–441
  configurations for, 445–446
  for invoice entry, 429–432
  loading, 433
  names for, 430, 438n
  printing, 443–445
  for start-up, 441–443
custom screen styles, 480–484
customer statements, 381
  ad hoc relationships for, 383–386
  format for, 386–390
  high level queries for, 382
CUSTQRY form, 333–334

D

.DAT files, 515
data entry, 4, 51–53
  for CUST, 410–414
  defaults for, 153–154, 164–165
  errors in, 31–33, 54–59
  exiting from, 63–64
  fields for, 27–28
  calculated, 41–42
  choice, 230–231
  formulas and functions for, 216–218
  modifying forms for, 334
  for orders, 368–374, 423–424

for PAYMENTS, 288–290
preventing, 41, 275
for record selection, 330–334
Records menu for, 49–50
reports from, 136–137
security for, 64
with sequencing and text conversion, 223–228
for shipment records, 362–368
shortcuts in, 59–63
for subforms, 263–267
in Table View, 89–90
variables for, 412–414
Data Selection screen, 513
Database Status command, 458–460
databases, 3
  backing up, 465–466
  building, 8–9
  copying files between, 457–465
  creating and naming, 11–13
  managing, 5–6
  restoring, 467–468
  sorting, 493
  terminology for, 4–5
DataEase menus, 429, 433–434
date fields, 29, 35, 50
DATE function, 213
dates
  current, displaying, 10
  entering, 210–211, 486
  fields for, 29, 35, 50
  formats for, 476–478
  in headers, 113–115
.DBA (form definition) files, 459–461
dBASE
  converting files, 505–506
  memo fields, 505
.DBG (GrafTalk chart) files, 515–516
.DBM (form data) files, 459–461
.DBR (procedure) files, 460
decimal places
  in dollar fields, 38
  in numbers, 29
decimal points (.) for number fields, 50
decision-making, 213–218, 369–374, 405–408

520 *MASTERING DATAEASE*

default records and entries, 60–63, 153–154, 164–165
default settings, 475–480
Define List Fields form, 102–103
Define Printers command, 479
Define Relationships command, 180
Define Screen Style command, 480
defining
    fields, 28–29, 33–44, 102–103
    main invoice form, 250–259
    queries, 308–313
    reports, 124–127
    subforms, 249–250
    system configuration, 475–484
    variables, 412–413
Del key
    for Form Definition screen, 30–31
    for record entry, 55
delete records command, 453–454
deleting
    choices in choice fields, 232
    lines from forms, 154–156
    records, 85–87, 452–456
    rows, 155n
DELORD procedure, 456
derivation formulas, 210–211
    for balances, 282
    for calculated fields, 40–42
    functions for, 213
    IF in, 215–216
    LOWER in, 219
    PROPER in, 219
    UPPER in, 220
descending sorts, 72, 102
designing
    custom formats, 386–390
    forms, 21, 27–29, 247–249
DICTIONARY form, 235–240
directories
    for buffer files, 476
    DataEase, 9–10
disk files, printing to, 118, 395–396
diskcopy command (DOS), 497
division, 41
documenting reports and queries, 353

dollar signs ($) in dollar fields, 38
DOS
    performing functions in, 468
    signing on from, 492
double borders for forms, 160
DQL (Data Query Language), 6, 304
    converting Quick Reports to, 305–307
    with data entry forms, 330–334
    defining queries in, 308–313
    modifying procedures for, 319–322
    for record deletion, 452–454
    for related forms, 314–318, 326–330
    relational operators with, 322–326
    for single form reports, 307–313
    See also high level queries
DQL menu, 305, 434
duplicate items, grouping, 74, 127–131
duplicate unique fields, 167
duplicating forms and records, 450–451, 453
Dynamic Lookup command, 180, 196–198

E

.E (exception) files, 460
editing
    DQL procedures, 319–322
    for Form Definition screen, 30–31
    records, 5, 84–87, 92–93
    See also modification
editing keys
    for Field Definition screen, 34
    for record entry, 55
electronic databases, 3–4
elite pitch, 240
else statement, 370
empty fields, 214
encrypted records, 485, 489
.end formatting command, 107
End key
    for Field Definition screen, 34
    for Form Definition screen, 30
    for menu selection, 15
    for record entry, 55
    for Table View, 88

INDEX 521

end query statement, 339
    with **if**, 370
    with **while**, 414
enter a record command, 368, 408
Enter key
    for Field Definition screen, 34
    for menu selection, 15
entering records. *See* data entry
entry order, viewing records in, 69–70
equal sign (=)
    with BLANK, 214
    for record selection, 119–120, 124
Erase Border command, 260
errors
    beeps for, 360, 476–477
    choice fields to reduce, 228
    data entry, 31–33, 54–57
    in DQL procedures, 319–322
    LOOKUP to reduce, 212
    modification, 156, 168
Esc key
    with current status, 407
    with menu selection, 15
exact matches with searches, 76–79
exception files, 168, 460
exclusive records, 94
exporting to GrafTalk, 510–516
expressions, **case,** 406
extended memory, 498–499
extensions, file, 396

F

fields and field values, 4
    adding, 147–150, 298–299
    attributes for, 36–44, 57–59
    calculated. *See* calculated fields
    choice, 29, 228–234
    comment, 147–150, 166
    common, 178, 196–198, 248
    comparing, 342–346
    copying, 180, 196–198, 212–213, 408–409, 411,
        453–454
    date, 29, 35, 50

    default, 164–167
    definitions for, 28–29, 33–44, 102–103
    DICTIONARY form for, 235–240
    duplicating data in, 60–63
    fixed point, 29, 39
    floating point, 29, 39
    help, 42–43, 52–53
    hiding, 252
    highlighting, 157–159
    incrementing, 220–223
    integer, 29, 39
    length of, 28, 111, 146–147
    missing, after conversions, 418
    moving, 150–152
    for names, 223, 225
    names for, 4, 28, 36, 299
    number, 29, 39–40, 102–103
    numeric string, 29, 36, 72
    placement of, 33–36
    prompts for, 4, 23, 28–33
    in queries, 306–307, 310–311
    in reports, 99–105
    required, 37, 57–58
    search criteria for, 76
    security for, 487–488
    statistics for, 307, 311, 323–325
    suppressing spaces in, 293, 295–296
    system, 114
    text, 29, 72
    time, 29
    totaling, 102, 252, 271–274, 322–323, 325
    types for, 28–29, 35
    unique, 37–38, 57–58, 167, 174–178
    width of, 260, 345
    yes/no, 29
files
    buffer, 476, 497
    copying, 457–465
    exception, 168, 460
    index. *See* indexes and index files
    locking, 7, 64, 469
    names for, 395–396, 458–460
    printing to, 118, 395–396
Files = statement (config.sys), 497
FINANCIAL function, 213

522 MASTERING DATAEASE

fixed point fields, 29, 39
floating point fields, 29, 39
footer margins, 297
footers, report, 112, 114–117, 138, 494
for query statement, 306–308, 339, 358
foreground color, 483–484
Form Definition menu, 21–22
Form Definition screen, 22–23, 30
form letters, 390–396
Form Relationship screen, 181
Form View, 68–75, 260
Format command (DOS), 468
formats, report, 99–100, 105–107, 109–112, 386–390
form data file (.DBM), 459–461
form definition file (.DBA), 459–461
forms, 4, 6, 21, 27–29
    available, 49–50
    borders for, 159–161
    conditions on, 213–218
    copying, 450–452
    dates on, 210–211
    default entries on, 153–154, 164–167
    definitions for, 21–23, 30, 44–46
    designing, 27–29
    DICTIONARY, 235–240
    enhancing, 157–159
    fields for
    adding, 147–150
    calculated, 40–42
    definitions for, 33–44
    help, 42–43
    length of, 146–147
    moving, 150–152
    special attributes for, 36–39, 43–44
    Form Definition screen for, 22–23
    help for, 23–27
    installing, 458–464
    lines on, adding and deleting, 154–156
    modifying, 144–145
    names for, 21, 46
    print attributes on, 163–164
    printing, 167

    properties of, 486
    ranges, 39–40
    related. *See* related forms
    reorganization of, 454–456
    security for, 46
    system, 444
    text on, 28–33, 161–163
    See also specific forms
Forms menu, 434
formulas
    for data entry, 216–218
    recalculating, 274–275
    referential, 298
    See also derivation formulas
function keys, 10
    with current status, 407
    with Field Definition screen, 33–34
    with Form Definition screen, 23–24
functions
    for case, 219–220
    combining, 225–227
    for data entry, 216–218
    with menus, 430–431
Furniture Palace MAIN MENU, 436–438

G

global changes, 357–359
global variables, 412
GrafTalk
    chart format for, 513–516
    export format for, 510–511
    graphs with, 511–513
graphs, creating, 511–513
greater than sign (>)
    for field comparisons, 342
    for record selection, 119–120, 124
groups
    headers and trailers for, 291–292, 387–388
    multiple, 290–300
    of records, 73, 102, 452–456
    report, 102, 127–131

H

hardware requirements, 496–497
header margins, 297
headers, 390
    group, 127–131, 291–292, 387
    multiple, 494
    report, 112–114, 138
help
    for commands, 23–27
    for fields, 42–43, 52–53
    for forms, 486
hiding fields, 252
high level queries, 308, 339
    ad hoc relationships with, 346–351
    calculated fields in, 340–346
    copying, 492–493
    for customer statements, 382
    for global changes, 357–359
    with interactive menus, 359–361
    multiple conditions in, 369–374
    for order placement, 368–374
    printing, 352–353
    for record selection, 375–378
    for shipment records, 362–368
high security level, 8
HIGHEST OF operator, 252, 322–323, 325, 371
highlighting
    fields, 157–159
    text, 161–163
Home key
    for Field Definition screen, 34
    for Form Definition screen, 30
    for menu selection, 15
    for record entry, 55
    for Table View, 88

I

.I (index) files, 459
if command, 213–218, 369–374
in order query statement, 310
in query statement, 358

incrementing, sequencing for, 220–223
indexes and index files, 37, 459–460, 505
    with choice fields, 229
    searching with, 83
    with Table View, 90–91
    viewing records with, 71–75
input command, 375–378, 405
Ins key
    for data entry, 55
    for Form Definition screen, 30–31
Insert mode, 31
inserting choices in choice fields, 232
install application command, 458
install form command, 458, 460
install procedure command, 458, 461
install program, 497–498
installation command files, 463
installing
    DataEase, 496–502
    files, 457–465
integer fields, 29, 39
intensify setting, 484
interactive menus
    with DQL, 308–313
    with high level queries, 359–361
INVENTRY query, 415–416
INVLIST form, 249–250, 254
    converting to DQL, 306–307
    copying, 462
    relating to ITEMS, 257–258
INVLISTP procedure, 313, 319–322
invoices and INVOICE form, 247, 250–259
    calculating balances for, 282–283
    converting to procedure, 417–419
    copying data to, 408–409
    custom menus for, 429–432
    for customer statements, 382
    designing, 247–249
    DQL with, 327–330
    for form letters, 390–396
    with high level queries, 343–346
    main form for, 250–259
    printing, 267–271

524 MASTERING DATAEASE

record selection from, 375–378
relating
  to CUST, 256
  to PAYLIST, 283–284, 347–350
  to SP, 257
selecting records from, 405–408
as subform, 284–287
subforms for, 249–250, 257–259
INVORD procedure, 372–374, 416, 422–423, 435
INVPRINT query, 418
INVPROC procedure, 420, 431
italic attribute, 163
.items area, 106, 311, 388, 393
ITEMS form and records
  copying, 460–462
  data entry on, 51–59
  designing, 22–44
  DQL with, 315–318, 323–326
  modifying, 145–167
  for order placement, 368–374
  queries for, 309–312
  Quick Reports for, 101–117
  relating
    to INVLIST, 257–258
    to ORDERS, 180–182, 190–198
    to VENDORS, 183–184, 198–206
  searching for, 75–84
  for shipment records query, 362–368
  totals for, 272–273, 275
  viewing, 68–75, 87–93
.items nosplit command, 444

K

key names, color for, 483
keys
  for Form Definition screen, 30
  for menu selection, 15
  for record entry, 55
  for subforms, 192
  for Table View, 88
keywords, DQL, 308
R(L(R
labels, mailing, 99, 396–399
LABELS procedure, 397–399

LAN (local area networks). *See* networks
language setting, 476
largest value for groups, 103
last modification date on forms, 211
LASTFIRST function, 223, 225–228
leading zeros, 221, 478
left printer margins, 297
length
  of fields, 28, 111, 146–147
  of lines, 105–106
less than sign ($<$), 119–120, 124
letters, form, 390–396
levels, security, 8, 12–13, 484–488
limits, field, 39–40
  for record selection, 123–124
  testing of, 58–59
lines
  in forms, 154–156
  between labels, 398
  length of, in reports, 105–106
linking. *See* related forms
list records command, 306–307, 310, 340–341, 358–359
loading
  menus, 433
  reports, 137
local area networks. *See* networks
locking files, 7, 64, 469
locking rules, 7, 139, 488
long:text fields, 147–150
LOOKUP command, 212–213, 215–216
LOOKUP CURRENT DATE command, 211
loops, programming, 414–416
Lotus 1-2-3 files, converting, 504–505
low level queries, 308–309
low security levels, 8
LOWER function, 219
LOWEST OF operator, 252, 322–323, 325

M

mailing labels, 99, 396–399
main form for invoice, 250–259
Main Menu (DataEase), 14–15, 434
MAIN MENU (Furniture Palace), 436–438

maintenance, 446
  backing up database, 465–468
  copying
  fields, 453–454
  files, 457–465
  forms, 450–452
  records, 450–452, 456–457
  deleting records, 452–453
  with DOS functions, 468
  reorganizing forms, 454–456
Maintenance menu, 434
margins, printer, 297
MATH function, 213
max statistic for reports, 103
MEAN OF operator, 252, 325
mean statistic for reports, 102, 323, 325
medium security levels, 8
memo fields, dBASE, 505
memory
  extended, 498–499
  requirements for, 496
MENU DEFINITION form, 430
menus
  custom. *See* custom menus
  help for, 26
  interactive, 308–313, 359–361
  Main, 14–15
  selections on, 15
message area, 22, 483
message command, 409–410
MFRORD procedure, 318
min statistic for reports, 103
minus sign (–) operator, 41
mode/cursor position indicator, 22–23
modification
  of choice fields, 231–234
  of config.sys file, 497–498
  of data entry forms, 334
  of DQL procedures, 319–322
  of forms, 144–145
  adding and deleting lines, 154–156
  adding fields and field values, 147–150, 164–167
  borders, 159–161
  default entries for, 153–154
  errors in, 156, 168

form enhancements, 157–159
  highlighting text, 161–163
  length of fields, 146–147
  moving fields, 150–152
  print attributes, 163–164
  saving, 156–157
  and unique fields, 167
  with high level queries. *See* high level queries
  of ORDERS, 451–452
  of print style, 297–298, 351–353
  of records, 5, 84–87, 92–93, 193–195, 357–358, 408–409
  of related forms, 257–258
  of reports, 109–112
  of start-up menu, 441–443
modify records command, 357–358, 408–409
moving fields, 150–152
Multi-Form command, 178, 190–191, 193–195
Multi-View command, 178, 186–196
multiple conditions, case for, 405–408
multiple criteria searches, 79
multiple groups in reports, 290–300
multiple headers and footers, 494
multiple procedures, 419–420
multiple subforms, displaying, 195–196
multiplication, 41

N

names
  for databases, 11–12
  for fields, 4, 28, 36, 299
  for files, 395–396, 458–460
  for forms, 21, 46
  functions for, 223, 225
  for menus, 430, 438n
  in relationships, 181, 198–200, 299
  user, 12, 446
networks
  backing up data on, 469
  and data entry, 64
  forms in, 46
  installing DataEase on, 498
  locking rules on, 7, 139, 488

526 MASTERING DATAEASE

and reports, 139–140
settings for, 479
sharing data on, 7
viewing records, 94
nosplit command, 268, 444
not operator, 119–120
null fields, 214
Null modification option, 257–258
number fields, 29
ranges for, 39–40
for reports, 102–103
numbering, sequencing for, 220–223
numeric criteria for record selection, 120, 123–124
numeric string fields, 29, 36, 72

O

Opening Screen, 10–11
operators
arithmetic, 41
for record selection, 119–120
relational, 314, 317, 322–326, 330
statistical, 102, 252, 271–274, 307, 371
optional form names for relationships, 198–200
or operator, 119
order
of choice fields, 232
of report fields, 102
order placement, high level queries for, 368–374
ORDERS form
adding records to, 216–218
consolidating data from, 422–424
creating, 174–178
DQL with, 316–318, 323–326
modifying, 451–452
for order placement, 368–374
relating
to ITEMS, 180–182, 190–198
to VENDORS, 182–183, 186–190, 195–196
for shipment records query, 362–368
ORDPLACED form, 423, 451–452
ORDREC form, 362–368
others keyword, 406
OVER120 relationship, 384–385
OVER120LET procedure, 392–395

P

.page command, 269, 387
page numbers, 114–117
paper, width of, 242
Paradox files, converting, 506–507
paragraphs, 393
partial search matches, 80–84
passwords, 13, 441–442, 489–490
past due accounts, selecting, 298
Paste command, 132–133
PAYLIST form, 279–281, 284–286
with DQL, 327–330
with high level queries, 343–346
relating to INVOICE, 283–284, 347–350
PAYMENTS form, 279–281
creating, 281–284
entering records to, 288–290
report from, 290–300
subforms for, 284–287
periods (.)
with DQL, 307, 311
with high level queries, 339, 344, 358–359
PgDn and PgUp keys
for data entry, 55
for Form Definition screen, 30
for subforms, 192
for Table View, 88
phone no format, 174
pica pitch, 240
pitch for reports, 240–243
placing orders, 368–374
plus sign (+) operator, 41
ports, printer, 17
precision of numbers, 29
Prevent Data-entry? option, 41, 275
previous record data, duplicating, 59–60
PRINT menu, 436–438
Print Style Specification form, 118, 352
printing, 6
attributes for, 163–164
custom menus, 443–445
to disk files, 118, 395–396
form definitions, 44–45
INVOICE form, 267–271
pitch for, 240–243

printer definition records for, 479–480
procedures, 353
README.txt file, 500
records, 63, 167
report definitions, 124–127
reports, 117–118
selecting printers for, 16–17
style for, 297–298, 351–353
procedures, 305
  ad hoc relationships for, 346–351
  control, 419–421
  converting INVOICE to, 417–419
  global variables for, 412
  installing, 458–461, 464
  modifying, 319–322
  printing, 353
  repeating, 414–416
Procedures menu, 434
processing commands, 340
programming. *See* DQL (Data Query Language);
    high level queries
prompts, field, 4, 23, 8–33
PROPER function, 219, 225–227
protection. *See* security

Q

QUARTERLY menu, 439–440
queries. *See* DQL (Data Query Language); high
    level queries; reports
Query by Example, 98. *See also* Quick Reports
    menu
Query screen, 308–309
question marks (?)
  for data entry forms, 331–332
  for searches, 80, 82
quick reports, 98, 100–101
  and choice fields, 234
  converting, 305–307, 314, 418
  from data entry, 136–137
  fields for, 101–105
  formats for, 105–107
  running, 107–109
  switching to, 365–368

Quick Reports menu, 99–101, 434
quotes (")
  for default entry text, 153–154
  for record selection, 120, 122

R

ranges, field, 39–40
  for record selection, 123–124
  testing of, 58–59
README.txt file, 500
recalculating formulas, 274–275
Record Entry format, 50
  for printing, 268
  reports from, 136–137
  See also data entry
record numbers
  restoring deleted records by, 86
  searching for records by, 75–76
  viewing records in order of, 69–70
records, 5
  copying, 450–452, 456–457
  default, 60–63
  deleting, 85–87, 452–456
  encrypted, 485, 489
  entering. *See* data entry
  exclusive, 94
  exporting, 510–516
  global changes to, 357–359
  grouping, 73, 102, 452–456
  locking, 7
  managing, 5–6
  modifying, 5, 84–87, 92–93, 193–195, 357–358,
    408–409
  printing, 63, 167
  with related forms, 184–191
  in reports, 99–100
  saving, 53–54, 89–90
  searching for. *See* searching for records
  security for. *See* security
  selecting, 91–92, 119–124, 330–334, 375–378
  subform, 263–267
  viewing. *See* viewing records
Records menu, 49–50, 434
referential formulas, 298

528 MASTERING DATAEASE

related forms, 178–180
   adding fields to, 298–299
   copying field values from, 180, 196–198,
     212–213, 408–409, 411, 453–454
   creating, 180–185
   DQL for, 314–318, 326–330
   menu of, 324
   modifying, 257–258
   multiple relationships for, 198–203
   record processing with, 184–191, 450–451
   reports from, 203–206
relational operators, 314, 317, 322–326, 330
relationships, 5
   ad hoc, 346–351, 383–386
   See also related forms
reorganizing forms, 454–456
repeated information for data entry, 59–63
repeating query statements, 414–416
Report Field Definition box, 110
reports, 6, 100
   converting, 305–307, 314, 418
   copying information in, 132–133
   from data entry, 136–137
   exiting from, 139
   fields for, 101–105
   calculated, 134–136, 340–346
   choice, 234
   formats for, 99–100, 105–107, 109–112, 386–390
   groupings for, 102, 127–131, 290–300
   headers and footers for, 112–117, 127–131, 138,
     387–388, 494
   installing, 462, 464
   loading, 137
   modifying, 109–112
   with networks, 139–140
   pitch for, 240–243
   printing, 117–118
   printing definitions for, 124–127
   from related forms, 203–206, 314–318, 326–330
   running, 107–109
   saving, 101, 117
   security with, 139
   selecting records for, 119–124
   single form, with DQL, 307–313
   width of, 106, 109–112

required fields, 37, 57–58
resource conflict messages, 7
Restore command (DataEase), 465, 467–468
Restore command (DOS), 468
restoring
   databases, 467–478
   deleted records, 86–87
Restrict modification option, 257–258
reverse order
   for report fields, 102
   viewing records in, 70–71, 75, 84
right printer margins, 297
rows, deleting, 155n
run command, 419–420
running
   control procedures, 420–421
   reports, 107–109

S

Salary field, 236
SALES information record, 442
SALES menu, 429–432, 435
salesperson form. *See* SP form
saving
   and choice fields, 232
   form definitions, 45–46
   modifications, 156–157
   queries, 339, 344
   records, 53–54, 89–90
   reports, 101, 117
SCIENTIFIC function, 213
screen format files, converting dBASE, 505
Screen Style form, 480–481
screen styles, settings for, 475–476, 480–484
searching for records
   exact matches, 76–79
   partial matches, 80–84
   by record number, 75–76
   in subforms, 191–193
security, 7–8, 12–13
   assigning levels of, 484–488
   for backing up data, 469
   for **copy all from** command, 424

for custom menus, 446
for data entry, 64
with DQL, 335
for form creation, 46
for menus, 430, 441–442
for modifying records, 378
passwords for, 489–490
for relationships, 206
for reports, 139
for transferring data, 469
for viewing records, 93–94
selecting
printers, 16–17
records, 91–92, 119–124, 330–334,
375–378
semicolons (;)
with DQL, 307, 310–311
with sequencing, 221
SEQUENCE FROM command, 220–223
sequencing, 220–228, 456
serial numbers
displaying, 10
for upgrades, 501
shading, 158
shared records, 7, 94
shipment records, queries for, 362–368
SHIPS report, 365–366
shortcuts
for copying queries, 492–493
for data entry, 59–63
for signing on, 492
signing on, 10–11, 492
single form reports with DQL, 307–313
size of fields, 105
slashes (/)
for date fields, 50
for division, 41
smallest value for groups, 103
Soc.Sec.No. field, 235
software requirements, 497
sort order for report fields, 102
sorting, 6, 71–75, 493
Soundex ("sounds like") searches, 81–83
SP form, 218
case functions for, 219–220

data entry for, 223–228
with high level queries, 340–346
relating, to INVOICE, 257
sequencing for, 220–223
totals for, 272
spaces
in menu names, 438n
suppressing, 293, 295–296
trailing, 478
SPELL function, 213
start-up menus, 429, 441–443
starting DataEase, 9–10
State field, 236
statements, DQL, 306–308
statistical operators, 102, 252, 307, 271–274,
322–325, 371
Statistics menu, 311–312
status of forms and procedures, 458–460
subdirectories, 9–10
Subform Definitions screen, 259
subforms, 190, 248
adding, to INVOICE, 259–263
arrow keys used in, 192
copying, 462
data entry for, 263–267
defining, 249–250
displaying multiple, 195–196
for PAYMENTS, 284–287
searching for records in, 191–193
substatements, 307
subtraction, 41
SUM OF operator, 252
sum statistic for reports, 102
summary fields, 323
summing operators, 102, 252, 271–274,
322–323, 325
SUMORD procedure, 423–424
suppliers. *See* VENDORS form
suppressing field spaces, 293, 295–296
Symphony files, converting, 504–505
syntax, DQL, 307–308
System Administration menu, 16, 441
system administration
of configuration settings, 475–484
menu for, 16, 441, 474–475

530 MASTERING DATAEASE

of passwords, 489–490
of security level assignments, 484
system fields, 114
system forms, 444
system variables, 406–407, 409

T

Tab key
    for Field Definition screen, 34
    for Form Definition screen, 30
    for queries, 339, 344
    for record entry, 55
    for subforms, 192
    for Table View, 88
Table View, 87–93
    hiding fields from, 252
    for related records, 190–191
    for subforms, 260
tables of related records, 190–191
tabs, setting automatic, 486
task menus, 15
telephone numbers, 173–174
temp variables, 412
temporary files, 476
text
    converting, 223–228
    default entry, 153–154
    fields, 29, 72
    on forms, 28–33, 161–163
    highlighting, 161–163
    for menus, 430
    for record selection criteria, 119–123
TEXT function, 213
tildes (˜) in Soundex searches, 82
time, displaying, 10
time fields, 29
TIME function, 213
title area, 22
top margins, 297
totals, field, 102, 252, 271–274, 322–323, 325
trailers, group, 127–131, 291–292, 388
trailing spaces, 293, 295–296, 478
Transfer Data command, 456–457

TRIG function, 213
truncation of fields, 146n
TYPE STYLE area, 240
types, field, 28–29, 35

U

unchecked data entry mode, 61
underlining attribute, 163–164
unique fields, 37–38, 57–58, 167, 174–178
upgrading, 500–502
UPPER function, 220
USER FILE ENCRYPTION field, 489
USER INFORMATION form, 441
USERIAAA.DBM file, 489–490
users
    information records for, 7–8, 12–13,
        441–443, 482
    menus for, 429
    names of, 12, 446
Utilities menu, 434

V

variables
    for data entry, 412–414
    system, 406–407, 409
VENDORS form
    choice field for, 228–234
    creating, 172–174
    relating
        to ITEMS, 183–184, 198–206
        to ORDERS, 182–183, 186–190, 195–196
versions
    compatibility between, 478
    upgrading, 500–502
video, settings for, 475–476
View Security field, 487
viewing records
    in Form View, 68–75
    on networks, 94
    for related forms, 178
    security for, 93–94

setting for, 486
in Table View, 87–93

W

while command, 414–416
width
    field, 260, 345
    mailing label, 397
    paper, 242
    report, 106, 109–112
wild card characters
    for data entry forms, 331–332
    for record selection, 378
    for searches, 80–81

windows for messages, 409–410
with statements, 306–307, 309
word-wrap, 166, 393
Write Security field, 487

Y

year setting, 476–477
yes/no fields, 29

Z

zeros, leading, 221, 478

Selections from The SYBEX Library

DATABASES

The ABC's of dBASE III PLUS
Robert Cowart
264pp. Ref. 379-1
The most efficient way to get beginners up and running with dBASE. Every 'how' and 'why' of database management is demonstrated through tutorials and practical dBASE III PLUS applications.

The ABC's of dBASE IV 1.1
Robert Cowart
350pp, Ref. 632-4
The latest version of dBASE IV is featured in this hands-on introduction. It assumes no previous experience with computers or database management, and uses easy-to-follow lessons to introduce the concepts, build basic skills, and set up some practical applications. Includes report writing and Query by Example.

The ABC's of FoxPro 2 (Second Edition)
Scott D. Palmer
308pp; Ref. 877-7
This fast, friendly introduction to database management is now in a new edition for version 2. Concise tutorials show you how to use essential FoxPro features and commands, while hot tips give you special pointers for avoiding pitfalls. Covers everything from simple customer files to multi-file databases.

The ABC's of Paradox 3.5 (Second Edition)
Charles Siegel
334pp, Ref. 785-1
This easy-to-follow, hands-on tutorial is a must for beginning users of Paradox 3.0 and 3.5. Even if you've never used a computer before, you'll be doing useful work in just a few short lessons. A clear introduction to database management and valuable business examples make this a "right-to-work" guide for the practical-minded.

The ABC's of Q & A 4
Trudi Reisner
232pp; Ref. 824-6
A popular introduction to Q & A 4, packed with step-by-step tutorials for beginners. Learn to create databases, use the word processor, print out reports, and more. Easy instructions incorporate practical business applications. With special coverage of the Intelligent Assistant.

Advanced Techniques in dBASE III PLUS
Alan Simpson
454pp. Ref. 369-4
A full course in database design and structured programming, with routines for inventory control, accounts receivable, system management, and integrated databases.

dBASE Instant Reference SYBEX Prompter Series
Alan Simpson
471pp. Ref. 484-4
Comprehensive information at a glance: a brief explanation of syntax and usage for every dBASE command, with step-by-step instructions and exact keystroke sequences. Commands are grouped by function in twenty precise categories.

dBASE III PLUS Programmer's Reference Guide SYBEX Ready Reference Series
Alan Simpson
1056pp. Ref. 508-5

Programmers will save untold hours and effort using this comprehensive, well-organized dBASE encyclopedia. Complete technical details on commands and functions, plus scores of often-needed algorithms.

dBASE IV 1.1 Programmer's Desktop Reference
Alan Simpson
1050pp. Ref. 539-5

This comprehensive seven-part reference is a must for dBASE programmers. It offers full details on every command and function, as well as practical techniques and algorithms for achieving specific programming goals. Fully cross-referenced and indexed by command, function, and topic.

dBASE IV 1.1 Programmer's Instant Reference (Second Edition)
Alan Simpson
555pp. Ref. 764-9

Enjoy fast, easy access to information often hidden in cumbersome documentation. This handy pocket-sized reference presents information on each command and function in the dBASE IV programming language. Commands are grouped according to their purpose, so readers can locate the correct command for any task—quickly and easily.

dBASE IV User's Instant Reference (Second Edition)
Alan Simpson
356pp. Ref. 786-X

Completely revised to cover the new 1.1 version of dBASE IV, this handy reference guide presents information on every dBASE operation a user can perform. Exact keystroke sequences are presented, and complex tasks are explained step-by-step. It's a great way for newer users to look up the basics, while more experienced users will find it a fast way to locate information on specialized tasks.

Mastering dBASE III PLUS: A Structured Approach
Carl Townsend
342pp. Ref. 372-4

In-depth treatment of structured programming for custom dBASE solutions. An ideal study and reference guide for applications developers, new and experienced users with an interest in efficient programming.

Mastering dBASE IV 1.1 Programming
Carl Townsend
546pp. Ref. 782-9

An in-depth introduction especially for applications developers, and for experienced dBASE users seeking programming skills. This up-to-date new edition covers 1.1 basics, structured programming and database design, and specific techniques for business application programming—with examples for general ledger and invoicing.

Mastering FoxPro 2 (Second Edition)
Charles Siegel
650pp; Ref. 808-4

This highly readable hands-on guide now covers FoxPro version 2.0, with its graphical interface and other powerful new features. Part I is a practical introduction to business database management. Part II adds macros, custom menus, and other special features. Part III is a concise introduction to structured programming with FoxPro 2.0 development language.

TO JOIN THE SYBEX MAILING LIST OR ORDER BOOKS
PLEASE COMPLETE THIS FORM

NAME _____ COMPANY _____

STREET _____ CITY _____

STATE _____ ZIP _____

☐ PLEASE MAIL ME MORE INFORMATION ABOUT **SYBEX** TITLES

ORDER FORM (There is no obligation to order)

PLEASE SEND ME THE FOLLOWING:

TITLE	QTY	PRICE
_____	____	____
_____	____	____
_____	____	____
_____	____	____

TOTAL BOOK ORDER _____ $_____

CUSTOMER SIGNATURE _____

SHIPPING AND HANDLING PLEASE ADD $2.00 PER BOOK VIA UPS _____

FOR OVERSEAS SURFACE ADD $5.25 PER BOOK PLUS $4.40 REGISTRATION FEE _____

FOR OVERSEAS AIRMAIL ADD $18.25 PER BOOK PLUS $4.40 REGISTRATION FEE _____

CALIFORNIA RESIDENTS PLEASE ADD APPLICABLE SALES TAX _____

TOTAL AMOUNT PAYABLE _____

☐ CHECK ENCLOSED ☐ VISA
☐ MASTERCARD ☐ AMERICAN EXPRESS

ACCOUNT NUMBER _____

EXPIR. DATE _____ DAYTIME PHONE _____

CHECK AREA OF COMPUTER INTEREST:
☐ BUSINESS SOFTWARE
☐ TECHNICAL PROGRAMMING
☐ OTHER: _____

THE FACTOR THAT WAS MOST IMPORTANT IN YOUR SELECTION:
☐ THE SYBEX NAME
☐ QUALITY
☐ PRICE
☐ EXTRA FEATURES
☐ COMPREHENSIVENESS
☐ CLEAR WRITING
☐ OTHER _____

OTHER COMPUTER TITLES YOU WOULD LIKE TO SEE IN PRINT:
_____
_____

OCCUPATION
☐ PROGRAMMER ☐ TEACHER
☐ SENIOR EXECUTIVE ☐ HOMEMAKER
☐ COMPUTER CONSULTANT ☐ RETIRED
☐ SUPERVISOR ☐ STUDENT
☐ MIDDLE MANAGEMENT ☐ OTHER: _____
☐ ENGINEER/TECHNICAL
☐ CLERICAL/SERVICE
☐ BUSINESS OWNER/SELF EMPLOYED

CHECK YOUR LEVEL OF COMPUTER USE

☐ NEW TO COMPUTERS
☐ INFREQUENT COMPUTER USER
☐ FREQUENT USER OF ONE SOFTWARE
　PACKAGE:
　NAME _____
☐ FREQUENT USER OF MANY SOFTWARE
　PACKAGES
☐ PROFESSIONAL PROGRAMMER

OTHER COMMENTS:

_____
_____
_____
_____
_____
_____
_____

PLEASE FOLD, SEAL, AND MAIL TO SYBEX

SYBEX, INC.
2021 CHALLENGER DR. #100
ALAMEDA, CALIFORNIA USA
94501

SEAL

SYBEX Computer Books are different.

Here is why . . .

At SYBEX, each book is designed with you in mind. Every manuscript is carefully selected and supervised by our editors, who are themselves computer experts. We publish the best authors, whose technical expertise is matched by an ability to write clearly and to communicate effectively. Programs are thoroughly tested for accuracy by our technical staff. Our computerized production department goes to great lengths to make sure that each book is well-designed.

In the pursuit of timeliness, SYBEX has achieved many publishing firsts. SYBEX was among the first to integrate personal computers used by authors and staff into the publishing process. SYBEX was the first to publish books on the CP/M operating system, microprocessor interfacing techniques, word processing, and many more topics.

Expertise in computers and dedication to the highest quality product have made SYBEX a world leader in computer book publishing. Translated into fourteen languages, SYBEX books have helped millions of people around the world to get the most from their computers. We hope we have helped you, too.

For a complete catalog of our publications:

SYBEX, Inc. 2021 Challenger Drive, #100, Alameda, CA 94501
Tel: (415) 523-8233/(800) 227-2346   Telex: 336311
Fax: (415) 523-2373

FORMULA & COMMAND REFERENCE

FORMULAS AND FUNCTIONS	CHAPTER
IF	8
LASTFIRST	8
LOOKUP	8
PROPER	8
SEQUENCE FROM	8
UPPER	8

HIGH LEVEL DQL COMMANDS	CHAPTER
assign	15
case	15
control procedures	15
define	15
delete records	17
end	12
enter a record	13
exit	15
for	11
if	13
input	13
list records	11
message	15
modify records	13
variables	15
while	15